CW01669872

Fault Lines

Ridinghouse

Fault Lines

Art in Germany 1945–1955

John-Paul Stonard

First published in 2007 by
Ridinghouse
47 Lexington Street
London W1R 3LG
www.karstenschubert.com

Distributed by
Cornerhouse
70 Oxford Street
Manchester M15 5NH
www.cornerhouse.org

Text © 2007 John-Paul Stonard
For the book in this form © 2007 Ridinghouse
For additional copyright credits see p. 371

All rights reserved.
No part of this book may be reproduced or transmitted in any form or by any means, electronic or mechanical, including photocopying, recording or any other information storage or retrieval system, without prior permission in writing from the publisher.

British Library Cataloguing-in-Publication Data
A catalogue record of this book is available from the British Library

ISBN 978-1-905464-02-9

Co-ordination and editorial supervision: Rosalind Horne
Picture Research: Caroline Thompson
Copy-editing: Melissa Larner
Design: Marit Münzberg
Print: die Keure, Belgium

The research for this book was completed with financial assistance from the British Academy, the DAAD, the University of London and the Paul Mellon Foundation.

The author wishes to acknowledge in particular: Shulamith Behr, Geoff Eley, Romy Golan, Ralf Forster, Stella Harpley, Keith Hartley, Yule Heibel, Iris Lauterbach, Elisabeth Nay-Scheibler, Br Norbert, Patricia Rubin, Sybille Schallenberg, Martin Schieder, Amy Schmidt, Karsten Schubert, Frederic Schwarz, Richard Shone, Aurélie Verdier, Sarah Wilson, Wolfgang Wittrock, Christopher S. Wood.

Contents

Zones of Occupation 1945

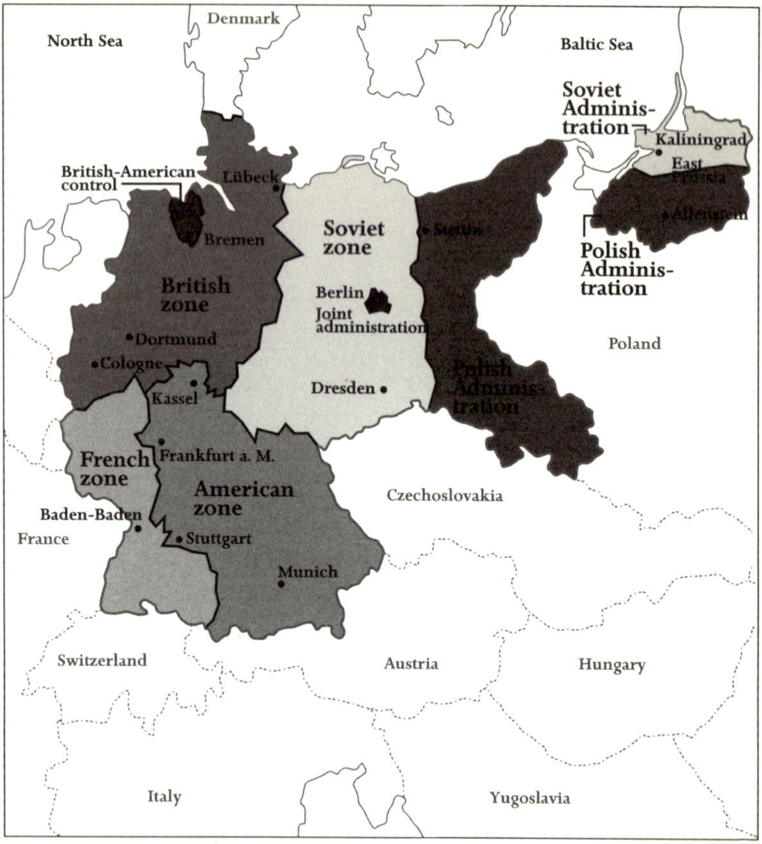

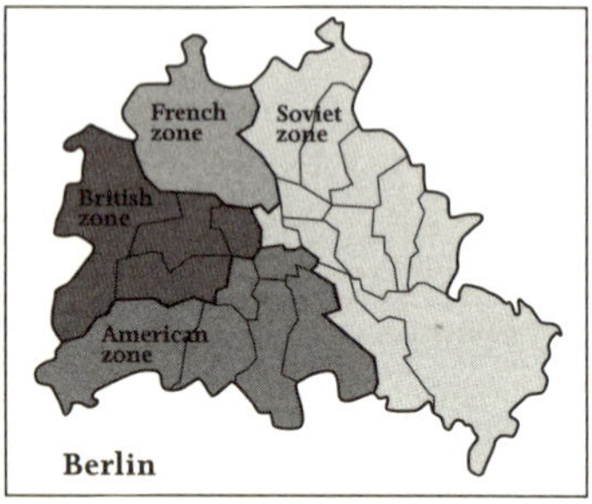

Chronology

1945

May: End of the Second World War
Germany is divided by the Allies into four military occupation zones
Mass expulsion from former German provinces in the East
July: Founding of the *Kulturbund* (Cultural League for the Democratic Renewal of Germany)

1946

The first major postwar exhibition, the *Allgemeine Deutsche Kunstausstellung*, opens in Dresden
The magazine *Das Kunstwerk. Zeitschrift für Moderne Kunst*, which supports modern and abstract painting, is founded in Stuttgart
Moderne Französischer Malerei, an exhibition of modern French painting, tours the Western Zones

1947

The Soviet-sponsored magazine *Bildende Kunst. Zeitschrift für Malerei, Graphik, Plastik und Architektur* is founded in Berlin
Publication of Thomas Mann's *Doktor Faustus*

1948

Hans Sedlmayr's influential account of modern art, *Verlust der Mitte*, is published
The exhibition *Christliche Kunst der Gegenwart* (Christian Art of our Times) opens in Cologne
June: Currency Reform. Soviet Union initiates 10-month transport blockade of West Berlin

1949

May: Founding of the Federal Republic of Germany
October: Founding of the German Democratic Republic

1950

The first exhibition of work by Henry Moore in postwar Germany opens in Hamburg

1951

The *Darmstädter Gespräch*, an important public debate about the representation of man in modern art, takes place in Darmstadt

1952

East Germany seals borders to the West

1953

The exhibition *Dritte Deutsche Kunstausstellung* in Dresden marks a high point of Stalinst Socialist Realism in Germany
March: Death of Stalin

1955

9 May: West Germany joins NATO
14 May: Signing of the Warsaw Pact between Soviet Union and its satellite states
July: The first documenta exhibition opens in Kassel
Werner Haftmann's book *Malerei im 20. Jahrhundert* is published

Preface

It was only in the mid-1950s, after a golden era that can be traced back at least to the time of Baudelaire, that Paris lost its status as Mecca for artists and as the international standard for contemporary art. Following victory in the war and the beginnings of a new engagement in world politics, America was the new centre of cultural gravity, with New York the source of aesthetic judgement. But as the French standard dwindled and art from the New World emerged from isolation, another story was unfolding. The mid-century saw the first signs of a resurgence of German art, and the gradual acceptance that there could be a legitimate 'national school' of German painting and sculpture.

The story of German art after the Second World War usually begins in the early 1960s, notably with the work of a young artist from the Rhineland, Joseph Beuys. It continues into the 1980s with the expressionist painting of Georg Baselitz, Anselm Kiefer and others, and with the re-invention of photography as grand-format museum art in the 1990s. This followed the reinvention of painting through the 'look' of photography by Gerhard Richter. Other major figures found their place in contradiction to this rather high-brow tradition, in particular Sigmar Polke, Martin Kippenberger and Georg Herold.

It may be considered extraordinary that barely four decades after the fall of the Third Reich such a diverse national school could arise. But there was a number of factors driving this success. A generation of postwar artists was burdened with the task of compensating for the damage of war, and the goal of fixing the broken national psyche. Further, that German artists were visible and acceptable on an international level was seen by the political elite of the Federal Republic as an essential part of 'democratic normalisation', a view that led to strongly supportive cultural policies. Benefits also arose from the renewal of traditions of private patronage and collecting at a time of unparalleled economic prosperity, and the ubiquitous construction of museums for contemporary art. From this perspective, the history of German art from the end of the Second World War to the turn of the Millennium is one of continuous expansion and extraordinary international success.

A true history of the German cultural 'miracle' would, however, show that there are two essential elements missing from this account. First are the events of the postwar decade. The impression that the ten years after capitulation were covered in rubble, beset by backward-looking debates about style, and devoid of significant artistic personalities can be countered by a more detailed look at the circumstances of destruction, defeat and division. Even in the first months after 1945, it became clear that following political disaster, cultural life, both in the form of artistic creation and national heritage, was all that was left to motivate rebuilding the broken country. Periodicals, exhibition catalogues, personal memoirs and official archives document numerous exhibitions and a considerable debate about the new functions of art in postwar society. Driving this activity was a euphoric idealism, latched to the epic task of reconstruction. The eventual disappointment of these ideals – the dousing of *mystique* with *politique*, to paraphrase Charles Péguy – was, however, virtually complete by the mid-1950s. Whereas those embarking on the task of cultural reconstruction believed that they were inaugurating a new epoch, now it appears instead a swan song for an older ideal, a detached, spiritual utopia of the early twentieth century that could not survive the new postwar world order.

The second area of neglect is the 'other' Germany in the East. Impressions of the Soviet Zone tend to focus on the imposition of state-sponsored Socialist Realism, and the attempt to regulate creativity and inner life. Again, a more detailed examination reveals not only the extent of resistance to official culture, but also that this official culture was nuanced by the interplay of German and Soviet traditions. Behind the iron curtain, cultural life was as complex and illuminated as in the West. The two were strongly interlinked, not least by the quantity of successful West German artists who had begun their careers in the East. Just as in the 1920s and 30s artists otherwise divided by politics were united by a certain faith in culture and ideas, so after the war the political divisions were in many cases effaced by a shared sense of a German cultural heritage. The more one looks, the clearer it becomes that Germany did survive as a cultural whole during the period of partition, not politically, but in terms of memories of a shared cultural past, and of aspirations for future reunification on the basis of that common culture. Received Cold War political divisions do not account for facts on the ground. Scholars have a duty to examine

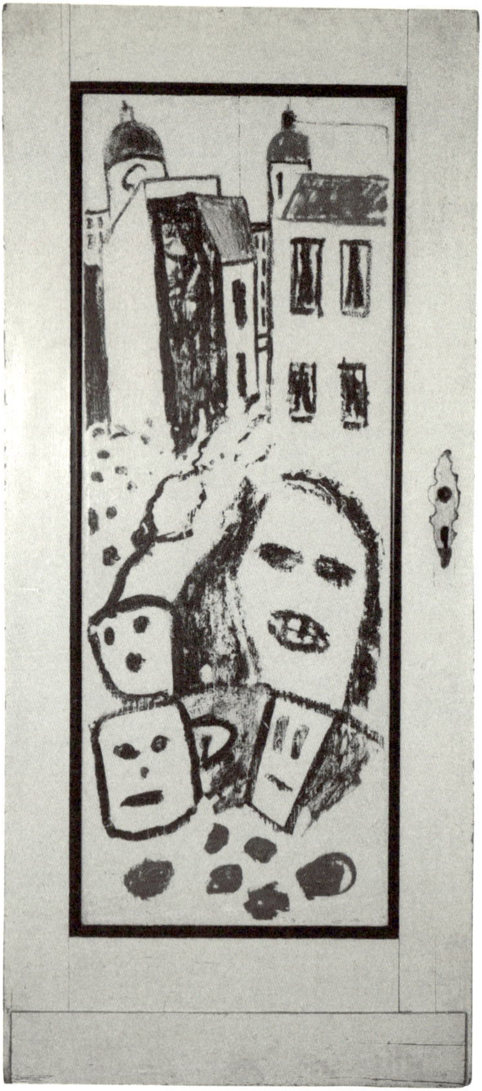

Werner Heldt, *Berliner Häuser, im Vordergrund Masken* (Berlin Houses and Masks), c. 1950, lipstick and other cosmetics on wooden door, 197 × 89 cm, Berlinische Galerie, Berlin

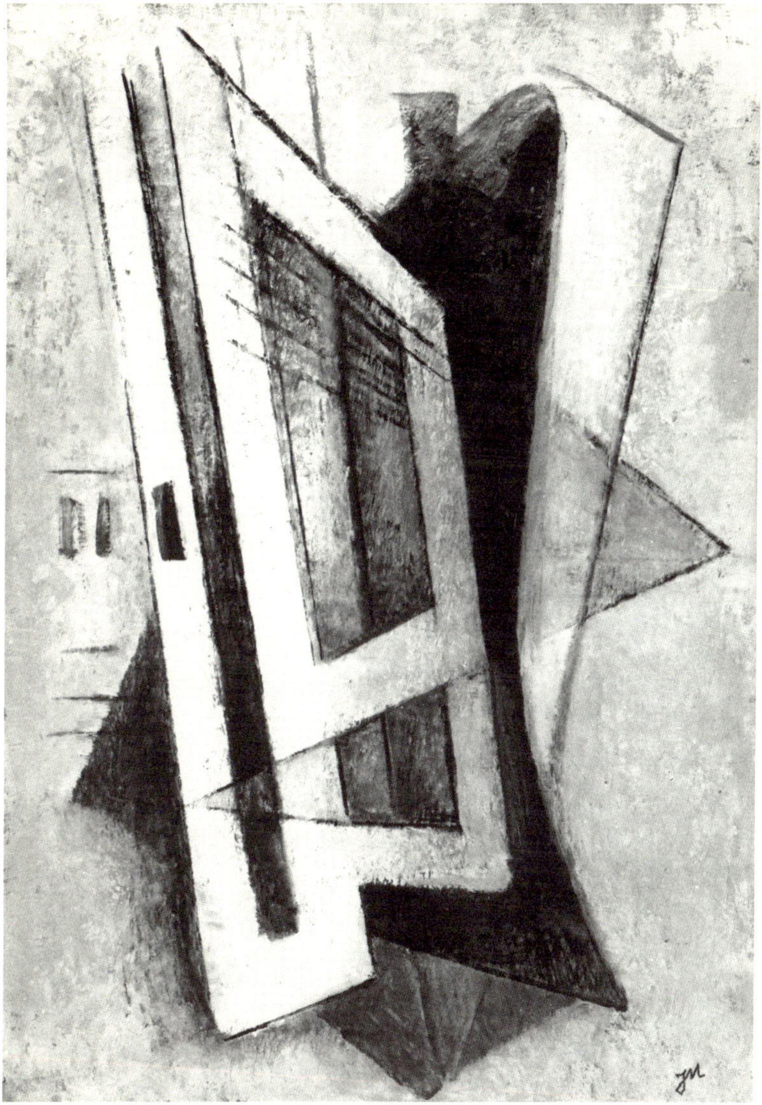

Jeanne Mammen, **Tür zum nichts** (Door to Nothing), c. 1945, oil on paper, 100 × 70 cm, Berlinische Galerie, Berlin

this period, as any period, in a manner that reproduces not political claims on objects, but the contingent life of objects themselves.

It is not difficult to see why these two areas – the postwar decade and East German art – have been neglected. Devotional monographs or surveys dependent on illustrating an established canon have little time for historical detail, marginalia or aesthetically problematic paintings and sculptures. This book builds on a handful of studies that correct such a blinkered view. The first significant exhibition to show West and East German art together was organised by Eckhardt Gillen in 1997 at the Martin Gropius Bau, Berlin. The

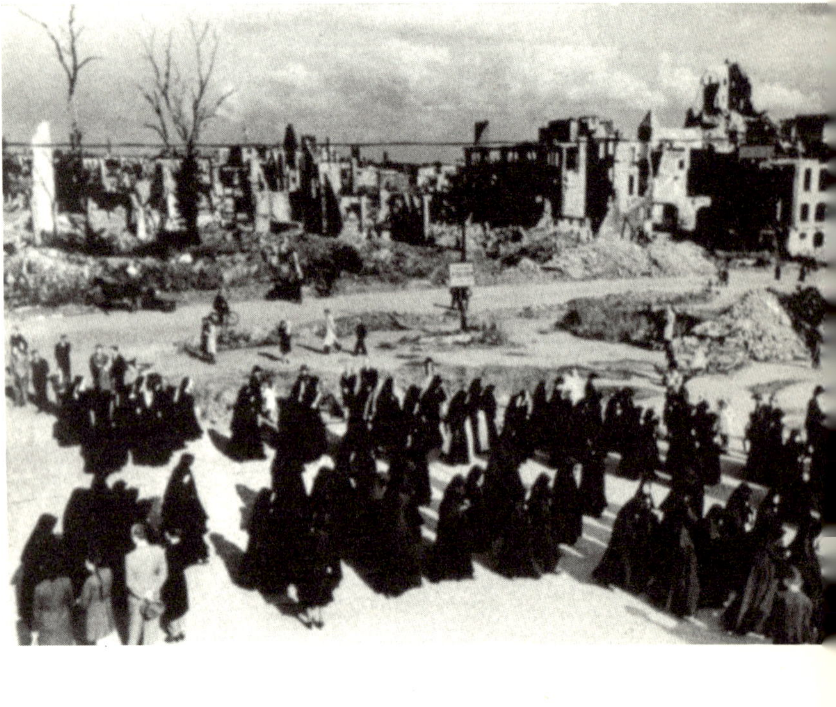

exhibition bore the title *Deutschlandbilder* (Images of Germany), a word conveying the idea of works of art floating above political divisions, allowing an ideal type of free cultural exchange.[1] In print, the art historian Karin Thomas has been one of the most persistent champions of the bilateral view.[2] As for the period directly after 1945, English readers are lucky to have an in-depth and strongly argued account of abstract painting and attitudes towards 'expression' in Yule Heibel's *Reconstructing the Subject*.[3]

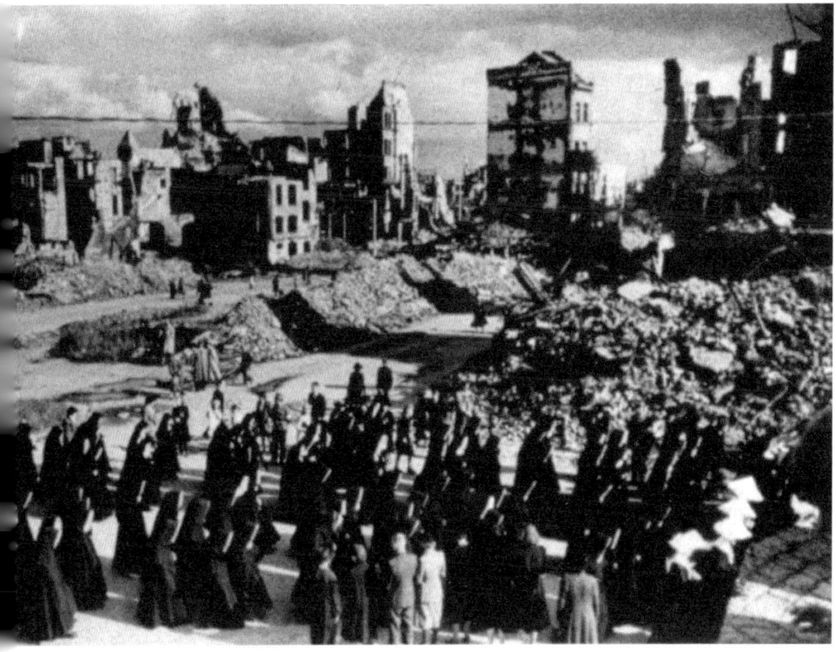

Hermann Claasen, 'Fronleichnamsprozession' (Corpus Christi Day Procession), 1946, published in *Gesang im Feuerofen*, Düsseldorf, 1947

The confusions of the postwar moment, the lack of any central location, idea or person against which to judge the welter of cultural manifestations, suggest a thematic survey as the least problematic approach. Although the themes chosen for this book are presented in roughly chronological order, no implication of historical progression should be drawn; rather, the chapter headings indicate the fragile 'coherences' of this moment. We can see them forming and elaborating on themselves, but at the same time becoming outmoded.

First are the far-reaching effects of the Allied bombing campaign. A significant debate about the literary representation of the bombing of Germany was initiated at the end of the 1990s by the writer W.G. Sebald, who argued that authors had failed in their task to represent the events of the Allied bombardment of Germany.[4] A similar question may be asked of the visual arts: how did artists respond to the extraordinary ruinscape? How was it possible to represent destroyed cities and towns that were themselves so eloquent on the complex political tragedy of the war? These questions are addressed in Chapter One. As with Sebald's contentious account, the answer is fragmented and unsatisfying. There were representations, but they served no useful public function. Contemporary ideas about tragedy and the literary representation of tragedy may be able to throw at least some light on this difficult debate.

The second context is the Allied occupation. The division of Germany into four sectors, Russian, American, French and British, was no less important than the Allied bombardment in defining postwar cultural life. The mid-1950s marked a thaw in Soviet policies, and also saw the final hand-over of sovereignty from the Western Allies to the Federal Republic. For this reason, the decade after 1945 may be referred to as the period of 'long occupation'. There has been no shortage of commentary on the extensive role played by art in the growing Cold War confrontation. Rivalries and alliances were nevertheless more complex than a simple East-West polarisation, which has often served to obscure the role played by German artists themselves during the period of reconstruction. Tensions in the field of cultural diplomacy between the French and British simmered throughout the occupation. Surprisingly, in comparison with Soviet, American and French cultural policies, which have been closely scrutinised, virtually nothing has been written about British policy for the visual arts. Exhibitions mounted by the British government, largely under the auspices of the British Council, most significantly of the work of Henry Moore, are examined in the second chapter of this book.

The third context is provided by the 1949 partition into eastern and western states. Exchange continued, even when differences made such interaction appear impossible: in 1953, for example, at the height of Stalinist cultural repression, 117 West German artists took part in a large exhibition of Socialist Realist art in Dresden. Many artists from the East were fleeing westwards, and a number of them (Gerhard Richter, Günther Uecker, Klaus Staeck, Georg Baselitz, Georg Herold etc.) were to become leading figures in the West German art scene. The conditions that enabled such movement led directly to the construction of the Berlin Wall in 1961, which by no means stopped the defections. By considering aspects of both East and West, such connections can be rescued from the simplifications of a polarised history. Rather than post-factum reconciliation, however, the question is of how two distinct yet 'interlocked' entities exerted an influence on each other. The idea of cultural unity, or a unified national cultural heritage within the context of a 'postwar renaissance' was central to this particularly intriguing episode of cultural exchange.

Yule Heibel's seminal book, mentioned above, is one of the starting points for a further theme, the turbulent dealings with the heritage of Expressionism. The strained engagement with this part of national visual history reaches to the heart of the postwar order. Germany's contribution to modern art was being rehabilitated, but at the same time historicised. It comes as some surprise to realise that the history of the Brücke artists' group was first treated seriously only after 1945. In some respects, art history itself was being invented anew at this moment, especially in those countries that did not, like Germany, have a tradition of scholarly, 'scientific' study of the arts.

Expressionism was also in trouble for more immediate, psychological reasons. Whereas Yule Heibel explains this 'withering' by referring to certain critical philosophers, notably Walter Benjamin and Theodor Adorno, another approach may be grounded in the 'damaged-language' theory of the philologist Victor Klemperer, and the postwar writings of Martin Heidegger. Heidegger's influence in the immediate postwar years should not be underestimated; it was at this moment that he experienced his 'aesthetic turn', and published the essay *Der Ursprung des Kunstwerks* (The Origin of the Work of Art), endowing art with the deepest mystical function of revealing human truth. This was a theme that artists were keen to address.

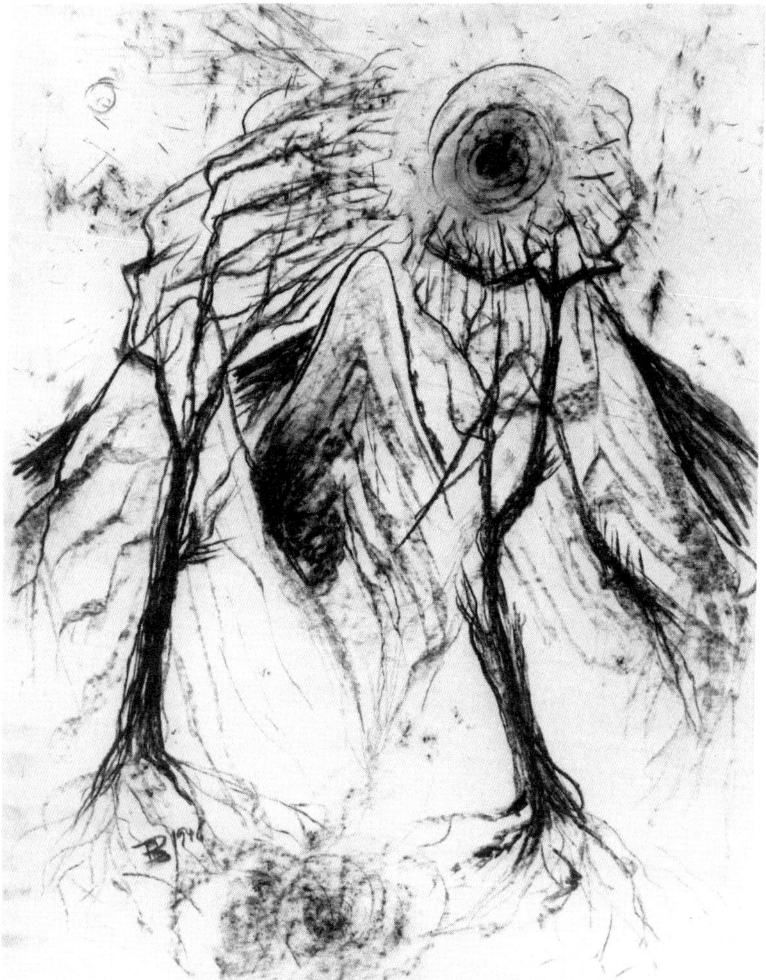

Theo Balden, *Landschaft* (Landscape), 1946, chalk on paper, 57 × 44.5 cm, Akademie der Künste, Berlin, Kunstsammlung

Although a documentary history of modernism was gradually appearing, reactionary forces were by no means absent. The huge influence of Hans Sedlmayr's conservative anti-modern diatribe *Verlust der Mitte* (The Loss of the Centre), must be taken into account. When he resumed his position at Munich University after the war, Sedlmayr's inaugural address took Pieter Brueghel's *The Parable of the Blind* as a focus for a revision of his earlier essay on the Flemish artist, a pungent choice of image at this moment to illustrate a theory of apperception that attempted an 'expressive' formulation of the art-historical imagination. *Verlust der Mitte* was written from the perspective of a Catholic for whom modern art was a secular nightmare. The strong position of the Catholic Church, and the enduring legacy of a tradition of anti-modernism that had been relentlessly stoked by opportunist Nazi propaganda meant that he was not alone in his views after 1945. There was, nevertheless, a considerable movement to reconcile the Church and contemporary art, mirroring the Art Sacré movement in France. The postwar boom of *Kirchliche Kunst* was fuelled not only by the West German Chancellor Konrad Adenauer's concept of the *Abendland*, a quasi-religious concept of European culture, and to a certain extent by the extensive rebuilding of damaged and destroyed churches (by 1960 over 8,000 churches and chapels had been reconstructed or built afresh; in the Catholic heartland of Cologne, 323 new churches were built in the postwar decade), but also by the more basic need to reinvest the fabric of everyday life with ethical meaning. Chapter Five of this book accounts for the postwar Catholic restoration in the West, and, despite changing attitudes in Rome towards 'modern art', suggests why this did not lead to a strong Catholic art movement as could be found in France.

As a thematic rather than chronological survey, certain important elements of postwar art find themselves outside the scope of this book. No full account of abstract painting is provided: it should become clear that only in retrospect is abstraction a dominant theme. The ideals and motives of western abstraction are nevertheless conveyed within broader revisionist headings. More pressing is the theme of exile and return. This may be hinted at here, but it is a huge topic that demands far more space. In addition, the account of modern reception cannot be complete without mention of the Bauhaus, but unfortunately this is all that this worthy institution receives here. The Deutsche Werkbund was formally reinstated in 1947 with the 'Rheydt Manifesto', and had numerous branches in the occupation zones. The fate of these linked institutions deserves a separate study. Further work on artists' organisations would begin with a consideration of the West German Künstlerbund (Artists' Federation), founded in 1950, with the painter Karl Hofer as first president. Individual biographies of those such as Hofer are dispersed throughout this book; it should be admitted that this does not help the fact that so many existing biographies stop around 1933, as if historiography should itself confirm post-Nazi extinction. This absence is dealt with here thematically, rather than monographically; there remains a need for fuller accounts of the individuals mentioned.

In geological terms, 'fault lines' are where tectonic plates clash, creating high levels of seismic activity. The driving force of ideology can be seen in the light of this terrestrial drama: the clash of beliefs generates historical circumstance. Germany, as has so often been pointed out, was the stage on which a world drama was played out in the years after 1945. Questions of guilt and responsibility were never far behind. The geological term in German is just as appropriate for this moment: *Störungszone*: 'disturbance-zone'.

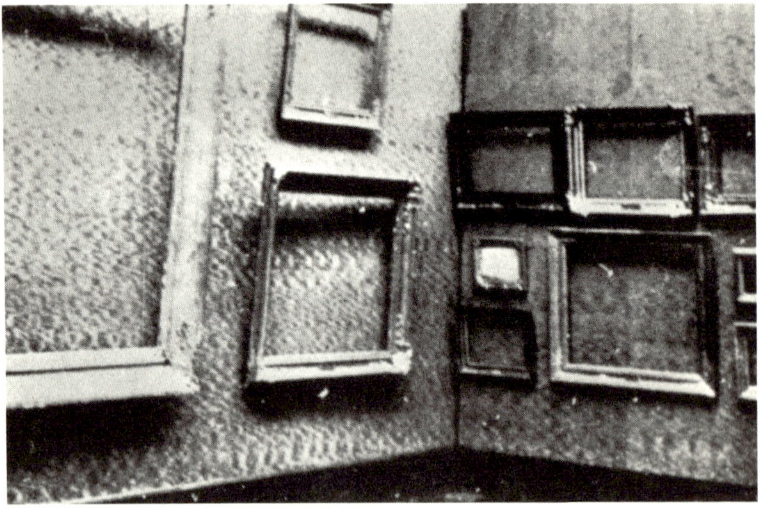

Anonymous, 'A corner of the Oslo Museum (Norway) after the destruction wrought by the Germans', from: George Mihan, *Looted Treasure. Germany's raid on Art*, London, 1944

1 Gillen, 1998.

2 Thomas, 1985; 2002.

3 Heibel.

4 Sebald.

Ruin and Reconstruction

Pictures of Destruction

[It is] a destruction that would cry to heaven if we who suffer were not ourselves laden with guilt. As it is, the cry is smothered in our throats [...]

Thomas Mann, *Doktor Faustus*, Berlin, 1947, 173

English and American planes bombed over one hundred German towns from the beginning of 1940 to May 1945. At first, attacks were directed towards strategic targets such as oil production and transportation, but the limited success of this approach led to the policy, developed by the British Bomber Command, of attacking civilian targets with the aim of disrupting life and lowering morale. The night-time bombing of the north German town of Lübeck on 28 March 1942 was the first in a series of raids that wrought destruction on a scale that was most often referred to with biblical analogies. Twenty-nine raids were directed at Berlin alone. Cologne was hit eighteen times, Hamburg sixteen. Heavy bombs known as 'blockbusters' were dropped on buildings to create holes for air to circulate and whip up fires caused by smaller incendiary bombs that followed. The complete destruction of Hamburg and Dresden by this method was the result of policies adopted by the British initially in the face of protests from the Americans, who preferred daylight raids, during which they could identify strategic, non-civilian targets. In Dresden on one night in February 1945, practically everything was destroyed apart from the military installations on the outskirts of the town. Berlin had emerged less than fifty years previously as the cosmopolitan capital of modern Europe; by the time of the last raid in April 1945 it had been reduced to a state described by some eyewitnesses as lunar, by others as prehistoric.

The legacy of the bombardments stretches deep into the recent history of postwar Germany, both East and West. To this day in Berlin, Dresden and most other major German cities, the open spaces of old bomb sites and wide gaps between solitary houses carry a physical memory of the air war. What can be said about this legacy? How can it be understood? In one of the first accounts of the bombardment, published in 1963, the historian Hermann Rumpf wrote that even 'seventeen years after the thunderous explosions in Germany's towns have died away' anyone attempting to bring up the topic would be reproached for 'disturbing the grass which has been so carefully grown over an old scar'. Rumpf continues: 'Have those past events any significance today? He will be asked... Considered as an historical event, the bombing war and its significance for the future has hardly taken root in the consciousness of the people'.[1]

Many eyewitness reports indicate that such indifference was an ordinary feature of life in the first postwar years. In her account of a visit to Germany in 1950, the philosopher Hannah Arendt records not only nightmarish scenes of poverty, destruction and displacement, but also the strange unconcern from Germans whom she met. They walk indifferently through the rubble, she writes, and send each other postcards of the destroyed cathedrals as if they were still standing. Discussions are so generalised as to forgo direct reference to the lost war, the defeated Reich, or the landscape of ruins. 'The average German looks for the causes of the last war not in the acts of the Nazi regime, but in the events that led to the expulsion of Adam and Eve from Paradise.'[2] Commenting on the everyday struggles that took precedent over historical reflection, the Austrian writer and victim of Nazi persecution Jean Améry wrote that the 'German walks around his destroyed streets, a worn briefcase on a string over his shoulder, hunting for a bit of bread or tobacco – or for some wood to make a coffin – or for some committee or other, from which he hopes to learn the whereabouts of his children, his wife, his mother'.[3] The American writer on architecture and technology, Lewis Mumford, designated this blank-eyed wandering figure as 'post-historical man', a new everyman who had more in common with the 'DPs' (Displaced Persons), refugees from the Eastern territories, and homeless from all over the country, than with any other type of citizen.[4]

Such indifference on the part of the general populace is perhaps not that remarkable: what does it mean to say that the defeated country should have showed an interest in the ruins? More remarkable was the silence of those artists and writers whose response, as Rumpf suggested, could have helped root the experience of bombardment in the postwar consciousness. The absence of any adequate literary response to the bombing attests to the suppression of memories attached to the 'nights of destruction', as the writer W.G. Sebald has more recently phrased it. Sebald's *Luftkrieg und Literatur* (1999, published in English as *On the Natural History of Destruction*, 2003) condemns postwar German literature for not responding adequately to the terror of aerial warfare.[5] Accounts of the bombardment presented in contemporary literature were, Sebald claims, characterised by stiff objectivity or kitsch sentimentality, wholly inadequate to representing the disaster. The true nature of the catastrophe and its effect on the German psyche remains unexamined: Sebald describes the thousands of unrecovered corpses which are the 'well-kept secret' in the foundations of the new state, a 'hidden history'.[6] What has failed to appear, he suggests, is a successful literary or artistic work that could provide a spur and standard for public discussion: 'I repeat, I do not doubt that there were and are memories of those nights of destruction', he writes. 'I simply do not trust the form – including the literary form – in which they are expressed, and I do not believe they were a significant factor in the public consciousness of the new Federal Republic in any sense except as encouraging the will to reconstruction'.[7] Hermann Kasack's *Die Stadt hinter dem Strom* (published in 1953 in English as *The City Beyond the River*) was considered at the time a profound reflection on the disasters of Nazism, though Sebald laments its mythologising tendencies and its resort to 'Expressionist fantasy'. He also describes Hans Erich Nossack's *Nekyia. Bericht eines Überlebenden* (1947) despite its valuable documentary quality, as 'metaphysical fraudulence'. More successful is Alexander Kluge's account of the air raid on Halberstadt, although, published in 1981, this was hardly a contemporary response.[8]

Many of the questions asked by Sebald, and the criticism he makes of literature, may be transposed to the visual arts. Although a significant number of photographers, painters and draughtsman responded directly to the ruined landscapes, their efforts reveal a complex relationship with the ruined country. The dilemma facing artists was acute: to dwell on the ruins was considered tasteless in a situation where reconstruction was imperative, but to avoid them was seen as dangerously escapist: 'To offer our contemporaries an escape into some idyll would have been too cruel for words', the writer Heinrich Böll later suggested.[9] Many felt that artists, like writers, had regrettably opted for silence: for one American observer, the lack of direct artistic response to the environment constituted 'the most astonishing aspect' of the reconstruction situation.[10] An official attempt in mid-1946 to stimulate artistic reflection suggested a deep unease with the silence: the town of Dortmund created a prize directed at artists in the Westphalia region for works expressing the suffering of the bombing raids in painting and sculpture.[11] There are no records of any overwhelming response to the prize, or memorable winning entries.

The history of postwar ruin representation in painting and photography is unresolved, a history of false-starts and fractured debates. Even with photography, the importance of which is suggested by the numerous half-tone images that illustrate *Luftkrieg und Literatur*, the problems of stylisation were not absent. What could be said, and how? The scale of the disaster was such that it appeared unencompassable with existing traditions. Sebald's book hints at this problem, as does a more recent book by the British philosopher A.C. Grayling that describes the Allied bombing campaign as an act of terrorism, impugnable as a war crime.[12] Both criticise the way in which the extraordinary events under discussion – thousand-bomber raids, firestorms of over 800 degrees centigrade, mass slaughter, the destruction of villages, cities, towns, whole cultures – have been represented. Both writers seek justice for human failure in the face of a disaster so vast that it appears not the work of man but of nature itself.

Amongst artists, the modern movement most commonly evoked during the first years of reconstruction was Surrealism, and a 'surrealistic' response was generally expected.[13] For one visitor, Berlin itself presented a tableau worthy of Lautréamont: 'an umbrella and a sewing machine on top of an operating table here would not have seemed at all out of place; the premises themselves seem to have no premise any more. To cultivate a derangement of the senses, as Arthur Rimbaud suggested, would have been superfluous; reality itself was insanity'.[14] The art historian Hans Sedlmayr recorded similar sentiments: 'The ultimate surrealist architecture is the result of total war – could anything be more surreal than the scenes of our ruined towns?'[15]

A short revival of Surrealist-inspired painting constituted one of the first coherent artistic events after 1945, and the only real significant genre of *Ruinenmalerei* (ruin painting). These works were shown in three notable exhibitions, two of which were held in Berlin at the Galerie Gerd Rosen. Rosen, who was primarily an antiquarian book dealer, had opened his gallery in August 1945 with the exhibition *Ausstellung junger Kunst* (Exhibition of New Art), which compared work by three young artists working in Berlin and classic modern works by those such as Paul Klee and Gerhard Marcks. The gallery was run at the time by the painter Heinz Trökes (1913–97), who, together with the sculptor Hans Uhlmann (1900–1975), established it as a showcase for abstract and surrealist painting, and a meeting place for young artists; the 'first sensation in the ruined metropolis', according to the writer Viktoria Ehrig.[16]

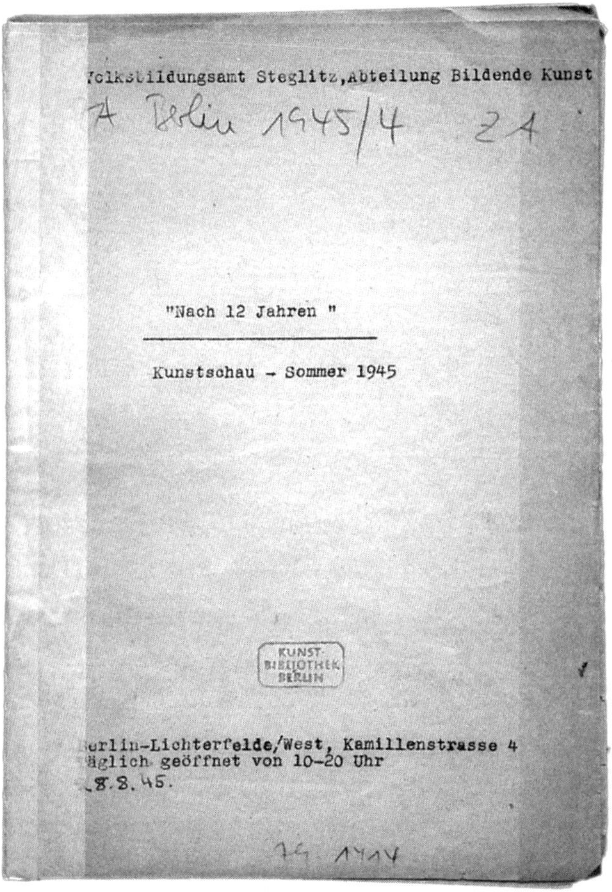

Hans Uhlmann, *Nach 12 Jahren* (After Twelve Years), cover of catalogue for an exhibition held at Kamillenstrasse 4, Berlin-Lichterfeld, Summer 1945

In February 1946, the *Fantasten-Ausstellung* (Fantasten Exhibition) showed work by Stephan Alexander (an American about whom little is known), Hannah Höch (1889–1978), Hans Thiemann (1910–77), Heinz Trökes, Hans Uhlmann, and Mac Zimmerman (1912–95), who constituted, chiefly for the purposes of this single exhibition, the Fantasten group. The effect of the works displayed was, however, compromised by the selective recuperation of surrealist stylistics, alighting on dream imagery at the expense of disruptive working methods. If such works avoided the more troubling side of the Surrealist imagination, they also avoided the disturbing aspects of contemporary reality, as critics observed at the time. Heinz Trökes' *Mit der offenen Tür* (With the Open Door, 1943), made by the artist while serving in an anti-aircraft unit in Berlin, is typical of the escapist tenor of Fantasten painting. Indeed, none of the works displayed in the *Fantasten-Ausstellung* indicate a significant will to measure modern styles against the postwar landscape.

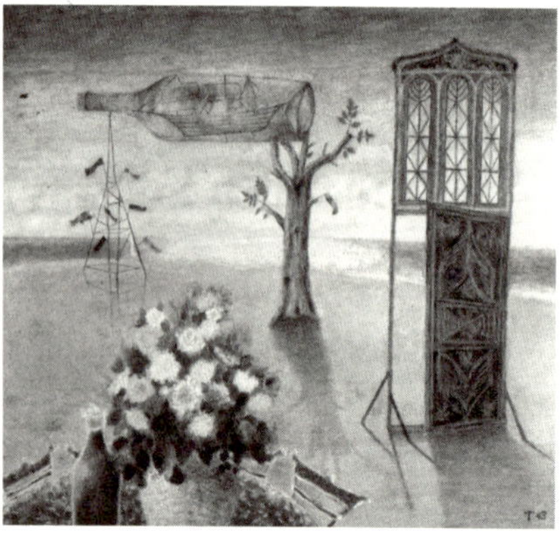

Heinz Trökes, *Mit der offenen Tür* (With an Open Door), 1943, oil on canvas, 60 × 70 cm, Berlinische Galerie, Berlin

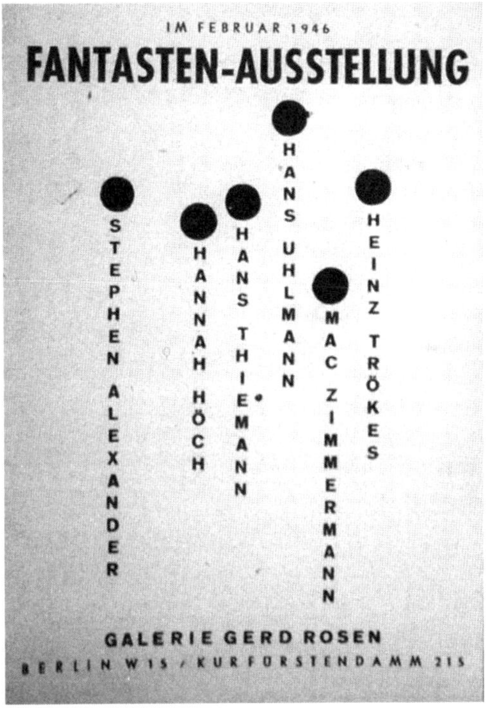

Fantasten-Ausstellung, cover of catalogue for exhibition held at the Gerd Rosen Galerie, Berlin, February 1946

Trökes, the spokesman for the Fantasten group, addressed this problem at the opening of the Rosen exhibition: 'Is a painting of its time [*zeitnahe*] because it shows a soldier returning to his ruined home? [...] Can naturalistic painting express a century that has seen two world wars, the discovery of relativity, psychology, in which mathematics has calculated a fourth co-ordinate, and thus created a new dimension!'[17] What in fact had occurred, Trökes continued, was that the world itself had become abstract and surreal, so that the works on display were effectively naturalistic imitations.

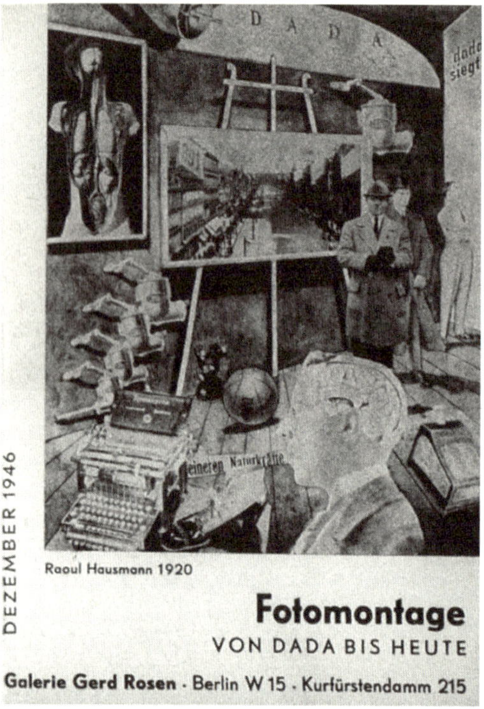

Fotomontage von Dada bis Heute (Photomontage from Dada to Today), cover of catalogue for an exhibition held at the Galerie Gerd Rosen, December 1946

The second exhibition at the Rosen Gallery, *Fotomontage von Dada bis heute* (Photomontage from Dada to Today), organised by Hannah Höch in December 1946, showed works by the Austrian Dadaist Raoul Hausmann (1886–1971), the Hungarian Juro Kubicěk (1906–70), and Höch herself.[18] (Kubicěk, incidentally, was the first artist to benefit from an exchange programme established by the American State Department, and spent the years 1947 to 1949 as visiting professor of painting at the University of Louisville in Kentucky). Many of the works exhibited, including Hausmann's photomontage *Dada Siegt* (Dada Victorious, 1920), which illustrated the cover of the catalogue, came from Höch's own collection, which she had kept throughout the war in her house in Berlin-Heilgensee.[19] Photomontage was central to the Berlin Dada movement, the critical spirit of which was a promising source for reflection on the ruins; the promise was, however, little fulfilled. Höch's short address at the opening was an isolated attempt to document and revalorise German Dada, in particular the photomontage, which she suggests deserves to be seen as an 'art form in its own right' (*selbständige Kunstform*).[20] She traces the birth of photomontage to the first public exhibition of works in the medium, in the rooms of Otto Burchard (she is referring to the *First International Dada Fair*, held in Berlin, 1920). Between 1920 and 1933, she continues, photomontage was used extensively in advertising and photo-reportage. Exhibitions of works by the Russian El Lissitzky (1890–1941) in 1919 and by the American photographer Paul Outerbridge (1896–1958) in 1929 are mentioned as formative moments, as is the activity of the Dessau Bauhaus. If she ends on a note of optimism about the future of the medium, however, the works exhibited in *Fotomontage von Dada bis heute* give little indication of contemporary events in the way that Höch's celebrated *Schnitt mit dem Küchenmesser. Dada durch die letzte Weimarer Bierbauch-Kulturepoche Deutschlands* (Cut with the Kitchen Knife. Dada through the Last Weimar Beer-Belly Cultural Epoch of Germany, 1919) had directly impressed on viewers the turmoil of the founding of the Weimar Republic. Most of the works on display in Rosen's gallery were made before 1933, suggesting a historical survey rather than a contemporary response. However, even those made after 1945, such as Juro Kubicěk's *Berlin* 1946 reveal little about the ruined city in which they were made. The satirical and destructive forces that had been brought from Zurich to Berlin by Richard Huelsenbeck in 1918 found little resonance in the reconstruction milieu after 1945.

The members of the Fantasten group exhibited together one last time, now as *Zone 5*, at the Galerie Franz in Berlin from September to October 1948. It was by this point impossible to avoid political realities; the Berlin Blockade, by which the Soviets had stopped all rail and road access to West Berlin, had begun in late June.

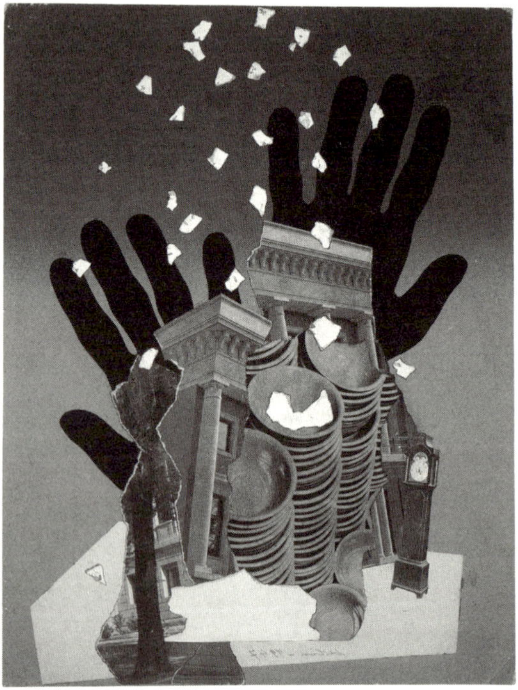

Juro Kubicěk, *Berlin*, 1946, collage, 39.2 × 45 cm, Berlinische Galerie, Berlin

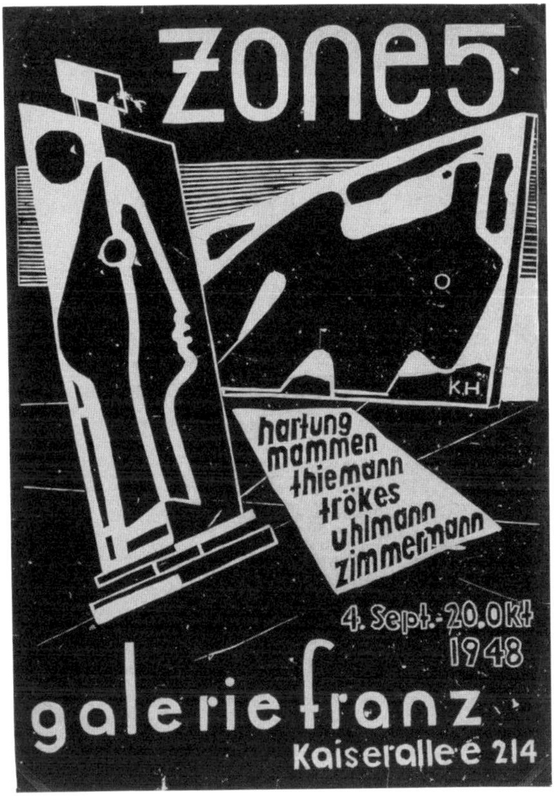

Poster for the exhibition *Zone 5*, Galerie Franz, 1948, Berlinische Galerie, Landesmuseum für Moderne Kunst, Fotografie und Architektur

The wish to escape from the four zones of Berlin could not have been expressed better, or perhaps with more irony, by the new name chosen by the group. If the 'fifth zone' was to be one of artistic freedom, then the symbol of this freedom was the increasingly strong influence of abstract painting, in particular the type of paintings being made by Willi Baumeister (1889–1955), Karl-Otto Götz (b.1914) and Ernst Wilhelm Nay (1902–1968), all based in the western zones. Solo displays of works by all three had been mounted at the Rosen Gallery. Paintings exhibited by Hans Thiemann in *Zone 5*, such as *Im Gelände* (On the Land, 1948) and *Bunte Reihe* (Colourful Row, 1948) show the gradual move away from surrealistic to abstract imagery.

Elsewhere, the 'cruel idyll' of which Heinrich Böll had warned may be discerned in the work of three artists not associated with the Fantasten group, Franz Radziwill (1895–1983), Werner Heldt (1904–54) and Edgar Ende (1901–1965). Radziwill, a painter based in the old Brücke haunt of Dangast on the North Sea coast of Friesland, was honoured in 1946 with solo exhibitions of his work in the Oldenburg Landesmuseum and the Alsterhaus Hamburg. For the critic Egon Vietta, his work combined the influence of Altdorfer and Brueghel with the coloration of the Expressionists and Neue Sachlichkeit painters.[21] Radzwill's refined technique may be compared with that of other artists, such as Otto Dix and Hans Bellmer, who sought to revive traditional Old Master methods of drawing and paint application. Their subject matter, however, was far from traditional. Vietta describes Radziwill as both a 'regionally bound' painter and as an artist striving after universal symbols. His apocalyptic naturalism frequently uses the motif of a fissure in pictorial space to signify the 'broken' postwar landscape, a landscape devoid of local or historical references.

Werner Heldt was, by contrast, a Berlin-based painter little interested in traditional working methods. He had served in anti-aircraft units during the war, and was subsequently held in a British prisoner-of-war camp. An exhibition of his works at the Galerie Gerd Rosen in March 1946 showed mostly works from the

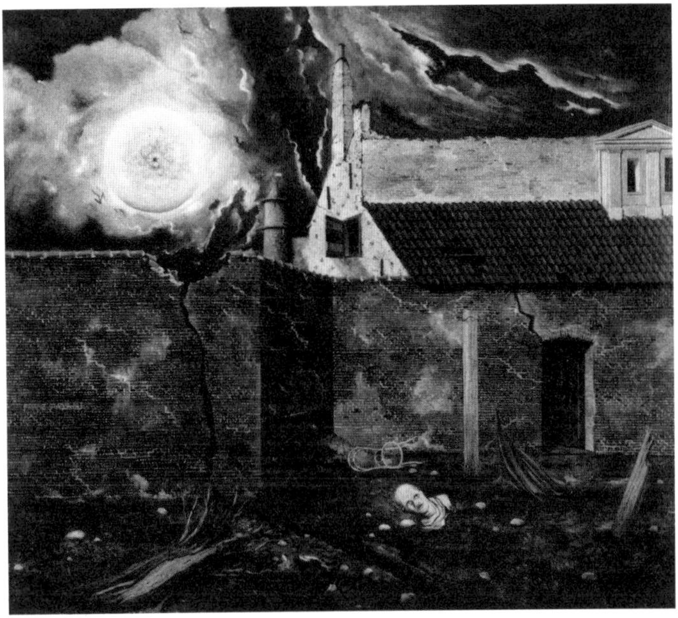

Franz Radziwill, *Der Riß im Hof* (The Fractured Courtyard), 1945, oil on wood, 101 × 115 cm, Städtische Galerie Wolfsburg

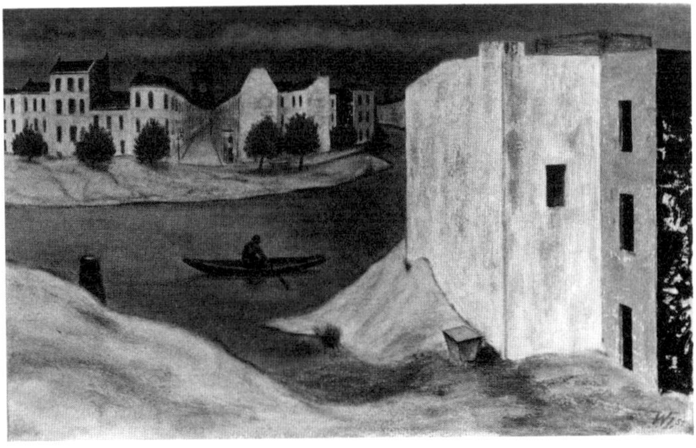

Werner Heldt, *Gewitternachmittag an der Spree* (Stormy afternoon on the Spree), 1951, oil on tempera, Akademie der Künste, Berlin, Kunstsammlung

1930s that he had been hitherto unable to exhibit.[22] He lived in East Berlin until the end of the Occupation, when he moved to the West. In 1947, a second exhibition of his works was held at the Galerie Anja Bremer in West Berlin, for which he wrote a short essay 'Berlin am Meer' (Berlin at Sea). Many of his works of this time took up the theme of an imaginary deluge of Berlin, and of a more general submission of humanity to natural disaster. The tone of these paintings and drawings is nevertheless consistently blithe, almost wistful; the ruins of Berlin are vaguely equated with Venetian decay. In comparison to works by older Berlin painters with whom he was associated, such as Heinrich Zille (1858–1929) and Lesser Ury (1861–1931), Heldt's images have no documentary value, and like those of Radziwill, no recognisable local detail. Both Radziwill and Heldt appeal to a realm defined by its lack of concrete historical or geographical references: the surrealist landscape is another country to which both artist and viewer can escape.

Works by Radziwill were exhibited at the only other exhibition of surrealist tendencies, *Vision und Magie* (Vision and Magic), at the Galerie Egon Günther in Mannheim in June 1948. Works by Max Ernst (1891–1976), Paul Klee (1879–1940), Radziwill and Rudolf Schlichter (1890–1955) were also exhibited alongside those by members of the Fantasten group: Thiemann, Trökes, Zimmerman, as well as Werner Gilles (1894–1951). Little more was heard from Surrealism after this moment. Despite Max Ernst's noticeable influence on young Berlin painters at the time, the failure of the large 1951 exhibition of his works organised in the Schloss-Augustusburg in the artist's birth-town of Brühl, was emblematic of the deeper distaste for Surrealism. 'Although many in Germany know his name', Lothar Pretzell wrote, 'only a few know his art [...] very little has changed since Alfred Flechtheim raised his admonitory voice [against Surrealism] in 1929'.[23] This view was shared by the critic Eduard Trier: 'If only the people of Brühl appreciated Surrealism!', he lamented, adding that the large financial burden that the exhibition placed on the local council, which was by no means sympathetic to Ernst's work, only exacerbated resentment.[24]

The case of the Munich-based painter Edgar Ende is equally telling. After a period serving in the Wehrmacht and as a prisoner-of-war, Ende returned to Munich and continued the type of painting with which he had established his reputation in the 1920s and 30s; small, sparse figurative compositions whose dream imagery is reminiscent of Giorgio de Chirico and René Magritte. His work was included in a number of exhibitions, including the 1946 *Erste Allgemeine Deutscher Kunstausstellung* in Dresden, the first large-scale survey exhibition of German art after the War (described in more detail in the following chapter), and also in *Vision und Magie*. In 1951 Ende was a founding member of the Internationalen Vereinigung der Surrealisten (International Society of Surrealists), an organisation instigated by the Swiss painter Walter Grab (1927–1989), whose sole manifestation was an exhibition of Surrealist painting held in the Saarland Museum in Saarbrücken in 1952. André Breton's forward for the exhibition catalogue, 'Trait d'union', emphasised the diplomatic function of the exhibition was a means of establishing connections between France and Germany. The essence of Surrealism,

Breton argued, resides in the 'profonde communauté de but' (profoundly communal nature of its aim).[25] The notion of such an international brotherhood was little upheld by the rest of the catalogue, which distinguished between artists belonging to the Surrealist movement, such as Bellmer, Ernst and Salvador Dalí, and those outside. The latter group included Ende, Schlichter and Grab. The Internationalen Vereinigung der Surrealisten was dissolved in 1953.

Surrealism, it seems, was a too dangerous and potentially disruptive idea to act as the basis of international accord, or as a symbol for the European Movement. As Freya Mülhaupt has written, German postwar interest in Surrealism stemmed less from French models and the influence of psychoanalysis than from the *Magischen Realismus* of the 1920s.[26] The artist and critic Franz Roh had instigated this critical trend in 1925; twenty years later, he showed little interest in the *Nachleben* of Surrealism, engaging rather with the legacy of Expression and the new spirit of abstraction.

The inadequacy of Surrealism as a ruin stylistic signalled a more general perception of painting's inadequacy at this moment. Many felt that the War was itself beyond representation: in 1954 the art historian Werner Haftmann wrote of the 'unanswerable' nature of the events, and suggested that the last conflict to find appropriate artistic response was the Spanish Civil War. He was evoking Picasso's *Guernica* (which toured Germany during 1955–6), itself a painterly response to terror bombing. More than any other subject, the effects of aerial bombardment exacerbated the long-standing confrontation of mechanical and manual artistic media – painting and photography – as legitimate ways to represent a changed world.

Ruin was the common fate binding East and West well into the postwar years. Dresden and Hamburg were the twin symbols of a German cultural heritage that had experienced the trauma of bombardment and the indignity of political division. Artistic responses to the disasters of war nevertheless diverged in the aftermath. Picturesque ruinscapes made in the West broadly contrast with works in the East that were determined by the imperatives of Socialist reconstruction, as well as Soviet stylistic demands. Soviet anti-formalist criticism, curiously anticipating Sebald, quickly latched on to the failure of western painting to respond adequately to the spectacle of destruction. Paintings by Fritz Kuhr (1899–1975), a former Bauhaus student, shown at the Berlin Galerie Franz in 1948, were criticised in the Soviet press for showing the 'phosphoric nights of aerial bombardment' as just an 'empty structure'. 'What does it mean when he paints a few curves onto the canvas subtitling them 'Lines of the *Trümmerfrauen* [rubble women]'? No randomly applied coloured scribbles can ever be testimony to social reality'.[27]

Working in a socially engaged, representational tradition, artists in the East were less prone to the dangers of escapism. It is nevertheless difficult to find works that directly 'testify to social reality', unmarked by the evasions evident in the West. Drawings by Wilhelm Rudolph (1889–1982) of Dresden ruins, in situ sketches with an important documentary character, or the two portfolios produced by Conrad Felixmüller (1897–1977), *Das Jahr des Malers* (The Painter's Year, 1947) and *Ich sah und schnitt in Holz* (I Saw and

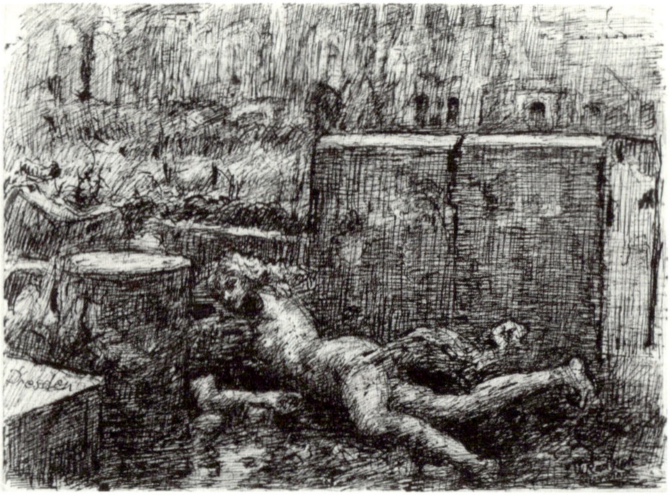

Wilhelm Rudolph, *Figuren vom Mozartbrunnen an der Bürgerwiese* (Figures from the the Mozart Fountain on the Bürgerwiese), 1945/6, ink drawing, 31.3 × 43.7 cm, Kupferstich-Kabinett, Staatliche Kunstsammlungen Dresden

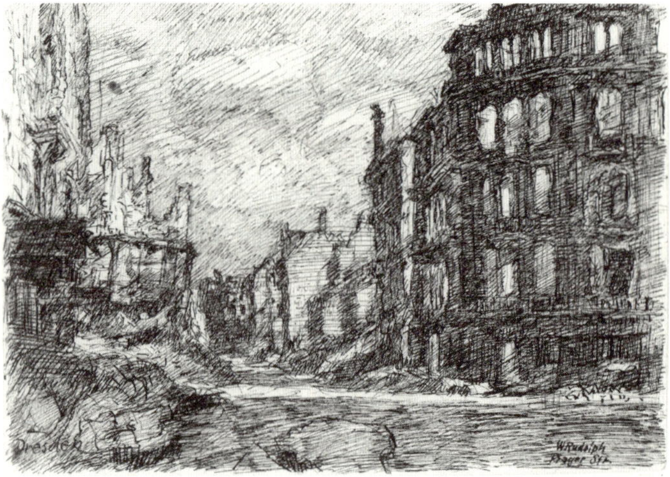

Wilhelm Rudolph, *Prager Straße*, 1945/6, ink drawing, 30.5 × 43.3 cm, Kupferstich-Kabinett, Staatliche Kunstsammlungen Dresden

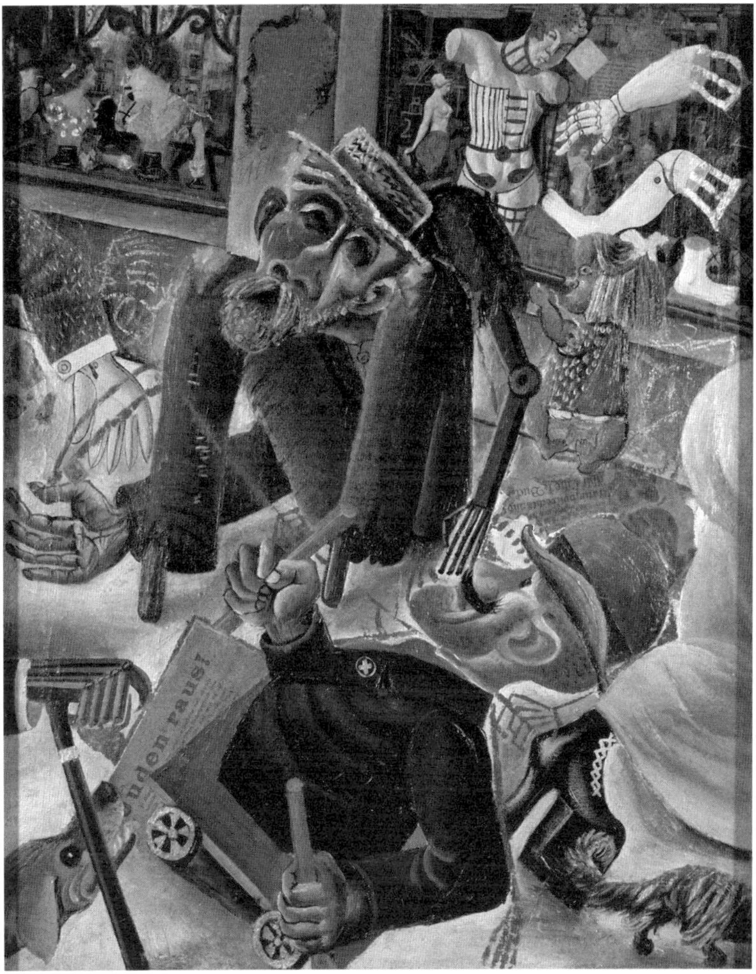

Otto Dix, *Prager Straße*, 1920, oil on canvas with collage, 101 × 81 cm, Staatsgalerie, Stuttgart. Peter Willi/ The Bridgeman Art Library

Cut in Wood, 1948), stand amongst the more successful attempts in traditional media to respond to the ruinscape. Rudolph began the portfolio *Das zerstörte Dresden* directly after the bombardments with a drawing of his own house, which had been destroyed, and completed the series of 150 sheets in early 1946. The most painful symbol of Dresden's destruction, the toppled statue of the theologian Martin Luther lying face down in front of the demolised Frauenkirche, formed the subject for one drawing. Rudolph was evidently proud of the eyewitness quality of his drawings – Richard Peters, whose photographic portfolio *Eine Kamera Klagt an* (The Camera Accuses, 1950) depicted the ruins of the towns, along with the first moments of rubble-clearance, 'arrived only in Autumn', according to Rudolph.[28] A comparison with Otto Dix's images of Dresden after the First World War, particularly his depiction of Dresden's famous Prager Straße, suggests however that Rudolph's drawings, whose even tone and texture may be likened to black and white photographic prints, convey little real information about the effects of the bombardments, showing rather the views of a wanderer on the edge of a town, reluctant to enter the area of silent desolation.

In his foundational essay on postwar stylistic debates, the art historian Peter Hielscher notes how work made after 1945 by left-wing artists appeared pale and spent in comparison with revolutionary art of the 1920s.[29] Some of the more compelling efforts were published in satirical anti-fascist journals that appeared both in eastern and western zones in 1946, particularly *Der Simpl*, *Wespennest* and *Ulenspiegel*.[30] *Der Simpl*, intended as a descendent of the satirical weekly review *Simplicissimus* (which ran from 1896

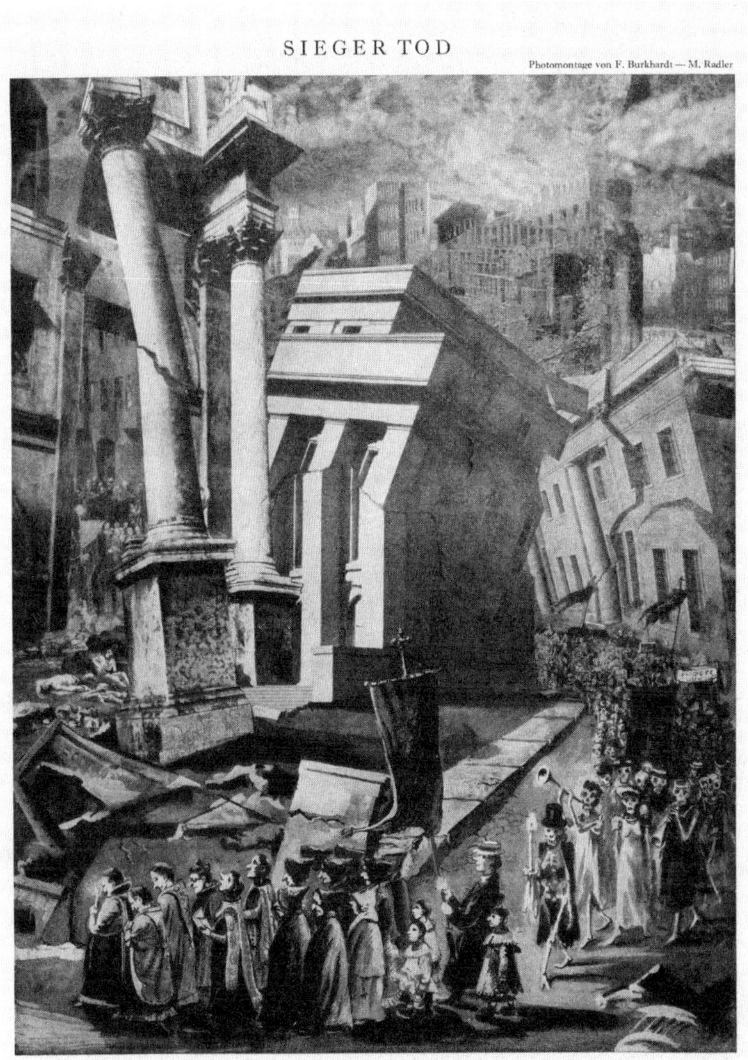

Fritz Burckhardt, *Sieger Tod* (Death Victorious), photomontage from *Der Simpl*, Munich, no.1, 28 March 1946

to 1944), appeared in Munich from 1946 to 1950, and targeted Bavarian Catholic culture and the (not inconsiderable) remnants of Nazism. Collages and illustrations by Fritz Burckhardt (1900–83) and his friend the painter Max Radler (1904–71), as well as other local artists, are a revealing window onto postwar life. Burkhardt's photomontage *Sieger Tod* (Death Victorious), which appeared in the first issue, depicts a Catholic procession of priests and skeletons in carnival mode beneath crumbling classical buildings and distant ruins.[31] *Wespennest* was published in Stuttgart between 1946 and 1949, and held an anti-CDU position. The best-known of these journals, *Ulenspiegel*, first appeared in Berlin in 1946, under American licence.[32] The involvement of a number of prominent artists, including Jeanne Mammen (1900–76), Oskar Nerlinger (1893–1969) and the former Bauhaus student Theo Balden (1904–95), who had returned from English exile in 1947 (see below), lent cultural weight to the anti-fascist programme.

In all these journals, the engagement with contemporary reality, as the art historian Jost Hermand has suggested, is nevertheless given a *kabarettistische* (cabaret-like) frame that renders it politically harmless.[33] Gathering political debates also tended to overshadow documentary intent. From an anti-fascist position, the ruins themselves were confirmation of the deleterious nature of modern art, the early modern abstraction of Wassily Kandinsky and the distortions of Picasso signalling the decline of European culture into secular ruin. By contrast, the new school of ruin painting projected in the East would neither romanticise nor demonise the ruins, but would use them as a symbol of the social and spiritual dimensions of reconstruction. These points were made in the Soviet-sponsored journal *bildende kunst* during 1948.[34] There is no evidence of any school appearing able to fulfil this role. Revealingly, what developed instead in the East was an incipient debate about the status of photography, pivoted on the documentary and aesthetic claims of the medium, whose status was far from clarified. Enthusiasm for photography as an 'art' was still very tentative.

These questions were addressed by the art critic Heinz Lüdecke, who warned in 1948 of the dangers of 'pictorial escapism'. Writing in *bildende kunst*, he described an image by the photographer Max Baur (1898–1988) as transforming the ruins of the Potsdamer Schloß into a 'romantic idyll' reminiscent of the 'impassioned' style of ruin painting that arose in the eighteenth century in the work of Giovanni Paolo Panini and Giovanni Battista Piranesi.[35] Baur, whose work was closely influenced by Bauhaus trends before the war, had returned to Potsdam from 'inner-emigration' in Munich to find his beloved Sanssouci in ruins. Other photographs, including those taken by Edmund Kesting (1892–1970) of Dresden, show that a 'subjective' use of photography can be historical and also convey information about the ruins. Kesting had been associated with Herwarth Walden's Expressionist Sturm circle in the 1920s, but then in 1932 joined the Deutschen Werkbund and became active as a photographer. He was banned from painting and exhibiting in 1934, but was able to continue photographic work. He was closely involved in cultural reconstruction in Dresden and then Berlin after 1945, both as an artist and a teacher of photography. Kesting's prints, among the most striking response to the ruins of Dresden, used a technique of printing from montaged and altered negatives. The example of his work fired Lüdecke's enthusiasm for the flexibility of photography to constitute both an *Abbild*, a copy of nature, and a *Sinnbild*, or symbol. Lüdecke's proposal implies something very important: that precisely because photography stopped short of full artistic status, it was an appropriate mode for the ruins. Other reflections on the artistic legitimacy of photography at the time demonstrate no driving wish to claim photography as one of the fine arts. 'It is an old and unfulfilled wish of us photographers for our work to be valued as real art', wrote the photojournalist Fritz Eschen (1900–64) in *bildende kunst*, 1949. He concludes that this is an unattainable goal, and that photography should be evaluated either as a craft or as photoreportage.[36]

Photography has been defined in many subsequent accounts as a 'counter-aesthetic' medium amongst the ruins. Walter Grasskamp has suggested that photography 'triumphed' over painting after 1945, but not strictly as an 'art'. If painting was obliged to abdicate its representational power in the face of the SS-State and Stalinism, as Grasskamp writes, then photography was a way of protecting images from dangerous human subjectivity: man could no longer be the measure in his formed arts, without prosthetic, mechanical assistance.[37] Though painting could convey individual experiences or personal feelings of humiliation and trauma, the formative influence of images on 'collective' historical consciousness was superseded, so this argument ran, by the documentary possibilities of photography and film. Peter Hielscher has also asserted that the documentary aspect of postwar ruin photography blocked the escape route into a *selbstgefertigte Kunstwelten*, or self-referential sphere of art.[38] However, as Lüdecke's comments in *bildende kunst* hint, and as many photographs of the time clearly show, this 'avoidance of avoidance' was by no means clear, and in many cases photographs took on qualities similar to those of ruin paintings.

Photographs of Cologne taken by Hermann Claasen (1899–1987) during the bombing raids of 1945 (when he risked not only the bombs but also a Reich prohibition on photography)[39] and his pictures of the ruins and reconstruction, were exhibited for the first time in November 1947, in the exhibition *Tragödie einer Stadt* (Tragedy

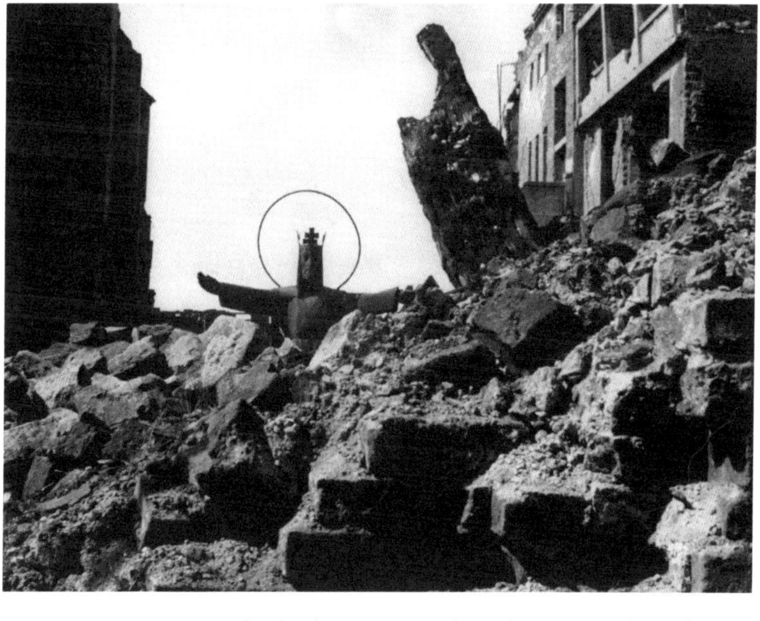

Hermann Claasen, 'Christus König vor der Kirche St. Maria in der Kupfergasse' (Convent Garden in the Kupfergasse), c.1945, published in *Gesang im Feuerofen*, Düsseldorf, 1947

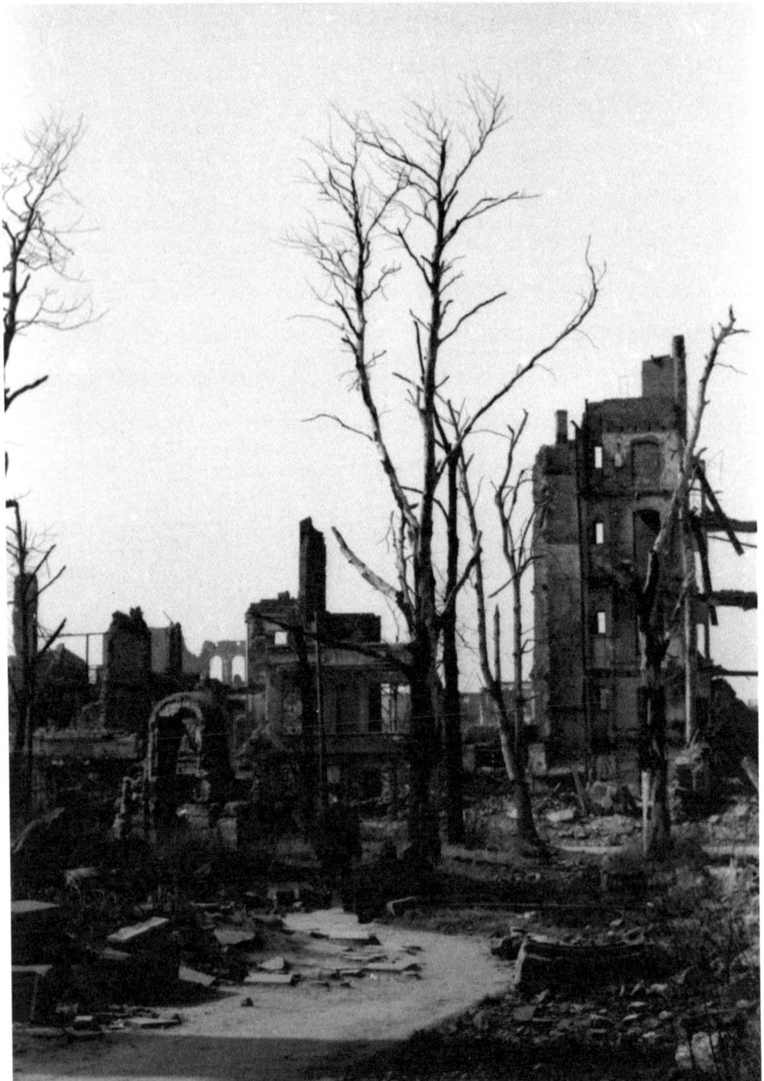

Hermann Claasen, 'Blick vom Wallraf-Richartz-Museum auf die Straße An der Rechtschule' (Near the Museum), c.1945, published in *Gesang im Feuerofen*, Düsseldorf, 1947

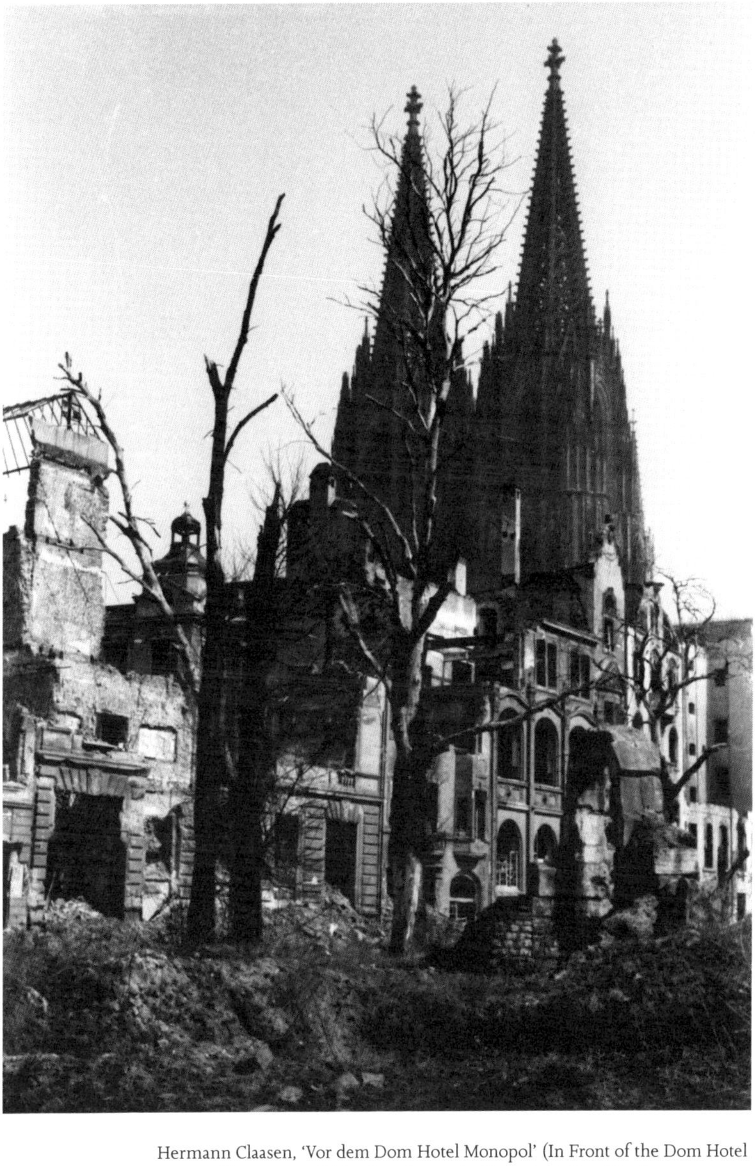

Hermann Claasen, 'Vor dem Dom Hotel Monopol' (In Front of the Dom Hotel Monopol), c.1945, published in *Gesang im Feuerofen*, Düsseldorf, 1947

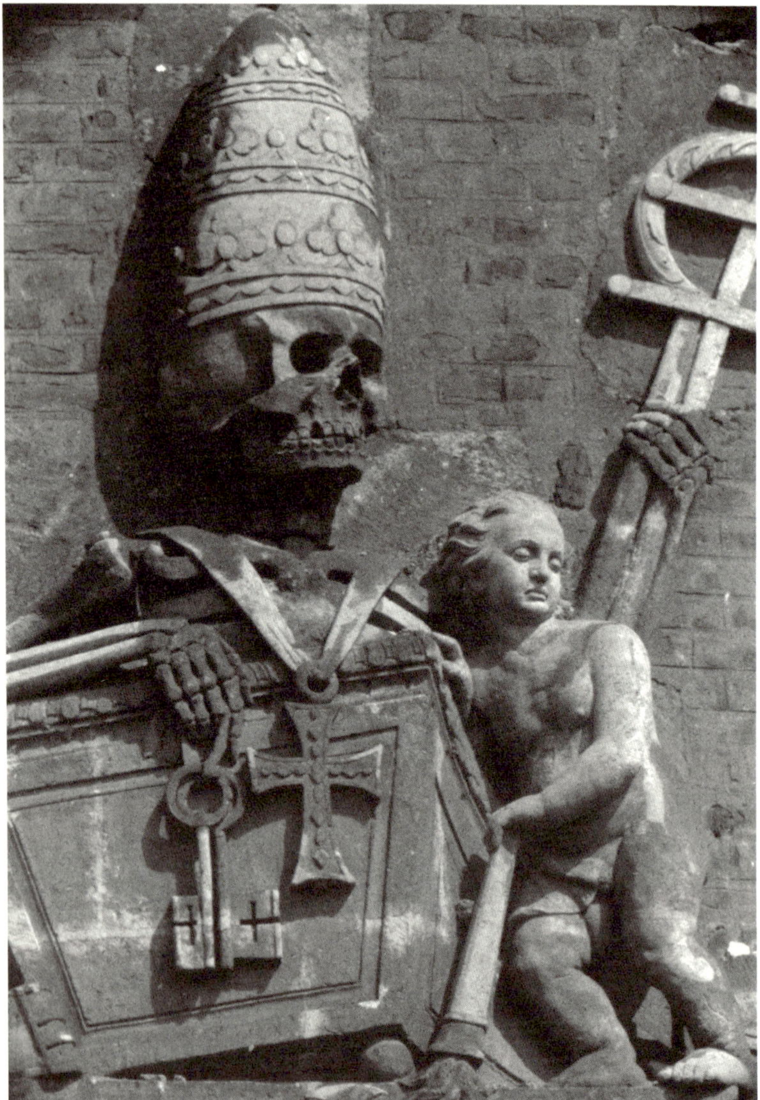

Hermann Claasen, 'Elendskirche' (Porch Coronal of the Elendskirche), c.1945, published in *Gesang im Feuerofen*, Düsseldorf, 1947

of a Town), and published the same year in the book *Gesang im Feuerofen* (Songs of the Furnace).[40] The title refers to the Old Testament story of the three Jews who refuse to worship a golden statue made by King Nebuchadnezzar. The Jews were thrown into a furnace, but miraculously survived. Consequently, Nebuchadnezzar decreed that anybody who blasphemed their names should be torn limb from limb, and their dwelling-places laid in ruins.

Based in Cologne and active as a freelance commercial photographer before the war, Claasen became well-known for his images of the ruined Rhineland. He had received a request from the local council of Düren, a small town to the West of Cologne, to photograph damage in the environs of Düren, Jülich and Hürtengewald. Düren itself had been completely destroyed on one night in November 1944. Claasen's attention was nevertheless most captivated by the spectacle of Cologne, photographs of which dominate *Gesang im Feuerofen*. Damaged, burnt and toppled statues are virtually the only human forms present in his photographs. Appearing again and again from different vantage points, Cologne Cathedral, apparently untouched by the bombs that had wrought unlimited destruction right up to its portals, constitutes an intact central point for Claasen's photographic wanderings.

Although the structure that remained could still give the impression of an intact building, damage to the cathedral had in fact been extensive.[41] It was for this reason that the Dom could be portrayed as martyred architecture. In the wake of bombing, such buildings became strong emblems of cultural endurance and spiritual hope – St Paul's Cathedral in London was a similar witness to the profane destruction. Just as the devastation of French medieval architecture during the First World War, particularly Reims cathedral, had stimulated a neo-medieval revival, and a historiographic claim for medieval art as a French phenomenon,[42] so in Germany after 1945 the medieval became charged with national significance. The Gothic cathedral was the emblem of a coherent Middle Age that stood opposed to the dislocated machine age, whose technologies of destruction had ravaged Europe. For those who had not witnessed the destruction, it was difficult to imagine the loss. The art historian Otto von Simson, working in exile in Chicago, elided the facts of European destruction:

> We may feel no closer to medieval civilisation than we do to ancient Greece or Egypt: indeed, our modern world came into existence as a revolt against the intellectual order of the Middle Ages. But the Gothic cathedral, the expression of that order, is intact and in use today; it is not the romantic ruin of a recent past beyond recovery, but still the center of nearly every European town [...][43]

Simson's indifference may be contrasted with the comments of the poet Stephen Spender, who visited Germany during 1945 and 1946. His description of devastated Cologne is powerful:

> The effect of these corpse-towns is a grave discouragement which influences everyone living and working in Germany, to Occupying Forces as much as the

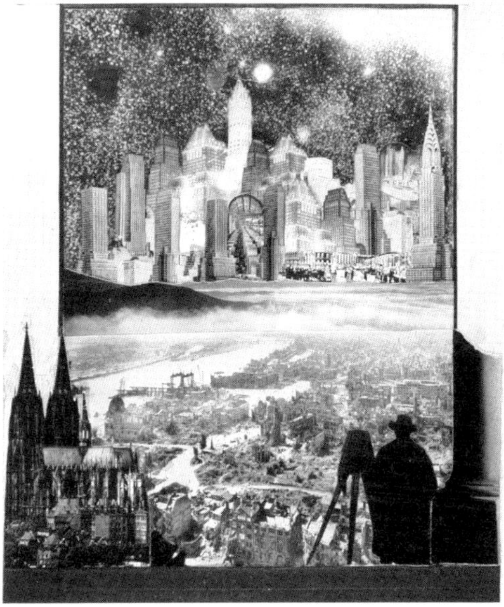

August Sander, collage for New Year's greeting, 1948–1949

> German. The destruction is *serious* in more senses than one. It is a climax of deliberate effort, an achievement of our civilization, the most striking result of co-operation between nations in the twentieth century. It is the shape created by our century as the Gothic cathedral is the shape created by the Middle Ages. Everything has stopped here, that fusion of the past within the present, integrated into architecture, which forms the organic life of a city [...][44]

The destruction, Spender suggests, hangs with bodily insistence in a timeless present. Claasen's pictorial account gives the cathedral and surviving statuary a living, anthropomorphic character, the survivors contrasting with the surrounding desolation. Only one photograph shows signs of human activity, but even here the theme is linked to the ecclesiastical monuments: a Corpus Christi procession through Cologne in 1946. The frieze of nuns in the lower third of the image compares with the band of destroyed buildings above. In-between, bystanders locate themselves vaguely on the pathways that have begun to be cleared through the rubble. The image is exceptional for *Gesang im Feuerofen* in showing organised social life amongst the ruins. Later revised editions of Claasen's portfolio dwell instead on the problems of daily life – a version published in the early 1980s, containing two short texts by Heinrich Böll, is made up almost entirely of human-interest images, emergency accommodation, the black-market, rubble-clearance.[45] The 1947 publication was the result of a different impulse, directed more towards rescuing the specificity, the 'placeness' of place, not only by emphasising the centrality of the cathedral, but also by referring, as had Wilhelm Rudolph, directly to street names and areas of town. This was clearly an imperative, though difficult task – Claasen reports that much of the character of the town was lost, and that he could well have been in Essen or Hamburg.[46]

Ruins are already symbols, allegories of their own histories. Delocalised, they become emblems of all damage: 'universal visual shorthand for the pity of war', in the recent words of one historian.[47] Would this not, as Simone de Beauvoir had noted, and Heinz Trökes implied, make any attempt at artistic interpretation superfluous, like making a painting of a painting? Why would one want to multiply these painful symbols? Photography too, it seemed, could not solve this problem, or exchange the stylistic question for one of historical analysis. Claasen's depictions of ecclesiastical statuary are no more able to ascribe historical meaning to the ruins than Rudolph's etchings or Heldt's scenes of flooded Berlin. The limits of photography as a medium were keenly evident. Whereas written history arranges the objects of the past according to a particular perspective or chronology, photography, by contrast, presents a promiscuity of detail that obliterates any perspective or ordering of historical traces: 'a person's history is buried as if under a layer of snow', as the Weimar theorist Siegfried Kracauer put it.[48]

If photography and Surrealism were divergent modes of response, they were also curiously interlinked. It was only by the appeal to Surrealist imagery that photography could attempt any kind of generic, interpretative look at the ruins. Postwar, Surrealist-influenced painting was in turn largely concerned with naturalistic imagery. That this brought with it the dangers of aestheticisation, escapism and the picturesque, indicates the dilemma facing artists. Only by an oblique vision can artists avoid the dangers of kitsch when representing disaster.

A different sort of evidence was captured in photographs taken in Germany in early 1945 by the American photojournalist Margaret Bourke-White (1904–71). These were published in *Life* magazine and then the next year in *Dear Fatherland, Rest Quietly*, a fascinating illustrated account of Bourke-White's experiences in Germany.[49] They follow largely the same formula as her portfolios of industrial photography, made in the 1930s whilst working for *Fortune* magazine, picture-stories that showed 'everything from the steam shovel to the board of directors'. Bourke-White had travelled to Germany in 1930 to photograph industrial subjects including AEG and IG Farben, the North German Lloyd shipping docks and other subjects in the Ruhr Valley. A further illustrated article on German rearmament appeared in *Fortune* magazine in January 1933.[50] The format she developed before the war for representing large-scale industrial processes was important for her later work in postwar Germany. The 1939 book *Newsprint. A Book of Pictures Illustrating the Operations in the Manufacture of Paper on which to print the World's News* used aerial photography to grasp the large scale, quasi-abstract commercial operations, such as the sprawling log-floats or hydroelectric dams, presenting as clearly as possible the industrial processes from beginning to end. Similarly focusing on cause and effect, the images in *Dear Fatherland* are chiefly concerned with the 'German' question of guilt and culpability. Faces of 'typical' Nazis are shown to excite a response of physiognomic stereotyping, for example in the unidentified portrait of a 'German Butcher and his wife' (whether the parody of August Sander was intentional is unclear; in the later German translation of her book, the caption reads '*Ein deutsches Ehepaar*' – 'A German married couple'). An aerial shot of a ruin landscape is presented as a symbol of the country as a whole, captioned 'Detail of any German city'. Similarly, an overhead view of the room containing the corpses of the Leipzig city treasurer and his family, suicides in advance of the Red Army, is compared to an aerial photograph of a 'prison pen' of German soldiers near Munich. The moral prerogative of a *vae victis*, or the victor's point of view, is barely concealed. To be German was to be guilty. Like Claasen's picturesque views, Bourke-White's images are

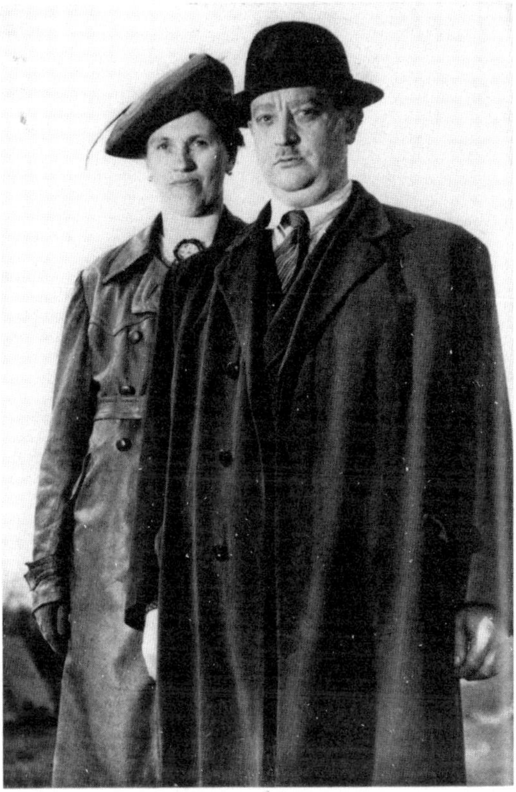

A German butcher and his wife.

Margaret Bourke-White, 'A German Butcher and his Wife', illustration from *Dear Fatherland, Rest Quietly*, 1946, unpaginated

delocalised in an allegorical manner. *Dear Fatherland, Rest Quietly* may itself be captioned with a penetrating analysis of the nature of allegory: 'Any person, any object, any relationship can mean absolutely anything else. With this possibility a destructive, but just verdict is passed on the profane world: it is characterized as a world in which the detail is of no great importance'.[51]

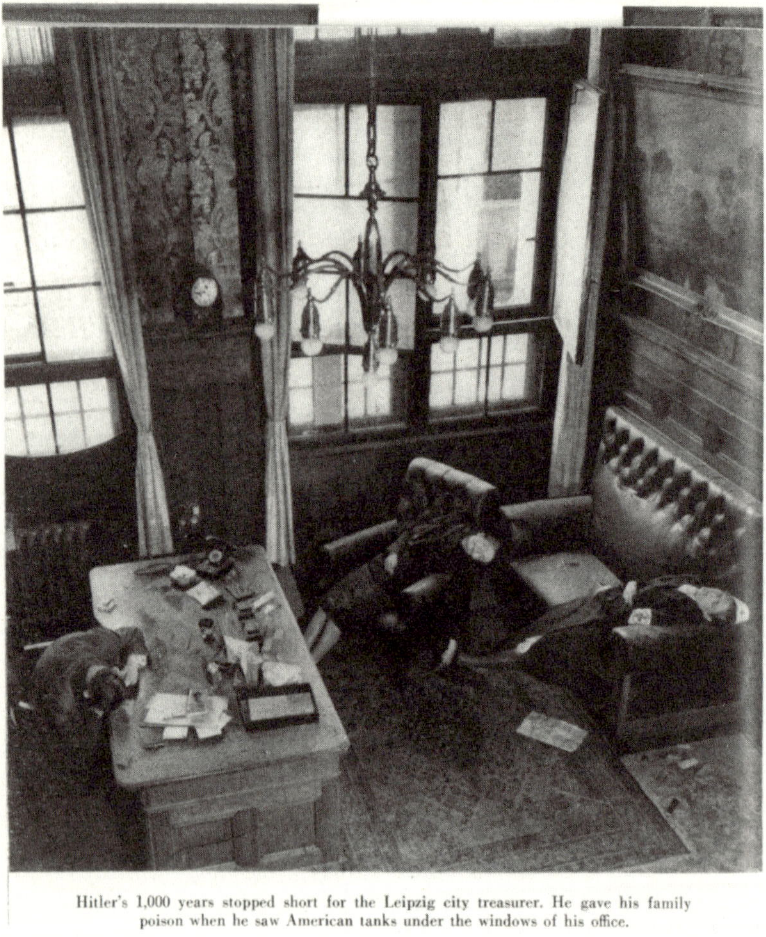

Hitler's 1,000 years stopped short for the Leipzig city treasurer. He gave his family poison when he saw American tanks under the windows of his office.

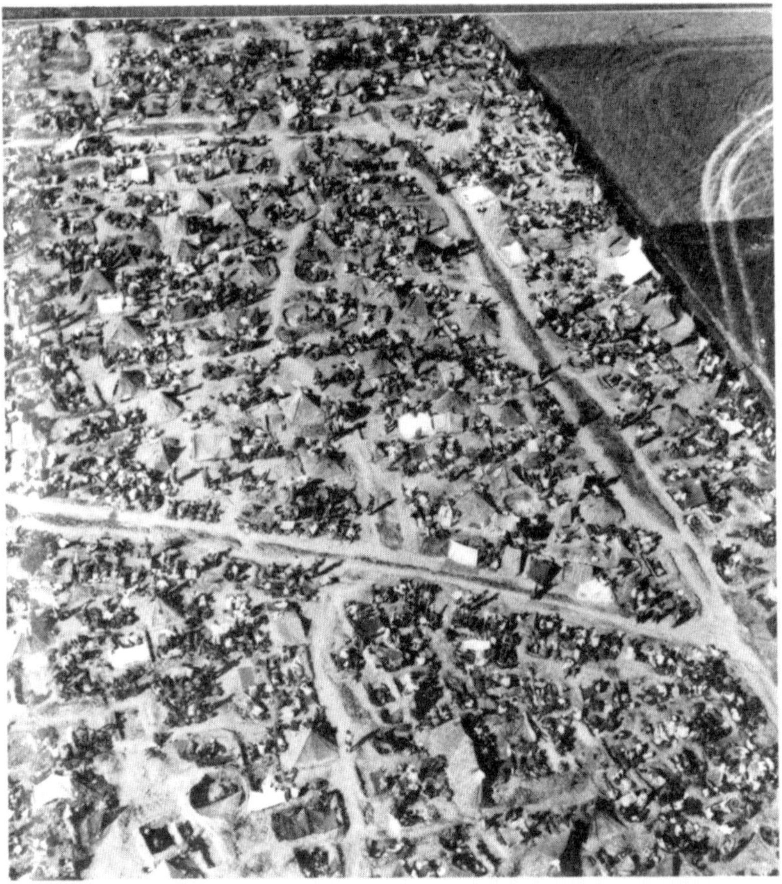

There were many prison pens like this one near Munich when whole armies began surrendering.

Left: Margaret Bourke-White, 'Hitler's 1000 years stopped short for the Leipzig city treasurer. He gave his family poison when he saw the American tanks under the windows of his office'. Right: Margaret Bourke-White, 'There are many prison pens like this one near Munich when whole armies began surrendering'. Illustrations from *Dear Fatherland, Rest Quietly*, 1946, unpaginated

The quotation is from Walter Benjamin's difficult work on the German tragic drama of the sixteenth and seventeenth centuries. Benjamin also observes that the allegorical imagination is attracted, with a melancholy, ruminative gaze, to the ruin: allegories are 'in the realm of thoughts what ruins are in the realm of things'.[52] Ruins for Benjamin emblematised the allegorical condition of modernity itself. The 'petrified, primordial landscape' of the ruinscape showed '[everything] about history that, from the very beginning, has been untimely, sorrowful, unsuccessful'.[53] With the peculiar quality of an image rather than a thing, and with clear historical connotations of romantic escape, the postwar landscape appeared to catch artists in an allegorical circuit that shut out real causes or effects. It is impossible to evade the problem of 'topographical sentimentality', which precludes all discussion of actual causes or historical circumstances.[54] An aestheticising impulse implies both a 'thrown-ness' and blindness to the situation, a resigned view that has no intention of invoking cause or culpability. A disturbance in nature has cut the objects in the world off from human relations, leaving no other option for a wanderer through the broken towns than a detached, blank gaze. His appeal to the picturesque appears as a weakness, or a turn away from reality, by which, at best, a certain attitude towards the material world after the war is brought to light.

Photographs by Bourke-White were exhibited for the first time in Germany at the 1951 *photokina*, a yearly trade-fair/exhibition inaugurated in Cologne the previous year. The exhibition was a conscious re-establishment of prewar traditions, for instance of the *Photo-Kino-Optik-Messen* – trade fairs that took place in Leipzig until 1938.[55] A further connection may be drawn to the *Film und Foto* exhibition held in Stuttgart in 1929. Instigating the exhibition series in September 1949, the curator and collector Fritz Gruber (1908–2005) described the 'cultural mission' of photography as a coalition both of professionals and amateurs, and also as a means to promote international relations within economic, scientific and cultural circles. The aesthetic status and value of photography was apparently not part of this mission. Gruber's ideas of photography as a 'world language' were realised at the 1951 *photokina* exhibition, with displays from eight countries, including contributions from the New York Museum of Modern Art and *Life* Magazine. Bourke-White's work was included as part of this display.[56] The emphasis was on international commercial exchange rather than aesthetics. The legitimate export of German cameras after their extensive use as a medium of exchange with Allied soldiers and officials during the occupation, described by Bourke-White in *Dear Fatherland*, is also cited in the 1950 catalogue as a symbol of the successful reintegration of German industry into an international market.

The inaugural exhibition in 1950, the *Photo-Kino Ausstellung*, did not, however, exclude 'aesthetic' photography. Here could also be seen the first public showing of 'subjective photography' by the fotoform group, co-founded the previous year by the photographer and teacher Otto Steinert (1915–78), with Peter Keetman, Siegfried Lauterwasser, Wolfgang Reisewitz, Toni Schneiders and

Ludwig Windstoßer. Although Subjektive fotografie was defined by Steinert in part as opposition to commercial and documentary photography, it drew on traditions of both. Typically, it adopted unusual viewpoints to create abstract imagery, or effects like long exposure to produce pictorial ambiguity, showing clearly the influence of 1930s experimental photography. In early 1948, Steinert had established a course in photography at the Staatlichen Schulen für Kunst und Handwerk (State School for Art and Crafts) in Saarbrücken, a Bauhaus-inspired school established by the French military administration in the Saar region. The first Subjektive fotografie exhibition, organised by Steinert in Saarbrücken in 1951, comprised a range of works, from the 'abstract' photography associated with the fotoform group, to documentary photography. It was billed as an 'international exhibition of modern photography', and showed work by a number of other European groups, including three from Italy, the English C.S. Association, the French Group de XV, and others from Holland, Sweden and Austria.[57] Also included were displays of photographs by László Moholy-Nagy, Man Ray and Herbert Bayer, indicating Steinert's debt to the experimental photography of the Bauhaus, and to Surrealism. The pedagogic environment of the Bauhaus was a strong influence on Steinert's work in Saarbrücken.

His efforts were, however, short-lived. The Subjektive fotografie movement can at best be seen as a bridge between the graphic, abstract concerns of Neue Sachlichkeit photography and postwar abstract painting. Steinert's school may also be considered as part of a postwar photographic milieu that bore little resemblance to the critical sphere that evolved around experimental photography and media theory during the 1930s. The art historian Klaus Honnef has described the number of Nazi photographers who readily found work after 1945, in particular in the democratic press established by the British occupation authorities.[58] Despite the publication in 1947 of the German translation of Siegfried Kracauer's *From Caligari to Hitler*, Honnef notes that Steinert and the photography milieu of his time were as unaware of Kracauer's theories of photography as they were of the writings of Walter Benjamin or Bela Balázs. 'The philistine spirit of National Socialism had taken its toll', he concludes.[59] Lacking such theoretical grounding, Steinert's photographic practice, extending a tradition nurtured by Claasen, slid into a defensive mode. After his success with photographs of the ruined Rhineland, Claasen's work, too, tended towards 'subjective' trends, and was included in exhibitions of subjective photography during the 1950s.

Following the difficult, and ultimately unsatisfactory trends of ruin painting and photography, which were hardly to develop into coherent genres, these developments show how little prewar intellectual traditions were available in the first few years of reconstruction. The indifference that Arendt had noted ran deep. Critical, media-oriented theories of those such as Kracauer, Benjamin and others had virtually no resonance: these left-wing Weimar theorists were simply not part of the *Wiederaufbau* (reconstruction) milieu. Benjamin was first brought to light in the postwar period by the publication in 1955 of his two-volume *Schriften* (collected writings), edited by Theodor and Gretel Adorno, and Friedich Podszus. *Einbahnstrasse* appeared the next year. Although two other books by Benjamin had appeared since 1945 – his *Spiegelungen*

Goethes in unserer Zeit, a series of studies on the poet published during the Goethe celebrations of in 1949, and *Berliner Kindheit um neunzehnhundert* (Berlin childhood around 1900) in 1950 – the broader impact of his 'neo-marxism' arose only in the context of the student movement a decade later. Current understanding of his work, and indeed impressions of 'radical' Weimar culture in general, are in debt to this rediscovery by a politicised generation born during or after the war. Adorno himself, although he may in retrospect have produced the most cogent philosophical expression of the broken spirit of the postwar years, had little impact through his writings at the time. The lack of interest in the 1947 *Dialektik der Aufklärung* (Dialectic of Enlightenment), out of print for over twenty years until its first reissue in 1969, is well known. The complete absence of Adorno's name from all art publications and periodicals during the late 1940s and 1950s (with the important exception of the Darmstädter Gespräch, described below) confirms his obscurity within aesthetic discussions.

Rather than the historical explanations of critical theory, the intellectual field during the decade after 1945 was dominated by three more dogmatic modes: Marxist-Leninism, Catholicism and Existentialism. Although, as has been shown, it is difficult to avoid figures such as Benjamin and Kracauer entirely, other sorts of texts must be sought to ground an understanding of the problems facing artists waking up in the ruined country. Such texts are marked by similar problems of representation.

Unsurprisingly, the theme of ruin was directly addressed by the major representatives of Existentialism after 1945, Martin

Heidegger and Karl Jaspers. Although their paths had separated in 1933 following Heidegger's assimilation into Nazism, a separation confirmed by Jaspers' dismissal in 1937 from his professorship at Heidelberg and subsequent *Publikationsverbot* (publishing ban), both philosophers appeared after the war as leading representatives of the tradition of Existenzphilosophie (Existentialism). The attention paid by such thinking to the ethical position of the individual and the subjective, personal dimension of life, acquired clear and understandable resonance in the postwar decade. Jean Améry was to note that the appeal of Existentialism was based at least in part on the word 'existence' itself, precious and magical after the disasters of war. Although the tenor is allusive, both were able to respond directly to the postwar landscape, suggesting ways in which it could be seen. Heidegger's 1951 essay 'Bauen Wohnen Denken' (Building, Dwelling, Thinking), first presented as a lecture in Darmstadt the same year, develops concepts directly from a sense of being in a 'broken' place. Dwelling is a basic character of mankind; 'Building as dwelling, that is, as being on the earth, however, remains for man's everyday experience that which is from the outset "habitual" – we inhabit it, as our language says so beautifully: it is the *Gewohnte*'.[60] Heidegger's concern is to salvage the original significance of words denoting building and dwelling, to return the essence of a lost meaning. The postwar housing shortage (to which he directly refers) becomes also a conceptual shortage, a de-signification or de-localisation of things for which he is anxious to compensate.

Despite the poetic weight of Heidegger's formulations, Jasper's lectures and publications had a greater general impact during the postwar decade. He was more accessible and vividly concerned with the practical application of philosophy. One contemporary compared the importance of Jasper's 1933 publication *Die geistige Situation der Zeit* (published in English the same year as *Man in the Modern Age*), as a source of solace and orientation, with the memorable impact of Max Weber's essays 'Wissenschaft als Beruf' (Science as a Vocation) and 'Politik als Beruf' (Politics as a Vocation) during the chaos following the First World War.[61] In his book *Die Schuldfrage*, published in Heidelberg in 1946 and in English translation the next year as *The Question of German Guilt*, Jaspers held that Germans who had not assisted with Nazi crimes but remained in Germany were politically, but not morally or metaphysically, guilty – 'Guilt, therefore, is necessarily collective as the political liability of nationals, but not in the same sense as moral and metaphysical, and never as criminal guilt'. Such political guilt had 'fearful consequences', but nonetheless 'leaves the soul untouched'.[62] The question of guilt was closely bound to the touchy question of *vae victis*, especially in relation to the Nuremberg Trials. Moral guilt could be incurred through passive acceptance of the regime; the right to pass moral judgement, however, should be reserved for the Germans themselves. Jaspers' argument ends with an appeal to the possibilities of purification, not only through dutiful reparation and genuine self-analysis, but also through 'purification of the soul', without which 'there is no political liberty'.[63]

Die Schuldfrage emphasises the experience of those who had lived the war in Germany. How could the Allies, who had not experienced daily life in Germany over the past few decades, cast judgement on those who had not risked their lives resisting the regime? It is true that few, if any, visual artists politically resisted Nazism from within Germany. More writers did so, but, as in the tragic case of Carl Ossietzky, their resistance led to nothing but great personal suffering and futile death. Yet after the war, the simple fact of not having left was of great import. The crucial qualification for intellectual leadership in the postwar period was having remained in Germany throughout the Third Reich. Thinkers and writers such as Adorno, Arendt and Ernst Bloch, as Jean Améry has noted, were therefore disqualified.[64] Thomas Mann's debate with the writers Frank Thiess and Walter von Molo, in which Mann criticised the concept of 'inner emigration', was one flashpoint for this widespread debate, which was largely decided in favour of those who had stayed.[65] Suffering was also a form of legitimacy for visual artists: underpinning the importance of Claasen's images was his proximity to real events as a witness and survivor. Paintings can, of course, be made after and away from the event, but they inevitably suffer for it: Werner Gilles's *Nach der Bombennacht* (After the Night Bombing, 1950) unmistakeably shows this distancing. The directness of drawing from life and photography have in this sense a moral dimension: only those with first-hand experience would be able to show things as they were. Max Ernst's failure during the postwar decade was at least in part based on his physical absence. Proximity was significant in other ways, too: the importance to artists' public reputations of having served at the front, documented in war letters, or having been branded *entartet* (degenerate) by the Nazis, is discussed below. Further, works of art themselves that showed scars of damage could be taken as

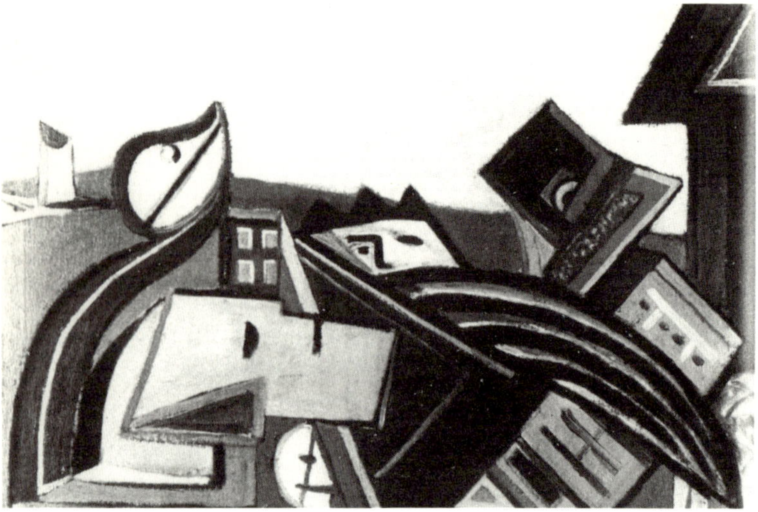

Werner Gilles, *Nach der Bombennacht*, (After the Night Bombing), 1950, oil on canvas, 67 × 95 cm, Kunstmuseum, Mülheim an der Ruhr in der Alten Post

legitimate representations of the destruction. Contemplating those survivals not only of the bombardment but also of the terrible fire in the air raid bunker at Friedrichshain in May 1945, whose cause is still disputed, one may concluded that suffering is indeed the only true source of historical knowledge.

Experience of the air raids was more widespread in the postwar decade than knowledge of the Holocaust, and it is for this reason that the focus can be placed here so strongly on the former. The impact of knowledge of the concentration camps on postwar German art, which has been documented in a number of books, is a story more properly taken up from a later date.[66] There is virtually no mention of the camps in literature on the arts that appeared in the postwar decade, and little evidence of an impact of the Holocaust

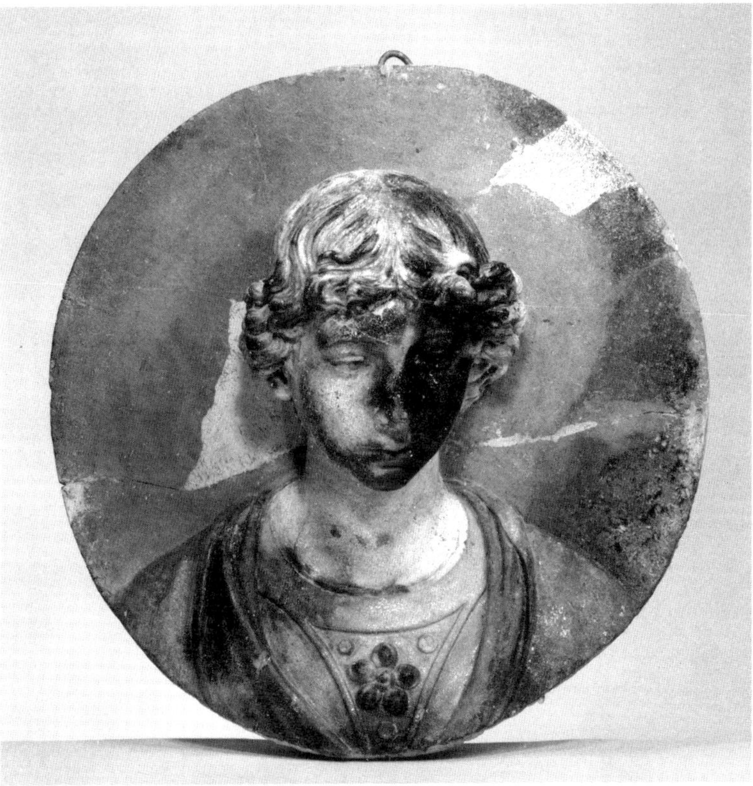

Andrea della Robia, *Portrait of a Youth*, c. 1470, relief with fire damage, Skulpturensammlung und Museum für Byzantinische Kunst, Berlin

on the visual arts. There were of course exceptions, in particular works of art made in the Soviet Zone by former political prisoners such as Hans and Lea Grundig, but these were generally perceived as contributing to the anti-fascist movement rather than affording atonement or recognition of the scale of the Holocaust, in particular the genocide of the European Jews. The effects of the bombardment still appeared in contemporary minds as a greater tragedy.

An indication of these priorities can be taken from a further book by Jaspers, *Von der Wahrheit* (On Truth), published in Munich in 1947. A short excerpt was translated into English and published as *Tragedy is not Enough* by the Anglo-Jewish publisher Victor Gollancz in London, in 1952. Gollancz's sympathy for Jasper's work was part of a much broader involvement in the 'German problem': he had visited the British Zone during late 1945, and published the illustrated book *In Darkest Germany* on his return, drawing attention to the plight of German civilians and criticising the moral underpinning of the Allied military governments. The book also reprinted many articles and letters that Gollancz had sent to the British press articulating these criticisms, which followed from his active opposition to fascism in the 1930s, as well as his attempt in 1942 to spread consciousness of the concentration camps. Following Jasper's concern to distinguish levels of guilt, Gollancz's publication of *Tragedy is not Enough* was part of a personal campaign to promote a more equitable view of Germans in England.

Tragedy is not Enough aims to salvage a concept of tragedy – a concept of genuine 'tragic knowledge' – to be set against the pseudo-tragedy of the 'arrogant nihilist', that is, the pathos and hubris of the Third Reich.[67] Jaspers projects the character of Hamlet onto the postwar German psyche – Hamlet quests after truth, despite the ruinous circumstances into which fate has thrust him. His predicament is exemplary: 'The time is out of joint. O cursed spite / That ever I was born to set it right!'[68] At the core of his argument is the idea that genuine tragic experience involves a discovery and interrogation of truth. If 'breakdown and failure reveal the true nature of things',[69] salvation can still be achieved by facing up to the tragic. 'Tragedy shows up in battle, in victory, and in defeat, guilt. It is the measure of man's greatness in breakdown and failure'.[70] To have survived tragic reality is to have been purified and elevated by tragic knowledge. That the 'tragic reality' is the ruined landscape is hinted at only once: 'Tragedy arises wherever in the world there is disunity, and where its consequences become visible. To be able to say this requires no deduction, but simply an elucidation of what is before us. This failure to achieve unity underlies the ruin of all we see around us'.[71] A human overcoming of tragedy is important, for tragic knowledge has its limits and becomes dangerous when assumed as a worldview. At this point '[it] lures us into an exalting realm of grandeur; and thus, despite all clear-eyed honesty, it obscures the truth'.[72]

Von der Wahrheit may be read as a call to artists and writers to respond to the ruins. Even if the universalising claims of tragedy brought with them the danger of 'metaphysical fraudulence' of which Sebald warned, his injunction to look directly at the ruined world as a source of knowledge is an important moment in the development of postwar art.

The alternative, of course, was silence. In his published memoirs of the postwar years, the legal theorist Carl Schmitt is highly critical of Jaspers' concept of 'collective guilt', preferring to join the community of those who chose not to speak or write in such an impossible situation. The 'silence' implied here is not an absolute muteness, but a refusal to contribute towards public discussion.[73] As a major twentieth-century political theorist and legal advisor to the Third Reich, Schmitt left a legacy that is without doubt as controversial as that of Heidegger. Although after 1945 Schmitt entered into a sort of postwar 'inner emigration' reserved for those who had been quite at home in the Third Reich, both the legacy of his Weimar theorising and his postwar work articulates many of the concerns of the reconstruction period, just as they had provided many of the leading political themes of the Weimar Republic. His anti-modernism and anti-liberalism voiced the concerns of those who thought that postwar culture in the West was too drastic a departure from tradition. Schmitt held that the problems faced by the modern state arose from liberal policies of economic freedom,[74] and the perilous move away from 'authentic' politics of decisionism and power struggle, towards the compromises of democracy.[75] Under threat was the authority of the Catholic Church, which for Schmitt, amongst many others, was the paragon of a coherent and substantial world-view, opposed to the meagre rationalism of economics and technology.

Schmitt is a fascinating figure, whose implication in the development of modern German culture – from his early friendship with the Dadaist Hugo Ball to his later involvement with the Third Reich – has yet to be adequately written. Despite his assumed muteness after 1945, he is nevertheless one of the few figures to have provided an adequate account of the situation of artists immediately after the fall of the Third Reich, albeit in a veiled manner. Schmitt often spoke out against the 'moral' basis on which the Allies framed their victory. What possibilities of legitimate expression could there be if the morality was all on one side, if the act of destroying the objects and erasing the names of the culture could find no echo in terms of culpability? His 1956 publication *Hamlet oder Hekuba. Der Einbruch der Zeit in das Spiel*, with which he broke his vow of silence, stands in a tradition of German political and philosophical writing that takes the figure of Hamlet as emblematic of a modern everyman. As Jasper's own work on tragedy had shown, the theme was by no means new. Victoria Kahn's outstanding account of Schmitt's interpretation of Hobbes and Shakespeare, one of the few commentaries available on *Hamlet oder Hekuba*, relates it to a tradition of 'Hamlet-reception' in German literature, including Goethe's *Wilhelm Meister*, Hegel's *Aesthetics* and Schlegel's *Über das Studium der griechischen Poesie* (On the Study of Greek Poetry) – she also refers to the compelling issue of the appropriation of Shakespeare by the Third Reich.[76]

Schmitt's theory of tragedy holds that for a work of art to be properly tragic it must be open to history, or be implicated in real historical events. He ascribes the tragic character of Hamlet, for example, to its intermingling of events at the end of Queen Elizabeth's reign with the political preferences of a Protestant London audience, for which Shakespeare had to cater. The suggestion is that in alluding to real events, authors communicate directly to audiences on the basis of a common culture or a shared history. Only those works of art that arise out of real circumstances are compelling enough to elicit feelings of catharsis, or a direct emotional response. 'An invented fate is no fate at all'.[77] Tragedy cannot simply be made up: it depends for its emotional effect not on the weight of aesthetic expression, but on how it coheres in a particular historical setting. The historical consciousness of the audience provides the authentic basis on which tragic circumstances can unfold. *Hamlet* is an open-ended play – formally imperfect, perhaps, but like an open-doored house through which historical draughts rush.

Letters written by the painter Hans Grundig from Dresden to his wife Lea, who remained in exile in Palestine until 1948, are a memorable contemporary document. Grundig, a committed left-wing artist who had strong ties with his native city, was in early 1946 made director of the Dresdner Academy, one of the few buildings that survived relatively intact. Wilhelm Rudolph was amongst those who returned to work with Grundig at the Academy. Alongside constant pleas for Lea to return to Dresden, despite the terrible living conditions, Grundig also describes the reconstruction of cultural life. In the Academy itself the exhibition *Sächsische Künstler stellen aus* (Saxon Artists' Exhibition) was held during March 1946. 'Here one can see everything that was hidden during the Fascist years', Grundig wrote. 'But it is shameful to consider the spiritual profile of such work. […] The worst thing is that there is no reflection of the terrible years that we have been through'.[78] He expresses similar sentiments while reflecting on the works which he and Will Grohmann had collected for the *Erste Allgemeine Deutsche Kunstausstellung*, held in Dresden in 1946: 'It can be said that this is the most important exhibition since 1927, the year of the large international exhibition. Yet, my dear Lea, all we have are generalities, just as in the recent exhibition of Saxon artists. Nowhere is anyone making any art that reflects the terrible years of the Third Reich'.[79]

Grundig's opinion was shared increasingly by those who had hoped for the emergence, from the catacombs, of work by artists made in secret during the years of fascism, that could act as symbols for inner resistance. Such work was not forthcoming.

If the text by Jaspers cited above may be read as a call to action, then Schmitt's *Hamlet oder Hekuba* may be considered a diagnosis, and explain some of the reasons for this failure. The lack of any meaningful artistic response to the Allied bombardment was a continuation of the muteness faced by those artists who remained in Germany throughout the Third Reich, in 'inner emigration'. If it was impossible to connect with traditions of German art, it was also impossible to reflect on the bizarre circumstances of everyday life. These conditions formed the foundations on which subsequent German art was to develop, and for which such art was in many cases to compensate. This situation may be clarified with a more detailed look at the material conditions of postwar life, in particular the problems arising from the occupation of Germany.

1 Rumpf, 9.
2 Arendt, H., 'The Aftermath of Nazi Rule', *Commentary*, no. 10, October 1950, 342–53, here 343.
3 Améry, 4.
4 Mumford, 15.
5 Sebald.
6 Ibid., 12.
7 Ibid., 81.
8 Kluge, 33-106.
9 Böll, 127.

10 Myers, B., 'Postwar Art in Germany', *College Art Journal*, vol. 10, Spring 1951, 251–6, here 251.
11 Dvorak, R., 'Kunst und Ruine. Preissausschreiben in Dortmund', *Die Welt*, 16 June 1946, 3.
12 Grayling.
13 Cf. Hans Galperin, 'Durchbruch zum Surrealismus', *Die Zeit*, 21 November 1946, 4; Ilse Langner, 'Wirklichkeit und Surrealismus', *Die Zeit*, 17 April 1947, 5; Barbara Klie, 'Übergangszeit. Drei Phasen der Kunst nach dem Krieg', *Der Monat*, no. 200, 1965, 100; *Der Simpl*, vol. II, no. 8, June 1947, special issue on 'irrealismus'.
14 de Beauvoir, 144.
15 Sedlmayr, 1961, 87.
16 Cited by Krause, 28.
17 Heinz Trökes, opening speech for the exhibition *Fantasten-Ausstellung*, Galerie Gerd Rosen, 11 February 1946. Reprinted in: Krause, 172–5, here 174.
18 Krause, 93.
19 Ibid., 94.
20 Hannah Höch, speech at the opening of the exhibition *Die Fotomontage von Dada bis heute*, December 1946. Reprinted in: Krause, 175–8.
21 Vietta, E., 'Franz Radziwill', *Das Kunstwerk*, no. 6, 1946, 42.
22 Krause, 64.
23 Pretzell, L., 'Zu Max Ernst und seinem Werk', *Max Ernst. Gemälde und Graphik 1920–1950*, exh. cat., Schloss Augustusburg, Brühl, 1951. Cited and translated in Spies, 232.
24 Trier, E., 'Surrealismus mit realistischem Defizit. Brühl schätzt zwar Max Ernsts Ruhm, doch nicht seine "Richtung"', *Die Neue Zeitung*, Frankfurt, no. 214, 12 September 1951. Cited and translated in: Spies, 234–5.
25 Breton, 6.
26 Mülhaupt, F., '…Und was Lebt, Flieht die Norm', in: Schulz, 192.
27 Lüd., 'Die Austreibung des Menschen. Zur Diskussion über abstrakte Kunst – Ausstellung und Zeitschriftenliteratur', *Berliner Zeitung*, no. 49, 27 February 1948.
28 Rudolph, 82.
29 Hielscher, P., 'Unbewältigte Gegenwart. Von der Schwierigkeit, Wirklichkeit Abzubilden', in: Schulz, 223–9.
30 Hermand, 1986, 119–21.
31 Fritz Burkhardt, *Sieger Tod* (photomontage), *Der Simpl. Kunst, Karikatur, Kritik*, year 1, no. 1, 28 March 1948, unpaginated (5).
32 Kuhirt, 60–5.
33 Hermand, 1995, 135.
34 E.L., 'Ruinenromantik, Ruinendämonie', *bildende kunst*, no. 7, 1948.
35 Lüdecke, H., 'Es Kommt auf die Einstellung an', *bildende kunst*, no. 7, 1948, 12.
36 F. Eschen, 'Ist Fotografie Wirkliche Kunst?', *bildende kunst*, no. 2, 1949, 70.
37 Grasskamp, 107–8.
38 Hielscher, P., 'Unbewältigte Gegenwart. Von der Schwierigkeit, Wirklichkeit Abzubilden', in: Schulz, 223–9, here 228.
39 Sachsse, R., 'Es wird nochmals ausdrücklichst darauf hingewiesen …' Aspekte der Bildzensur im NS-Staat und im Zweiten Weltkrieg', in: Deres and Rüther, 11–62.
40 Claasen, 1947, 1979; Scheurer; Honnef, 1995.
41 Kleff, W., 'Der Dom im Kriege', *Kölner Domblatt*, no.1, 1948, 50–60; Weyres, W., 'Die Schaden an unserem Dom', *Kölner Domblatt*, no. 1, 1948, 61–5.
42 Golan, 29.
43 von Simson, xxvii.
44 Spender, 24.
45 Thorn-Prikker.
46 Thorn-Prikker, 12.
47 Judt, 16.
48 Kracauer, S., 'Photography' (1927), in: Kracauer, 1995, 47–63, here 51.
49 'The Battered Face of Germany', *Life*, vol. 18, no. 3, 4 June 1945, 21–7; Bourke-White, 1946.

50 'Germany's Reichswehr', *Fortune*, vol. 7, no. 1, January 1933, 49–57.
51 Benjamin, 175.
52 Ibid., 178.
53 Ibid., 166.
54 Grasskamp, 113.
55 Messegelände, 1950, 7.
56 Reuter, N., 'Ten Years of photokina. The Cultural Achievement', in: Messegelände, 1960, 5–11.
57 Koenig, 400.
58 Honnef, K., 'From Reality to Art. Photography between profession and abstraction', in: Honnef, 1997, 140.
59 Ibid., 143.
60 Heidegger, M., 'Building Dwelling Thinking', in: Heidegger, 1978, 323–9, here 325–6; Originally 'Bauen Wohnen Denken' in: Heidegger, 1954, 145–62.
61 Schaeder, H.H., 'Karl Jaspers und sein kritiker', *Die Zeit*, 12 May 1949, 4.
62 Jaspers, 1947, 61–2.
63 Jaspers, 1947, 121.
64 Améry, 190–1.
65 Grosser.
66 Cf. Hornstein.
67 Jaspers, 1953, 101.
68 Cited by ibid., 1953, 61.
69 Ibid., 41.
70 Ibid., 45.
71 Ibid., 103–4.
72 Ibid., 99.
73 van Laak.
74 Schmitt, 1976, 28
75 Schmitt, 1922.
76 Kahn, V., 'Hamlet or Hecuba: Carl Schmitt's Decision', *Representations*, no. 83, Summer 2003, 67–96, here 93.
77 Schmitt, 1985, 47. Translation: David Pan 'The Source of the Tragic', *Telos*, no. 72, 1987, 133–51.
78 Grundig, 93.
79 Ibid., 107.

Occupation

Twelve years of oppression and struggle now lie behind us, a struggle against a cultural oppression pursued with a treacherous and devilish cunning unprecedented in German history.

Hans Uhlmann, 'Freiheit des Kunstschaffens', in Uhlmann, *Nach 12 Jahren*, exhibition catalogue, Kamillenstrasse 4, Berlin, 1945, unpaginated

As director of the Berlin National Gallery from 1937 to 1950, Paul Ortwin Rave was in a privileged position to observe the obliteration of Weimar cultural life by National Socialism. He recorded these observations in the first documentary account of art and the Third Reich, *Kunstdiktatur im Dritten Reich* (The Arts under the Third Reich), first published in 1949. The story told in this fascinating book accords with Jean-Michel Palmier's more recent assertion that '[...] it is impossible to analyse the richness of Weimar culture without raising the question of its destruction and survival after the advent of National Socialism'.[2]

Rave orients his discussion of cultural policy with an examination of the ways in which modern art was promoted as a national symbol abroad. At the beginning of the century, he notes, there was scant exposure of modern German art outside the country, and no official interest in supporting such ventures. Meagre showings at world fairs, the Venice Biennale, or else via private initiative did little to make the names of leading German artists known abroad.[3] All this changed towards the end of the First World War, when the propaganda value of art exhibitions was first appreciated. The success of exhibitions organised in Switzerland by Harry Kessler whilst German attaché in Bern, and also by Gustav Hartlaub in Gotenburg,

daransetzt, Künster heranzubilden, deren Werke Bestand haben. Auch am Sonntag hat Max Pechstein junge Maler bei sich, die er unterrichtet. Es sind Angehörige der

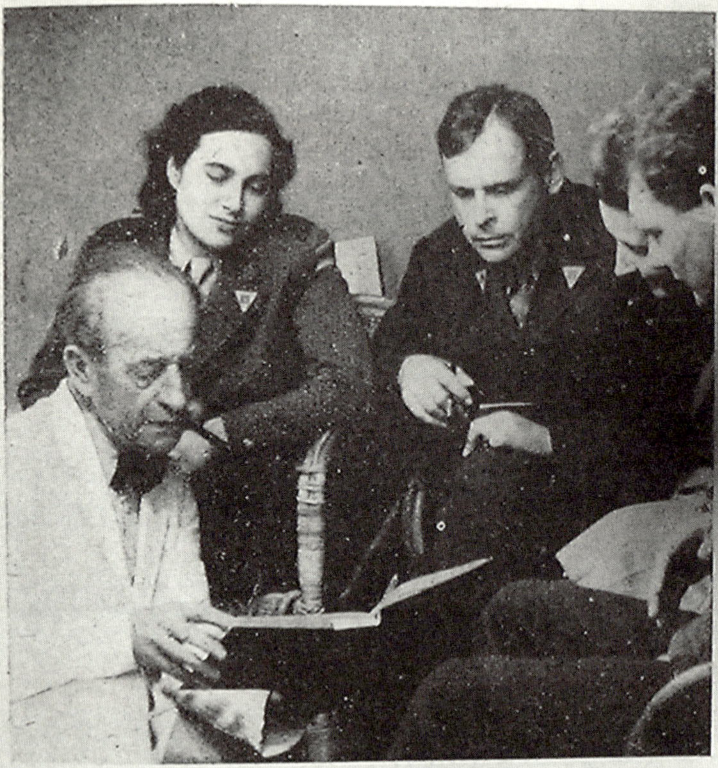

Professor Max Pechstein
beim Unterricht amerikanischer Offiziere

amerikanischen und englischen Armee, die mit Hingabe bei der Sache sind und nichts mehr wünschen, als recht lange in Berlin bleiben zu können, um die Ausbildung nicht vorzeitig unterbrechen zu müssen.

'Max Pechstein teaching American officers', 1946, *Die Aussprache* vol. 1, 1946, 7

led to the appointment, in the last months of the war, of the first art historian to the Legationsrat (Legation Council) of the Foreign Office, Johannes Sievers, who over the next fifteen years instigated numerous events to promote German artists abroad. Rave notes Siever's support, for example, of Gustav Pauli's exhibitions of German art in Stockholm and Helsingfors in 1922, as well as an exhibition of German art shown in London in 1925, organised by Emil Waldmann, the director of the Bremer Kunsthalle. An exhibition of German art toured America from 1925–7. The bannings, expulsions, confiscations and *Schandausstellungen* (Shame-Exhibitions) of the 1930s and beyond are set in this manner against the leading international role played by Germany in promoting modern art during the 1920s, a direct result of national feeling during the First World War.

Strikingly similar diplomatic attention was given to the promotion of German art after 1945. Following 'twelve years of oppression and struggle', as the sculptor Hans Uhlmann put it, artists and their supporters had a double task: to re-establish links with prewar art and national traditions that had been scorched by Nazi philippics, but also to catch up with and contribute to international developments. The new struggle was to revalidate German art in the eyes of the civilised world. For the first few years after 1945, this struggle was part of the military occupation of the former Reich by American, British, French and Soviet forces. During this period, which lasted well beyond 1949, Germany became a patchwork of international rivalries and interests. Although the country had been occupied after 1918, the political symbolism ascribed to the arts after 1945 was unprecedented.

Division of the country amongst the Soviets, Americans and British was discussed during the last two years of the war. The inclusion of the French completed the quadripartite Allied Kommandatura, the four-power authority with the all but impossible task of administering the chaotic remains of the country. During this short, strange time, Germany ceased legally to exist as a sovereign state. The Western military governments operated until the founding of the Federal Republic in 1949, although they retained sovereignty over Germany until 1955 with High Commissions. The Russian military government, the first to be installed after the fall of Berlin to the Red Army on 8 May 1945, co-operated as part of the Allied Kommandatura until March 1948. Although relations were initially optimistic and co-operative, it became increasingly apparent both to Soviets and Western Allies that continuation of such friendly terms was unfeasible. Mounting hostility, in part based on Soviet reaction to the economic union of the western zones, led to the Berlin Blockade, which, together with the February 1948 Communist coup in Czechoslovakia, was one of the first steps in the Cold War, confirmed by the founding of the two separate states at the end of 1949. Mounting confrontation led the Western Allies to reverse their policy of dismantling German industry and 'pastoralising' the country, opting rather to build western Germany up as a bulwark against Communism.

Cultural histories of this period have tended, quite naturally, to focus on the confrontation of East and West, read through a battle of styles: western abstraction versus Soviet Socialist Realism. Although there is little doubt that superpower confrontation had a major effect on the creation and display of works of art, however, it would be wrong to read the art made during this period solely in terms of this confrontation. The legal disappearance of Germany had by no means been accompanied by the vaporisation of cultural nationalism, or of an indigenous artistic tradition. The image of Max Pechstein giving art lessons to American officers published in the Soviet-sponsored information sheet *Die Aussprache* may be taken as a symbol of a relative freedom of exchange – of note is the enthusiasm with which the American officers are studying the unknown lesson.

In considering the period of 'long' cultural occupation, as it may be called, until the middle of the 1950s, two major forms of national cultural expression can be discerned. First, the strong desire for national unification on the part of Germans both fired the recovery and rehabilitation of past national styles, and drove efforts to create a new German art, as we shall see. The second instance was more short-lived, but equally important for the future development of art in both East and West Germany: the 'national projection' of each of the four Allied governments within the occupied country. If the legacy of the postwar occupation was the establishment of a democratic political culture ('political culture' here referring to the subjective dimensions of political life, perceptions, attitudes and behaviour), then the period of occupation produced one of the most important and lasting political revolutions in German history, predicated on national, rather than supranational, terms. Later on, the art made within the *demokratische Streitkultur* in Germany, a political culture that fostered and incorporated dissent, was similarly emblematic of this spirit; dissenting, critical art, which developed in both East and West Germany over the following decades, may be traced directly back to this formative moment of national cultural interchange.

Exhibitions, publications and discussions marshalled for the task of national projection were largely determined by the policy of *Umerziehungen* – 're-education'. Compared to the problems of denazification – determining degrees of allegiance to Nazism and culpability for war crimes – re-education, or the potentially fraught task of 'conveying conviction about democracy',[4] in the words of one commentator, was an open assignment that could be pursued through a number of different channels. The core intention was simply to set a good example, and provide information that had been denied to ordinary Germans during the Third Reich. Quite what this example was, however, and what type of information was provided, varied from one Zone to the next, and was inevitably informed by national priorities.

Promotion of modern art became a central aspect of re-education, for immediate and pragmatic reasons. The liberalising potential of modern idioms was considered essential in the face of negative public opinion about modern art, largely carried over from the Nazi period. Many freely held that avant-garde experimentation of an abstract or Surrealist nature was aberrant, and morally wrong. A number of contemporary reports give evidence of this situation.

Most prominent was the 'Augsburger Diagnose', recorded in January 1946 by the writer Erich Kästner.[5] Visitors to an exhibition of contemporary South German painters at the Palais Schäzler in Augsburg had been given with their entrance card a *Stimmzettel*, or short questionnaire, asking which pictures they preferred and whether they would like to see more exhibitions. The reaction was largely negative, particularly to a room of paintings by Ernst Geitlinger, reminiscent of Paul Klee: 'These are obnoxious and mock German art!', 'Down with artists like Schlichter, Geitlinger and Blocherer', 'No more *entartete Kunst*'. All these comments came, Kästner noted, from young people, schoolchildren and students. This was cause for grave concern – were not the young supposed to support modern art? Kästner's generation, he notes, discussed and supported Expressionist poetry and the paintings of Dix, Kokoschka, Kandinsky, Marc and Feininger; 'We loved the modern and respected older art'. The younger generation had grown up in an atmosphere of hatred for modern art, ignorant of developments abroad, and with no ability to think for themselves.

One month later, the painter Heinz Trökes, speaking at the opening of an exhibition of Surrealist art at the Galerie Gerd Rosen in Berlin, pointedly summarised contemporary public opinion: 'We should paint like Feuerbach again; the paintings in this exhibition are incomprehensible; this is just a repeat of the artistic chaos after 1918 [...] this is neither art for the people nor has it anything to do with contemporary life'.[6] Tröke's comments were not necessarily straw dolls for his advocacy of non-figurative art, and confirm Kästner's summary of the situation: the restoration of modern art, in particular abstract art, provoked two reactions – frenetic interest and astounding intolerance.[7] After twelve years of repression, the possibility of once again expressing opinion led to a flood of letters to newspapers, despite severe shortage of paper and ink. The *Neue Zeitung* received two thousand letters a week, Kästner reports, many of them of considerable length, almost all signed with name and address. Painting became a key part of this craze, Kästner continues, a *Toleranzthema*, or a gauge of tolerance levels.

The phenomenon was by no means short-lived or isolated. Six months later, in August 1946, Ilse Nehemias, an officer for the American Information Control department in Berlin, recorded the reactions of ordinary Berliners to a display of paintings by Picasso (part of the exhibition *Rückblick und Vorschau*, a survey of the first year of the gallery's activities) in the window of Gerd Rosen's gallery:

> 'Look, this looks like a bombed out woman. This should be forbidden, look at such craziness' [...] A woman looking up at the front of the house: 'What is his name? One should smash his windows. This is outrageous' [...] 'What a waste of paper. Here we are short of it, and there it is used for such nonsense' [...] 'What has become of our wonderful clean German art again? We were so proud, when finally we got rid of our "*Entartete Kunst*" [...] and now they have the nerve to show us dirt again.'[8]

Similar sentiments were recorded the next year in the catalogue of an exhibition of French art, *Die Meister französischer Malerei der Gegenwart* (Masters of Contemporary French Painting), organised by the French occupation authorities in Freibourg. That the 'freely expressive' art on display was supposed to foster democratic awareness of freedom of expression in visitors is clearly evident from the section of the catalogue that records in detail 'Judgements' of the exhibition by members of the public, garnered apparently from a questionnaire or visitors book: 'I feel sorry for those who must see the world like this – or perhaps it is the only way they can see: completely in ruins, terribly distorted, frightfully deformed'.[9]

Significantly, there was no general recognition that dislike of modern art was informed by Nazi cultural policy. In May 1946, the art critic Franz Roh was able to discuss the question 'Are the fundamental objections to Modern Art valid?' with no mention of *verfemte Kunst* (ostracised art).[10] Six years later, Roh was still concerned by the 'opposition in certain circles', though by this time he had recognised that the new, open political situation had created a much larger audience, and therefore more possibility of dissent: 'Since our modern democratic newspapers encourage readers to express their opinions, people who would never have been asked, now talk and write in Germany. This may perhaps have created the impression of an "overly pessimistic public response"'.[11] The success of Hans Sedlmayr's viciously anti-modern book *Verlust der Mitte*, first published in 1947, indicates, as we shall see, the extent to which a reactionary, conservative position still dominated thought about modern art in the public mind, and was not necessarily associated (by its readers at least) with Nazism.

How much the prevailing reactionary feeling was a result of the Nazi *Entartete Kunst* campaign, and to what extent it had its roots in a broader cultural movement that began in the late nineteenth century was therefore an open question. In the first few years after 1945, the answer was usually given in terms of a longer tradition of anti-modernism, minimising the effect of the *Entartete Kunst* campaign. A writer in the Hamburg-based newspaper *Die Zeit* (founded in February 1946) traced the rejection of modern art back to the violent reaction against Manet's *Olympia* at the Paris World Fair of 1867. The politicisation of culture after the First World War was the prelude to the Soviet ban on modern art in the early 1920s, an act of censorship that was itself a model for the Nazi campaign. Hitler's rage against modern painting is illustrated by the story of him ripping a painting from the walls of an exhibition in Munich, trampling it underfoot and shouting, 'I want to see finished pictures!'.[12] The degree to which this tradition had been 'spun' by Nazism in such a way as to normalise anti-modern feelings and root them in everyday language and behaviour was not generally appreciated. Goebbels had certainly tapped into a strong tradition of anti-modernism, but had given it his own pernicious twist. In the postwar period, it is thus important to separate the language in which this anti-modernism was expressed, clearly informed by Nazism, and the strong distaste for modern art itself, a much older feeling.

That modern art was a crucial *Toleranzthema* in the re-education campaign was clear to the Allies, and strongly influenced cultural policy. Dislike of modern art was emblematic of a threat perceived as very real. If democracy was the goal, then the enemy was not just the saturation of Nazi ideology, but the belief during the first years of occupation that Nazism still existed in very real terms, and could quite easily rise up again as a dangerous political force. Nazism was still an unknown quantity. In his lectures on 'The Spiritual Situation in Germany', given in Heidelberg as early as the winter semester 1945–6, Karl Jaspers felt it necessary to warn that National Socialism could not just be partially rejected, but had to be dispensed with completely.[13] Spruille Braden, the American Secretary of State, made clear the perception that Nazism had been driven underground rather than defeated: 'We find it flourishing in the midst of our international community, ready for the day when, if we allow it to do so, it will become resurgent.'[14] The British intelligence officer George Clare notes in his memoirs that a Nazi revival appeared such a very real danger at the time, that anything carrying an 'anti-fascist' label was immediately given a sympathetic hearing.[15]

In this precarious context, the battle for public opinion was crucial. Within the democratic re-education programme, tolerance towards modern art played an indexical role in relation to general political attitudes: 'modern art', as it was understood, became a test-case for democratic adjustment and awareness. The ability to answer the challenges of non-naturalistic art was seen as evidence of having internalised the spirit of tolerance necessary for the new freedoms of democracy.

During the occupation, relations between German artists and the Allied officials were largely defined by the official requirements of denazification and re-education. The licensing of exhibitions, organisations and journals, often based on the notorious 'black' and 'white' lists determining individual involvement with Nazism, formed the first point of contact. Extreme material circumstances also raised for the Allies more philosophical questions about the value of art (ironically, questions that may have been clarified by reference to a German tradition of aesthetic thought). These included the distinction between the 'living arts' – referring to the exhibition of contemporary art in Germany and the attempt to stimulate creativity as a socially beneficial activity – and the 'dead' arts, largely referring to the monumental task of restoring works of art to their legal owners and museum homes. In the early years of occupation, responsibility for 'living' and 'dead' arts was still an ambiguous issue. Michael Josselson, the chairman of the Cultural Affairs Committee, requested clarification from the head of the Fine Arts and Museums Committee on this point in April 1946, stating that the latter was responsible for the 'dead art', and that 'all matters pertaining to contemporary, living artists, such as the organizations, the arrangement of exhibits, etc', were under the jurisdiction of the Cultural Affairs Committee.[16]

The Central Collecting Points, where vagrant, mostly looted cultural objects were collected and stored, became the theatres in which this dual cultural function was played out. The four main Collecting Points, at Munich, Wiesbaden, Marburg and Offenbach, grew out of a number of such centres that were established in the first weeks of occupation. When the Marburg Point closed in June 1946, the other three became specialised: Wiesbaden in German-owned material – for instance, loot from German museums; Munich in material subject to restitution, as well as the collections of the Bavarian State Museums; Offenbach in Jewish cultural objects. Offenbach was closed in June 1949, and the Wiesbaden and Munich Points in August 1951. A fascinating series of exhibitions held at the Munich Collecting Point began in 1949 with *Kunstschaffen in Deutschland* 1930–1949; this was followed in early 1950 by the first exhibition of the Zen 49 group, covered in more detail below. Entries for the Blevin Davis-Preis, a prize for modern painting sponsored by a New York theatrical producer, were shown in February and March 1950.

When the question of responsibility for restitution of cultural property was raised in late 1949, the importance of the Wiesbaden and Munich Collecting Points was given strong emphasis:

> Needless to say the exhibition galleries in the two Collecting Points are major focal points in our cultural relations and re-education programs [...] It is suggested that in the two Collecting Points, with the immense prestige they have earned among the German public and rich in technical resources, lie our greatest potential assets. As staging and primary exhibition places they are unsurpassed.[17]

The dual function of the Collecting Points often resulted in a clash between military and cultural apperception of works of art; places, as one contemporary report put it, 'where one party tends to consider the objects as so many items of property comparable to nuts and bolts, [while] the other party feels under compulsion to treat the objects with the individual care and concern due to unique and irreplaceable elements of our cultural heritage'.[18] William Constable, a former director of the Courtauld Institute and at that moment a curator at the Museum of Fine Arts in Boston, was contracted as an art consultant for the US government and completed a 'tour of duty' in occupied Germany. He reported in late 1949 on the deficiencies of military property regulations that were unable to distinguish between works of art and machine parts. For Constable, art is 'unique and cannot be duplicated', even when private property 'is also a matter of interest and concern to a much wider circle so that the owner becomes in some measure a trustee'.[19] The task of restituting objects to claimants, an activity that had considerable diplomatic import, was carried out by members of the Monuments, Fine Arts & Archives section (MFA&A), American and British cultural officers who had co-operated with the advancing Allied forces in protecting cultural treasures and gathering information that would spare their destruction and aid with postwar restitution. Such measures were unprecedented, and therefore experimental. After the surrender, MFA&A was reconstituted on a national basis.[20] The promotion, in winter 1948 and spring 1949, of certain 'non-restitutional functions', namely exhibitions, by MFA&A and Cultural Affairs officers, was recognition of the importance of the Munich and Wiesbaden Collecting Points for public relations and also for re-education.[21] Such recognition was part of the gradual realisation, on the part of the British and Americans, of the distinctive status accorded to 'high art' in Germany, as a source of personal salvation, but also as the basis of a national community – the *Kulturnation* opposed to the political sense of belonging encapsulated in the notion of *Staatsnation*. This realisation came as a surprise after years of wartime propaganda in which the Germans were depicted by their very nature as the barbarians of Europe, and was treated with circumspection. *Kultur* was, in the American view, a 'dangerously indefinite word', with theological overtones: '"Kultur" is a magic word. Today many hope to save "Kultur", and many hope to be saved by it. For some, it is the last refuge in defeat and disaster'.[22]

The paucity of accounts of British cultural policies during the occupation, in particular of the role played by the Fine Arts, has been explained by the concentration on Soviet-American relations, leading to a 'tendency to relegate Britain to the level of a faded imperial power living on past glories'.[23] This impression of Germany as another addition to the British Empire was not completely out of keeping with postwar sentiment; many Germans saw this as an inevitable development, and were keen for the British to clarify what kind of status Germany was going to have as a colony.[24] In the early days, the British assumed that the occupation would last for twenty years. It was to be run along the lines of a colony, the Germans gradually re-educated and the political vacuum only slowly replenished. For one senior civilian officer, who, like many others, had previously been a British colonial servant in India, the Germans were 'a specially intelligent tribe of Beduins', and were simply not ready for the type of democratic society to which most other western Europeans were accustomed.[25]

Within three years, the slow-burn colonial model had to be seriously rethought. The Communist coup in Prague in February 1948 had a decisive impact on perceptions of the Soviets, the effects of which were felt very keenly in Berlin. As one government advisor put it:

> [...] there is little doubt that the Revolution in Czechoslovakia has had a very great effect in Berlin, causing a general loss of confidence and a fear that similar tactics may be employed there ... What we have to fear particularly is a movement by Germans in Berlin, who had previously co-operated with us, to insure against future Russian domination, either by ceasing to involve themselves with us, or by actually co-operating with the Russians. Once this starts, the rot might spread quickly.[26]

By the summer of 1948, denazification had been radically demoted on the list of British priorities. Re-education was now to be carried out by emphasis on a projection of 'British civilisation' as a model for democratic adjustment and Western integration. The cultural offensive that the British mounted as a result was, however, hardly the result of a sophisticated propaganda machine. Financial limitations and organisational problems were the initial barriers. The structure of the British Control Commission was complex and shifting,[27] making it difficult for any individual to implement well-thought-out cultural programmes. In contrast to the Marxist-Leninism of the Russians (which from May 1945 formed part of a cogent and persuasive propaganda culture), and to the cultural policies of the French (which began in 1946), or even in comparison to the eventual propagation by the Americans of a triumphant liberal-democratic world-view in which Jackson Pollock's vast paintings were equated with western freedom, for the British there was little ideological co-ordination of aims. Indeed, there was no definite ideology on which to draw, apart from vague ideas of fair play and the parliamentary tradition.

Even areas in which Britain was traditionally strong, broadcasting and publishing (of which the newspaper *Die Welt* and the British-language radio station NWDF, Nordwestdeutscher Rundfunk, modelled on the BBC, were the two most important creations),[28] showed acutely the limitations of an imposed culture. The clear contradiction of imposing liberalism by authority was the central problem for the re-education programme, and for the occupation as a whole. This difficulty was evident for British cultural officers: 'No nation with any self-respect will willingly accept the word of an Occupying Power, particularly when this power is concerned not only with teaching a new way of life, but also with condemning much that forms part of the individual German's heritage'.[29]

These problems were not without historical precedent. The highly successful propaganda campaign developed by the Ministry of Information and the Department for Enemy Propaganda during the First World War was discontinued in 1918. The British Council (then known as The British Committee for Relations with Other Countries) was established by the Foreign Office in November 1934 to project a positive image of Britain abroad after a long period when such propaganda, considering the extent and success of the Empire, was seen, if not as infra dig, then at least as unnecessary. Bolstering the British position was necessitated not only by the declining fortunes of Imperial might, but also by the increasingly evident lag between British inactivity and the highly developed propaganda initiatives of the French, Germans and Italians. These initiatives showed that a new era of publicity consciousness and political rapprochement with the mass media was well under way. The first significant uses of cultural propaganda for diplomatic purposes took place in France and Germany around the turn of the century: the French government instituted the Maison de la Presse, essentially the propaganda department of the French Foreign Affairs Ministry, which also operated the Service des oeuvres françaises à l'étranger, a service for schools and education. Both followed the institution of the Alliance Française in 1880, the dissemination of French culture by the French Catholic teaching missionaries in the Near and Far East, and other organisations such as the Mission Laïque and the Ligue de l'Enseignement, all essentially concerned with the French language. Similar efforts took place in Germany, particularly under the influence of Bernhard von Bülow, one of the first statesmen to use the press for political purposes (an activity to which Bismarck was completely averse), and with the foundation of organisations such as the Verein für das Deutschtum in Ausland, dedicated to the spread of German *Kultur* overseas.[30] Throughout the twentieth century, the growing need to project a national image both at home and abroad, accurate or not, was motivated not only by the increase of mass political movements and the need to influence voting behaviour, but also by the necessity to restore a sense of 'centre' and national pride at a time when both war and imperial decline, and the challenges of new imperial domains, were humbling the old European powers.

Although cultural policies were at first based on traditional, national principals, priorities were soon to change. French attitudes were initially informed by fear of renewed German aggression, and led to punitive policies such as the use of German economic resources to sustain French reconstruction. This position soon changed, however, to the Anglo-American model of economic independence for Germany and reintegration into a Europe of self-determining nation states. The shift from attitudes of superiority to equality was reflected in the exhibitions mounted as part of the *rayonnement culturelle*, the enlightening dissemination of French culture abroad. These included two major displays of French art. The first, *Moderne Französischer Malerei* (Modern French Painting), comprised 130 paintings 'from Impressionism to the present day', and toured from 1946–7. The second was *Die Meister Französischer Malerei der Gegenwart*, organised by the French cultural officer Maurice Jardot in collaboration with Kurt Martin, director of the

Karlsruhe Kunsthalle, and the dealer Daniel-Henry Kahnweiler, which opened in Freiburg in October 1947, and showed six works by each of seven 'French' artists: Braque, Picasso, Léger, Gris, Matisse, Chagall and Rouault. 'Who would have thought that just two and a half years after the horrors of war, the most famous French painters would send their work to us here in Freiburg?', the organisers asked. The exhibition, which was held on the second floor of the Friedrichsbau in Kaiserstrasse, presaged a significant series of solo exhibitions of French artists around Germany: Léger, Masson and Rouault appeared in 1949, Braque, Matisse and Maillol in 1951. Picasso, perhaps perceived as too dangerously challenging even then, and at any rate a member of the Communist Party, had to wait until 1955 for an exhibition commensurate with his reputation. Visitor numbers indicate the success of these exhibitions: *Moderne Französische Malerei* totalled 150,000 in all its venues, more than documenta (130,000) in 1955.[31]

While the Soviets and the French were developing significant cultural programmes, the British had little to offer in the first two years of the occupation. When it did appear, the programme consisted of exhibitions and publications, rather than exchanges or visits from artists. A minor exception was the Scottish painter William Gear, who, after being posted to Germany in 1945, became part of the MFA&A, living, painting and staging exhibitions in Celle in the British Zone.[32]

The background to this development of cultural policy was the marked increase in Britain of state intervention in public culture, and what has been termed a 'nationalisation of culture' following the Labour victory of 1945.[33] Cultural foreign policy was

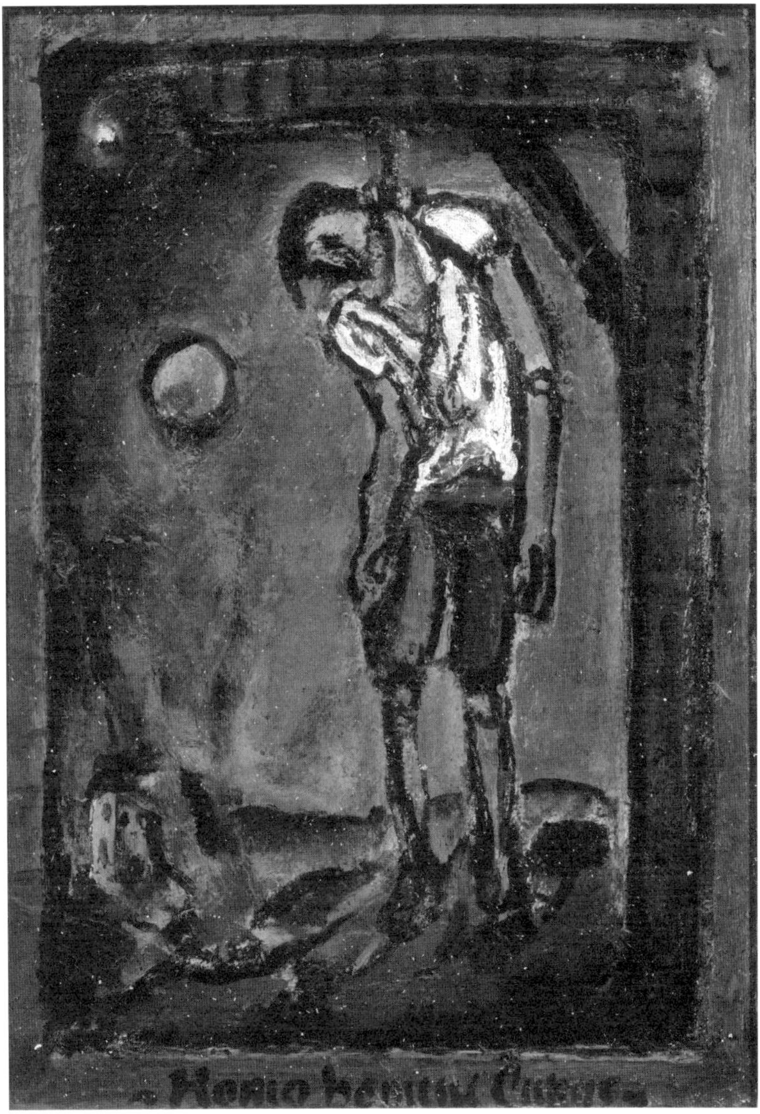

Georges Rouault, 'Homo homini lupus' (Man is a Wolf to Man), 1944–1948, oil on paper laid on canvas, 64.7 × 46 cm, Centre Georges Pompidou, Paris. Included in the exhibition *Moderne Französischer Malerei*

nonetheless diffuse. The emphasis, derived from a vague notion of implicit national values, was on increasing the amount of cultural exposure to specifically British ideas, through for instance lectures and supplies of books. Such resources were requested from Germany by the British Office of the Educational Adviser (OEA) in a telegram to the Foreign Office on 19 May 1948.[34] By this time, it had become impossible to ignore the confrontation of East and West and the need for national assertion. The Foreign Office had already suggested in April that the OEA should become more active in promoting British culture in Germany. Emphasis was placed on the importance of 'Entertainments and Exhibitions', in particular, 'A really good exhibition of painting, especially of British pictures'. There was, however, a clear preference for public events that could reach the widest possible audience.

British Council activities began in earnest in early 1948, as the organisation's review described: 'At this stage we can do little more than scratch the surface of the field, but it is none the less satisfactory to have made a start'.[35] A festival of music and theatre from the time of Elizabeth I, staged in the British Information Centre in Berlin in late 1948, took up much of the initial energy. Although this was part of a conscious 'cultural offensive', the lines between the British and Soviet sector had not completely hardened, even within the incipient blockade: the organiser requested from Military Government headquarters that the publicity for the festival appear particularly in the Russian sector, and even that an invitation be sent for a lecturer to speak on Russian ideas about Shakespeare as part of the programme.[36]

Logisitical, rather than political issues tended to determine the cultural policies of all four Allied powers. In the British case, these material restraints were particularly acute, thanks to the war-drained domestic economy. Foreign Office documents show that plans to extend to Germany the tour of the exhibition *50 Years of Modern British Painting*, travelling during 1946 to Warsaw, Prague, Rome and Madrid, were shelved due to lack of funding.[37] In March 1947, the Foreign Office again recommended extending the tours of existing exhibitions to Germany, but it was not at all clear which organisation would be responsible.[38] Although the possibility of the British Council taking over various tasks from the Control Commission was negotiated as early as August 1946, it would not be for another two years that the Fine Arts Committee (established in 1935 to promote the foreign exhibition of British art) would raise the question of sending Fine Arts exhibits to Germany.[39] To those present at a meeting in September 1948 (including Clive Bell, Anthony Blunt and John Rothenstein), Herbert Read read out letters that he had received from two German art historians requesting art exhibitions to tour the occupied country.[40] Although Read had replied stating that he was only able to work through the Control Commission, the British Council, as cultural organ of the Control Commission, stepped up its activities considerably in the last two months of 1948.

At the time Read made his appeal, two exhibitions were already in place in Germany. It is not easy to divine the reasons behind the choice of the first British Council exhibition, *Das Englische Bühnenbild* (English Stage Design), held at the Berlin

Information Centre during August 1948. Organised by the British Council Drama Department and James Laver of the Victoria & Albert Museum, the exhibition had opened earlier that year at the Art and Industry Museum in Cracow. There may have been some feeling that this represented a neutral and optimistic contribution that could draw on an area that was at once 'fine' and 'popular' art. This was followed, during September and October, by an exhibition of contemporary British printmaking, *Ausstellung über Graphische Kunst von zeitgenössischen britischen Künstlern* (Exhibition of Graphic Art by Contemporary British Artists), which toured Hamburg, Hanover, Berlin and Kiel. The exhibition contained 127 works by just over one hundred artists, the sole criterion for inclusion of a print being that it was made by a British artist. In most cases, the artists were living, but many of the more prominent had recently died – Eric Gill (d. 1940); Eric Ravilious (d. 1942); Walter Sickert (d. 1942); Christopher Nevinson (d. 1946) and Paul Nash (d. 1946) – adding a layer of nostalgia to the idea of 'Britishness' that was being propagated. The rather hopeful deduction of such a quality from the works on display is laid out in the catalogue essay:

> British artists have first and foremost always been individualists. They do not easily align themselves with a certain programme, or a certain school. Nonetheless, the continental visitor will no doubt be able to detect the predominant taste, even style underlying the works included in this exhibition. British preference for landscape, British admiration for professional finish,

even British tolerance, basis of the often ridiculed '*phlegme britannique*', all these imponderable things can be found in this exhibition, which we hope will contribute, through its appeal to connoisseurship, to the reciprocal understanding of the European people, something the world is much in need of.[41]

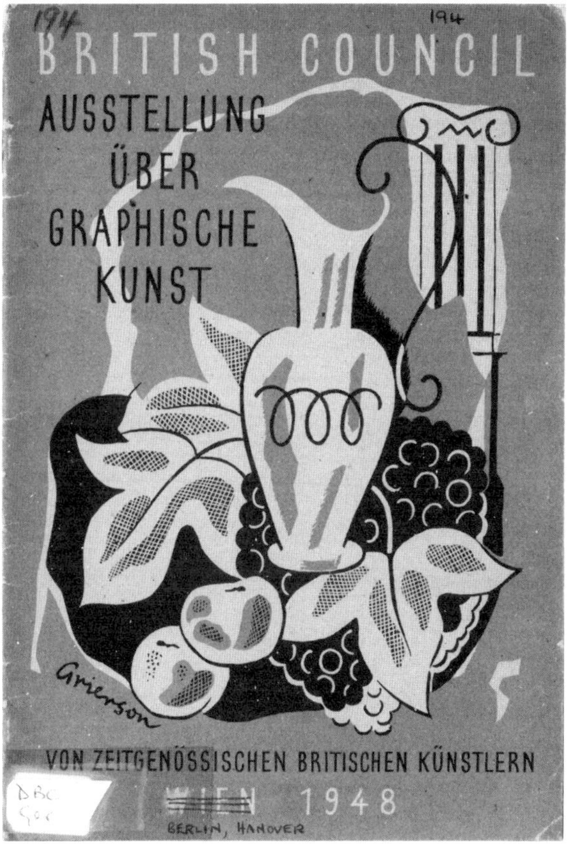

Cover of exhibition catalogue *Ausstellung über Graphische Kunst*, Hamburg, 1948

Commenting on the Berlin installation of the exhibition, the art critic Will Grohmann had different ideas about the British and their art: for him, the interest of the prints on display was purely technical – they were handicrafts (*Handwerk*) rather than art. According to Grohmann, the only British artist of European stature was Henry Moore – an exception because the English had 'always been better at appreciating than making art'. Art is a different quantity for the Germans, as Grohmann explains: 'nothing can part us from our commitment to the arts, nor would we wish otherwise, although they will no doubt cause us concern this century'.[42]

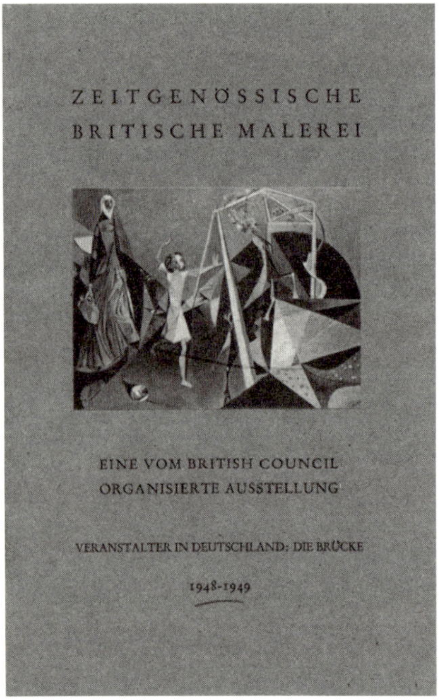

Cover of exhibition catalogue *Zeitgenössische Britische Malerei*, (Contemporary British Painting), showing John Craxton's *Poros*, 1947

Such a conventional exhibition of British graphic art would have had little impact as cultural propaganda. A meeting of the Fine Arts Committee in December came to the rather obvious conclusion that such a conservative display could not compete with the strong tradition of graphic art in Germany. It was becoming increasingly obvious that it was not possible to rival German traditions in certain areas.

Thus a revised position was soon evident. *Zeitgenössische Britische Malerei* (Contemporary British Painting), which toured 1948–9, and *Die Grossen Maler Englands von Hogarth bis Turner* (Great English Painters from Hogarth to Turner), which travelled around Europe 1949–50, stopping in Hamburg in late 1949, were the first important signs of success. They took place at the crucial moment between the currency reform and beginning of the Berlin Blockade in mid 1948, and the founding of the two separate German states in May 1949. *Zeitgenössische Britische Malerei* was deemed a success by the British organisers, who expressed 'a sense of relief that it was not of the academic nature to be feared in an official exhibition'.[43] The exhibition contained an impressive array of work from twelve painters, including the twenty-five year old John Craxton, whose painting *Poros* of 1947 was used to illustrate the cover of the catalogue. German visitors would also have been able to see works by Stanley Spencer, including *The Temptation of Saint Anthony* (1946), Ivon Hitchens, L.S. Lowry, John Minton, Ben Nicholson, Matthew Smith and Graham Sutherland. With a few exceptions, the exhibition comprised work made since the end of war, allowing the influence of the conflict to be seen, as Herbert Read noted in the catalogue, as self-reliance and independence resulting from wartime isolation from European trends. It is striking that Read should make such a claim for English painters at a time when German art life was itself opening out after twelve years of isolation. Read is also at pains to suggest an affinity between the English art and a German tradition in terms of style: 'A general overview of a representative cross-section of English painting suggests that it is rather expressionistic than realistic, rather expressionistic than constructivist'.[44] Read stresses that pluralism, of an international range, is a characteristic of British painting, which leads to the perplexing conclusion that 'internationalism' is a 'national' characteristic.

Die Grossen Maler Englands von Hogarth bis Turner, installed in the Hamburg Kunsthalle from October to November 1949, was by far the most prestigious exhibition put on by the British. To transport to Germany such works as Gainsborough's *Robert Andrews and his Wife* and Constable's *Flatford Mill on the River Stour*, amongst many others, was certainly a statement of confidence in the security of the British Zone. As a large-scale exhibition dedicated to the highest expressions of a national cultural tradition, *Die Grossen Maler Englands* stands as a rival to the French exhibitions *Moderne Französische Malerei* and *Meister Französische Malerei der Gegenwart*, which had toured Germany in 1946 and 1947. As one British Cultural Relations official reflected:

> The Germans, as a body, considered the exhibition to be extraordinarily well-timed and believed that it was a deliberate demonstration of confidence in the newly

> formed West German government, since previously no great classical exhibition has been sent during the period of occupation. The French, whilst being most complimentary about the exhibition, were clearly ruffled by its success, and complained that they were never allowed to show French national treasures from the Louvre and similar galleries in Germany. There is no doubt that an exhibition of this kind arouses nation-wide interest in Germany, whereas the smaller modern exhibitions sent by the French (and hitherto by us) arouse only local interest in the towns in which they are shown, and the interest of a limited number of cognoscenti.[45]

Anglo-French cultural rivalry was of course nothing new. Even exhibitions staged in part by exiled artists in London and Paris before the War, as responses to the *Entartete Kunst* campaign, were subject to such competition. The exhibition *Freie Deutsche Kunst* (Free German Art) was organised by the Paris-based Freie Künstlerbund and the president of the Association des écrivains et artistes révolutionnaires, Louis Aragon, and took place in the association's headquarters in November 1938. The London exhibition *20th Century German Art* was held at the Royal Academy earlier the same year. The French organisers accused the British of avoiding a political stance, and also of showing work by the 'Nazi' sculptor Georg Kolbe. The confrontation after 1945 was heightened by a new situation in which geographical boundaries had been diminished.

This new intimacy helped keep the national question dominant. *Turner Watercolours*, which opened in Düsseldorf on 8 October 1949, presented Turner as 'the greatest English painter of the Romantic period', and, as Romanticism was integral to English creativity, so the catalogue held, 'Turner must be the greatest English painter'.[46] The art critic Geoffrey Grigson's essay for the exhibition catalogue of *Moderne Englische Zeichnungen und Aquarelle* (Modern English Drawings and Watercolours)[47] also concerns itself with national characteristics, but argues that the period of aggressive nationalism in the arts, and the identification of art by national schools was coming to an end. 'When the Japanese publish books on Picasso and when Chinese poets acknowledge the influence of T.S. Eliot and W.H. Auden, it becomes apparent that the internationalism of art extends well beyond Europe and that humanity is again recognised as the fundamentally most important factor'.[48] Grigson stresses the possibility of being both national and international, echoing Herbert Read in the suggestion that nationality is a simply a subcategory of a larger, more humanistic classification of mankind.

It was becoming increasingly apparent that in an age of international politics the best ambassadors were artists – or moreover, works of art, which could be made to say all sorts of things, yet simultaneously had the politically desirable characteristic of hanging silently and saying nothing at all.

Following the disjointed series of exhibitions mounted in 1948 and 1949, the second phase of the British cultural occupation in the early 1950s was dominated by the work of Henry Moore. Between 1950 and 1953 there were three large solo exhibitions of Moore's work, which toured between them to ten locations, including one at the Haus am Waldsee in Berlin. There was a considerable response to the exhibitions, and Moore was quickly appreciated as the leading international figure of 'modern art'. Moore was infinitely suited as a generic model for the role of art in a reconstructing society and an emblem of the 'new agencies of state culture',[49] and thus spearheaded the British Council's campaign in the newly founded Federal Republic from 1950. There was most probably a great sense of relief that the English had an artist to rival Picasso – just as Pollock was to do for the Americans a few years later.

Enthusiastic reception of Moore in Germany was not immediate. The opening of the first exhibition, *Henry Moore. Ausstellung von Skulpturen und Zeichnungen* (Exhibition of Sculpture and Drawings), in Hamburg in early 1950 came at a time of poor Anglo-German relations, and was marred by a controversy concerning the demolition by the British of one of the largest docks in Hamburg, as part of the soon abandoned policy of *démontage*, the deconstruction of German industry.[50] Moore could nevertheless be described in the German art press as a vital and disturbing artist, one of the most 'unsettling artists of the twentieth century, whose international reputation arrived late in Germany'.[51] There was at this moment no extensive knowledge of his work, which remained 'unknown' in Germany, according to Hann Theodor Flemming in 1947. Moore's well-known drawings of bomb shelters in the London Underground, Flemming writes, may be closely compared with the drawings of another sculptor, Ernst Barlach, but were unknown to German artists.[52] Although a bronze maquette for the Northampton *Madonna and Child* had been included in an exhibition of religious art mounted in Cologne in 1948, the response to it was as muted as that received by a display of his work at the 1948 Venice Biennale. Moore was awarded the first prize for sculpture by the Venice jury, but for one German reviewer, echoing Grohmann's comments on British printmaking, it was doubtful that his sculpture amounted to more that a 'refined handicraft' (*raffiniertes Kunstgewerbe*).[53]

For the art historian Werner Haftmann however, Moore was one of the few artists able to break through the general discontent with modern art and exhibit successfully to a worldwide public. The foundations of this success, for Haftmann, were the new synthesis of ideas common to modern sculptors from Maillol to Brancusi, and from 'primitive' art to Alexander Calder.[54] That such non-naturalistic works epitomised public aversion to new art, meant that they could be situated in public places as a way of probing and 're-educating' public opinion. Moore's work, broadly speaking, resonated in this heuristic manner. Alfred Hentzen, the director of the Hannover Kestner-Gesellschaft, in the catalogue for the third British Council exhibition of Moore's drawings and sculptures, which opened in Hanover mid-1953 and toured to six further locations, describes Moore as an exemplary modern sculptor working in an uncontested, international and public sphere. His sculptures for Battersea Park, the Festival of Britain and St Matthew's, Northhampton, 'are just a few of many examples [of Moore's works], and one cannot emphasise too strongly how far Germany has fallen behind in such matters and will have to catch up over time. It is amazing how hesitant one still is to place contemporary art into the public sphere and when one does how much noise it provokes!'[55] Adolf Frisé also referred to the success of the Battersea Park exhibition in his review of the Hamburg show. It is unprecedented, Frisé wrote, that so conservative a country as England, with no tradition of avant-garde sculpture, could be so supportive of a sculptor like Moore, adding that all the works on display came from private collections.[56]

If some critics tended to respond enthusiastically to Moore's cryptic nationalism, others were drawn to the 'humanism' embodied in his work. His drawings of underground bomb shelters found resonance in Germany, where these types of experience were still part of a largely undiscussed public trauma. Although none were shown in the 1950 Hamburg exhibition (which travelled to Düsseldorf), six of the Bunker drawings appeared in an exhibition mounted in Berlin during 1951. In style they bear comparison with Wilhelm Rudolph's drawings of ruined Dresden, but in the human empathy of the subject matter there is marked difference. For Will Grohmann, the 'community of experience shared by those affected by the war, and the directness of portrayal, made these drawings universally understood'.[57] Niklaus Pevsner had put forward a similar view in 1945. For him, the Northhampton Madonna showed a human compassion that went far beyond Moore's previous tendency to aesthetic purism, and a type of formalism with which a general public would not identify.[58] In western newspapers, the most frequently

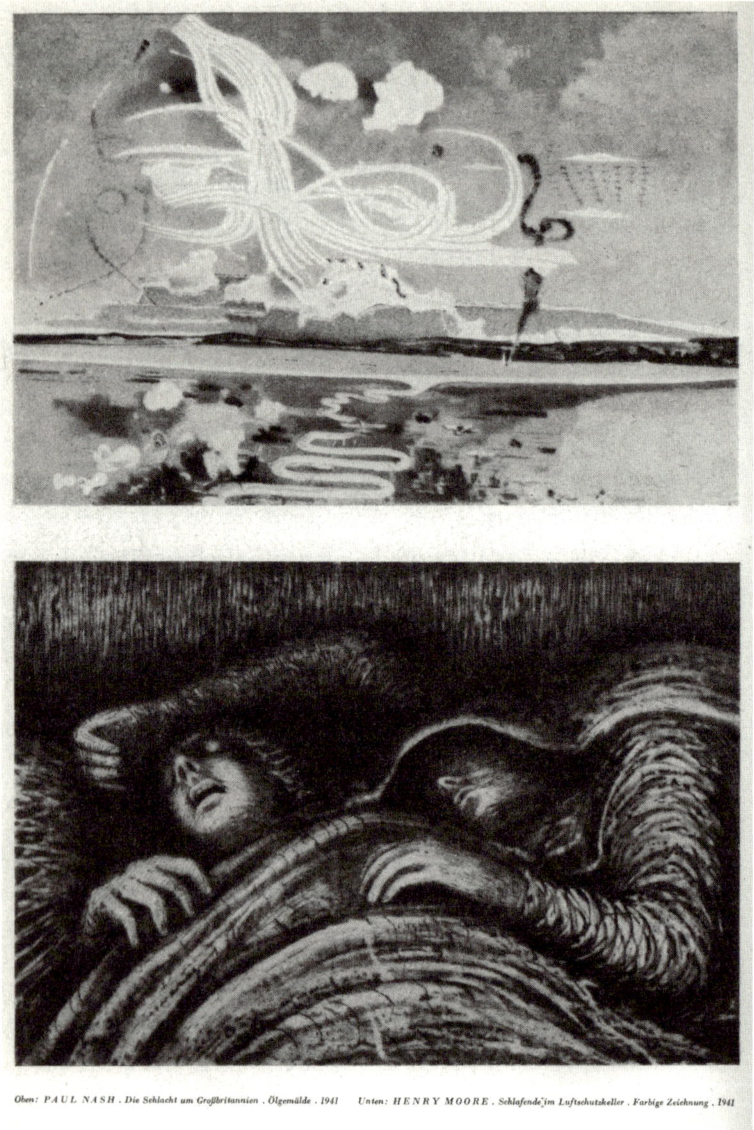

Montage in *bildende kunst*, 1949. Paul Nash, *Battle of Britain*, 1941 and Henry Moore, *The Two Sleepers*, 1941

evoked comparison was with Wilhelm Lehmbruck: the 1950 show of Moore's work in Düsseldorf reminded one reviewer of the exhibition of Lehmbruck's sculpture the previous year; works by both artists were distinguished by a 'symbolic power', rooted in an understanding of human nature.[59] Such an interpretation was manifested indirectly in an uncaptioned montage reproduced *bildende kunst*, combining Paul Nash's *The Battle of Britain* and Moore's *The Two Sleepers*, both made in 1941, the year of the heaviest bombardment of England by the Germans. Against Nash's inhuman, abstract, decorative image, the identification with the innocent victims of war in Moore's drawing is clear, and refers to a typical element of the anti-fascist movement with which the Soviet journal would certainly have identified: that ordinary people in all capitalist countries were manipulated by authoritarian regimes, and were therefore not liable to share the burden of guilt for war crimes committed in their name. Nevertheless, Moore's 'formalism' did not go without criticism: in response to the Düsseldorf showing, the left-wing newspaper *Freies Volk* pronounced his work 'symptomatic of artistic disintegration in capitalist lands'.[60]

As part of the 1951 *Berlin Festwochen* (these week-long festivals were instigated as a way of bolstering public spirit and focusing cultural resources), the exhibition *Henry Moore Zeichnungen und Kleine Plastik* (Drawings and Small Sculpture) was staged at the Haus am Waldsee. It was perceived by the German organisers as a symbol of solidarity with western Europe – 'As part of the Berlin Festival the exhibition serves as a sign of solidarity between West Berlin and the great European nations'.[61] Alongside a large Max Beckmann exhibition and the *Ausstellung des Deutschen Künstlerbundes*

1950 (an exhibition of Western-oriented professional artists), as well as a show of sculpture by Bernhard Heiliger (who was termed by one newspaper the '*Berliner Moore*', and often compared to the English artist),[62] Moore's contribution was described as part of a new European dialogue. His status as a 'western humanist' had been written into the 1948 Venice display by Herbert Read, who noted not only his concentration on the human figure, but also the compassion of his wartime shelter drawings. The problem arose, however, that in trying to satisfy such a diffuse ideology, the presentation of Moore's work lost any direct political focus. The generic quality of his sculpture was surely at the root of this: the flexibility of images such as the 1944 *Mother and Child*, able to slide between emblems of a caring welfare state and more traditionally grounded religious iconography, meant, as his reception in Germany showed, that he was in the end to please nobody. Neither eastern nor western agencies identified fully with the work, fearing perhaps that such a move could be taken as a compromise. Rosa Schapire's short article celebrating Moore's work published in *Die Weltkunst* towards the end of 1953 suggests something of this disassociation. 'The revolutionaries of today will become the classics of tomorrow', she suggested, although it seems that the process had already taken place.[63] Moore's engagement with postwar Germany culminated in the exhibition *Das Bild des Menschen in Meisterwerken europäischer Kunst* (The Image of Man in Masterpieces of European Art), held in Recklinghausen, mid-1955. Organised by Thomas Grochowiak, this showed an epic swathe of figurative art by some 100 artists from Altdorfer to Picasso. Moore was particularly well represented with three sculptures and three drawings, and gave a speech at the opening of the exhibition. The formal comparison of works from different ages was clearly meant to establish a tradition in which modern forms could be placed, counteracting the anti-modern arguments of those such as Hans Sedlmayr, covered in more detail below. Moore's *Helmet Head no.2* (1950) was strikingly compared with a Romanesque reliquary bust of St Vitalis from the church of St Lamberti in Düsseldorf.

Martin Schieder's illuminating work on the reception of Picasso in postwar Germany provides a comparison with attitudes towards Moore.[64] Before the war, Picasso had traditionally found strong support in Germany amongst the dealers Heinrich Thannhauser, Alfred Flechtheim and Daniel-Henry Kahnweiler, the critic Carl

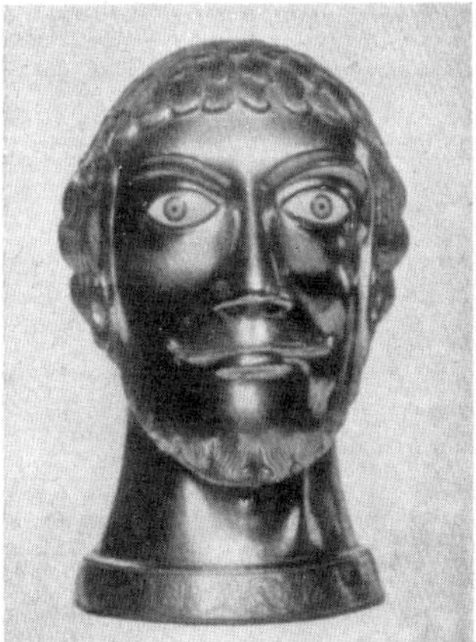
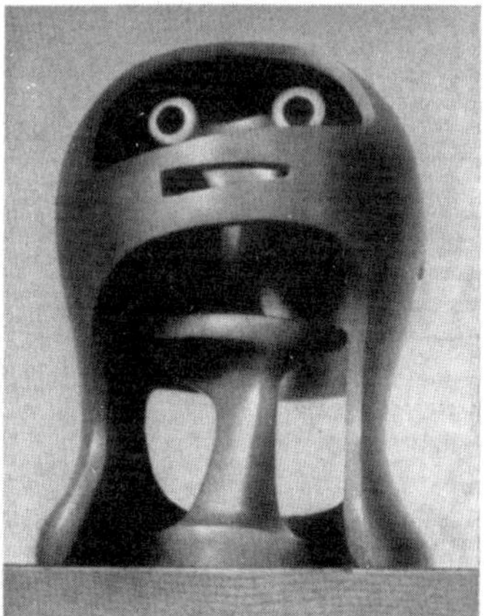

Illustration from: Städtliche Kunsthalle, Recklinghausen, *Das Bild des Menschen in Meisterwerken europäischer Kunst*, exh.cat., 1955; right: Henry Moore, Helmet Head no.2, Bronze, h. 30cm, Museo d'Arte Moderna – Ca'Pesaro, Venice, left: Reliquary Statue of St Vitalis, c.1160, h. 28cm, St Lamberti, Düsseldorf

Einstein, and Alfred Hagelstange, who as director of the Wallraf-Richartz-Museum in Cologne was responsible for the first entry of a work by Picasso into a public museum, in 1912. This support stopped, as Schieder notes, in 1933. Given Picasso's pre-eminence, it may seem surprising that even after 1945 he received such an ambivalent reception, and had to wait a full ten years before his works were adequately exhibited, in the first documenta at Kassel. Picasso had remained in Paris during the occupation and was known to have defied the Germans, yet the potential appeal of this to the culture of 'inner emigration' was attenuated by his membership of the Communist party. *Guernica* was shown for the first and only time in Germany in the retrospective organised by Maurice Jardot, which

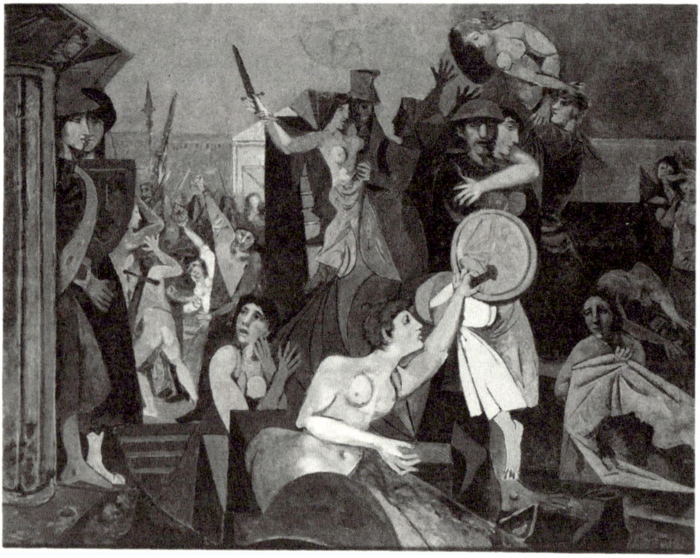

Willi Sitte, *Raub der Sabinerinnen* (Rape of the Sabine Women), 1953, oil on board, 126.5 × 165 cm, Nationalgalerie, Staatliche Museen zu Berlin

started in Paris, and, through the agency of Alfred Hentzen and the art dealer Michael Hertz, toured Munich, Cologne and Hamburg in 1956–7. Unsurprisingly, *Guernica* had more resonance in the East, where it connected with the anti-fascist campaign. Yet, as Schieder demonstrates, this enthusiasm was soon to be doused by Stalinist anti-formalism, at least on an official level. Questions were still asked and public debate conducted on the question of whether Picasso was a realist or not. How was it possible to reconcile the non-naturalistic aspect of his images with the traditional realist demands of Socialist art theories? If he was driven out of the Politburo, as Schieder puts it, for failing in this respect, he was nevertheless able to take refuge in the studios of a number of artists, both in East and West. Willi Sitte's *Raub der Saberinnen* (Rape of the Sabine Women) of 1953 suggests that the *Picasso-Fieber* (Picasso Fever) was far from cured by Stalinist doctrine. Ironically, it was in the West that Picasso's example was most strongly rejected on a formal basis. Faced with the apparently 'complete' formal world that Picasso had created, younger artists felt condemned to epigony, Scheider writes. The 'absolute' art of Informel provided a way of overcoming the omnipresent style of Picasso. Mac Zimmerman's *P.I.C.A.S.S.O.* (1949) is an earlier homage by a western artist that shows little will to step out of the shadow of the *Übervater* of modern art. The title of the work transforms the artist's name into what may be seen as the acronym of an international organisation, perhaps pitting Picasso against the universal claims of NATO and the Warsaw Pact. Zimmerman chooses to echo the smooth, anthropomorphic forms of Picasso's bather series of the late 1920s and early 1930s, rather than the distressing and often unrecognisable world of Cubism. In doing so, he produces a work that also closely resembles a homage to Moore. What was important to postwar German artists in Picasso, it seems, may have been found in a purer, politically untainted form in the work of the English artist, which would explain the far greater success of Moore's work in the first half of the 1950s.

Nevertheless, Moore's actual influence on young German artists (and for that matter young British artists) was limited, and was soon made redundant by changing ideas of artistic representation, by which Moore's largely allegorical, semi-abstract approach to form was seen as outmoded. An ambiguous filtering of his monumental symbolism can nevertheless be seen in the work of Theo Balden. Balden spent his formative Weimar years in the company of left-wing intellectuals, studying at the Bauhaus 1922–3, and joining the revolutionary artists' group ASSO (Assoziation Revolutionärer Bildener Künstler Deutschlands – Association of Fine Artists in Germany) in 1929. He lived in exile in Prague from 1936, but later moved to England, where, apart from a short internment in Canada, he remained for the duration of the war. In London, Balden had contact with Moore, and it is clear from some of his drawings dating from 1943–50 that his work was strongly influenced by Moore's stylistic. He was later on to publish a number of articles about the English sculptor.[65] On his return to Berlin in January 1947, he became once more active in the East, and remained to live and work in the DDR. Though Moore's influence is visible in the first few years of this period, for instance in the 1948 drawing *Lesender*, it was soon displaced by an approach to form largely dictated by the popular

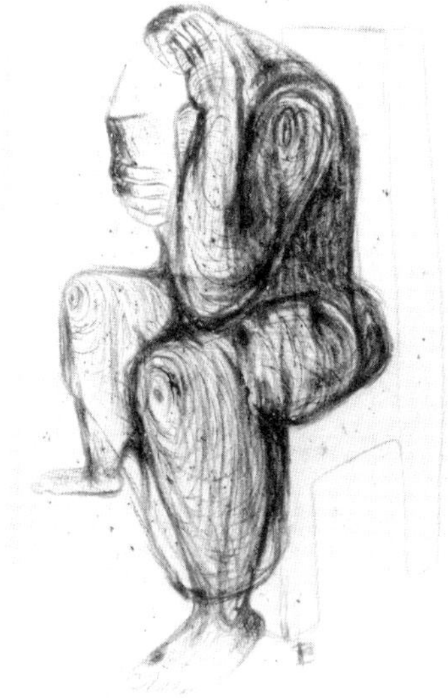

Theo Balden, *Lesender*, (Woman Reading), 1948, oil pastel on paper, 58.4 × 47 cm, Akademie der Künste, Berlin

requirements of Soviet cultural policy, seen for instance in the highly 'finished' and naturalistic portrait-bust of a young Korean girl, *Koreanisches Mädchen*, of 1954. As with his compatriot, René Graetz, who had also remained in London during the war, and travelled to Berlin in 1946, and had had contact with Moore, Balden found that the international formalist language absorbed during exile caused difficulties in Soviet zone.

Three years after Moore's first large showing in Berlin, the 1954 *Berlin Festwochen* was marked by an exhibition of paintings and drawings at the Haus am Waldsee by the other great hope of British art at this time, the painter Graham Sutherland. Although the organisers hoped that Sutherland would have a similar impact to Moore, a report written by Nicholas Powell for the British Council illustrated how changing conditions had diminished the effect:

> As I believe is usual with Sutherland, the exhibition was more a success with the informed than the general public; by this I mean that the impact of Sutherland on Germany was not the bombshell that the first showing of Henry Moore was, coming at a time when there was little or no competition nor any idea of what was being done in the contemporary world outside this country.[66]

By spring 1954, it would appear, much of the isolation remaining from wartime circumstances had disappeared. The supposed carte blanche presented to the four military governments in 1945 to impose, through whatever means, their own particular political will had by this point been forfeited, although not just as a result of Cold War build up. Negotiations with German organisations, which had their own preoccupations, continued to play an important part. Something of the character of these negotiations can be seen by turning to reorganisation on the German side.

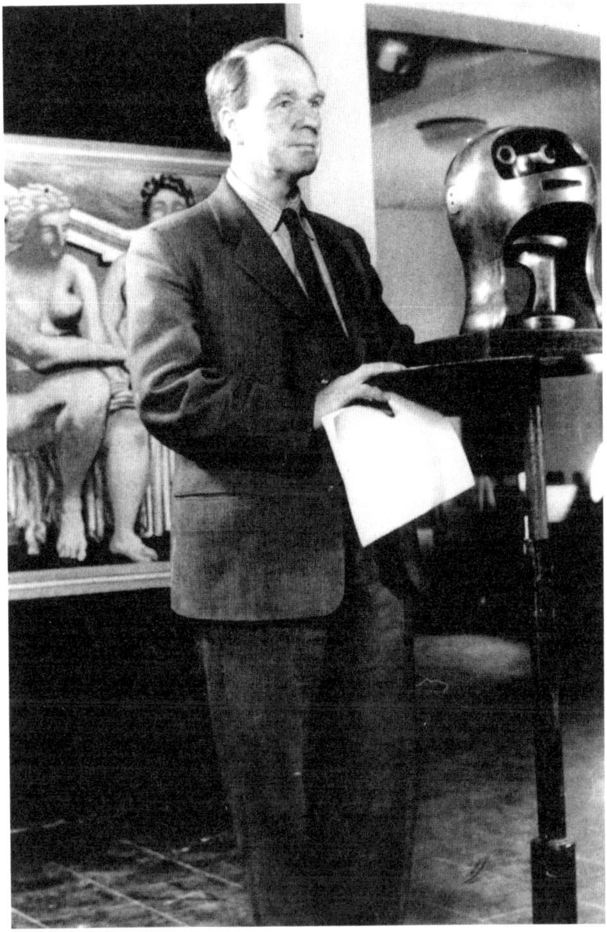

Photograph of Henry Moore at the opening of the exhibition *Das Bild des Menschen in Meisterwerken europäischer Kunst*, Städtliche Kunsthalle, Recklinghausen, 1955. Moore is standing with *Helmet Head no.2*, 1950

1 Uhlmann, H., 'Freiheit des Kunstschaffens', in: Uhlmann, unpaginated.

2 Palmier, 15.

3 Rave, 15–16. Easton, 256.

4 Bance, 13.

5 Kästner, 25–31.

6 Heinz Trökes, opening speech for the exhibition *Fantasten-Ausstellung*, Galerie Gerd Rosen, 11 February 1946. Reprinted in: Krause, 172–5, here 172.

7 Kästner, 25.

8 NA/OMGUS/ISD/007. Fine Arts/Ilse Nehemias, 'Proposal of Features on Modern Art on US-Controlled Radio Stations', 26 August 1946.

9 'Beurteilungen der Ausstellung', in: Friedrichsbau, 41–52, quote 45.

10 Roh, 1948, 44–7.

11 Roh,F., 'German art in the 20th Century', in: Offenburg, 7–10, here 7.

12 Tüngel, R., 'Häßliche Kunst', *Die Zeit*, 24 July 1947, 4.

13 Schölzel, K., 'Die Entlastung des Geistes', in: Glaser, 1989, 310–15, here 310.

14 Braden, S., 'Lost Remnants of National Socialist Ideology', *Department of State Bulletin*, 27 January 1946; cited by Lee, 76.

15 Clare, 118.

16 NA/OMGBS/ISD/Chamber of Creative Artists/165.01/Michael Josselson, 'A Request for Clarification of the Operating Scope of the Committee', 29 April 1946.

17 NA/OMGUS/ECR Cult Ex/Monuments and Fine Arts (Breitenbach & Heinrich)/Edgar Breitenbach and Theodore A. Heinrich, 'Assumption by E & CR Division of Cultural Restitutions Responsibility', 1 August 1949, 2–3.

18 NA/OMGUS/ECR/Cult Ex/211. Memo: 'Assumption by E&CR Division of Cultural Restitutions Responsibility', 1 August 1949, 3.

19 NA/OMGUS/ECR/5, Constable, W., 'Art and Reorientation', September 1949, 3.

20 Breitenbach, B., 'Historical survey of the activities of the intelligence department, MFA&A section, OMGB, 1946–49', *College Art Journal*, vol. IX., no. 2, Winter 1949–50, 192–8; Leonard Woolley's introduction to: Lord Methuen, xv–xviii.

21 Henke, J., 'OMGUS. Education and Cultural Relations Division (ECR)', unpublished archive description, NA/USGCC, 1944–5, Boxes 1–23.

22 OMGBW/ISD/Report no. 22, period ending 25 July 1947, 13.

23 Turner, I., 'Research on the British Occupation', in: Turner, 1989, 327–58.

24 Spender, 28–9.

25 Annan, 1983, 7.

26 PRO/FO 1012/166. Memo from Mr R. Birley, Educational Advisor, CCG(BE), 12 March 1948. Cf. also: Birley, R., 'British Policy in Retrospect', in: Hearnden, 46–63.

27 Birke, Booms and Merker, vol. 1, viii–xxi.

28 Greene; Welch, D., 'Priming the Pump of German Democracy', in: Turner, 1989, 215–38, here 216–9.

29 PRO/FO1056/93.

30 Cf. Taylor, 1981; Lauren; Lee.

31 Schieder, 2003, 68–70.

32 McEwen, 23–6; Junge Kunst; Karl & Faber, 2–3.

33 Taylor, 1999, 167.

34 PRO FO 1012/166.

35 'News From Home and Overseas', *Monthly Review of the British Council*, no.8, January 1948, 245.

36 PRO FO 1012/166, Letter from F.G.A. Wint, Political Liaison Officer, OEA, CCG(BE) to Brigadier E.R. Benson, British Military Government, Berlin, 21 July 1948.

37 PRO FO 946/50.

38 PRO FO 946/50, Memo from D.H. Whyte, 15 March 1947. Cf. also excerpts from the AIA Bulletin of Autumn 1945 in: Morris, 76.

39 PRO BW 1/135.

40 BC FAC, 22 September 1948.

41 British Council, 5.

42 Grohmann, W., 'Aber wieviel Mut dazu gehört. Randbemerkungen zu einer Ausstellungspromenade', *Die Neue Zeitung*, 26 October 1948, unpaginated.

43 BC/FAC, January 1949.

44 Read, 1948, 4.

45 BC/FAC, quoted in meeting of February 1951.

46 Isaacs, 5.

47 The exhibition toured Stuttgart, Wiesbaden, Munich, 1950–1.

48 Grigson, 1950–1, 3.

49 Stallabrass, 14.

50 BC/FAC, July 1950.

51 Poley, J., 'Ausstellung Henry Moore in Hamburg', *Das Kunstwerk*, no. 4, 1950, 59–61, here 59.

52 Flemming, H.T., 'Moore and Sutherland', *Das Kunstwerk*, no. 8/9, 1946–7, 59–51, here 51.

53 Peiffer-Watenphul, M., 'Biennale di Venezia', *Das Kunstwerk*, no. 8, 1948, 35–6, here 36.

54 Haftmann, W., 'Der Bildhauer Henry Moore', *Die Kunst und das Schöne Heim*, no. 2, November 1949, 53–5, here 53.

55 Hentzen.

56 Frisé, A., 'Henry Moore in Hamburg', *Deutsche Zeitung und Wirtschafts Zeitung*, no. 25, 29 March 1950, 11.

57 Grohmann, 1960, 137.

58 Pevsner, N., 'Thoughts on Henry Moore', *The Burlington Magazine*, no. 503, February 1945, 47–9.

59 Erben, W., 'So arbeiten wie der Natur … ', *Rheinische Post*, no. 100, 29 April 1950.

60 K.L., 'Repräsentiert Henry Moore England?', *Freies Volk*, no. 108, 10 May 1950.

61 'Dr Jannasch and Dr Skutch', foreword to: Grigson, 1951.

62 Buesche, A., 'Rückkehr zum Gesamtkunstwerk', *Tagesspiegel*, 11 September 1951; Dargel, F.A., 'Vorstoß ins Neuland. Ausstellungen von Henry Moore und Bernhard Heiliger', *Telegraf*, 11 September 1951.

63 Schapire, R., 'Henry Moore', *Die Weltkunst*, vol. 23, no. 18, 15 September 1953, 2, 4, here 4.

64 Schieder, 2005, 333–63.

65 Cf. Balden, T., 'Erbe in Dienst eines Streitbaren Humanismus', *Bildende Kunst*, vol. 23, 1975, 381; idem. 'Henry Moore', *Sonntag*, 21 September 1986.

66 BC/FAC, May 1955, Report from Nicholas Powell.

Reorganisation

Berlin ... sprawled flat between mountains of ruins. Emptied squares, in which the wind swirled twisters of debris. Brick dust between one's teeth. Arguments about everything. Representational versus nonrepresentational art: Hofer on one side, Grohmann on the other. Over here and over there: here Benn, there Brecht. Cold War by loudspeaker. And yet the Berlin of those years, for all the shouting, was a place as silent as the dead.

Günter Grass, *Writing After Ausschwitz*, in 'Two States – One Nation?', trans. K. Winston and A.S. Wensinger, London, 1990, 104–5

At the beginning of 1946, the art historian Adolf Jannasch, reporting to the Berlin Magistrate, summarised the requirements for cultural reconstruction in the city. Before all else, Jannasch stated, the connection between art and the people (*Kunst und Volk*) should be re-established, and, through exposure to the visual arts, ordinary Germans be taught to see again. Leading artists (he cites Gerhard Marcks, Erich Heckel, Otto Dix, Karl Schmidt-Rottluff, Alfred Mahlau, Alfred Kubin and Hans Meid) should be supported, and given teaching jobs if necessary. With the obvious exception of Nazi art, all artistic directions and forms were to be encouraged, in particular 'degenerate art': those artists condemned by Nazism must become once again legitimate public figures. Next on Jannasch's list were art schools, in particular a school of decorative arts, and the planning of exhibitions, not only of works by living artists – he lists Max Pechstein, Karl Hofer and René Sintenis – but also memorial exhibitions for those such as Barlach who had died during the Third Reich and had not received proper commemoration. 'Perhaps the happiest task is forming collections of the younger generation, the future masters', Jannasch adds, referring to the important collection of twentieth-century art, the Galerie des 20. Jahrhunderts, that he and Ludwig Justi had instigated within the Berlin Magistrate, which was to form the basis of the collection of the Neue Nationalgalerie. In addition, public awareness of the arts should be promoted through a central exhibition building and the publication of an educational arts journal. Only with these measures would Berlin regain the status of a 'living and leading art city'.[1]

For many, the activities unleashed by this enthusiasm resulted in a period of excitement and creativity that harked back to the golden years of Weimar culture in the 1920s. Berlin was the centre of this activity, as Jannasch hoped, just as it had been twenty years previously. To see all of the exhibitions in Berlin, wrote Paul Fechter in March 1947, would require at least three exhausting days; he refers to the overwhelming amount of activity as a *Kultursündflut*, a deluge of culture.[2] Although at the time it appeared that a real and magnificent restoration had occurred, this nevertheless turned out to be short-lived. The Soviet Blockade of supplies to Western Berlin was the first major step in the breakdown of the wartime Soviet-Western alliance. An idealistic spirit of cultural renewal was soon doused by postwar realpolitik, and Berlin was to remain, as always, a politically divided and materially impoverished city. The dissipation of energy that had created such excitement in the first few years after 1945 continued with the growing exodus of artists from East to West that began in the early 1950s. Postwar Berlin was to be no new Weimar.

The divisions that emerged were by no means solely East versus West. Although the conflicting promotion of Socialist Realism and abstraction was a major contemporary phenomenon, there was no public debate or event where these forces really clashed.

It was a diffuse battle in comparison to debates in the West over the status of abstraction, and also in comparison to the 1951 Darmstädter Gespräch, at which conservative and liberal forces with the West clashed over the issue of modern art. As Günther Grass noted many years later, the public focus for 'all the shouting' about realism and abstraction was in fact an embittered dispute within the West between the painter Karl Hofer and the critic Will Grohmann. Although much of the antagonism was motivated by Hofer's own annoyance with what he saw as the sectarian nature of the support for abstract art, he was by no means an agent for Soviet cultural policy. At the opening of the fourth exhibition of the Berlin-based Künstlerbund, Hofer lamented the vanishing of the *Menschenbild*, or human image, in contemporary painting. Grohmann, surrounded by those painters who had left the Künstlerbund in protest at Hofer's polemical stance, kept aloof from direct engagement with Hofer, though was unwavering in his support for artists such as those connected with the Zen 49 group – Willi Baumeister, Rupprecht Geiger, Theodor Werner and Fritz Winter – the avatars of abstraction in postwar Germany. The debate ceased after Hofer's death in 1955.

But if these divisions implied weakness, there was a far stronger will to reconstruct after 1945 than after 1918, a result of the fact that the war damage was much greater. This will existed despite the absence of many figures who could have reconciled the problems of style and acted as a bridge for older ideas: amongst others, Max Beckmann and Walter Gropius were in exile; Paul Klee and Oskar Schlemmer were no longer alive. Arguably, with the exception of Otto Dix, not one major artist remained in Germany from the former period, and even Dix could not make anything to rival the historic antheses of Expressionism, Bauhaus and Sachlichkeit.

The lack of towering individuals can be contrasted with the proliferation of artists' groups, societies and unions, amateur and professional, from small, revolutionary caucuses to large, conservative, country-wide associations, which began appearing soon after 1945. This was a busy time. These groups contributed in a number of different ways towards the enormous task of cultural reconstruction. In the face of a critical, frequently hostile, public, whose views on modern art, as we have seen, kept the spirit of Goebbels alive, such groups provided the platform upon which difficult artistic styles and ideas about art were discussed, and found legitimacy. More pressing than the need for spiritual and intellectual support, however, were the problems posed by financial and material insecurity, which in many cases meant near starvation. Membership of groups entitled artists to public assistance, especially after the currency reform (the replacement of the Reichsmark with the Deutsche Mark) in 1948. The short-term effect on artists of the reform was considerable: prices plummeted and many enterprises folded. In one instance, in late 1949, the Berufsverband (Professional Union) Nordrhein-Westfalen and seven Landesverbände (Regional Unions) made a plea to the authorities for financial relief. Although the fall in market prices was a blow for artists and dealers alike, it also had the unexpected benefit of driving out of the temple the 'charlatans' and 'kitsch-merchants' who sold over-priced, substandard work, according to a report in *bildende kunst*.[3]

In the face of such 'kitsch-merchants', professional organisations sustained the distinction between 'genuine' and merely amateur art. Upholding this divide was crucial, as the two often appeared in the same exhibition spaces – a result of material difficulties in transporting and circulating 'professional' work, and of the generally haphazard way in which many exhibitions were organised in the first few years of occupation. Professional groups closed ranks in the search for definite boundaries between 'genuine' and 'false' art. In 1948, the information sheet of the Schutzverband Bildender Künstler (Protective Association of Fine Artists – a trade association founded in March 1946 and active throughout Germany before being incorporated in 1951 into the Verband Bildender Künstler Deutschlands – Association of German Fine Artists – the central East German artists' association), printed a letter from a member suggesting methods of fighting 'kitsch-production', the low-quality work sold in ordinary shops and by venal art dealers, which constituted a market stealing trade from professionals. The solution was not to wait for the public to become more discerning, but to create a quality-control guarantee in the form of a label that could be affixed to the back of each work produced by a member.[4] Such a seal had in fact already been instituted by the Berufsband Bildender Künstler (Professional Association of Fine Artists) in Munich during 1946.[5]

Artists' groups were thus essential for survival – just as they were throughout Second Empire Germany and the Weimar Republic. Certain postwar groupings were direct revivals of earlier institutions. The Schutzverband Bildender Künstler, for instance, was the heir to the Reichsverband Bildender Künstler Deutschlands e.V. (Reich Association of Fine Artists in Germany, 1913–33), an association that protected many artists from dire poverty throughout the First World War and its aftermath. As well as evincing continuity and survival, postwar artists' groups created a bridge between individual artists and civic authorities. In the absence of a sovereign state, it should be remembered, authority took the exceptional form of a quadripartite military government that was by no means a coherent, happy whole. As we have seen in the case of re-education, the alliance of modern art and political democracy became crucial. If the relation of artists to the nation state is taken as a key theme of modernity, and art is considered as a means of testing the bounds of civic freedom in response to the legal monopoly of the state, then the situation of Allied occupation provides a fascinating case study of this relation exacerbated to an extreme.

More prosaically, the relation was determined first by judicial enquiries that produced 'black' and 'white' lists to determine how involved individuals had been with the Nazi Party, and thus their suitability for participation in postwar public life, and second by the obligation to issue licences for all cultural activities. In the first months of the occupation, military governments gave licences only to democratic political parties and trade unions. By 1946, however, artistic organisations such as the Künstlervereine (Artists' Societies) were beginning to reappear. As part of a liberal tradition of civic responsibility, clearly opposed to the centralisation of the Nazi Reichskulturkammer (Reich Chamber of Culture), the 'Vereine' were highly significant for the 'democratic adjustment' of postwar society, and were thus largely favoured by the authorities in the West, and readily licensed. In comparison with these liberal groupings, however, which took time to develop into influential structures, the left-wing groups that arose swiftly after the fall of Berlin to the Red Army had a far more strained relationship with the Allied military governments, a relationship that hinged around the formal question of licensing.

At the root of these difficulties was the primacy of the Soviets in determining cultural life in Berlin. SMAD (Sowjetische Militäradministration), the Soviet Military Government for Occupied Germany, was established in Berlin on 9 June 1945, well before the other Allies arrived. The leading cadre of the KPD (Kommunistisches Partei Deutschlands – the German Communist Party) returned from Soviet exile, landing on Tempelhof airfield, and reconstituted themselves as a political force over the next few days. In an announcement published in Berlin on 13 June, the KPD admitted that it would be inappropriate to foist the Soviet one-party system on Germany, advocating instead an anti-fascist democratic regime.[6] Stalin's decision to allow the founding of competing political parties and cultural organisations acknowledged the difficulties that a totalitarian state would have, not only with the indigenous population but also with the other three powers. This decision had a direct effect on cultural reconstruction, creating a relatively liberal environment in which artists could work in a variety of styles, and within which discussion was not restricted by political mandate. It was precisely this liberal environment, and the mobility that it allowed for ideas, particularly those relating to the question of the cultural basis of German nationalism, that led to a stand-off between the Western Allies and the Soviets, and the beginning of a more repressive period of cultural policy.

The Kammer der Kunstschaffenden (Chamber of Creative Artists), was created on the orders of Nikolai Berzarin, the Soviet Commandant of Berlin, on 6 June 1945. It was the only cultural organisation to be officially recognised by all four military authorities. In the temporary absence of any unions or professional associations, the Kammer was set up to handle all cultural affairs in Berlin, and was thus divided into sections for theatre, dance, music, the fine arts and film. Within the bureaucratic hierarchies of the Berlin Magistrate (which had been reinstated only ten days after capitulation on 12 May), the Kammer was financed as part of the Volksbildung department, the section of the Magistrate charged with 'popular' education and cultural matters. As such, the Kammer was not a professional organisation with paying members, but an organisation run by a civic authority, and was clearly intended to fulfil many of Adolf Jannasch's desiderata, cited above. For example, the Fine Arts section of the Kammer, led by the Socialist art historian Carl Linfert and the painter Albert Klatt, was immediately involved with the rehabilitation of defamed artists. The choice of the first two large touring exhibitions, Käthe Kollwitz (the exhibition toured Dresden, Leipzig, Berlin and Potsdam) and Ernst Barlach (which toured Rostock, Güstrow and Schwerin), nevertheless suggests that this was a very selective recuperation, both artists having associations with prewar revolutionary styles and organisations. The same department was also responsible for mounting one of the first exhibitions in postwar Berlin, which appeared in July. A photograph in the official Soviet newspaper, the *Tägliche Rundschau*, shows that this was by no means a politically radical showing, mixing the tasks of rehabilitation and support of living artists. The review accompanying the image notes the inclusion of Ernst Ludwig Kirchner's *Die Wohnstube* (The Sitting Room) and Ernst Wilhelm Nay's *Boote* (Boats) and *Dorf am schwarzen Meer* (Village on the Black Sea), and criticises them both for their formal preoccupations, and lack of attention to 'social themes'.[7] The painter Karl Hofer on the other

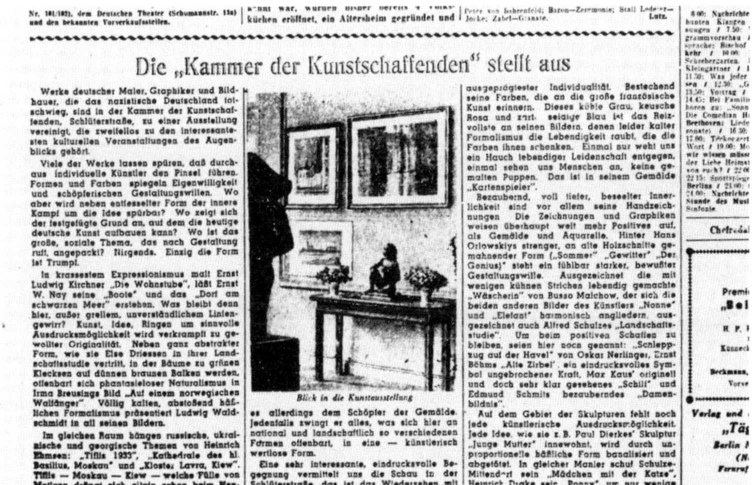

Nr. 181/182), dem Deutschen Theater (Schumannstr. 13a) und den bekannten Vorverkaufsstellen.

küchen eröffnet, ein Altersheim gegründet und

Peter von Ehrenfeld; Baron—Zeremonie; Stall Lederer—Jocke; Zabel—Granate. Lutz.

Die „Kammer der Kunstschaffenden" stellt aus

Werke deutscher Maler, Graphiker und Bildhauer, die das nazistische Deutschland totschwieg, sind in der Kammer der Kunstschaffenden, Schlüterstraße, zu einer Ausstellung vereinigt, die zweifellos zu den interessantesten kulturellen Veranstaltungen des Augenblicks gehört.

Viele der Werke lassen spüren, daß durchaus individuelle Künstler den Pinsel führen. Formen und Farben spiegeln Eigenwilligkeit und schöpferischen Gestaltungswillen. Wo aber wird neben entfesselter Form der innere Kampf um die Idee spürbar? Wo zeigt sich der festgefügte Grund an, auf dem die heutige deutsche Kunst aufbauen kann? Wo ist das große, soziale Thema, das nach Gestaltung ruft, angepackt? Nirgends. Einzig die Form ist Trumpf.

In krassestem Expressionismus malt Ernst Ludwig Kirchner „Die Wohnstube", läßt Ernst W. Nay seine „Boote" und das „Dorf am schwarzen Meer" erstehen. Was bleibt denn hier, außer grellem, unverständlichem Liniengewirr? Kunst, Idee, Ringen um sinnvolle Ausdrucksmöglichkeit wird verkrampft zu gewollter Originalität. Neben ganz abstrakter Form, wie sie Else Driessen in ihrer Landschaftsstudie vertritt, in der Bäume zu grünen Klecksen auf dünnen braunen Balken werden, offenbart sich phantasieloser Naturalismus in Irma Breusings Bild „Auf einem norwegischen Walfänger". Völlig kalten, abstoßend häßlichen Formalismus präsentiert Ludwig Waldschmidt in all seinen Bildern.

Im gleichen Raum hängen russische, ukrainische und georgische Themen von Heinrich Ehmsen: „Tiflis 1933", „Kathedrale des hl. Basilius, Moskau" und „Kloster Lavra, Kiew". Tiflis — Moskau — Kiew — welche Fülle von Motiven drängt sich allein schon beim Nennen dieser drei Namen auf. Nicht so erging es allerdings dem Schöpfer der Gemälde. Jedenfalls zwingt er alles, was sich hier an national und landschaftlich so verschiedenen Formen offenbart, in eine — künstlerisch wertlose Form.

Blick in die Kunstausstellung

Eine sehr interessante, eindrucksvolle Begegnung vermittelt uns die Schau in der Schlüterstraße, das ist das Wiedersehen mit Karl Hofer. Hofer ist ohne Zweifel der Künstler ausgeprägtester Individualität. Bestechend seine Farben, die an die große französische Kunst erinnern. Dieses kühle Grau, keusche Rosa und zart seidige Blau ist das Reizvollste an seinen Bildern, denen leider kalter Formalismus die Lebendigkeit raubt, die die Farben ihnen schenken. Einmal nur weht uns ein Hauch lebendiger Leidenschaft entgegen, einmal sehen uns Menschen an, keine gemalten Puppen. Das ist in seinem Gemälde „Kartenspieler".

Bezaubernd, voll tiefer, beseelter Innerlichkeit sind vor allem seine Handzeichnungen. Die Zeichnungen und Graphiken weisen überhaupt weit mehr Positives auf, als Gemälde und Aquarelle. Hinter Hans Orlowskiys strenger, an alte Holzschnitte gemahnender Form („Sommer" „Gewitter" „Der Genius)" steht ein fühlbar starker, bewußter Gestaltungswille. Ausgezeichnet die mit wenigen kühnen Strichen lebendig gemachte „Wäscherin" von Busso Malchow, der sich die beiden anderen Bilder des Künstlers „Nonne" und „Elefant" harmonisch angliedern, ausgezeichnet auch Alfred Schulzes „Landschaftsstudie". Um beim positiven Schaffen zu bleiben, seien hier noch genannt: „Schleppzug auf der Havel" von Oskar Nerlinger, Ernst Böhms „Alte Zirbel", ein eindrucksvolles Symbol ungebrochener Kraft, Max Kaus' originell und doch sehr klar gesehenes „Schilf" und Edmund Schmits bezauberndes „Damenbildnis".

Auf dem Gebiet der Skulpturen fehlt noch jede künstlerische Ausdrucksmöglichkeit. Jede Idee, wie sie z. B. Paul Dierkes' Skulptur „Junge Mutter" innewohnt, wird durch unproportionelle häßliche Form banalisiert und abgetötet. In gleicher Manier schuf Schulze-Mittendorf sein „Mädchen mit der Katze", Heinrich Drake sein „Ponny", um nur wenige Arbeiten herauszugreifen. — Seng

Газета «Ежедневное обозрение». Издается Советской Военной Администрацией в Германии.

'Blick in die Kunstausstellung', (Installation View), installation photograph of an exhibition organised by the Kammer der Kunstschaffenden in Berlin, July 1945, published in the *Täglicher Rundschau*, 28 July 1945, 4

hand (who happened to be the president of the Kammer at that moment), is praised for his *Kartenspieler* (Card Players), despite the 'dangers of formal reduction' noted elsewhere in his work. Although the review assumes the democratic intentions of the Kammer, which had been announced in the *Tägliche Rundschau* the previous month, it is clear that the review and exhibition were both informed by Soviet sympathies. Apart from Hofer, the painters Hans Orlowsky, Bussow Malchow, Alfred Schulze, Oskar Nerlinger, Ernst Böhm, Max Kaus and Edmund Schmit were given a positive mention, all artists working in a realist tradition compatible with Socialist notions of realism and human empathy.

Suspicion of the Kammer der Kunstschaffenden quickly mounted amongst the Western military governors. The very name of the organisation evoked its predecessor organisation, the Nazi Reichskulturkammer. Although a common term, no cultural organisation before 1933 had been designated as a *Kammer*, or 'chamber'. The idea of a hierarchical organisation subdivided into various chambers was a direct continuation of the form taken by the Reichskulturkammer. The impression of continuity was not helped by the fact that the Kammer der Kunstschaffenden was housed in the former headquarters of the Reichskulturkammer, at 45 Schlüterstrasse, in the British Zone. However, whereas the Reichskulturkammer was based on the authority of one individual, the Kammer der Kunstschaffenden was divided between the four zones, with each of the local administrations that covered the twenty districts of Berlin answerable to the Military Government under which that district had been placed.

As heir to the Reichskulturkammer, the Kammer was for the Allies both a problem and a source of useful information. The meticulous records kept by the Nazi administration, the Hinkel archives, named after the administrative head of the Reichskulturkammer, were inherited by the Kammer der Kunstschaffenden, and provided the Intelligence Section of the Allied ISC (Information Services Control) with invaluable data for the arduous procedure of denazification in the cultural field. These archives were open to use by the Soviets as early as May, and were utilised as part of the political classifications of artists that determined what type of ration card they would receive – extremely important in the light of severe food shortages.[8] By the end of 1945, the Allies were centralising the files and dispatched a representative of each of the four governments to work in the Kammer archives, and created a committee to draw up black and white lists for future employment.[9] These advisors would presumably have worked alongside the existing German office of denazification, the Spruchkammer. This had been formed with representatives from the Kulturbund (described below), the Berlin Magistrate, and the Kammer itself, with the job of recommending individuals, in the light of the Kammer's archives, for employment in the cultural field.[10] By late October 1948, the British were keen to pass on responsibility for the archives:

> The archives contain records relating to the careers of all Germans who were active in the cultural field during the Nazi regime, and have therefore been of great value in vetting applications for licenses. Now that the

responsibility for licensing has been passed to German committees, however, with merely a right of veto retained by military government, we are anxious to dissociate ourselves from the routine of screening applications and encourage the Germans to do this themselves.[11]

By this time, however, the Kammer der Kunstschaffenden had ceased to exist. According to Jutta Held, it was dissolved on 23 November 1945, after complaints from Otto Winzer, head of the Volksbildung department of the Berlin Magistrate, concerning organisational difficulties and fears that the Kammer der Kunstschaffenden in the British Sector was becoming a centre of Western opposition.[12] American military records suggest, on the contrary, that it functioned until the end of March 1946. The American Cultural Affairs committee had nevertheless decided in December 1945 to do away with the Kammer, in part due to its affinities with the Reichskulturkammer, but also because it was trying to spread its jurisdiction throughout the four zones, and was thus a challenge to Allied governance.[13] Although they were satisfied that the Reichskulturkammer had been 'thoroughly liquified', according to one American report,[14] and that the Kammer der Kunstschaffenden had been legitimately constituted, American and British government officials evidently feared the hidden political aims of the organisation. To replace the Kammer der Kunstschaffenden, a new department was established by the Western Allies, dealing with film, theatre, music and the visual arts, and was deliberately detached from the Sovietleaning Berlin Magistrate in the hope of politically neutralising cultural matters.[15] The problem presented by the Kammer der Kunstschaffenden was clear: although such organisations were essential for artists facing material plight, it was important to avoid 'top-down' bureaucratic organisations that were open to Soviet manipulation.

Only in the early months of 1948 did this confrontation of Soviet principles and the needs of the Western Allies begin to determine relations. Up to this moment, exhibitions and organisations mounted in the East were more likely to be determined by feelings of German nationalism than by Soviet sympathies. Combined with Soviet concessions to democracy, however short-lived, the result of this was a period of relative tolerance and pluralism in the arts, a period nevertheless quickly forgotten in the West during the years after 1947. A decade later, Will Grohmann could write that 'only in the Russian Zone was there no resumption of artistic activity: the regulations regarding art that were laid down by the Russian authorities were like those of the Third Reich'.[16]

Grohmann's remark is particularly perplexing given his involvement in a major exhibition organised in 1946 in Soviet-Zone Dresden, the *Allgemeine Deutsche Kunstausstellung*, an 'all-German' event symptomatic of the early years of occupation. The exhibition took place largely thanks to Grohmann and the painter Hans Grundig, who toured Germany, securing works from all zones. (Although sixty to seventy works were secured from the British Zone, none arrived, most probably for logistical reasons rather than due to anti-Soviet feeling).[17] That most of the works came from the collections of the artists not only indicates the virtual or complete absence of public collections, but also entailed that few works by artists who had not remained in Germany throughout the war were shown. As such, it was an exhibition of those who had stayed. Abstract and figurative works were shown, and no political distinction made between the styles. The organisers clearly wished to create an ecumenical atmosphere. The effect was of a reassembling of forces after a prolonged period of suppression and dispersion.

The point was consciously defended: amongst speeches at the opening of the exhibition, which reinforced the broad-based anti-fascist position, Theodor Plievier, the author of the novel *Stalingrad* (1945), defended the exhibition against charges of partisanship. Plievier argued that the role of art in democratic renewal

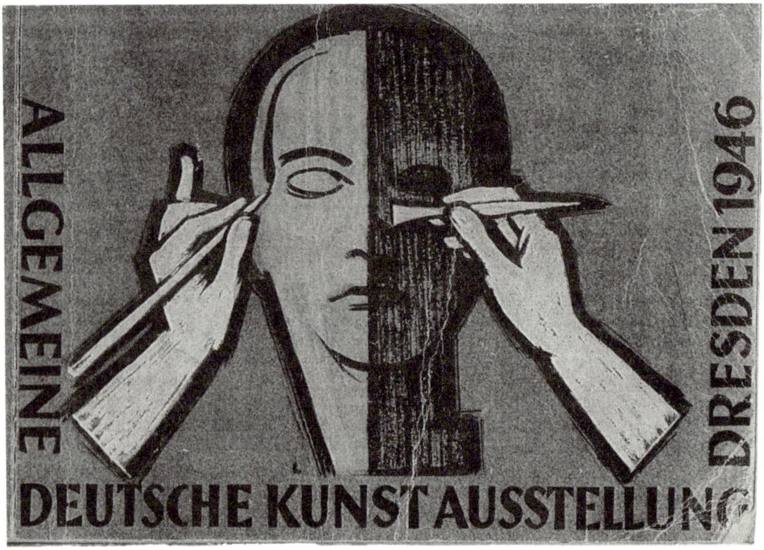

Exhibition Catalogue, *Allgemeine Kunstausstellung*, Stadthalle Nordplatz, Dresden, 1946

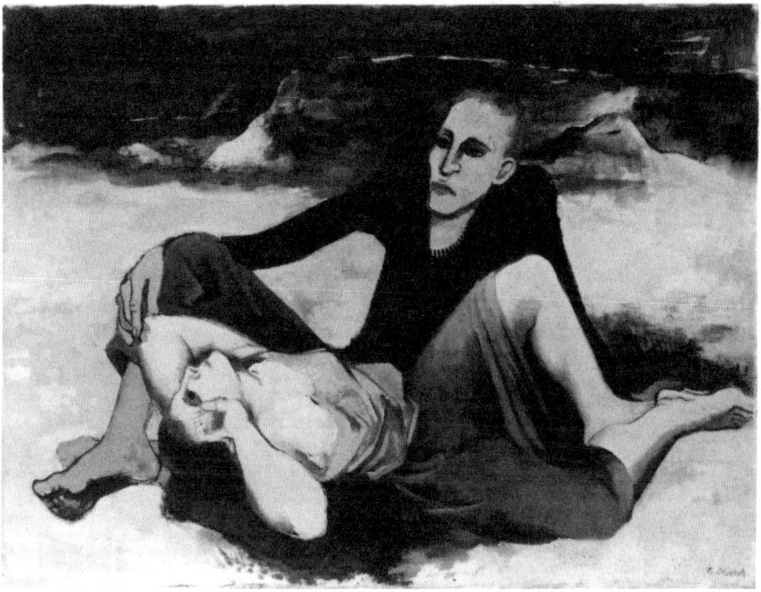

Fritz Duda, *Ruhendes Paar,* (Leisure Time), 1934/6, oil on canvas, 85 × 115 cm, Nationalgalerie, Staatliche Museen zu Berlin

was not linked to a narrow political viewpoint, but to the 'support and promotion of the concept [of democracy] itself'.[18] Inclusiveness also meant showing works by the sculptors Richard Scheibe and Georg Kolbe, both of whom had exhibited in the Nazi *Große Deutsche Kunstausstellung* (Great German Art Exhibition) nine years previously, alongside paintings by the radical left-wing artist Fritz Duda. Rudolf Schlichter's surrealistic *Lebendiges Sprengt Totes* (Life Vanquishes Death, 1946), Willi Baumeister's fully abstract *Bild mit farbigen Zonen* (Painting with Coloured Zones, 1946) and Curt Querner's Dix-like proletarian-realism portraits of farmers from Saxony further suggest the range of works on display. The sculptor Herbert

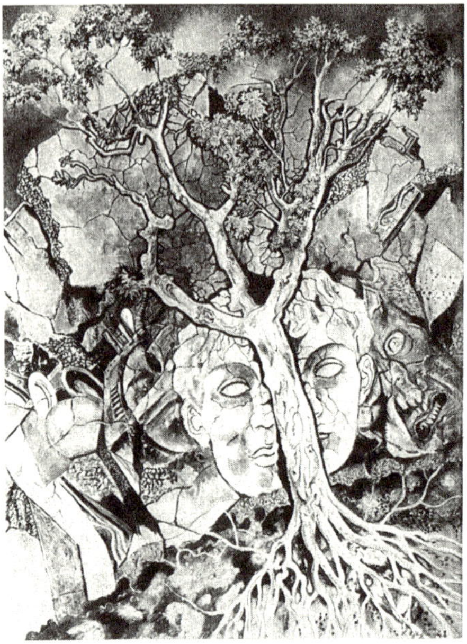

Rudolf Schlichter, *Lebendiges Sprengt Totes* (Life Conquers Death), 1940, oil on board, 100 × 74,5 cm, © Viola Roehr v. Alvensleben, Munich

Volwahsen, in his speech delivered at the opening of the exhibition, described another purpose of the exhibition; artists from Dresden had not forgotten that the *Entartete Kunst* exhibition had appeared first in their city twelve years previously. The *Allgemeine Deutsche Kunstausstellung* would show that art involved work not just for the artist, but also for the viewer: 'It is not the intention to make things easy for the average viewer. He will not find himself lulled by an uncomplicated, sugarcoated, decorative pseudo-art'.[19]

Despite these broad intentions, over half of the works came from the Soviet Zone, and the inclusion of many associated with the ASSO group resulted to a certain degree in a retrospective

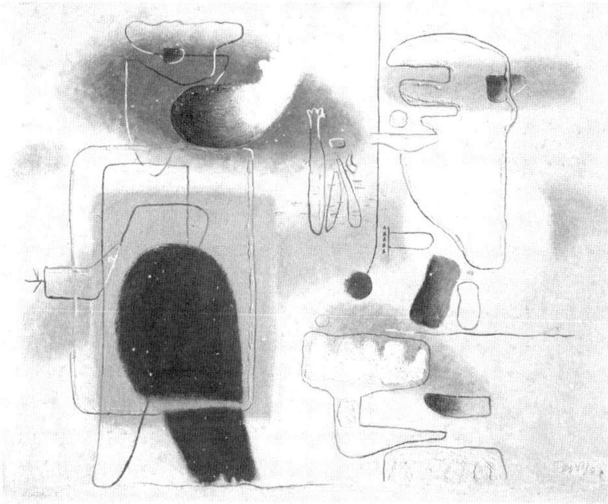

Willi Baumeister, *Bild mit farbigen Zonen* (Picture with Coloured Areas), 1946, oil and resin on cardboard, 54 × 65 cm, location unknown

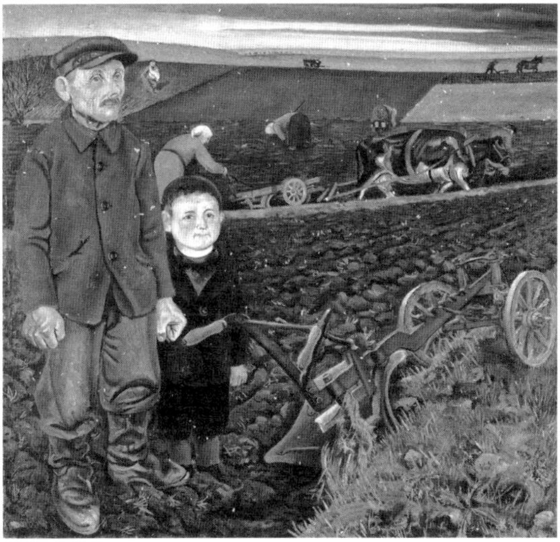

Curt Querner, *Bauernbild* (also: *Märzbild*) (Farmers, or March Painting) 1933, oil on canvas, 134 × 146 cm, Stiftung Moritzburg, Kunstmuseum des Landes Sachsen-Anhalt

and rehabilitation of this prewar, revolutionary association. Works by Hans and Lea Grundig, Wilhelm Lachnit, Curt Querner, Otto Griebel, Oskar Nerlinger and Conrad Felixmüller, all prewar ASSO members, were shown. As the Stuttgart-based journal *Das Kunstwerk* reported, whereas artists associated with the Brücke group were represented 'above all', only three stands were 'left over' for abstract and Surrealist work.[20]

Behind the scenes simmered a more overt political tendentiousness. An accompanying artists' congress revealed a highly exclusive view of official art, and marked the first occasion on which the Zhdanovist anti-formalist doctrine was aired in public.[21] Oberst Tjulpanow, representing the cultural department of the Soviet Military Administration, concluded his opening address with an appeal against the 'Nazi wild abandon and the decadence of abstraction'.[22] These views were clearly a reflection of the 'reassertion of ideology' that had been launched by Andrei Zhdanov in the Central Committee of the Soviet Union in August, around the same time that the Dresden exhibition was opened.

Soviet eagerness to form corporate bodies regardless of Western opinion led to inexorable differences. This was particularly acute in the case of union organisations, the real purpose of which was to ensure that artists were aware of their responsibility to the workers' movement, and that cultural reconstruction took place along politically acceptable lines – that is, in accord with the wishes of the SED

(Sozialistische Einheitspartei Deutschlands – Socialist Unity Party of Germany), formed under Soviet pressure in 1946 from the existing Socialist and Communist parties. Such cultural organisations were perceived increasingly, especially by the Americans, as evidence of Soviet infiltration by cultural means and therefore as a threat to the zonal division of Germany.[23] These fears were most evident with the largest cultural organisation established in Germany in the postwar decade, the Kulturbund zur Demokratischen Erneuerung Deutschlands (Cultural League for the Democratic Renewal of Germany). The Kulturbund was founded in Berlin on 3 July 1945 as an anti-fascist cultural league to unite German artists and intellectuals. Given a large amount of support from the Soviet authorities, the Kulturbund quickly developed into the most important cultural organisation of the immediate postwar years. Numerous branches were established in all four zones and, largely due to the energetic efforts of the first president of the organisation, the poet Johannes R. Becher, fresh from Moscow exile, influential figures such as the painter Karl Hofer, the philologist Victor Klemperer, and the writers Ricarda Huch and the elderly Gerhard Hauptmann were enrolled. While Klemperer, involved in both the Dresden branch and Berlin executive committee, describes in his diaries the mixture of otiose speechmaking, privileges for members, internal political wrangling, and eventual submission to Soviet doctrine that characterised the organisation, he also admits the unique importance of the Kulturbund as an institution of reconstruction. It provided a cultural arena that other discredited or reactionary institutions, such as the universities, were unable to fulfil. It also served a practical function: for many émigrés returning to

Berlin, the Kulturbund office (at 45 Schlüterstrasse, the former address as the Kammer der Kunstschaffenden, and also the home of the Allied denazification committee) was, as the cultural historian Wolfgang Schivelbusch writes, an 'information and travel agent and employment and housing office in one'.[24] In the manner of political organisations, it was able to propagate its message through the Berlin Radio and a publishing house, the Aufbau Verlag. These organs, combined with the Kulturbund's hierarchical, departmental structure, comparable to that of the Nazi Reichskulturkammer, and the distinct communist credentials of Becher himself – a 'Stalinist hack' for one Allied Intelligence officer – gave strong overtones of political tendentiousness that the organisation itself adamantly denied.

Precedents for the Kulturbund were the anti-fascist popular front organisations of the 1930s, and cultural-political ideals such as those expressed at the 1935 International Writers' congress in Paris. In addition, both the Freie Deutsche Kulturbund in Großbritannien (Free German League of Culture in Great Britain), founded by German exiles in London at the end of 1938, and the Freie Künstlerbund founded in Paris in 1937 (but only named as such in April 1938), served as a model of anti-fascist resistance.[25] Though the Kulturbund took on the character of a national cultural front, it nevertheless became increasingly clear that this was an enforced status, an imposition that led to struggles within the organisation. If the Kulturbund was the largest and most effective means for intellectuals and artists to engage in public debate, the nature of this debate was less anti-Nazi, or anti-bourgeois, than a struggle between pro- and anti-Soviet feeling as a basis for German national unity.

Two statements issued by Johannes Becher around the time of the founding of the Kulturbund indicate this ambivalent status, caught between Soviet and German demands. In June 1945, Becher wrote to the Military Commandant of Berlin requesting official sanction for the organisation. Although he made no reference to Communism, the pro-Soviet sentiment is clear: 'The aim of this organisation is to reach on the basis of democratic and anti-fascist principles the broadest representation of the intelligentsia (academics, artists, students)'.[26] He went on to outline the goals of the organisation, beginning with the elimination of fascist ideology, and the exposure of the historical distortions that led to militarism and fascism. The respect of the people of other countries would have to be won again, 'especially the people of the Soviet Union'.

Becher's manifesto for the Kulturbund, printed a week later in the *Deutsche Volkszeitung*, suggests that this special relationship with the Soviet Union had to co-exist with a move towards German national unity, in the interests of reconstruction and renewal:

> The Cultural Union for the Democratic Renewal of Germany addresses one of the most challenging tasks facing the nation today: to unite all those German men and women committed by honest and uncompromising will to contribute to the intellectual and cultural renewal of Germany ... The Cultural Union for the Democratic Renewal of Germany considers itself as an organisation

> supporting unfettered thought and feeling, with the aim of stimulating the nation's consciousness … We aim to introduce the German people to the cultural achievements of all nations, above all also those of the Soviet Union … The men and woman who have launched the Cultural Union for the Democratic Renewal of Germany will lead by example in their vision to rebuild German life from the ruins and rubble, moreover to build a firm intellectual basis for the renewal of the people.[27]

Becher's political orientation leaves little room for interpretation. The historian David Pike has shown how Becher's manifesto and guidelines for the Kulturbund drew directly on his experiences in Soviet Exile, and describes the tension between the public face of non-partisanship that organisations such as the Kulturbund were obliged to cultivate, and their clear origin in Stalinist policy.[28] Planning documents drawn up on the same day that the Soviet military government was constituted in Berlin ascribe responsibility to the veteran Communist Wilhelm Pieck, at that moment chairman of the KPD in the Soviet Zone, for the formation of a Kulturbund in occupied Germany, and leave no doubt that the Kulturbund was not the result of an independent grass-roots initiative.[29] Stalin's decision to allow organised political activities and democratic elections acknowledged the fact that any obvious confrontation with the Allied powers would reduce the possibility of spreading the influence of the KPD into the other zones.

Cultural bodies thus offered a covert mode of achieving party dominance, but also allowed a certain amount of latitude in the aims of local organisations, especially those in the western zones who argued for national unity from a non-partisan position. Branches of the Kulturbund were founded in the West at the discretion of military governors, who in some cases instructed the organisation to form under a different name, such as the Kulturliga (Cultural League) in Munich, and the Freie deutsche Kulturgesellschaft (Free German Cultural Society) in Frankfurt. The most successful regional branch was Nordrhein-Westfalen, founded in Düsseldorf in May 1946. The success of the Freie Deutsche Kulturbund in Großbritannien, the cultural organisation founded by German exiles in London during the war, contributed to the British military government's readiness to accept the founding of the Düsseldorf Kulturbund, and its expansion later that year into the Kulturbund for the whole British Zone.[30]

For the West as for the East, national unity was the driving force behind cultural renewal. When, in December 1947, a London Four-Power conference failed to resolve the question of the eastern border, or of unification and reparations, the newsletter of the Düsseldorfer Kulturbund reported the disappointment of its members, and referred back to the goal stated in the Kulturbund's founding manifesto: 'The re-awakening and promotion of all those authentic and valuable national cultural traditions that belong to our people, and their further development in the spirit of democratic renewal'.[31] This call for national unity on the basis of a German culture was repeated in official publications that stressed the fundamental nature of spiritual unity: that it was a pre-requisite for any German state; that it was older than any political or economic unity; and that it represents a culture that could not be reduced to anyone of the Länder, or to the defunct Prussia.[32] Johannes Becher was certainly one of the most vociferous proponents of this nationalism. Rebuffing any authority of the occupying powers, stating that true democratic renewal could only come from within (a point with which the British and American governors largely agreed), Becher made his aims clear: 'We are therefore a German movement, we look onto Germany, and we orientate ourselves in terms of Germany's renewal. We serve Germany [...] Thus our relationship to the occupying powers is neither to serve one or the other, but to serve Germany'.[33]

The banning of the Kulturbund in the American and British sectors of Berlin has been described as part of the gathering Cold War polarisation.[34] The problems faced by the organisation arose equally from questions of German cultural and political unity, and the responses provoked by such wishes in the occupying governments. The Western Allies were wary of cultural-political forces assembling across the sectors, and tried to keep activity contained within the military zones. This imperative led ultimately to the outlawing of the Kulturbund. During March 1946, the Soviets had tried for the first time to obtain quadripartite approval of the Kulturbund, but were told by the other three powers that such approval was not necessary or desirable, and that the organisation should continue to operate on a zonal basis.[35] At a meeting of the Cultural Affairs

Committee of the Allied Kommandatura on 14 June 1946, the British representative showed distinct unease with the increasing tendency of the Kulturbund to adopt a national character, especially with branches in different towns uniting. Officially recognising the Kulturbund would contradict the fact that the Allies had banned the Kammer der Kunstschaffenden on the grounds that it had adopted a nation-wide structure. The Kulturbund was really the same organisation but under a different name.[36]

Whereas British fears tended in the early moments of the occupation to focus on the 'national question', American objections to German cultural organisations must be seen in the light of broader policy reversals taking place mid-1947. The Truman Doctrine directed at the containment of Soviet subversion in the Eastern Mediterranean and Turkey appeared in March. Marshall Aid, the European recovery programme stimulated by the need to build up Germany against the Soviet Union, was announced in June. A CIA intelligence report on the Kulturbund of August 1947 indicates the depth of suspicion that was being entertained of Soviet organisations operating in Germany.[37] The report focuses on the status of the Kulturbund as the most powerful cultural organisation in Berlin and the Soviet Zone, and describes its use of a non-partisan public image. It dwells in particular on the Communist backgrounds of the leading figures. Heinz Willman is credited as being the 'true leader' of the Kulturbund, having been sent from Moscow to set up the organisation. Despite the presence of CDU members on the Präsidialrat (Membership Committee), true power is exercised by a four-man Arbeitsausschuss (Working party), or 'inner sanctum' of

Becher, Heinz Willman, Alexander Abusch and Klaus Gysi, able to 'operate without interference from the CDU or other non-SED members'. Active in the KPD before the war, Heinz Willman was then exiled in Czechoslovakia, France and the USSR. On his return to Berlin in 1945, he was a co-founder of the Kulturbund and its General Secretary. Alexander Abusch had also been an active member of the KPD before the war, and editor of the party newspaper, *Die Rote Fahne*. From 1933–46 he was in exile in France and then Mexico. He was Chief Secretary of the Kulturbund, and subsequently Minister of Culture and Deputy Prime Minister of the GDR – 'one of the most smoothly functioning wheels in the Stalinized cultural bureaucracy of the GDR', according to Wolfgang Schivelbusch.[38] Klaus Gysi was chief editor of the Kulturbund journal *Aufbau* and Federal Secretary of the Kulturbund, and later the GDR Minister of Culture. American suspicions of this caucus were not completely fanciful: in his postwar diaries, Victor Klemperer, himself a member of the Kulturbund, noted his own frustrations with the way in which the organisation was run: 'I have the impression, that everything is fixed in a small circle, 35 of 40 Executive Committee members are supernumerary, Becher, Willman, Gysi, Kleinschmidt do everything'.[39] (Karl Kleinschmidt, a Protestant Minister and Socialist, was vice-president of the Kulturbund 1947–9). This fact was widely acknowledged at the time. In a Berlin newspaper report in May 1947, Walter Karsch described the Kulturbund as 'serving [...] this four-man party [Becher, Abusch, Willman and Gysi] as a camouflage for the realization of their political programme'.[40]

American Intelligence sources based their assumption of political subordination on a number of points. Luxurious, well-funded facilities including cheap midday meals are mentioned as part of the 'physical' rather than political recruitment method. Numerous connections between the Kulturbund and left-wing cultural and political organisations, such as the FDGB (Freier Deutscher Gewerkschaftsbund – German Federation of Trade Unions) and Volksbühnen (Peoples' Theatres) confirmed political connections between the Kulturbund and the Soviet Military Government. Propagandistic use of the Aufbau Verlag and the dismissal of the original manager, Kurt Wilhelm, who possessed a 'good anti-Nazi record' and genuine non-partisan credentials, is cited in the CIA report as further evidence of the organisation's true nature. An American report published earlier in 1947 described the 'strongly Communist tendency of the chairman Becher', the 'oriental tendency' of the literature published by the Aufbau Verlag, and the fact that the monthly Kulturbund publication, *Die Aussprache*, published 'methods of recruitment'.[41]

US and British suspicion of the Kulturbund as a Soviet Trojan Horse was matched by debate amongst members themselves concerning the partisan nature of the organisation. The attempt to arrange cultural activity was too reminiscent of Nazi cultural policy, and did not fit into the individualist tenor of the times, upsetting both conservative and liberal factions. A report produced by the Württemberg-Baden American Military Government details some of the criticisms made by one of its members, Dr Clara Menck.[42] Her views encapsulate the liberal argument against the Kulturbund that was to form the basis of its rejection by German cultural figures in the West, and were cited at some length in the American report:

> Dr. Menck first of all asked that high-sounding phrases like '*kulturschöpferisch*' (literally: culture-creating) should be dropped from the program. [...] She suggested that the Kulturbund should come down to earth and consider itself merely as 'neutral ground' for the exchange of ideas, not as an esoteric society charged with the task of guarding and interpreting culture. [...] Secondly, Dr. Menck warned against too much organisation: 'It is only natural that today we feel the desire to be real individualists again'. [...] Thirdly, Dr. Menck asked that the Stuttgart Kulturbund should avoid affiliation with the Berlin group: 'It would be best to disassociate ourselves, discretely, from the semi-official activities carried on in the Eastern zone in the name of the Kulturbund. I believe those things must be more or less known by now; the fact that we have the same name discredits our organization.[43]

Similar rifts were growing between eastern and western branches elsewhere, the report continued. The efforts of the Berlin Kulturbund to 'infiltrate', or at least establish contacts with those in the western zones was confirmed by a visit paid by 'Herr Willman' – Heinz Willman, whom the CIA had already suspected of being the secret Communist leader of the Berlin Kulturbund – to the Heidelberg

Kulturbund. Members questioned the Berlin representative closely about the need for having such a large organisation, as opposed to a 'federalized, liberal development of single groups', and also about the large expenses for the Berlin club house, 'and its furnishings and equipment'.[44] Willman's insistence that stronger links should be established between the Berlin headquarters and the Heidelberg chapter reportedly only increased the suspicion of the Heidelberg members. The American report was, of course, far from being impartial, and although a fascinating source of local detail, must be set against German accounts. A passage from Victor Klemperer's diaries, describing a meeting of the Dresden branch at which Willman was present, can be cited in the latter's defence: 'Berlin's [i.e. Willman's] view, and Gute's [art teacher, writer, former ASSO member, at that moment cultural officer for Saxon State administration], was that the management had to be unpolitical, placing 'culture', scholarship, literature exclusively at the centre.[...] Central to W.'s [Willman's] report: No imitation of the parties – only culture and the arts'.[45]

The crucial moment for the Kulturbund came on 23 January 1947, when a special order was given stating that all existing political groups in Berlin had to apply for a licence, and would otherwise be banned, as from 1 November 1947.[46] The American Military Government requested such an application from the Kulturbund, which refused on the grounds that it was a non-political organisation that had been formed before the Allied Kommandatura had taken control of Berlin on 11 July 1945. The Soviet forces had issued an order at this point, stating that 'All existing regulations and ordinances issued by the Commander of the Soviet Army Garrison and Military Commandant of the City of Berlin, and by the German administration under Allied control ... shall remain in force.'[47] It was clear to the Western Allies by late 1947 that the Kulturbund was largely an SED organisation under neutral cultural cover, and its banning by the American Military Government on 1 November 1947, and by the British on 12 November, was inevitable. Although the Kulturbund, according to a letter of 30 October, had refused to apply for a licence on the grounds that it was a non-party political organisation, it is more probable, as a British Military Government Brief of November 1947 made clear, that the Soviets were reluctant to acquiesce to regulation of one organisation out of fear that this would sanction attacks on other unilateral Russian orders issued before 11 July 1945.[48] The British were at pains to state that the banning of the Kulturbund was not politically motivated, but rather a result of its failure to submit an application. A brief of 6 January 1948 made it clear that the Kulturbund could have expected a favourable response had it submitted such an application, however difficult to imagine this may have been. Considering the increasingly antagonistic climate, which was to lead a few months later to the currency reform and the Soviet Blockade of West Berlin, it seems unlikely that the Kulturbund would have been tolerated for long as a 'German' organisation.[49]

1 NA/OMGBS/ISD/Chamber of Creative Artists/Adolf Jannasch, 'Referat Bildende Kunst', 25 January 1946.
2 Fechter, P., 'Kultursündflut', *Die Zeit*, 8 March 1947, 3.
3 Anon., 'Bildende Kunst nach der Währungsreform', *bildende kunst*, no. 1, 1949, 38.
4 'Mitteilungen des Schutzverband Bildender Künstler', *bildende kunst*, no. 3, March 1948 (unpaginated).
5 'Ma'., 'Der Kampf gegen den Kitsch', *Süddeutsche Zeitung*, 18 January 1946, 3.
6 'Aufruf der Kommunistischen Partei', *Deutsche Volkszeitung*, 13 June 1945.
7 Seng, 'Die "Kammer der Kunstschaffenden" stellt aus', *Tägliche Rundschau*, 28 July 1945, 4.
8 Werner, 5; Schivelbusch, 42–3.
9 NA/OMGBS/ISD/84.
10 Cf. Schivelbusch, 43.
11 PRO/FO/1014/63. ISD memo, 5 October 1948.
12 Held, J., 'Die Kammer der Kulturschaffenden und der Schutzverband Bildender Künstler in der Berliner Kunstpolitik von 1945 bis 49', in: Staatliche Kunsthalle, 33–48, here 35.
13 NA/OMGBS/ISD/84.
14 NA/OMGBS/ISD/Chamber of Creative Artists/165.01/Major Douglas Waples, 'Disposition of Reichskulturkammer Organizations', 15 October 1945, 1.
15 Held, 35.
16 Grohmann, W., 'Germany, Austria, Switzerland', in: Grohmann, 1958, 155–220, here 155.
17 Martin-Gropius-Bau, 1988, 356.
18 Stadthalle Nordplatz, 1946, unpaginated.
19 Ibid.
20 Anon., 'Allgemeine Dresdner Kunstausstellung', *Das Kunstwerk*, no. 3, 1946/7, 43.
21 Cf. Matthias, C.E., 'Künstlerkongress in Dresden', *bildende kunst*, no. 1, 1947, 3–11.
22 Ibid., 5
23 PRO/FO/1012/166.
24 Schivelbusch, 83.
25 Cf. Holz; Roussel, H., 'Die emigrieten deutschen Künstler in Frankreich und der Freie Künstlerbund', in: Koebner, 173–211.
26 Becher, J. R., 'Brief an den Militärkommandanten der Stadt Berlin', 27 June 1945, reprinted in: *Frankfurter Kunstverein*, 176.
27 'Aufruf zur Gründung des Kulturbundes zur demokratischen Erneuerung Deutschlands', Berlin, June 1945. Cited in: ibid., 176–7.
28 Pike, 85.
29 Ibid., 5–6.
30 Held, J., 'Die Kammer der Kulturschaffenden und der Schutzverband Bildender Künstler in der Berliner Kunstpolitik von 1945 bis 49', in: Staatliche Kunsthalle, 257–8.
31 *KB Mitteilungsblatt des Kulturbundes zur Demokratischen Erneuerung Deutschlands Landesverband Nordrhein-Westfalen e.V*, no. 1/2, January/February 1948, 9.
32 Cf. 'Geistige Einheit-Nationale Einheit', *Die Aussprache*, no. 1, July 1946, 2.
33 Becher, J.R., 'Drei Fragen – Drei Antworten', *Die Aussprache*, no. 1, January 1946, 1–2.
34 Cf. Hermand, J., 'Modernism Restored: West German Painting in the 1950s', *New German Critique*, no. 32, Spring-Summer 1984, 23–41, here 29.
35 PRO/FO 1012/166.
36 NA/OMGBS/ISD/86.
37 NA/CREST/ 'Kulturbund zur Demokratischen Erneuerung Deutschlands', 11 August 1947.
38 Schivelbusch, 105
39 Klemperer, 2003, 227.
40 Karsch, W., 'On Democratic Reconstruction. A Chapter of New German Cultural Policy', *Der Tagesspiegel*, 25 May 1947. Translation: NA/OMGBS/ISD/Kulturbund (For the Democratic Revival of Germany).
41 NA/OMGBS/ISD/86. Report 'The 'KULTURBUND', 30 January 1947.
42 NA/OMGBS/ISD/86/Kulturbund/ 'Report no. 22'.

43 Ibid., 10.
44 Ibid., 13.
45 Klemperer, 2003, 90.
46 'Procedure for the Recognition of Organisations of a Political Character', Allied command order BK/o (47) 16; cited by Schivelbusch, 98.
47 Berlin, 1946.
48 PRO/FO/1012/166. Brief from P.H. Scott, head of Government Structure Branch, 3 November 1947. Cf. also: PRO/FO/1049/1095.
49 For the Kulturbund's side of the argument cf: 'Freiheit dem Kulturbund!', *Die Aussprache*, no. 10, December 1947, 1–6. This feature contains the transcript of a letter sent from various public figures in England, supporting the work of the Kulturbund.

Salvage and Salvation

Old Masters of Modern Art

Yes indeed, when the war is over someday, what then in Germany? Will there be an artistic Germany along with a political Germany?

Franz Marc, 'Im Fegefeuer des Krieges', *Kunstgewerbeblatt*, Leipzig, 1915

The art critic and educationalist Adolf Behne was a leading figure in the post-1918 reaction against Expressionism. After 1945, he once again found himself dealing with the legacy of Expressionism, but in quite different circumstances. Of all survivors from the former period, he was singularly well-placed to re-engage with German modern traditions following the Second World War, and to contribute towards cultural reconstruction. This position reached back to his early engagement with German modernism in its expressive and *sachlich* modes during the Weimar Republic, as well as his continuing devotion to public education, but also to his first-hand knowledge of Nazi cultural politics. Although he was banned in 1933 from teaching due to his involvement with the international free-speech organisation PEN, he nevertheless remained in Germany throughout the Third Reich, writing inoffensive articles for non-political journals. Behne's activities after the war were numerous: he was called to teach at the newly instituted Hochschule für bildende Künste in Berlin, was an active member of the Kulturbund, and also sat on the advisory board of *bildende kunst*. Alongside these institutional connections, he published a significant number of essays and reviews in defence of modern art. His death in 1948 came at a moment when euphoria at the freedoms of the postwar world was disintegrating into Cold War reality.

Barely a month after capitulation, 'so soon after we had emerged from the cellars', as he later recalled, Behne gave a talk in Wilmersdorf, in the British Zone of Berlin, 'Entartete Kunst – eine Hitlerlüge' (Degenerate Art – A Nazi Lie). As he noted in the published version, this was one of the first attempts at a public rehonouring (*Ehrenrettung*) of disgraced modern art.[1] The lecture, which had been planned by the Volksbildungsamt (Department of Public Education) Wilmersdorf as early as 13 May, just eleven days after the fall of the city to the Red Army, was indeed the first step in the rehabilitation of modern German artists. Behne was well aware of the need for such a campaign:

> As [...] the first exhibitions opened to the public, exhibitions that attempted, at first in an unprogrammatic manner, to identify what was still alive, what had survived, the resistance of a certain portion of the general public to modern art was quickly apparent. When a gallery on the Kurfürstendamm [Galerie Gerd Rosen] showed modern art, this antipathy escalated to open hostility, even to a menacing hatred.[2]

He refers to Erich Kästner's report of suggestions by visitors to a modern art exhibition in Augsburg that the artists should be 'shot, hung, gassed'. Goebbels himself, Behne writes, would not have believed that the *Entartete Kunst* campaign could have left such an indelible stain, particularly amongst the young.

Behne's 'defence' of modern art in his 1945 lecture was based as much on a sense of honouring the dead as on rational argument. Using photography as a foil with which to contrast painting (further indication of the artistic primacy accorded to hand-painting at this moment), he argues that traditional techniques represent the world by means of an 'ordering concept' that determines all parts of an image. Photographic technique does not allow such conscious discrimination in reproduction (unless it self-consciously assumes the methods of painting, in which case it ceases to be photography, Behne suggests). A photographic image cannot constitute a *Bild*, in the sense of an art-image, so defined due to its 'refined interconnection of parts'.[3] Painting necessarily deviates from actual appearances in that it is representation ordered by intelligence. For Behne art is thus 'modern' because it is non-naturalistic. He nevertheless draws a line between legitimate, non-naturalistic art and abstraction. Abstract painters, who constituted a minority, Behne suggests, should rather be tolerated as part of a democratic culture. As Martin Papenbrock remarks, Behne was continuing a conciliatory view of modern art from a Socialist perspective that he had already aired in the 1920s.[4] Creating a bridge between recondite artistry and a lay public entailed finding a middle-ground between realism and abstraction, but from the vantage point of the former. Behne's choice of artists to illustrate his point was relatively conservative and, as Papenbrock points out, referred back to the canon established by Carl Einstein in his 1926 survey *Kunst des 20. Jahrhunderts*: Liebermann, Barlach, Kollwitz, the artists of the Brücke and Blaue Reiter groups, and the

Bauhaus.[5] With the exception of the Bauhaus, Behne's account of modern art was thus largely a defence of Expressionism, even though his notion of the ordered artistic image was more indebted to theories arising from Cubism. The choice of an established national canon was not suprising: Expressionism was the most salient emblem of German modernism in the visual arts, and it was therefore natural that it should be placed at the centre of the rehabilitation campaign.

Significant steps were also taken to rehabilitate the Bauhaus. In addition to Otto Steinert's revival of experimental photography, the large exhibition mounted in 1950 at the Haus der Kunst in Munich, *Die Maler am Bauhaus* (Painters of the Bauhaus), comprised a didactic display of Bauhaus history, and Bauhaus traditions were reintroduced in the Hochschule für Gestaltung at Ulm, founded by Max Bill in 1951. But the absence of key personnel through death (Klee, Schlemmer, Kandinsky) or emigration (Moholy-Nagy, Gropius) diminished the role played by memories of the Weimar School in postwar consciousness.

As the main signifier of German modernism, however, Expressionism carried a troubled legacy. The problem, as Behne made clear, was that Expressionism had already been 'overcome' after the First World War and was no longer available as an aesthetic model. New art could not simply rejoin an Expressionist tradition after the rude interruption of the Third Reich. For a general public who had yet to accept modern art, it was clearly difficult to appreciate that these movements were already national heritage. The quandary was acute: just as the reputations of modern artists were being reinstated to counteract negative public opinion, it was becoming clear that access to the creative moment of modern art was closed for good. Expressionism was in this way central to the contradictions of the postwar world: the need for restoration and stability, and the need for new ideas and images; the friction between the older 'tainted' and the younger 'lost' generation; the competing claims of nationalism and internationalism. Modern art had become after 1945 a highly ambivalent symbol both of living freedom and archivable heritage.

Not all studies of Expression as a historic avant-garde need concern themselves with an enquiry into what makes a work of art 'expressive'. When the 'expressive' quotient of Expressionism comes to determine a moment of its reception and interpretation, however, as it did after 1945, the two terms are crucially linked. Questions of national history and national language are almost indistinguishable in a moment when both have been collapsed into the same disturbed zone.

What was actually left of Expressionism after 1945? Just over a decade later, Will Grohmann looked back and summarised the surviving legacy.[6] Schmidt-Rottluff, Heckel and Pechstein were among those who had been immediately honoured with teaching posts. Of all the 'originals', Max Beckmann appeared to be the most influential, despite his physical absence (he was exiled in Amsterdam from 1937 and then from 1947 in America), but for Grohmann, the younger generation was unable to emulate the breadth of Beckmann's experience and Dantean vision of the world. Kandinsky, who had died in Neuilly-sur-Seine in 1944 after eleven years of exile in Paris, also appears as one of the most influential artists, according to polls amongst young painters cited by Grohmann. Pupils of first-generation Expressionists, notably Alexander Camaro, Rolf Nesch and Werner Gilles, are credited with a minor contribution towards a continued tradition, though in all cases the change of stylistic preferences was clear: 'Expressionist features gradually yielded to Symbolism'. To Grohmann's list should, of course, be added Otto Dix, who had remained in Germany throughout the war, and arguably some of the artists connected with the prewar ASSO group who regrouped, as we have seen, in Dresden in the 1946 *Allgemeine Deutsche Kunstausstellung*.

The public presence of certain key figures was, however, in stark contrast to the public absence of their works. As a result of Nazi confiscation, no significant works of modern art remained in public collections. The Nazi policy of 'cleansing' the museums was never formally declared illegal, and unlike the fate of works confiscated from Jewish private collections, most of the seizures were never compensated. Attempts to reintroduce modern art into the public eye were therefore dependent on private collections that had been protected in one way or another during the war and remained in the country. In place of a fuller account, which would require another book, a few of these exceptionally important dealers and collectors can be briefly mentioned.

Restoration in the East was primarily shaped by the predominance of SED-funded cultural organisations and the consolidating doctrine of anti-fascism. In July and August 1945, for example, the Kammer der Kunstschaffenden staged one of the first large exhibitions to be mounted in Berlin after the war (mentioned above on page 147). Brücke artists dominated the presentation of rehabilitated Expressionism, which included works by Kirchner, Pechstein, Heckel and Schmidt-Rottluff. Max Beckmann was also represented. In addition, the Kammer was responsible for the touring exhibitions of Ernst Barlach and Käthe Kollwitz in 1946 – both promoted as examples of a politically engaged, 'expressive' figurative art. Dissolution of the Kammer, too close to an outdated activism, and dangerously close both in name and purpose to the Reichskulturkammer, signalled part of the shift from earlier revolutionary models Socialist Realism.

Exhibitions mounted by the Kulturbund, by contrast, demonstrate a far less activist, more pluralist policy. Although the 1946 *Allgemeine Deutsche Kunstausstellung* was not overtly shaped by ideological considerations, Dresden as a location and Pechstein's presence on the jury made essential a special focus on the Brücke group – it was given a separate room. Two of these works, Kirchner's *Sich kämmender Akt* (Nude Combing her Hair), of 1913, and Heckel's *Frühling in Flandern* (Spring in Flanders), of c. 1916, were obtained from the collection of Ferdinand Möller by Will Grohmann. With the exception of Klee, there were no representatives of the Blaue Reiter. Although not programmatic, clear preference was given by official bodies in the East to the Brücke heritage.

Remarkably, several commercial galleries in East Germany were able to continue business and show works by prominent modern artists throughout the hard-line early years of the Socialist Republic. Apart from those dealers listed by Martin Papenbrock in his survey of exhibitions in the East – Rudolf Richter in Dresden, Ercha in Wittenberg and Engelwald in Leipzig – the most prominent was Eduard Henning, who put on numerous exhibitions of works by Pechstein, Schmidt-Rottluff, Otto Müller, Ernst Barlach, Karl Hofer and Erich Heckel at his gallery in Halle.[7] The gallery opened in May 1947 and was able to show an astonishing variety of 'formalist' work over the next fourteen years. Hans-Georg Sehrt, in his valuable account of Henning's enterprise, notes that the first exhibition in divided Germany of works by Braque took place at Henning's gallery in April 1950. The survival of the gallery, despite attacks on its 'decadence', was due in part to Henning's own diplomacy and support from a broad network of artists and patrons, as well as personal fortitude (which finally gave way in 1962, in despair at the contacts severed by the Berlin Wall). It was also due to the relative lenience of SED cultural policy in Halle – such a gallery could certainly not have survived the heyday of Stalinism in Berlin.

Henning's gallery was nevertheless an isolated case. The main body of dealers and collectors who took on the political re-centering of 'difficult' art was, naturally, located in the West. Here, the effort to reinstate modern art took on different sorts of political significance. Regional and civic pride were invariably behind acts of private sponsorship and generosity; the donation of collections to large regional museums, for instance, not only compensated for the campaign of confiscation from state museums, but also counteracted Nazi centralisation by re-establishing local traditions.[8] Such was the effect of the series of exhibitions that appeared in the Augsburg Schaezler-Palais, beginning with *Maler der Gegenwart* (Contemporary Painters) in December 1945, and comprising two exhibitions of artists from Augsburg during the next year, before the better-known exhibition *Extreme Malerei* (Extreme Painting) in 1947, which showed works by the most progressive German artists such as Baumeister and Fritz Winter.[11] In Berlin itself, as Paul Fechter noted in 1947, the fact that various localities could instigate their own art exhibitions acted as a means of re-establishing local centres in the face of severe transportation difficulties.[10] In the broader field, the traditional federal structure of cultural life was reinstated by the activities of a number of important individuals. In Frankfurt, Hanna Bekker vom Rath displayed her collection in her private house throughout the war, and afterwards in the Frankfurter Kunstkabinetts in 1947, and the Hagemann collection was donated to the Städel Museum in Frankfurt.[11] Hamburg benefited from the activities of the collectors Martha and Paul Rauert.[12] Bernhard Sprengel, a key supporter of Emil Nolde, stored thirty paintings and 870 drawings and watercolours by the persecuted artist in his chocolate factory in Hanover, and then in further safe locations in Harz and Ammerland when the Allied bombardment, which destroyed Kurt Schwitters's immovable *Merzbau*, became severe. In November 1945, Bernhard and Margit Sprengel were able to mount an exhibition of their Nolde collection. Works by Nolde were also shown as the inaugural exhibition of the Kestner-Gesellschaft, which opened in Hanover under the directorship of Alfred Hentzen in 1948.[13]

The support of Nolde by Bernhard and Margit Sprengel began, ironically, after they had seen his work in the 1937 *Entartete Kunst* exhibition during their honeymoon in Munich. As a result of this visit, they bought two watercolours by Nolde, both now lost, from the dealer Günther Franke. Franke was a leading supporter of modern art in the 1920s, and, despite Nazi cultural policy, was able to buy and sell modern art covertly in Munich throughout much of the Third Reich.[14] He had worked for the dealer I.B. Neumann in Berlin between 1918 and 1923, and had established contact with Max Beckmann, the artist with whom he became most closely associated. He transferred to run Neumann's Graphisches Kabinett in Munich in 1923, and was eventually to take over the running of the business. In 1937, the Kabinett took his name and moved to the Palais Almeida in Munich, around the same time that the *Entartete Kunst* exhibition opened in the Hofgarten.[15] Franke's gallery was closed down by the Reichskammer der bildenden Künste on 1 September 1944, as he related to the painter Georg Meistermann in a letter shortly after the event.[16]

When Franke reopened his gallery in early 1946, using the premises of the Villa Stuck on the Prinzregentstraße, it was acclaimed by the critic Franz Roh during one of his regular postwar radio broadcasts on cultural themes as a vital symbol of newly won freedom.[17] The exhibitions mounted by Franke show that the regional basis on which public interest in Expressionism was being revived also determined the type of art being displayed: Franke's interest in a lyrical, non-revolutionary tradition of Expressionism was in contrast to the tendency in the East towards a Brücke heritage.

The programme of the Villa Stuck gathered steam during the summer of 1947, when two large exhibitions devoted to Max Beckmann opened, followed by an exhibition of works by Franz Marc at the end of the year. The methods by which the works of both artists were repackaged for a largely unsympathetic public contrast intriguingly with the rhetoric of anti-fascism in the East. Hans Eckstein, in a review of the Marc exhibition, noted that the public was uniquely well prepared for the Bavarian artist's work, due to the publication in 1940 of an edition of Marc's letters written from the front during the First World War.[18] Knowledge of Marc's *Heldentod* (Hero's Death) on the front would seem in the public eye to overwrite the *entartete* nature of his pictures, and give him special status, as a number of contemporary critical responses would suggest.[19] The importance of Marc's letters was also noted by Will Grohmann, who identified Marc as one of the four artists (including Nolde, Barlach, Kollwitz) who retained popular appeal throughout the Third Reich.[20] Marc was indeed tolerated by the Nazis well into the 1930s, and was the subject of a major retrospective in Hanover in 1936. Most striking of all was the withdrawal of his *Der Turm der blauen Pferde* (Tower of Blue Horses, 1913) from the *Entartete Kunst* exhibition as a result of a letter from the German Officer's Federation expressing astonishment that an artist who had won the Iron Cross could be subject to public disgrace. 'Military honour', as Karl Jaspers had insisted in 1946, was distinct from political meaning: 'purely soldierly' values could not be burdened with guilt, and such values, if 'unstained by evil acts', could in fact provide the 'foundations of the sense of life'.[21] A 'purely soldierly' sense of life expressed in abstract forms appealed to conservative critics for whom such a position highlighted the definition of most modern art as 'un-soldierly'. For conservatives such as Ernst Jünger, joining the army was the aristocratic form of emigration; antifascism for the nobility. 'We who are at the front breathe an air that is freer and more spiritual', as Marc himself had written in 1915.[22] The arch anti-modernist Hans Sedlmayr, quoting from the war letters, responded positively to Marc's visions of primitive purity; in an article written for the Catholic journal *Wort und Wahrheit*, Sedlmayr writes of Marc as a religious artist for whom animals were the symbolic traces of a lost paradise of *Unschuld* (guiltlessness).[23] Such dispensation for soldier-painters may have been the motivation for the printing of excerpts of Beckmann's letters from the front to his wife Minna Beckmann-Tube, written in April and May 1915, in the *Süddeutsche Zeitung* around the time of the summer exhibitions in 1946.[24]

As the authorities in the East were identifying with the revolutionary potential of the Saxon-based Brücke artists' group, the twin moment in German modernism, Blaue Reiter, was finding favour in the West as a nationally and regionally bound source for 'international abstraction'. The regional aspect was indeed important in the major exhibition *Der Blaue Reiter*, opened at the Haus der Kunst in Munich in September 1949. Ludwig Grote's historical survey of the group in the exhibition catalogue places it firmly in a local tradition: 'Since Adolf Hildebrand's appearance, considerations regarding style and form have dominated art in Munich'.[25] In comparison to Ludwig Grote's admiration of Kandinsky as the pioneer, theoretician and catalyst of Blaue Reiter, however, Werner

Haftmann's review of the 1949 Haus der Kunst exhibition dismisses him in a few lines. As a Russian, Kandinsky may have been less well placed to embody a spirit of national renewal. Like Picasso, who was tarnished by his association with Communism, Kandinsky had to wait until 1953 for his place in the restoration campaign with a solo tour around the Federal Republic. Only with Gabriele Münter's donation of many of his important pre-1914 works to the Städtische Galerie im Lenbachhaus in 1957 was a proper assessment of his work feasible. The legacy of the Blaue Reiter was also taken up by other artists' associations founded in the West around 1950, and often quoted by supporters such as Ottomar Domnick, described in more detail below. Marc and Kandinsky were, however, present more in word than deed: new formal concerns led swiftly away from traditional Expressionist imagery.

Similarly unresolved connections with prewar Expressionism were initiated by Joseph Haubrich's donation to Cologne of his collection of modern art, which foregrounded Expressionism and was particularly rich in Brücke works.[26] It was toured as an exhibition to Mannheim, Hamburg, Stuttgart, Wiesbaden and Düsseldorf during the next two years. Haubrich's own role as a private collector who was able to retain his collection when most 'modern' work was being sold for foreign currency or destroyed by the Nazis was seen as the essential base on which Expressionism could be assessed as a historical movement, and part of a national heritage, after 1945. 'In the same way the Nazis banned modern art from German museums, he took responsibility for it: forty-five works he acquired between 1933 and 1945, forty-five times he saved German art!'.[27] Haubrich's donation contained a number of works that he had bought himself to prevent them from leaving the country, including Otto Dix's *Bildnis des Dichters Theodor Däubler* (Portrait of the Poet Theodor Däubler), of 1927, from the Berlin Kronprinzenpalais.[28] The public appearance of such works provoked a reaction that, in the case of one newspaper article, raised probing questions about the significance of Expressionism as a historic, national style:

> We Germans have a strange relationship with Expressionism. Whereas most art movements become in time dated and part of established history, Expressionism, so it seems, has remained a living and up-to-date phenomenon, and can still be the cause of heated debates. It is a good idea to take a step back from these heady arguments for and against the validity of Expressionism, and to remember that the founders of the movement are no longer youthful rebels, and are now either the *éminences grises* of the academy or in the grave. Although Expressionism is still often described in Germany as 'the art of today' [junger Kunst], it is well to remember that it has for a long time been part of history.[29]

Only with the private initiative of Haubrich, the anonymous article concludes, was an engagement with the historic phenomenon of Expressionism 'from 1906 to 1932' made possible.

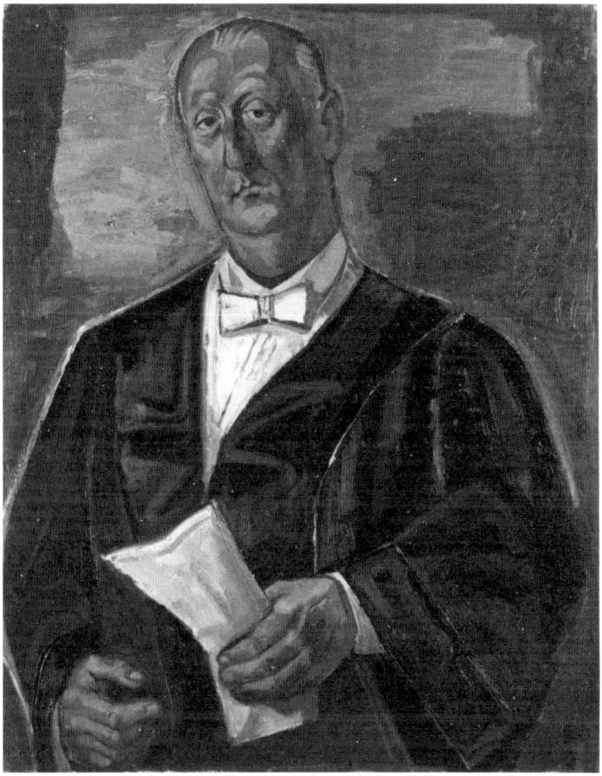

Otto Dix, *Bildnis Rechtsanwalt Dr Josef Haubrich* (Portrait of the Lawyer Dr Josef Haubrich), 1951, oil on canvas, 100 × 81 cm, Sammlung Haubrich, Museum Ludwig, Cologne

Haubrich's own intention, as he recorded in a short article published in *Die Zeit* in 1950, was to create a bridge between the revolutionary intentions of modern art and a largely conservative audience. Cologne was the traditional location for such a bridge, as the Sonderbund exhibition of 1912 had proved: 'An exhibition of modern art! And yet the honorary council, even the organising committee, contained well-known conservative members', Haubrich noted.[30] The city of Cologne had remained after 1945 the centre for *expressionistische Kunst* in West Germany, Haubrich wrote, continuing the tradition of the Sonderbund. This status was reinforced not only by the presence of important artists such as Gerhard Marcks and Ewald Mataré, but also by the move of one of the most important supporters of Expressionism, the dealer Ferdinand Möller, to Cologne from Berlin in 1950.

Möller was indeed one of the most important figures in the postwar reassessment of Expressionism anywhere in Germany, and it is of particular significance that he chose to move to the Rhenish capital. Like Haubrich, Franke, and indeed Behne, Möller had been one of the original promoters of Expressionism, largely of works by the Brücke that, as a conservative enthusiast of German nationalism, he had actively placed in a tradition of nineteenth- and twentieth-century German painting. Möller's position in the 1920s was to counter the predominance of French art, and the influence of critics such as Julius Meier-Graefe and Carl Einstein, and dealers like Alfred Flechtheim, who acted as advocates of French art in Germany.[31] As Möller made clear in 1927, this preference was not exclusive, and was based as much on economic principles – 'buy German' – as it was on chauvinistic preferences.[32] His distinctly partisan position was reflected by exhibitions put on in the Berlin Kronprinzenpalais in 1928 promoting modern German art – indeed, Ludwig Justi's 'New Section of the National Gallery', opened in June 1919, where work by living artists was on view, was central to Weimar debates concerning contemporary art and national identity.[33] Justi's 'germanophile' policy met with criticism from both left and right

– as a member of a specially formed *Kunstklub* (art club), Adolf Behne was one of those who attacked Justi for his chauvinism.[34]

Echoes of this connection between contemporary art, national identity and the domestic market occur in Möller's activities both during the war and after 1945. His involvement with the Third Reich, as one of the four dealers contracted to carry out the famous auction held by the Galerie Fischer in Lucerne at which the Nazis sold off a selection of the art they had plundered for foreign currency (the other three were Bernhard A. Boehmer from Güstrow, who was closely linked with Ernst Barlach; Hildebrandt Gurlitt from Hamburg; and Karl Buchholz from Berlin), is a particularly important part of this narrative, linking the prewar National Gallery and the postwar salvage campaign.[35] Salvage meant just that – physical rescue – as can be seen from Eberhard Roters's account of Möller and Rudolf Hetsch (an enthusiast of German modern art who nevertheless worked as a Nazi cultural official) rescuing the seized works from the fanatical clutches of Franz Hoffmann, the chairman of a committee established by Goebbels for the 'handling' of confiscated art, who had successfully sued for permission to burn 1,004 paintings and 3,825 drawings in Berlin.[36] Against the orders of the Reichspropagandaministerium (Reich Ministry of Propaganda), Möller had kept as much looted art as possible in the country through sales to private collectors and dealers – records indicate that he was dealing in 'entartete kunst' up until October 1943. It was the heavy Allied bombardment of Berlin, it has been suggested, rather than Nazi strictures that forced him to stop (the Allied air offensive against Berlin reached a peak in late 1943 – early 1944).[37] Paul Ortwin Rave lists the galleries of Möller in Berlin,

Franke in Munich and Alex Vömel in Düsseldorf as the 'last stands' of modern art in Nazi Germany.

Möller's involvement with the Reich complicates the view of opposition and 'inner emigration' – it seems that it was only by collaboration that he was able to oppose Nazi cultural policy. He spent the latter years of the war in retreat, in a house designed by Hans Scharoun, situated in the countryside far north of Berlin. Here he staged in 1946 his initial postwar exhibitions, the first of which, *Freie Deutsche Kunst* (Free German Art), organised with the Amt für Volksbildung (Office for Adult Education), Neuruppin, showed works by Brücke artists, as well as Kollwitz, Barlach and others. Despite calls from various quarters to return and contribute to the cultural reconstruction of Berlin, Möller was aware that the West offered greater commercial possibilities, and eventually chose Cologne as the location of his new gallery. His aversion to Berlin was also due to events surrounding the loan of two paintings from his stock to the 1946 *Allgemeine Deutsche Kunstausstellung*. After the exhibition, these were seized by the Soviet authorities and returned to the Moritzburg Museum in Halle, as part of that museum's collection that had originally been confiscated by the Nazis.[38] In his protests to the authorities he pointed out the importance of his collections as a resource for art historians and artists for the history of German Expressionism, and also stated that he had written to the Folkwang Museum in Essen offering to negotiate about the works seized from their collection.[39] That the resolution of this conflict, the permanent loan of six of Möller's Expressionist works to the museum, was not an end to this bitter saga came with the confiscation of these paintings by Soviet Cultural officials after Alexander Dymschitz launched the anti-formalist campaign in November 1948.[40]

Although Josef Haubrich's gift to the town of Cologne was predominantly of Expressionist works (given a broad application of this term), there was no specific attempt by Haubrich or the Stadtmuseum to promote Expressionism in a chauvinistic manner. The first exhibition at the re-instated Galerie Ferdinand Möller (more a small museum, as Will Grohmann observed),[41] *Die Alten Meister der Modernen Kunst in Deutschland* (Old Masters of Modern Art in Germany) was certainly more programmatic in this respect. The exhibition took place in two parts, the first, in November 1951, showing larger works by all of the key members of the Brücke and Blaue Reiter groups, and sculpture by Wilhelm Lehmbruck, Gerhard Marcks, Georg Kolbe, Richard Scheibe and Ewald Mataré, amongst others. The exhibition highlighted Kirchner's *Eine Künstlergruppe* (An Artists' Group, 1926), itself a highly selective historical reconstruction, painted over a decade after the group's dissolution in 1913. Kirchner's painting had hung in the Kronprinzenpalais as part of the pioneering display of German contemporary art in the late 1930s. Möller had acquired the painting from the Entartete Kunst collection, after it was included in the 1937 Munich exhibition, thus saving it from either Hoffmann's auto-da-fé or sale abroad. Published documents show that Möller also exchanged more conservative works from his stock for confiscated modern art. During January 1940, for example, the Reich passed on 222 prints by leading Expressionists for one drawing by Adolf Menzel.[42] The price Möller paid for *Eine Künstlergruppe*, $200, may not appear much, but was significantly more than most of the other works mentioned in this particular handlist – Kirchner's iconic *Ins Meer Schreitende* (Striding into the Sea, 1912), seized from Halle and now in Stuttgart, was purchased for just $60. The monetary value ascribed to Kirchner's group portrait is significant, and the question may be asked whether the work was valued because of its relatively sober, naturalistic style, or whether it was seen in a more totemic fashion, as a physical survivor of an important period of modern German art.[43]

After showing in the 1951 exhibition, Möller donated Kirchner's painting to the Wallraf-Richartz-Museum, to join the Haubrich collection. Also included by Haftmann in the first edition of his *Malerei im 20. Jahrhundert*, 1954, as one of the few paintings illustrating the protagonists of the now legendary modern movement, Kirchner's work became a new kind of 'constructed' historical document of a previous founding moment, though one belonging to an epoch that now appeared lost for good.[44] Möller was clearly attached to the painting, valuing it as a historical witness. It is indeed the only image, in the absence of any photograph, of the group together, minus Pechstein. The sense that works such as Kirchner's *Eine Künstlergruppe* were now part of a 'dead', rather than 'living' contemporary narrative is palpable from Möller's showing. Old Masters they were, surrounded by the aura of historical witness and marked by the significance of their own survival.

The second part of Möller's 'Old Masters' exhibition continued this historical effort, with the two branches of Expressionism, Brücke and Blaue Reiter, as well as the Bauhaus, representing modern German art – although the emphasis in this

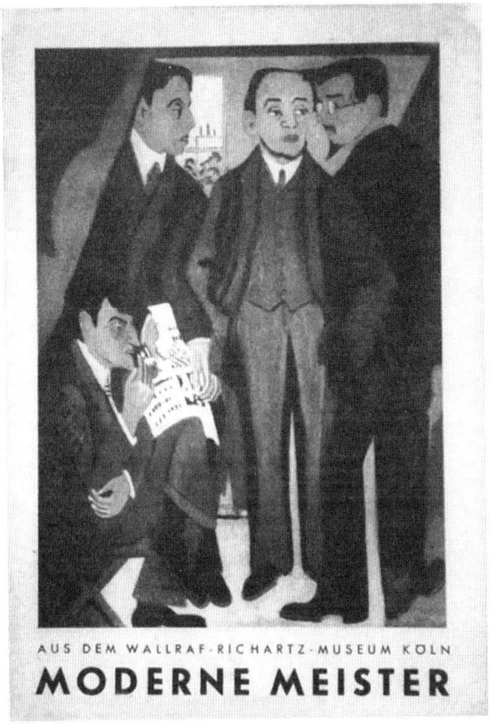

Front cover of catalogue for the exhibition *Moderne Meister* (Modern Masters), Wallraf-Richarts Museum, Cologne, 1955. Illustrated: Ludwig Kirchner, *Eine Künstlergruppe*, 1926

exhibition was certainly on Expressionism. Putting across such a national agenda clearly needed some diplomatic couching. Möller showed himself up to this task in the introduction to the exhibition catalogue: 'we have repositioned ourselves internationally', he wrote, 'we have been able to adopt a position that seemed to have been lost by the cultural politics of the past "era"'.[45] That Möller was sending works to the Venice and São Paolo Biennales, and to an exhibition at the Carnegie Institute, indicated beyond any doubt that the 'days of 'cleansing', as he put it, were over, and that German art could once again represent Germany internationally.

Whether this meant that the German public had been awakened from the stupor brought on by Nazi propaganda was less apparent to Möller. In June 1950, he wrote to Grohmann congratulating him on his article 'Das Unbehagen an moderner Kunst' (On Discontent with Modern Art), stating the importance of all positive attitudes towards *moderner Kunst*.[46] Möller was clearly aware of the importance of such public statements, which, like Behne's lecture and publication on the subject of Entartete Kunst, aimed to disentangle 'ordinary' prejudice from the effects of Nazi propaganda. Because the average man still feels justified in criticising Nolde, Klee and the abstracts, and soon resorts to the accusations *nichtskönnen* (incompetent) or *entartet*, Grohmann was obliged to remind his readers that such a 'litany' had been heard before in Paul Schultze-Naumburg's *Kampfbund für Deutsche Kultur* (Combat League for German Culture) and Wolfgang Willrich's *Säuberung des Kunsttempels* (Cleansing of the Art Temple). In early 1950, such reactionary sentiment was without *politische Begleitsmusik* (political accompaniment), yet, Grohmann asks, how long can this last?[47]

Grohmann's concern that reactionary forces were still abroad, a feeling widely shared at the time, produced, as we have seen, an anxious reassessment of public attitudes towards modern art. Crucial was the fact, intuited by both Möller and Grohmann and by Behne before them, that Expressionism could not simply figure as part of a triumphant restoration. It was clear that a return to the Golden Age of Expressionism, lauded in many postwar exhibitions, was impossible. The conditions that had created the historic Expressionist avant-garde were simply no longer present; the cosmopolitan city as stage for modern social relations had been largely destroyed; the distinction between city and country had been confused; decay and destruction were no longer aspects of a revolutionary aesthetic, but facts of daily life. Museums and the clutter of national heritage indeed had been burnt to the ground. The social base for psychological drama had also changed – the younger generation had no meaningful cohort with which to identify and mount a challenge that could re-enact the 'Revolt of the Son'. Above all, hope was pinned not on exultant overcoming but on dogged survival. If one of the central aims of Expressionism had been to uncover the reality behind appearance, to find 'the bridge that leads from the visible to the invisible', as Beckmann had it, then that reality had now been destroyed, or exposed as hollow, a fact of brute power and personality cults rather than revitalising authenticity. The 'withering of expressive potential' in the postwar era was the result not of philosophical notions of the image of man, but of the damaged reality that lay all around. However necessary the salvage campaign was to 'right' public opinion and rescue national heritage, Expressionism had now died twice over. For these reasons, the idea of 'expressivity' as an aesthetic attitude was to meet strong resistance within the different milieus of reconstruction society.

1 Behne, 1947.
2 Ibid., 11.
3 Ibid., 23–4.
4 Papenbrock, M., 'Spiel und Zufall, Ordnung und Gesetz. Adolf Behne und die Rehabilitierung der modernen Kunst in Deutschland nach 1945', in: Bushart, 2000, 273–86, here 278.
5 Ibid., 281.
6 Grohmann, W., 'Germany, Austria, Switzerland', in: Brion, 1958, 155–220.
7 Papenbrock, 2000. Sehrt, H-G., 'Die Galerie Henning in Halle 1947–62', in: Feist, 1996, 237–50.
8 Schulz-Hoffmann, C., 'Patterns of postwar patronage', in: Rogoff, 216–20.
9 Schaezler-Palais.
10 Fechter, P., 'Kultursündflut', *Die Zeit*, 8 March 1947, 3.
11 Meyer-Ellinger.
12 Caspers.
13 Heinzelmann.
14 Roh, 1962, 95.
15 Billeter, 125–7.
16 'Günther Franke am Meistermann', 5 September 1944, in: Germanisches Nationalmuseum, 35.
17 Roh, 1948, 24.
18 Marc; Eckstein, H., 'Wiederbegegnung mit Bildern von Franz Marc', *Süddeutsche Zeitung*, 19 November 1946, 5. Cf. Demisch; Lankheit, 1950.
19 Cf. Heise, C.G., 'Franz Marc zum Gedächtnis', *Die Zeit*, 28 February 1946, 5; Lankheit, K., 'Franz Marcs Skizzenbuch aus dem Felde', *Zeitschrift für Kunst*, no. 2, 1950, 140–6; Walden, H., 'Nekrolog für Franz Marc', *Das Kunstwerk* no. 5, 1952, 12 (originally published in *Der Sturm*, 1916); Zahn, L., 'Franz Marc und der Krieg', *Das Kunstwerk*, no. 5, 1952, p. 14; Wagner, F.A., 'Zwischen Chaos und Maß. Das Deutsche und Europäische im Werke Franz Marcs', *Das Goldene Tor*, no. 7, 1948, 627–34.
20 Grohmann, W., 'Der Fall Ernst Barlach', *Die Neue Zeitung*, 2 November 1948.
21 Jaspers, 1947, 64–5.
22 Marc, F., 'Im Fegefeuer des Krieges', *Kunstgewerbeblatt*, Leipzig, 1915.
23 Sedlmayr, H., 'Franz Marc oder die Unschuld der Tiere', *Wort und Wahrheit*, no. 6, June 1951, 430–8.
24 '...eine solche Passion für die Malerei' aus Kriegsbriefen des Malers Max Beckmann', *Süddeutsche Zeitung*, no. 66, 15 August 1946, 4. Cf. Gallwitz, 117–37.
25 Grote, 5.
26 Cf. Fuchs, 91–113.
27 Ibid., 33.
28 Ibid., 34.
29 Anon, 'Historische Moderne. Die Sammlung Haubrich in Hamburg', *Die Welt*, 31 October 1947, 5.
30 Haubrich, J., 'Umgang mit modernen Malern', *Die Zeit*, 14 September 1950, 17.
31 FMS/Gercken, unpublished manuscript, 8.
32 Möller, F., 'Wer trägt die Verantwortung', *Deutsche Allgemeine Zeitung*, 7 November 1927; quoted in Roters, 93–6.
33 Cf. Gee, M., 'The Berlin Art World 1911–33', in: Gee, 63–83, here 75–8.
34 Cf. Janda, A., 'Die Berliner Nationalgalerie im kampf um die moderne kunst', in: Barron, 1992, 106–20.
35 Cf. Nicholas, 3–25.
36 Roters, 170–6.
37 FMSA/Ferdinand Möller sales ledger. The question of Möller's cessation of dealing was raised in a conversation with Wolfgang Wittrock, February 2004.
38 Roters, 194–205.
39 Ferdinand Möller to Gerhard Strauß, 20 January 1947, cited in: ibid., 197.
40 Ibid., 1984, 204–5; Romanus, 112–3.
41 Cf. Grohmann's obituary for Möller, *Berliner Tagespiegel*, 19 January 1956.
42 Roters.

43 Cf. Stonard, J-P., 'Old Masters of Modern Art', in: Weikop, C., (ed.), *Bridging History: Perspectives on Brücke*, forthcoming.

44 Exhibition details of this work are provided by Grisebach, 287–8.

45 Möller, unpaginated.

46 FMSA/Ferdinand Möller to Will Grohmann, 6 June 1950.

47 FMSA/Grohmann, W., 'Das Unbehagen an moderner Kunst', typed unpaginated copy, published in *Die Neue Zeitung*, 30 May 1950.

Expression

All expressivism is really lament.

Thomas Mann, *Doktor Faustus*, Berlin, 1947, 145

The dispute after 1945 about Expressionism as national heritage was nothing new: it had persisted since the first critical voices at the beginning of the century. If artists were international, then the art they produced, in the eyes of critics and public, was not. Franz Marc's warning that 'narrowness of feeling and national ambition' would only impede cultural renewal, had in fact little echo.[1] Paul Fechter, in his book *Der Expressionismus* (1914) defines Cubism, Futurism and Expressionism as French, Italian and German respectively. Building on Wilhelm Worringer's *Formprobleme der Gotik* (Form in the Gothic, 1911), Fechter sets the 'gothicness' of Expressionism against Renaissance classicism and naturalism. That artistic style is the natural frame for national feeling is made clear: 'Expressionism is not a matter of will or determination, but destiny: the inner equilibrium of humanity requires this balance'.[2] Fechter's definition of Expressionism as the 'fate' of a people is concerned with a conservative delineation of the 'sacred' and 'profane' of national culture. A similar claim was made at the same moment by Adolf Behne: 'German in its innermost essence', Expressionism 'brings a strengthening of the national element in art, since it is built on will and fantasy'.[3] Even more uncompromising was the definition offered by Hans Arp and El Lissitzky in 1925, in their description of 'the isms of art': 'From cubism and futurism has been chopped the minced meat, the mystic German beefsteak: expressionism'.[4]

Much has been written about the attempt to revive Expressionism as the 'true' German art under National Socialism. The 'gothicness' of Expressionism, as Magdalena Bushart has described, informed its use as a stepping stone to a pre-modern yet avowedly German idyll.[5] Such national differentiation was equally present in the critical reception of the now 'Old Masters' after 1945, indeed, some of the key figures such as Worringer, Behne and Fechter were still present (though the articles and reviews written by Fechter for *Die Welt* show none of his former enthusiasms, and Worringer's 1948 *Problematik der Gegenwartskunst* – Problems in Current Art – published when the author was living in Halle, added little to the debate about contemporary art). But after a short period of enthusiasm, disillusion quickly followed, leading to a strong antipathy to expressive modes in both East and West.

In both cases, the rejection was based on what was perceived to be the essential error of Expressionism: subjective overload. In the West, the need for a new stylistic model for young artists was fired by mistrust of Weimar politics and culture, the experiments and failures of which were to be avoided: 'Bonn ist nicht Weimar', as a CDU slogan was later to proclaim. For critics in the West, Expressionism as a 'Weimar style' was a hypertrophic manifestation that had soon lapsed into mannerism and inauthenticity. It could certainly not act as a model for art in a new world. Although similar arguments did appear in the Soviet Zone,[6] here expression was rejected on theoretical and political, rather than psychological grounds. As noted above, by focusing on an anti-fascist heritage, which meant valorising the 'common people' against the capitalist factions allegedly responsible for the war, SED politics was able to avoid problems of collective guilt for German war crimes. In this schema, the German psyche was left intact, and difficult questions about subjectivity and language eluded, at least for the time being. Aversion to emotive idioms in the East provoked a decisive drift away from traditions of revolutionary painting and radical attitudes in general. Although prewar anti-fascist traditions had been closely associated with revolutionary groupings, in particular ASSO, both these groups and the Expressionist stylistics with which they were associated were quickly suppressed after 1945. Artists for whom such traditions constituted a rallying point were left with no alternative but to join the monolithic official cultural bodies that came to define East German cultural life. Towards the end of 1945, the painter Fritz Duda had assembled former ASSO members to form the Arbeitsgemeinschaft Sozialistischer Künstler (Working Group of Socialist Artists). The group had close connections with the KPD, mounting their first exhibition in the KPD headquarters on August-Bebel Platz. They also installed an exhibition space on Unter den Linden to promote socially engaged art, a gallery that became known as Bild der Zeit (Image of the Times). The *klassenkämpferische* (class-struggle oriented) aspect of Duda's group did not sit easily with the SED, and Duda eventually received the pointed instructions from Anton Ackermann, the SED Secretary of Culture: 'Ackermann says: no more ASSO'.[7] Duda's group was dissolved in 1949, its members transferring to the official artists' organisation for East Germany, the Verband Bildender Künstler Deutschlands. Other prominent members of the ASSO movement were equally absorbed into the neutralised Bündnispolitik of the SED: As noted above, Hans Grundig, who spent the war in KZ Sachsenhausen, became rector and professor of the Dresden Akademie der bildender Künste (1945–8); Lea Grundig, who was exiled in Palestine 1940–8 also taught in Dresden on her return, and was later (1964–70) President of the Verband Bildender Künstler Deutschlands. Both artists were members of the Dresden-based group Das Ufer (The Shore), a quarter of whose members had belonged to the Dresden ASSO group before 1933. Das Ufer was absorbed into the Verband Bildender Künstler in 1952. A similar transitional role was played in Leipzig by the Künstlerkollektiv 48 (Arts Collective 48, 1948–9), and in Halle by the group Die Fähre (The Ferry, 1947–9), another group whose name referred back to the legendary Brücke group.

Other critics of Expressionism in the East picked up on more traditional anti-modern themes. In 1949, the art historian Heinz Lüdecke (1906–72), at that moment Cultural Editor of the *Berliner Zeitung*, wrote an article for *bildende kunst* ascribing the frantic, contradictory rhetoric of Expressionism to its economic and social basis. That Lenin's *Imperialism, the Highest Stage of Capitalism* appeared in 1917 at the height of the Expressionist movement confirmed for Lüdecke the connection with Imperialism. The 'questionable and ghostly' relations of the middle-classes with reality, evinced in the phantasms of Expressionism, were raw symptoms of the effects of capital concentration on traditional life. Expressionist art was merely a theatrical gesture: 'The reform-oriented petit-bourgeoisie acted in art as in politics: fake-revolutionaries'.[8]

Lüdecke's attack on the Expressionist pose echoes many left-wing critiques that appeared in the 1920s and 30s. The Marxist philosopher and critic Georg Lukács' well-known denunciation of Expressionism and the ensuing debate served in particular to inspire postwar positions such as that of Lüdecke. For Lukács, the opposition made to bourgeois capitalism by the Expressionists was purely tokenistic – claims for the revolutionary status of the Expressionists ignore the fact that their contribution was a 'subjective idealism' that could not elude ideological entanglement with German Imperialism. Their efforts led to an 'emptying' of the concept of revolution and an ideological disenfranchisement of culture in general.[9]

Although rejection of Expressionism was common both to East and West after 1945, there were then significant differences. Whereas in the East the stakes were determined by official political requirements – about defining a specific relation to a 'true' German heritage, whilst avoiding the type of rhetorical excesses allegedly common to both Expressionism and fascism – in the West the question was whether or not the 'modern' as a category of taste, in particular Expressionism, was operative or not for the younger, postwar generation. Both were defined by a new political culture within which older ideas of revolutionary change had no place – the political failings of the Weimar Republic constituted a common memory. The fact that Expressionism was discussed at all after 1945 may, in the light of these strictures, appear surprising – it shows not only how deeply the question of national heritage was embedded in the postwar moment, but also how, as Ernst Bloch put it in the context of the 1930s *Expressionismusdebatte*, it remained relevant fifteen years later: 'The passions of an earlier period still stir controversy'.[10]

New priorities were however to define the frame in which this controversy unfolded. Ideas about an 'absolute', apparently non-referential abstract art developed swiftly after 1945, as if a void was being rapidly filled. Willi Baumeister was the leading producer and theoretician of such work. He had spent the war in 'inner emigration', aided notably by the lacquer manufacturer Kurt Herbert, who employed Baumeister and Oskar Schlemmer from 1937 until late 1944. In 1946 Baumeister was appointed professor at the Stuttgart Kunstakademie, where he had studied with Schlemmer in the 1920s. The Swabian regional capital retained its status after 1945 as the stronghold of advanced painting, although it was only in the postwar period that a version of allegedly 'pure', non-figurative painting arose. The *Menschenbild* debate that this provoked, covered in more detail below, occurred in the absence of Schlemmer, a crucial figure whose ideas on the human image in relation to modernity and technology were regrettably absent after 1945. Schlemmer died in 1944, exhausted from persecution. A memorial exhibition of his work was toured during 1949–50 in Frankfurt, Kassel, Berlin and Mannheim. Schlemmer's concept of the *Menschenbild*, based on clarity, certainty and sovereign subjectivity, was an approach to the human figure influenced by classicism and mysticism. For one postwar commentator, he was the 'modern Masaccio'.[11] His absence was symptomatic of a move away from such a 'modern' image of man, in particular a move away from the belief that man could be reconciled with the technological advances of the machine age, to a type of image that made no reference to the human body.

The development of Baumeister's work from constructed human form to a world of ambiguous, esoteric abstract imagery, epitomises this shift. The postwar series of 'ARU' paintings, for example, are based on the motif of a black void pushing to the edges vagrant patches of primary colour, clearly relinquishing all the utopian anthropomorphic elements of paintings such as *Apoll* from 1922. Works from other series, such as the 'Zwei Weltalter' (Two Epochs) and 'Metaphysichen Landschaften' (Metaphysical Landscapes), begun in 1947, show very similar concerns with composition, colour and surface. Although the shift had begun in his oeuvre around 1930, Baumeister's elaboration of these ideas in his 1947 publication *Das Unbekannte in der Kunst* (The Unknown in Art) embeds them firmly in the reconstruction milieu. A defence of abstract painting was published by the critic Leopold Zahn in the Stuttgart-based journal *Das Kunstwerk* in early 1947. The entire issue was devoted to abstraction, carrying descriptions of what such painting entailed, but also a 'Kleines Lexicon Abstrakter Maler', a sort of trade directory listing the names of abstract painters, most living in Germany. Zahn offers a fiery defence of abstract painting as the 'true' art of modern man, despite all political attempts at a 'naturalistic restoration', and despite the obvious discontent of the general public: 'All modern forms of art, however different they may appear from one another, have a common denominator in the turn away from nature'.[12] Abstract art seeks its sources in archaic and primitive art, hill and rock drawings, the work of children and folk art, rather than the Renaissance tradition of perspectival drawing and anatomical exactitude. Further, Zahn asserts, anti-natural modern painting is numinous: such art displays a religious feeling of fear in the face of the unknown.

Baumeister would have agreed with this description. In an open letter to André Malraux, published in the same issue of *Das Kunstwerk*, Baumeister compares his own description of experimental artistic activity with the explorations of science.[13] Malraux's article 'Der Mensch und die künstlerische Kultur' (Man and Creative Culture), which had been published in *Die Neue Zeitung* on 14 July 1947, carried similar ideas, wrote Baumeister. In comparison to other epochs, the current time is that of the *Formkünstler*: 'The formal artist (in painting), in contrast to the content-artist, comes to the fore only in the epoch of the individual artist. Individual art is not contract-art [*Auftragskunst*]'. Baumeister sums up the ideas that he presented in *Das Unbekannte in der Kunst*, which he describes as having written 'behind closed doors' in 1943, and published four years later.

The focus for interest in abstraction was the circle that formed around the doctor and collector Ottomar Domnick. Domnick was a key supporter of abstraction and published an important statement of abstract painting in 1947, *Die Schöpferischen Kräfte in der abstrakten Malerei: ein Zyklus* (The Force of Creativity in Abstract Painting: a Cycle).[14] This contained lengthy descriptions and justifications for the work of five painters working in an abstract idiom: Max Ackermann (1887–1975), Willi Baumeister, Georg

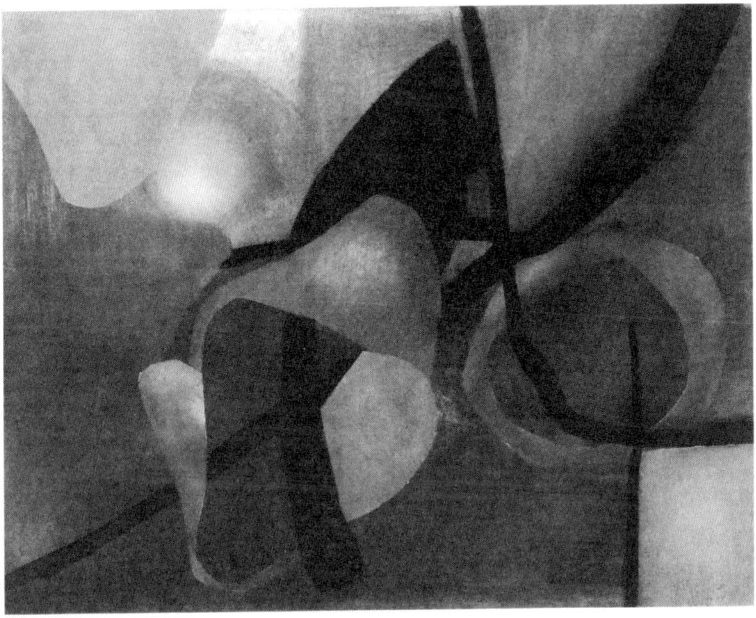

Fritz Winter, *Komposition III*, 1950, mixed technique 48.5 × 62.5 cm, Märkisches Museum der Stadt Witten, Witten

Meistermann (1911–1990), Otto Ritschl (1885–1976) and Fritz Winter (1905–1976). Original signatures by four of the five artists appeared on the inside cover of the first 250 copies of the book. As he was still in a Russian prisoner-of-war camp, the book explains, Fritz Winter's signature appears as a facsimile. The book accompanied a series of five 'Kunstwissenschaftlicher Veranstaltungen', symposiums accompanying displays by each artist, which took place on consecutive weekends in early 1947, in Domnick's home in Stuttgart. In 1948, he was asked by the French military government to organise the inclusion of German painters in the 2. *Salon des Réalités Nouvelles*, and the following year, Domnick was to organise the *Wanderausstellung französischer abstrakter*

Malerei, a touring exhibition of French abstract painting, including works by Hans Hartung, František Kupka and Pierre Soulages, which travelled to seven locations during 1948. The contacts he created led him to publish the next year a trilingual monograph on the painter Hans Hartung, whom he was particularly keen to support.

If the rhetoric surrounding the types of work that Domnick collected was posited on personal freedom, then the work itself was usually quite similar and frequently tame. In retrospect, the most appropriate context for such work, as Christine Mehring has argued, may be the interdisciplinary nature of postwar art and design, and the decorative impulses of the 1950s.[15] Clement Greenberg's warning of decoration as the 'specter that haunts modernist painting' is particularly appropriate for the postwar decade, a time for ghosts of many different sorts.[16] Artists had not yet found a way, as Greenberg prescribed, to use decoration against itself. In comparison with American painting, European abstraction conformed to a decorative standard that places it in a long tradition of concern with painterly decorum, against which the indecorous efforts of the Americans increasingly stood out. Such broad historical reflection was not, however, available for postwar artists and critics, who were anxious to re-establish a German aesthetic legacy. Postwar abstraction in this tradition was broadly considered as a filtering of the Blaue Reiter image world through both the technical experimentation and Eastern mysticism of the Bauhaus.

By far the most luminous moment in the elaboration of these ideas was the foundation in July 1949, in the Galerie Otto Stangl in Munich, of the Gruppe der Gegendstandlosen (Non-objective

Group). The history of the group, the support of the American administration and also notably of the British Consul John Anthony Thwaites has been well documented.[17] Apart from Baumeister, the six other founder members, Fritz Winter, Rolf Cavael (1898–1979), Gerhard Fietz (1910–77), Willi Hempel (1905–85), Rupprecht Geiger (b. 1908) and Brigitte Meier-Denninghoff (b.1923), all lived in Bavaria. The self-conception of the group was as South German, and the intention to provide a continuation of the tradition of the Blaue Reiter was evident,[18] although once again the sense of belatedness was present, one critic noting that 'it is unmistakable that the "Sturm und Drang" and the theoretical foundations of the "Kandinsky-period" are over'.[19]

For their first exhibition, held at the Central Art Collecting Point in Munich, April 1950, the group took the name Zen 49. The exhibition, which toured to a number of German towns, incorporated works from twelve 'guest' artists, including the American artist and curator Hilla von Rebay, a significant supporter of the group. Most of the 'absolute' painting on display was of a type similar to Baumeister's, forms and gestures floating within the frame of the picture. Paintings such as Fritz Winter's *Komposition III*, 1950, show that the claim of 'absolute' abstraction is difficult to sustain – crucially, these are works dependent on a representative effect. Illusion is obtained through traditional pictorial ideas of composition and atmospheric perspective; although the forms may be unrecognisable, the method of depiction is transparently naturalistic. A direct comparison may be made with subjective photography, which attempted to depict abstract, or non-recognisable forms, with traditional photographic techniques (an exception can be made in the case of photograms). Neither the traditional apparatus of painterly illusion nor the traditional means of photographic exposure and chemical revelation had been abandoned. In the case of Zen 49, an arguable exception was the work of Rupprecht Geiger, who provided the closest to a Minimalist or proto-Pop idiom with works such as 76 E (1948), an irregular shaped canvas with minimal colour areas. Yet his monochrome passages still show gradations of tone that suggest the effects of natural light, and the illusion of a highly abstract landscape, or cosmic scenario.

Aside from problems with the idea of 'pure abstraction', a claim more transparently supported by paintings and sculptures from members of the Zero group, which emerged from the abstract painting milieu in Düsseldorf in the late 1950s, the Zen 49 group was by no means considered at the time as a conservative appropriation of painterly traditions. On the contrary, the need was for mutual support for difficult art. Franz Roh anticipated criticism and incomprehension in his catalogue essay, which included a series of 'thesis' and 'antithesis' concerning abstract art: the objections (written by Roh himself) are telling: 'The new art is unreligious, even atheistic [...] Although this art is mistakenly derived from developments in physics, physicists would laugh at it [...] Is absolute painting not just a fashion, and is it not already outmoded? [...] Many people are simply bored by this art'.[20]

Zen 49 held three further exhibitions, in 1951 (shown in Lübeck, Düsseldorf and Munich), 1953 (Munich) and 1955 (Munich, Hamburg and Cologne), and a further exhibition that toured to nine locations in America during 1956 and early 1957. These may be considered as a survey of changing trends in postwar abstraction, notably the introduction of trends pertaining to Art informel. A number of smaller groups are associated with the introduction of the more 'existential' strain of abstraction from Paris, the first of which, junger westen, was established in Recklinghausen, in the industrial Ruhr region, in 1948. Informel painting was considered in some quarters as an alternative to the 'official' abstract painting of Baumeister and Zen 49, and it is indeed striking that a movement of 'anti-formal' painting should establish itself at the same time that official culture in the East was campaigning against dangerous 'formalism'. It is also noteworthy that those groups associated with Informel painting arose outside of the major artistic centres of Berlin, Munich, Stuttgart and Cologne. Introducing a survey of the group in 1957, Albert Schulze Vellinghausen noted the 'radical decentralisation' integral to cultural reconstruction.[21] Although the first exhibition of the junger westen, in a hotel in Recklinghausen, included works by thirty-one artists of varying styles, the core group, Gustav Deppe (1913–1999), Thomas Grochowiak (b.1914), Ernst Hermanns (b.1914), Emil Schumacher (1912–99), Heinrich Siepmann (1904–2002) and Hans Werdehausen (1910–77), all worked in a manner more or less influenced by Informel trends. The group was supported by the local town council, which funded a yearly prize and created an exhibition space in an old air-raid bunker.

A further group, Quadriga, formed by Karl-Otto Götz (b.1914), Otto Greis (1913–2001), Heinz Kreutz (b.1923) and Bernard Schultze (1915–2005), acted as a parallel conduit for Art informel trends into Germany. The first exhibition of the group was held in Klaus Franck's Zimmergalerie in Frankfurt from December 1952 until the end of the following February, consisting of thirteen paintings by the artists, none of which were sold.[22] During his introductory speech, the radio critic Leo M. Faerber stated that although this was Expressionism, it was no *Wiederholung* (repetition), rather an *Erneuerung* (renewal).[23] The term 'Expressionists' was quickly dropped when the name 'Quadriga' was discovered. An important influence on the loose gestural painting shown by Franck was the exhibition *Amerikanische Malerei, Werden und Gegenwart* (American Painting, Past and Present), which appeared as part of the 1951 Berlin Festwochen. Karl-Otto Götz's contacts with the artists associated with the COBRA group in Amsterdam was also formative, as was a general awareness of developments in Paris: although as we shall see, it would be wrong to suggest that the group was too open to international trends in the early 1950s.

Mention must also be made of Gruppe 53, which formed in Düsseldorf the next year, as an exhibition society for artists interested in Art informel. It was out of Gruppe 53 that the founders of the Zero group – Heinz Mack (b.1931), Otto Piene (b.1928) and Günther Uecker (b.1930) – forty years younger than Baumeister, developed a more impersonal, collective and critical art that reacted against the *huis clos* of postwar abstraction.

In her pioneering work on abstract painting in West Germany after 1945, *Reconstructing the Subject*, the American art historian Yule

Heibel has described the 'regrounding of subjectivity' that took place in the western half of the country after the war. Expressive and abstract painting styles, Heibel argues, played a considerable role in the reconstitution of emotional life. Although her account does not touch on the reception of the historic avant-garde of Expressionism, it nevertheless describes in compelling detail the 'withering' of 'expressive potential' in abstract painting during the period of reconstruction.[24] With the exception of Ernst Wilhelm Nay (1902–1968), whose work Heibel keenly supports, abstract painting developed away from corporeal and organic ideas, towards a floating, 'higher' ideal. Aversion to Expressionism as a stylistic choice was the result, says Heibel, of a 'crisis of subjectivity' in the wake of the War and the Holocaust, through which a stigma was attached to 'affective' and 'expressive' abstraction. This crisis led to a blandness of expressive content and a tendency to work in an obviously derivative manner. The philosophical 'regrounding' of a *Menschenbild*, or model of subjectivity, she argues, involved a rejection of the Nietzschean tradition of vitalism, expressivity and romanticism, which were associated with war, totalitarianism and an older, Berlin-based, 'eastern' artistic style. The shift towards a more autonomous, absolute concept of art found its theoretical justification in the aloof existential speculations of Martin Heidegger. The soldier-painters may have gone into the 1914–18 war with *Zarathustra* in their pocket, but they returned from the next war to the legacy of *Being and Time*.

Heidegger was indeed the philosopher of the moment. Although Heibel makes a connection between Theodor Adorno's criticism of this focus on 'pure being' at the expense of historical representation and the 'bodily', historical painting of Nay,[25] it is clear from the available evidence that Adorno's influence was minimal in comparison to that of Heidegger – the philosophy of the latter 'triumphing', as Hermann Glaser put it, in the 1950s and 60s over that of the former.[26] Heidegger's appeal, as Adorno himself recognised, was to have turned the negativity of the postwar world, its lack of formal possibility – simply stated, the lack of ideas and styles for artistic representation – into a virtue. Where history and subjectivity have been pulverised, the thinker who provides alternative grounds for aesthetic meaning will exert the stronger appeal. Heidegger's 1950 publication *Holzwege*, a collection of essays from the 1930s and 40s, provides a starting point for consideration of his postwar influence. 'The Age of the World Picture' in particular is an attempt to locate the essential and distinctive grounds of modern experience. The Modern Age is distinguished from Antiquity and the Middle Ages by the emergence of a *Weltbild*, a picture of the world, a fact strongly related to the emergence of a self-grounding, or self-aware subject, and consequently to the emergence of Humanism. 'There begins that way of being human which means the realm of human capability as a domain given over to measuring and executing, for the purpose of gaining mastery over that which is a whole', Heidegger writes.[27] The appeal that such an argument had for those in the West promoting the sort of non-visceral, all-encompassing abstraction described by Heibel is clear. An expressive subject was inserted into a technologically unified world, retaining all power of independent thought. That the position of such a subject could be calibrated by aesthetic reflection was suggested by Heidegger's turn to aesthetics in his essay *Der*

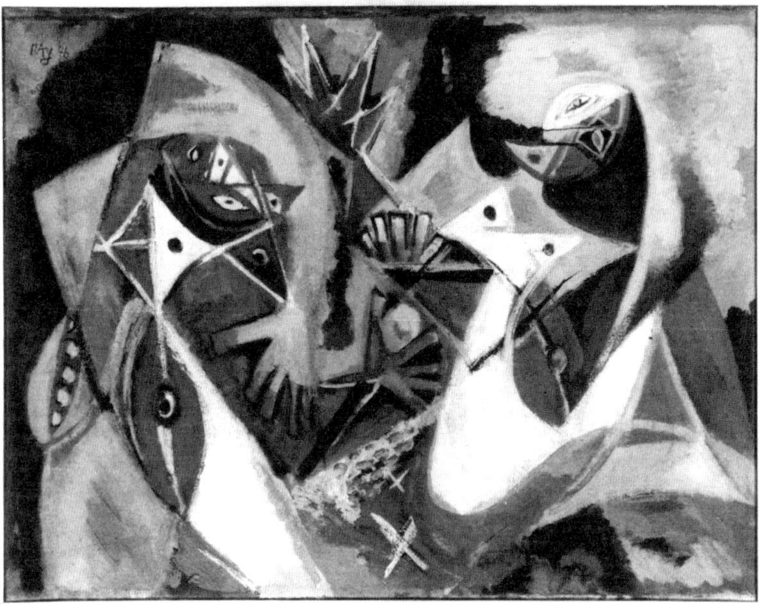

Ernst Wilhelm Nay, *Gespräch* (Discussion), 1946, oil on canvas, 61.5 × 81 cm, Westfälisches Landesmuseum für Kunst und Kulturgeschichte, Münster

Ursprung des Kunstwerks (The Origin of the Work of Art), first published in 1950, which imbues art with the deep philosophical task of revealing human truth.

Adorno's importance for Heibel lies in the criticism he made of Heidegger's 'jargon of authenticity'.[28] The philosophical confrontation is extended to painting. The restoration of modern modes, for example, in the work of the Zen 49 artists, incapacitated critical thought, and led to the 'fetishisation of autonomy'.[29] Heibel uses Nay, and to a lesser and more allusive extent, Dix, to criticise the 'higher formlessness' of Baumeister and Zen 49, and the ideas of their promoters, principally Ottomar Domnick: Nay's paintings offer a 'somatic', expressive type of abstraction with a critical potential that the work of Baumeister and the Zen 49 group, to their detriment, lack. This argument is convincingly backed with contemporary material – an exhibition of Hanna Bekker vom Rath's Frankfurt gallery, for instance, presented Baumeister and Nay as 'opposing poles' of modern German painting.[30] It is also true that Nay was one of the most interesting figures of this moment – and produced undoubtedly his best work around 1945, when it was reminiscent of the phosphorescent expressivism of early works by Christian Schad, and seems genuinely touched by the world. Whether his work, which so quickly drifted into the disengaged sphere of abstraction presaged by his mythological titles of the late 1940s, can really sustain this role, is another question. In discerning a 'rift' in western painting, Heibel appears to be compensating for her outright rejection of East German culture, which for her, exhibits an 'astonishing provincialism', a rejection that obliges the search for a dialectical partner for abstract painting in the West itself.[31] This may in the end be a more troublesome 'denial of difference' than the suppression of Nay's 'expressive' work in the West. As the evidence of Heidegger's alleged 'triumph' suggests, the critical spirit of Adorno was little present in the postwar decade. His attack on Heidegger was first published in 1964. As we have seen in the case of Weimar theorists of photography, such critical spirit was absent from reconstruction culture. The attempt to read this defecit back into the moment inevitably causes disappointment. Another lacuna, which has received extensive commentary, that of comment or reflection on the Holocaust, is equally absent, to Heibel's understandable frustration: 'It is a curious and at times irritating paradox that Nay, whose ambition was appropriate to the scale of the calamity, never once made that calamity (genocide and Holocaust) the express subject of his art'.[32] He would nevertheless have been isolated had he done so, and would have had little resonance with his time. As she goes on to concede, 'no one had the moral distance, the breadth of horizon to encompass this. It was unheard of, unbelievable, incomparable.'[33] Heibel's reflections here are of exceptional importance.

In response to these problems, and to build on Heibel's account, two further themes may be brought into play: the fate of the German language, and the figure of exile.

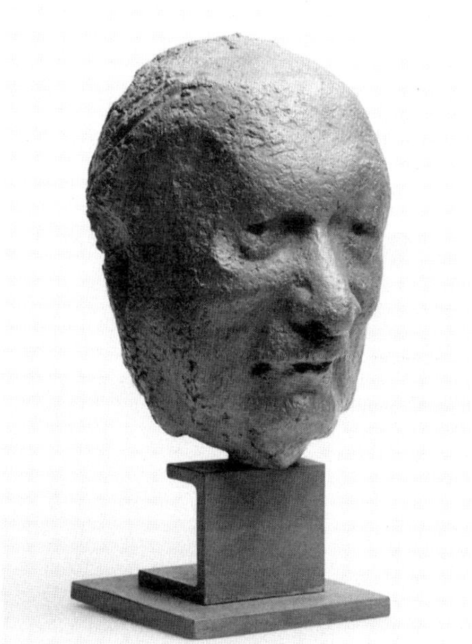

Bernhard Heiliger, *Martin Heidegger*, 1964, bronze and cement, Bernhard-Heiliger-Stiftung, Berlin

A comparison with contemporary literature, rather than philosophy, may do more to cast light on the troubled dealings with Expressionism after 1945. The Swiss writer Urs Widmer's doctoral thesis, published in 1966, on the subject of German literature in the wake of war, points to the *Sprachskepsis* (Language-Scepticism) of the younger generation, for whom the basic means of expression, the German language, had been stained by Nazism. The language appointed to propagate state violence infiltrated non-political areas such as science, and modes of private communication. Even anti-fascist writing and exile journals could not escape the Nazi *Wortschatz* (vocabulary), and, as Widmer demonstrates with numerous examples, postwar writers were also faced with the problem of a language littered with concepts – *Relikten* – defined by National Socialism. To write again meant to reinvent language, and necessitate what was termed by the writer Wolfgang Weyrauch as a *Kahlschlag*, a 'clear-felling'. Yet in the first few years after 1945, this was hardly possible.[34] Hans Werner Richter's Gruppe 47, originally constituted from those who had contributed to the banned radical journal *Der Ruf*, forms the literary focus for this debate in the late 1940s.[35]

For Widmer, the obligation to start from scratch indicates that there was in fact a strong, deep affinity between Expressionism and art of the postwar period. Widmer describes this affinity in terms of generations – where the Expressionist generation coalesced around the need to overcome the art of the nineteenth century, and struggled against a stuffy Prussian opposition, the postwar generation coalesced around the need to overcome Nazi culture. Both generations had the 'will to a new language'. Both reacted against traditional ideas of beauty. But if postwar writers were looking back to earlier models (Widmer highlights in particular the Sturm circle around Herwarth Walden), then the epigones were just that: latecomers. 'The achievements of the father were emulated by the son, but in a diluted and popularised form'.[36] Postwar writers were so implicated with the language and culture of the Third Reich that it was impossible simply to designate a 'year zero' and begin again.

The classic account of these conditions is provided by Victor Klemperer's *LTI Notizbuch eines Philologen* (LTI, lingua tertii imperii. A Philologist's Notebook), written throughout the period of the Third Reich and first published after the war, in Germany, 1947.[37] 'LTI' – Lingua Tertii Imperii – was the abbreviation used by Klemperer in his wartime notebooks to identify words that had acquired a fetishistic and propagandistic value within the Third Reich. He opens his reflections with the observation that the word *Entnazifizierung* (De-Nazification) was of a form, using the prefix 'Ent', commonly employed by the Nazis as part of an extensive rhetoric that 'permeate[d] the flesh and blood of the people'.[38] The prefix was most obviously related, though he does not mention it, with the concept of *Entartung*. The suggestion that even those concepts designed to destroy Nazism were of Nazi origin indicates the sense of entrapment described within the *Notizbuch*. The problematic resonance of certain linguistic forms is further complicated by the parallel drawn by Klemperer between Fascist language and that of the Expressionist avant-garde – a comparison predicated on 'certain ways of expressing the importance of the will and a fervently thrusting forward momentum'. The words *Sturm and Aktion* are two particularly prominent survivors. The zig-zag 'SS' symbol, for which there was a special key on Nazi typewriters, is also used as a point of comparison – the symbol was part of the Nazi thrust towards visualisation that found a historical source in Expressionist painting and literary language.[39] Ultimately, Klemperer is not denigrating Expressionism in any programmatic manner; rather, he is exemplifying what he describes as the 'blurred boundaries' of stylistic categories such as 'Expressionism'. He reinforces this blurring by pointing out that such an avant-garde could produce both an Ernst Toller, driven to exile and suicide by the Nazis, and a Hans Johst, who became president of the Nazi Reichsschrifttumskammer in 1935.[40]

A reading of Klemperer's account might suggest that Heibel's concern with 'withering' may be supplemented by examining the 'entrapment' of linguistic modes. The identification of fascism with Expressionism described by Klemperer created the need for new 'international' idioms after 1945. The vitiation not just of language but of whole attitudes towards the world needed to be isolated and countermanded; the double problem was that the language of this countermanding itself so often unconsciously repeated Nazi formulas. Soviet cultural agencies took pains to distinguish their idea of a politicised culture from that of the Nazis, particularly as they were often attacking the same modern formulas. Anti-fascist rhetoric was compromised, haunted by entrenched fascist idioms. Despite his apparent commitment to Socialist reconstruction, Klemperer began keeping another word-diary in June 1945: *LQI – Lingua Quarti Imperii*, noting, 'I must slowly begin to pay systematic attention to the language of the fourth Reich. It sometimes seems to me, that it is less different from that of the third than, say, the Saxon of Dresden from that of Leipzig'.[41] The transition from Nazism to Soviet-Communism had involved, it appears, in some places no more than a quick costume change.

In the West, the search for forms of language to escape the terrible 'entrapment' described by Klemperer were equally problematic. Claims for abstraction as a *Weltsprache* (universal language), as we have seen, were posited on contrived and exaggerated claims for the works of art in question. On the one hand, modernist myths of the primitive were revived to explain a prehistoric source of inspiration, a type of ur-human pool of ideas and images that informed a universally applicable language. For a number of critics, Willi Baumeister was able to tap such a 'primordial language', a shaman with profound intuition of the world, a Franz Marc who had survived two wars. By contrast, another strategy of redefinition in the West took the possibilities of vision enabled by atomic physics, and the 'regression' of vision, as it were, to a sub-atomic level, as a startling form of escape from difficult postwar realities. Herbert Read insisted on a transnational language of art that appealed to scientific knowledge: 'the forms that the artist creates derive their significance from the fact that they are forms that are echoed throughout the cosmos – in the structure of metals, fibres, organic tissues, electron diffraction patterns, frequency modulations, detonation patterns etc.'[42] One of the key publications in this field was György Kepes' *The New Landscape in Art and Science* (1956), juxtaposing images typical of the new reaches of scientific imaging, and abstract paintings and drawings. Franz Roh's concern to counteract the criticism that physicists would be clueless in front of such work noted above shows the dilemma of the scientific metaphor. The paintings in question, often more decorative in effect, could barely sustain the epic configurations of primitive or scientific thought projected onto them, resulting in a clear mismatch between word and image.

Problems of language are closely associated with the history of the Weimar exile, not least as writers formed one of the most persecuted of groups, and also stage some of the most memorable, if eventually futile, acts of resistance. Compared to the problems of language described by Klemperer, the 'exile condition' involved a different sort of withering, that of the creative individual disconnected from native cultural life and traditions. How German artists fared in exile, and how the momentum of tradition was or was not sustained is a vast, largely unchartered topic. One example, that of the painter Wols, may be taken to illustrate the theme of Expressionism and exile, from the vantage point less of the fate of prewar traditions (that theme would be most dutifully served by a description of Max Beckmann, whose story has been told elsewhere),[43] more of a postwar culture of expression and its limitation.

Hans Hartung, working as a painter in Paris after war service with De Gaulle's Free French, wrote in August 1947 to Will Grohmann about the 'real revolution' taking place in the Parisian art scene.[44] Hartung's letter reads like an intelligence report listing all the new artistic modes, the rising stars of a younger generation, and the galleries in which they could be seen. One of these new names may have caught Grohmann's eye. In addition to the paintings of Alfred Manessier, Jean Le Moal and Gustave Singier, 'colour-rich, abstracting, loosened-up painting that still hangs on to remnants of figuration', the Galerie René Drouin was showing new works by a little-known German painter named Wols, who, according to Hartung, displayed 'a variety of influences: Lyonel Feininger, Klee, Botany, abstraction and a technique of 'random-production (*technischen Zufallsprodukten*)'.[45] Like Hartung, Wols had chosen Parisian exile at least in part for aesthetic reasons: on joining the Bauhaus in 1932 in its short-lived Berlin manifestation, he had been advised by Moholy-Nagy to move to Paris, and did so the same year, eventually settling there the next year. Hartung's letter to Grohmann had been describing Wols's second exhibition at the Galerie Drouin, in May 1947. Although no more a commercial success than Wols's first show, at the end of 1945 there was a significant critical response to this second exhibition that anticipated Wols's importance for those artists associated with the 'loosened-up' painting that came to be termed Art informel.

It is uncertain whether Grohmann knew in 1947 that 'Wols' was the pseudonym of Alfred Otto Wolfgang Schulze, whom he most probably encountered during the late 1920s as part of the Hirsch circle in Dresden, a loose grouping of diverse cultural figures who met around the collector Fritz Bienert. The circle continued its weekly meetings until the evening of the 13 February 1945, the night of the first devastating bombing raid on Dresden, as we learn from the account written by Fritz Löffler, himself a member of the group.[46] Fritz Bienert was the son of Ida Bienert, whose collection of 'new' art was published by Grohmann in 1933 as part of an intended series on private collections of modern painting in Germany.[47] Another member of the Hirsch circle, during his stay in Dresden, was Otto Dix, who arrived in Dresden in 1927, five years before Wols departed for Paris. This early connection has been used by the art historian Birgit Schwarz to compare Wols's work to the ubiquitous decay and disintegration found in Dix's images of war, particularly the now lost *Der Schützengrabe* (The Dugout, 1920–23).[48] When he closed his eyes to draw, Schwarz claims, Wols was not plumbing the depths of his subconscious in the Surrealist manner, but rather drawing wistfully on *tieferes Bildgedächtnis*, (deep image-memories) of his early viewings of Dix's work. Such martial image-memories may have been triggered during his time in an internment camp for fourteen months from September 1939. This argument speaks less of Wols's work than it does of a tendency towards critical repatriation. Wols did not deviate from contemporary opinion in holding French painting in the highest regard, and was not untypical in his struggle to distance himself from his native landscape and become part of the École de Paris. Readings of his work are equally anxious, however, to bring him back home and place him within a German tradition. Birgit Schwarz, for instance, underlines her argument by pointing to the strong influence of German art on the Parisian scene after 1930.[49] Her thesis takes its place among many attempts, perhaps initiated by Hartung's comparison with Klee and Feininger, to place Wols within an entirely German tradition of painting.

Tracing such an enthusiastic 're-nationalisation' of Wols within later criticism comes after an equally discernible period, continuing for a few years after his death in 1951, during which his work remained unknown in Germany. Heinz Trökes' lyrical response to the artist, published in 1954, stands as one of the first significant responses to his work in the Federal Republic.[50] That Wols, as one of the prime initiators of Pariser Fleckenmalerei (Parisian Taschism), achieved success in Paris after the war is evinced not only by the sale of his paintings to American collectors, but also by the information that Picasso and Sartre paid his rent in the Rue de Seine, 'where he slept, drank, and painted'. This is compared by Trökes to the complete ignorance of him in Germany, as late as 1954.[51] Such neglect should perhaps be no great surprise. The collapse of the distinction between normal and abnormal in the works of those such as Jean Dubuffet was part of a general movement that sought a renewed dynamic via the authenticity of psychosis. The 'normative' in Germany was now the difficult goal, and it is little surprise that such debates found fallow ground there.

Wols's work remained unknown in Germany until the mid-1950s, when a 'restoration' of sorts took place, primarily by his inclusion both in Werner Haftmann's highly important postwar publication *Malerei im 20. Jahrhunderts*, and consequently the first documenta exhibition, in 1955. Works by artists associated with Art informel begin to show the influence of Wols around this time, in particular paintings by Karl Fred Dahmen, Emil Schumacher and Bernard Schultze, which echo Wol's motif of a visceral, bristling wound, or a central head or body-like figure constructed out of a dirty, scrubbed mess of filaments, such as in *Manhattan*, of 1947, which was included in the 1955 documenta. Haftmann's influential interpretation grounded the later view of Wols as an Expressionist through and through, although this was by no means immediate. In the first edition (1954) of Haftmann's book, Wols is mentioned only briefly as an important German painter within the École de Paris. The entry increases for the second (1957), Wols infiltrating Haftmann's photographic pantheon with a disarming self-portrait. By the fourth edition (1965), Wols is given a great deal more coverage. Here, Haftmann carefully traces the tradition in which Wols can be placed: the narrative art of James Ensor and Alfred Kubin, the descriptive sobriety of the early Grosz, the inventive freedom of Hieronymous Bosch and the Surrealists, the psychic improvisation of Klee, the free drawing style of Kandinsky. Although his *haute-pâte* may have been inspired by Jean Fautrier's use of the technique as early as 1942, again this was originally derived from Klee.[52] Such a concern to 'establish' Wols within a largely German tradition may be compared with the French painter Georges Mathieu's typically hyperbolic declaration after seeing the 1947 Drouin show, that Wols had 'pulverised' the past, and cut himself free of tradition – 'He has annihilated Picasso, Kandinsky, Kirchner and Klee, all at the same time [...] After Wols, everything has to begin again'.[53] The only comparison in recent art history, according to the effusive Mathieu, was Van Gogh. For Werner Haftmann, however, in the age of world abstraction, Van Gogh was best represented by a photograph of his headstone in Auvers-sur-Oise.

In 1957, Albert Vellinghausen described Wols as one of those artists who from exile had exercised a *Rückstrahlung*, a 'shining-back' onto native German art.[54] Hartung was in a similar position, although his art was so in keeping with the decorum of postwar abstraction that it is difficult to discern an actual influence. Vellinghausen adds Max Ernst to this trio of artists in exile whose influence was nevertheless to be felt – although, as we have seen, the influence of the latter was short-lived.

By the time Grohmann did write about Wols, in an article for the journal *Quadrum* in 1959, attention had turned away from Expressionism and cultural heritage towards the new artistic constellations of the postwar world. Wols's influence on painters associated with Art informel was not evident in the early manifestations of such work, for instance the first showing of the Quadriga artists in 1952. In describing the development of his own work during this period, Karl-Otto Götz, undoubtedly the best travelled and best connected artist associated with Art informel, dismisses the influence of Wols, along with that of Hartung and Mathieu.[55] If Wols was being reintegrated as a German artist, and as heir to a tradition of Expressionism, then his influence on contemporary artists was minimal. Expressionism was now abstract, or not at all. New stylistic debates derived from world views by which reality was constituted either by social relations, in the case of Soviet Socialist Realism, or by a world unified by technology and scientific knowledge, and new possibilities of micro- and macro-vision. In both cases historic Expressionism, with its legacy of spiritual overcoming and dazzling individual insight into the world, was of little help as a *vade-mecum*.

1 Marc, F., 'Im Fegefeuer des Krieges', *Kunstgewerbeblatt*, Leipzig, 1915.
2 Fechter, 29.
3 Behne, A., 'Organisation, Deutschtum und Kunst', *Zeit-Echo*, vol. 1, nos. 23–4, 1915–16, 364.
4 Arp, 8.
5 Bushart, 1990.
6 Cf. Bergen, G., 'Veteranen des Expressionismus und ihre Epigonen', *bildende kunst*, 1949, no. 4, 232.
7 Feist, 1996, 131.
8 Lüdecke, H., 'Die Tragödie des Expressionismus. Notizen zu seiner Soziologie', *bildende kunst*, 1949, no. 4, 109–12, here 109.
9 Lukács, G., 'Grösse und Verfall des Expressionismus', *Internationale Literatur*, no. 1, 1934, 153–73. Cf. Schmitt, 1973.
10 Bloch, E., 'Discussing Expressionism', in: Jameson, 16–27, here 25.
11 M.R., 'Zum Gedächtnis Oskar Schlemmers', *Die Zeit*, 20 October 1949, 4.
12 Zahn, L., 'Abkehr von der 'Natur'', *Das Kunstwerk*, no. 8/9, 1946–7, 3–6, here 3.
13 Baumeister, W., 'Offener Brief an André Malraux', *Das Kunstwerk*, no. 8/9, 1946–7, 79.
14 Domnick, 1947, 1982.
15 Mehring, C., 'Decoration and Abstraction in Blinky Palermo's Wall Paintings', *Grey Room*, 18, Winter 2004, 82–107.
16 (Cited in ibid.) Greenberg, C., 'Milton Avery', in: O'Brian, 39–44, here 43.
17 Cf. Poetter, 1986.
18 Cf. Cavael, R., 'Überlegungen zum Entwurf der ZEN-Zeitung'; cited in: Poetter, 1986, 345.
19 Petzet, W., 'Spaziergang durch Münchner Galerien', *Münchner Merkur*, 8 April 1950; cited in: Poetter, 1986, 349.
20 Roh, F., 'Gegenstandlose Kunst', Central Art Collecting Point, 2–5.
21 Vellinghausen, 14.
22 Martin-Gropius-Bau, 416–25.
23 Cf. Remszhardt, G., 'Quadriga malerischer Avantgarde', in: de la Motte, 31.
24 Heibel, 2.
25 Ibid., 38–44.
26 Glaser, 1989, 315.
27 Heidegger, 1977, 132.
28 Heibel, 40; Adorno.
29 Heibel, 64.
30 Ibid., 77.
31 Ibid., 88.
32 Ibid., 14.
33 Ibid., 19.
34 Weyrauch, 213. Cited in: Widmer, 14.
35 Cf. Neunzig.
36 Widmer, 106.
37 Klemperer, 1947. All citations taken from Martin Brady's 2000 translation.
38 Klemperer, 2000, 15.
39 Ibid., 68.
40 Ibid., 67.
41 Klemperer, 2003, 13.
42 Read, 1968, 257.
43 Cf. Guggenheim Museum.
44 Hans Hartung to Will Grohmann, 20 August 1947. Quoted in: Gutbrod, 162–7, here 162.
45 Ibid., 165
46 Löffler, 1981, 35; Löffler, F., 'Expressionismus in Dresden', *Imprimatur, Neue Folge*, vol. III, 1962, 235–9, here 239.
47 Junge, H., 'Vom Neuen begeistert – die Sammlerin Ida Beinert', in: Junge, 1992, 29–37.
48 Schwarz, B., 'Dix und Wols: Zur Biographie einer künstlerischen Revolution', *Jahrbuch des Staatlichen Kunstsammlungen in Baden-Württemberg*, no. 30, 1993, 104–24.
49 Ibid., 121–2.
50 Trökes, H., 'Flecken, Flecken. Hommage à Wols's, *schri kunst schri. ein almanach alter und neuer kunst* 1954, Baden-Baden (Woldemar-Klein Verlag), 1953, 41–4.
51 Ibid., 44.
52 Haftmann, 1965, 474.
53 Mathieu, 1963, 35.
54 Vellinghausen, 13.
55 de la Motte, 143–4, here 144.

Miserere

L'Européen le plus moderne c'est vous Pape Pie X

Guillaume Apollinaire, 'Zone', in *Alcools*, Paris, 1913

After a short period serving in the Volkssturm, Hitler's last-ditch national militia, Otto Dix was captured in the Black Forest and interned in a prison camp near the French town of Colmar, where he remained until February 1946. Although he was fifty-five years old, and had been exhausted by the experience of war, Dix neverthless continued painting, as he had throughout the Third Reich. During 1945 he completed an altar piece, commissioned by the camp authorities for the prison's Catholic chapel, in the studio of Robert Gall, a painter from Colmar whom Dix had befriended. The *Madonna mit Stacheldracht* (Madonna with Barbed Wire) shows Saints Peter and Paul in irons, amongst the ruins, while the central figure of the Virgin, who averts her eyes from the child that she holds, sits sequestered by barbed wire in the ruined landscape around the village of Logelbach, where the prison camp was situated. The painting eventually made its way to the Maria-Frieden church in a southern district of Berlin, where it can still be seen. Although the *Madonna mit Stacheldracht* has been compared to other fifteenth- and sixteenth-century Marian paintings from the Upper Rhine, including Matthias Grünewald's Issenheim altarpiece, further correspondences may be drawn with a tradition often considered eccentric to the history of modern art, that of twentieth-century religious painting.[1] Dix produced

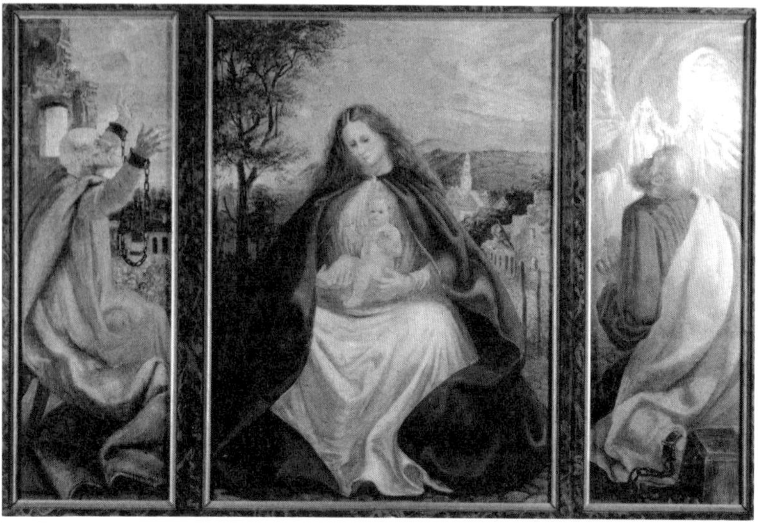

Otto Dix, *Madonna mit Stacheldracht* (Madonna with barbed wire), 1945, oil on wood, Maria-Frieden Church, Berlin

religious images throughout his career, yet the evidence of his oeuvre as a whole gives no indication of a particularly devout attitude, nor of a self-image as a Christian painter. His Madonna, so scarred with the violence of a secular age, raises the question of whether any rapprochement could be made between traditional religious iconography and art in the modern age.

This question became particular pressing for Germany in the wake of the Hitler. It was asked by a broad range of people for whom the notion of modern religious art held particular appeal, and for whom an entirely secular definition of modern art was difficult to accept. Christian subject matter, in particular the crucifixion, as well as formats traditionally suited to liturgical use, such as the triptych, were by no means abandoned by painters in the first half of the twentieth century. The art historian Klaus Lankheit has described the rebirth of the triptych in the modern age, with Hans von Marées and Max Beckmann as the principal artists.[2] Lankheit's is one of numerous publications dealing with religious art published in Germany since the end of the First World War, which together constitute a corpus unrivalled by any other European country.[3] In all these books, and of course within the art itself, the question is posed insistently: can there be such a thing as modern religious art?

The scope of the question was largely determined by the confrontation of Christian traditions, predominantly Catholic, with modernism, a confrontation that produced one of the most active fault lines of nineteenth- and twentieth-century art history. This was nowhere more true than in Germany, where the utopias of the Catholic Middle Age and the Modern Machine Age came repeatedly into conflict in reformist artistic movements and institutions. Theological debate remained living and present in daily life. Although the last of the Christian kings, Wilhelm II, had fled the country in 1919, the social and political roles of the Catholic and Protestant Churches persisted in Germany well into the twentieth century. During the Weimar Republic, the standing of the Catholic Church was considerably strengthened as a solid alternative in times of political and economic turmoil.

For these reasons, religious feeling simmers beneath, or not far away from, much of the art made in Germany at this time. Memorable instances may be found in the work of Barlach, for example his bronze *Pieta* of 1932; the chapel painted by Erich Heckel and Kirchner for the Sonderbund exhibition in Cologne, 1912;

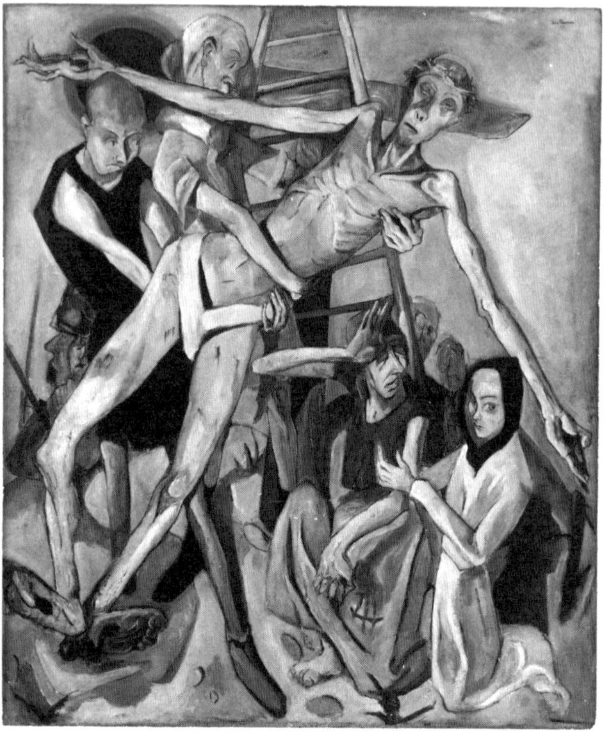

Max Beckmann, *The Descent from the Cross*, 1917, oil on canvas, 151.2 × 128.9 cm, Museum of Modern Art, New York

Beckmann's *Deposition*, made in Frankfurt in 1917; or the monastic ideal of the early Bauhaus. Even when the 'Cathedral of Socialism' that many had dreamt of in 1918 was suppressed in favour of a more industrialised approach to art, the place of traditional religious ideas in advanced art was by no means devalued. As Oskar Schlemmer wrote in the late 1920s: 'Might this be the key: a Catholic can still be saved, despite Enlightenment and Steiner. An oil painter can still be an artist, in spite of film and phosphorescent paint'.[4] Even if

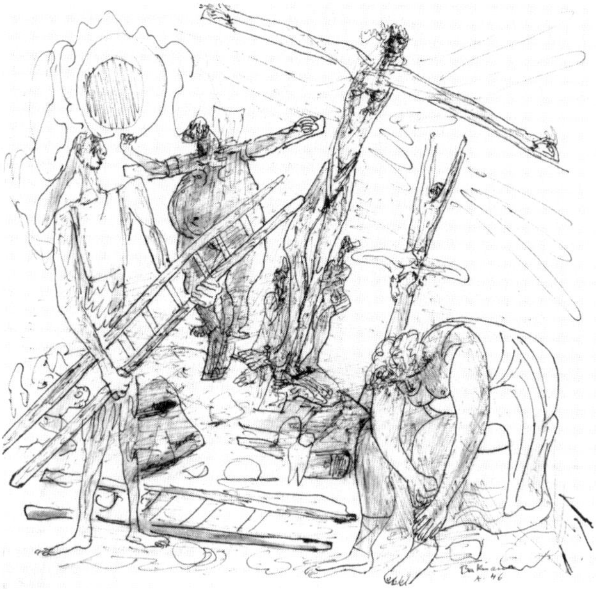

Max Beckmann, *Deposition*, 1946, ink drawing, 31.5 × 32.8 cm, Pfalzgalerie, Kaiserlauten

Schlemmer was expressing a private hope about the spiritual impact of his own work, his comments indicate a broader consensus that traditional art forms could be identified with religious salvation.

In 1949, more than 90 percent of the population belonged to either the Lutheran or the Roman Catholic Churches.[5] Catholic salvation and the persistence of painting, as Schlemmer implied, could still be equated – indeed, after the disasters of war such an equation combined the only two institutions unsullied by Nazism. The Catholic Church was the most important large-scale international institution that survived in Germany through the war and after 1945, and was the only institution judged by the Allies as non-culpable. Both Catholic and Protestant Churches gave a sense of continuity and form of leadership that the secular modern state, in the wake of fascism, appeared unable to provide. The resistance mounted by certain Catholic churches to the Third Reich (although there had also been a degree of collusion, largely a result of the Reich Concordat of July 1933, which gave the Catholic Church power of self-government in return for keeping out of politics) greatly increased their standing and offered an alternative to the belief systems of Communism and Existentialism. 'Modern art', largely understood as non-naturalistic representation, provided for the postwar imagination a similar belief system distinct from Nazism. We have already seen in the context of the Allied occupation how the freedoms of modern art, defined in terms of expression, originality, uniqueness, were considered emblematic of democratic consciousness both in East and West (though in very differing ways), and the basis for reconstruction.

Given this background, the considerable effort to restore and reform a movement of modern religious art in Germany after the war comes as no surprise. That these efforts were ultimately a failure indicates not only the frustrations of the period, but also a major shift away from the notion that an artistic style could carry ideological meaning.

A prominent example introduces the difficulties presented by modern religious art at this time. The Rhenish painter and stained-glass artist Georg Meistermann was one of the better-known Catholic painters to achieve success after 1945. He saw himself as part of a tradition stretching back to the late-nineteenth century, a tradition that sought to free Christian art from the stranglehold of kitsch. The efforts of Pierre Puvis de Chavannes, Rimbaud, Huysmans and Léon Bloy, directed towards the renewal of an art that had enjoyed its Golden Age in medieval Europe, for him stood at the beginning of this movement. Meistermann secured his reputation after 1945 with a series of stained-glass commissions; despite being banned from studying or exhibiting in 1933, he had completed his first such commission in 1938, for St Engelbert's in Solingen-Mangenberg. He carried on working throughout the war, producing windows for St Ulrich's, Frechen-Buschbell, in 1943–4. Much of his early work was destroyed in a bombing raid in 1944. His numerous postwar commissions include five windows for St Markus in the south-western town of Wittlich, in 1949.[6] Despite these activities, he achieved widespread recognition for the painting *Der Neue Adam* (The New Adam, c.1950), which won the 'Blevins-Davis' prize in 1950, a nationwide competition for artists born since 1910, sponsored by a theatrical producer from New York and held at the Central Art Collecting Point in Munich. Meistermann won 4,200 Marks and a trip to the USA (second prize was a trip to Rome, third a trip to Paris).[7] *Der Neue Adam* was cautiously described by Will Grohmann as being 'in the style of Picasso in his late period'.[8] Picasso was indeed the source of Meistermann's rather insipid semi-abstract image. 'One result of his religious devotion', wrote Werner Haftmann in 1955, 'is his bitter resistance to the secularisation of painting deriving from the casual dallying with colour forms. He feels he must grasp in his art the greater formative force at work behind the visible world'.[9] What we see in his prize-winning painting is difficult to square with either the artist's clearly religious intentions or with the enthusiastic claims made in response to the work. It was nevertheless sufficiently impressive to be included in Ottomar Domnick's *Die Schöpferischen Kräfte in der Abstrakten Malerei: ein Zyklus.*[10] As a painting giving off unmistakable modern signals, made by a believer for secular display, *Der Neue Adam* may be contrasted with Dix's *Madonna mit Stacheldracht*, a painting by a non-believer, in a traditional naturalistic style, intended for liturgical use.

The debates surrounding such works provide an essential insight into the politics and culture of the postwar West. That a theological interpretation of images was still possible suggests a link between religious art and modernism that has generally been

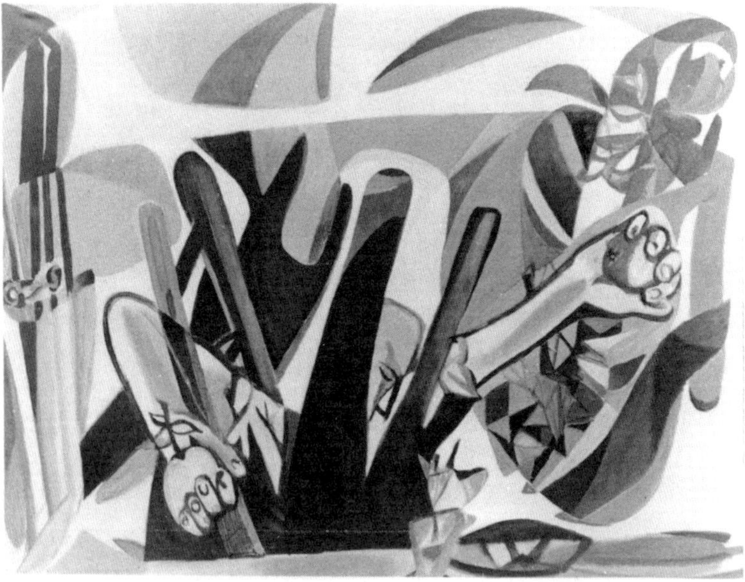

Georg Meistermann, *Der Neue Adam* (The New Adam), oil on canvas, Germanisches Nationalmuseum, Nürnberg

overlooked. Before the numerous 'postisms' that came about from the new critical climate of the early 1960s, a form of belief remained circumscribed in artistic styles that was never entirely foregone. One conclusion that may be drawn from the longevity of the Christian iconographic tradition in German art, and the continued interest in the possibility of modern religious art is that in the latter part of the twentieth century German art remained far more closely linked with modern formations than the 'neo avant-gardes' of France or America.

Given the fractured territories of postwar Germany, we should be cautious of drawing such neat conclusions. Discordant voices claimed attention in the discussion about modern art and religion. Three of these are prominent: the conservative anti-modern viewpoint; a political viewpoint; and the liberal view from the church itself, which saw modern art as a popular medium to combat the appeal of Communism and Existentialism. By examining each of these points in turn, through the example of a key spokesman, the shape of the postwar movement to renew a tradition of modern religious art may be drawn.

Although now largely forgotten, *Verlust der Mitte*, written by the Austrian art and architectural historian Hans Sedlmayr and first published in 1948, was undoubtedly the most influential art historical book to appear in the postwar decade.[11] The contents caused a sensation in the professional art world, and beyond, for years after its appearance. The 'loss of the middle' became a widespread slogan that

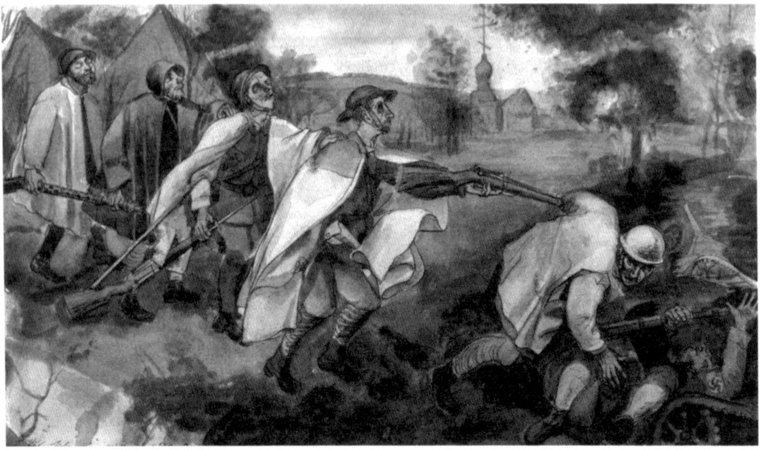

Karl Schleswig, *Das Gleichnis von den Blinden* (The Parable of the Blind), 1947, ink and watercolour on paper, 24 × 43 cm, Galerie Remmert und Barth, Düsseldorf

was used by conservative critics opposed to the avant-guardists who advocated abstraction.[12] Sedlmayr's jeremaid went far beyond simply lamenting the depletion of a traditional life-world, against which the conservatives railed: *Verlust der Mitte* is an extremist diatribe informed by hardline anti-modernist opinion. As a former Nazi and a committed Catholic, Sedlmayr himself was directly implicated with anti-liberal institutions. He had been driven out of his post as *Ordinarius* (full professor) at Vienna's Technische Hochschule in 1945 for his involvement with the Austrian Nazi Party and finished *Verlust der Mitte* during the ensuing period of unemployment in Bavaria, before being appointed (amid much protest) professor at the Munich Ludwigs-Maximilians-Universität in 1951.

The argument of Sedlmayr's book is at heart simple – modern art is an aberration that reflects the disintegrating and morally polluting effects of modernity itself. The composite arts of the Middle

Ages have been forever squandered by the isolation and degeneration of modern life. Nietzsche provides Sedlmayr with a resonant image of the horror of modern life: 'Are we not continually falling? – backwards, sideways and in all directions? *Do top and bottom still remain?* Are we not wandering through infinite nothingness? Is not the breath of empty space in our faces? Has it not grown colder?'[13] From Ernst Jünger, Sedlmayr gained support for the idea that nineteenth-century museum culture introduced a relativising attitude accompanied by a deadening impulse: 'it is in this museum-urge [*im musealen Trieb*] that our learning shows a face turned towards the death of things'.[14] Sedlmayr's scholarly references and compelling prose were the principal reasons for the success of *Verlust der Mitte* after 1945. Kenneth Clark described it as 'Nazi theory very intelligently done'.[15] After years of wearying Nazi rhetoric, such erudition and clarity of expression were refreshing, especially as it gave justification to a position – the moral rejection of non-figurative art – to which most adhered. Sedlmayr's book also provided an opportunity for conservative anti-modernists to shuck the undesirable association with Nazism by using Catholicism as the basis for their position. The art historian Frederic Schwartz has described *Verlust der Mitte* as a 'fine exercise in the gentle art of academic rebranding', suggesting that Sedlmayr was simply taking Nazi cultural policy and reframing it with the new 'alibi' of Catholic conservatism.[16] It may equally be read the other way around: Sedlmayr took a tradition of Catholic anti-modernism (of which Carl Schmitt was another prominent representative) and embellished it with elements of Nazi propaganda, in structure, language and tone. Apart from the rhetorical violence, the use of captions to denigrate the images reproduced is reminiscent of the bitter commentaries accompanying the exhibits of 'degenerate' art before the war. Georges Seurat's *Le Cirque*, for instance, is captioned 'Bald darauf wird bei Seurat der Mensch wie eine Holzpuppe, ein Mannequin oder ein Automat erscheinen' (According to Seurat, man will soon become a wooden puppet, a mannequin or an automaton).[17] It should nevertheless be remembered that Nazi propaganda was hardly likely to enlist traditional Christian imagery. If *Entartete Kunst* contained a section deriding modern religious art, then the alternative was not the Gothic cathedral, but heroic classicism.

In appealing to a post-Nazi world, Sedlmayr was playing to a like-minded audience rather than trying to make any new converts. It may seem astonishing now that he was not more roundly attacked for his fanatical account, which described modern life as being 'as though the gate to the nether world had been opened, and that world now pours into the whole life and infects every part of it'.[18] It must be remembered that at the time, there was little widespread scholarly attention being given to modern art. This was a moment when modernism itself was silently passing into history – a curious moment of overlap when the first documentary studies of the major movements could be read by the erstwhile protagonists of those movements. After 1945 it seemed that just about anyone expressing a scholarly interest, regardless of the views, was able to publish with authority a narrative of modern art – Sedlmayr himself did exactly this, writing the highly popular Rowolts Deutsche Enzyklopädie edition on the subject of *Die Revolution der modernen Kunst* (The Revolution of Modern Art).[19]

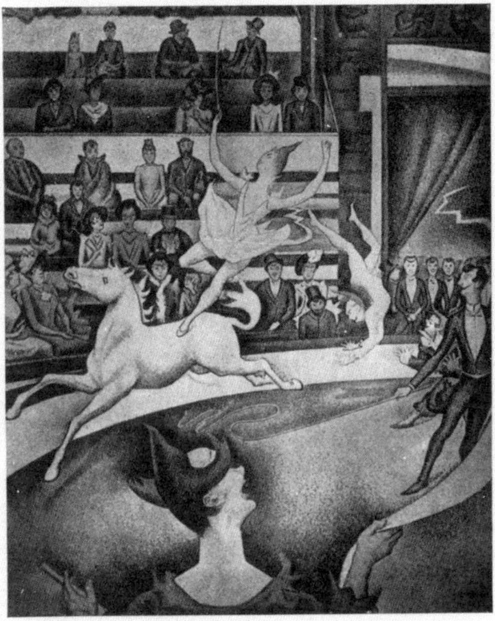

Abb. 52
SEURAT, DER ZIRKUS, 1890
Bald darauf wird bei Seurat der Mensch wie eine Holzpuppe, ein Mannequin oder ein Automat erscheinen (Seite 127)

Illustration of Georges Seurat's *Le Cirque* (The Circus), from *Verlust der Mitte*, Salzburg, 1948

Verlust der Mitte was contested in two notable public discussions. The first, the 1949 German art historians conference in Munich,[20] at which Werner Haftmann vigorously rejected Sedlmayr's book, was a preamble to the more historic Darmstädter Gespräch

(Darmstadt Debate) held in the middle of the next year, a 'cultural parliament', and a *cause célèbre*, where the heated confrontation between Sedlmayr and Baumeister came to symbolise the postwar confrontation of abstraction and figuration, under the heading of '*Das Menschenbild in unserer Zeit*' (The Image of Man in Our Time).

The published protocol of the Darmstädter Gespräch stands next to Sedlmayr's book as a crucial document of the time. Both books rotate around a philosophical discussion of the 'image of man', a discussion that provided intellectuals with the possibility of contributing to reconstruction culture. How this actually worked out in Darmstadt is equally revealing. Although the matters discussed and the positions taken where not new, the timing of the debate, less than a year after the founding of the Federal Republic, lent it the air of an intellectual christening. It was intended as an interdisciplinary conference lasting three days, but turned into a confrontation between Sedlmayr, his allies (very few), and his critics, primarily Willi Baumeister. As Adolf Schmoll's introduction to the exhibition catalogue made clear, the premise of the debate was to challenge the anthropocentrism of Sedlmayr's argument.[21] Nevertheless, papers given by a theologian (Adolf Köberle), a sociologist (Alfred Weber), a neurologist/clinical psychologist (Alexander Mitscherlich), a biologist (Wulf Emmo Ankel) and a philosopher (Karl Holzamer), gave a semblance of universalism to the debate. Theodor Adorno was also present. Apart from Baumeister, the artists Conrad Westphal, Rolf Cavael and Johannes Itten attended, the latter giving one of the two opening addresses: 'On the Possibilities of Modern Art', to which Sedlmayr replied with his observations 'On the Dangers of Modern Art'.[22]

The prospect was of a historic confrontation of conservative and liberal positions in the arts, a new public statement of ancient versus modern. The opportunity was, however, sadly missed. In the protocol of the conference Baumeister's speech stands as an uncompromising critique of Sedlmayr, and, importantly, the first one that made any reference to Sedlmayr's involvement in the Third Reich.[23] It is refreshing reading, the entrance of history and material conditions into an otherwise conceptually sealed debate. Unfortunately, due to the fact that Sedlmayr was absent, Baumeister chose not to deliver his prepared speech, and instead gave a talk about his own work. The disappointment that must have been felt at the time can only be marginally greater than that subsequently felt by historians of the period. The debate can at least be textually reconstructed with a rehearsal of Baumeister's address.

Baumeister's mention of Wilhelm Hausenstein in the title of his talk, 'Verteidigung der Modernen Kunst Gegen Sedlmayr und Hausenstein' (Defending Modern Art against Sedlmayr and Hausenstein) – refers to the book published by the critic in 1949, *Was Bedeutet die Moderne Kunst?* (What is Modern Art?), in which Hausenstein laments that the artists he supported before the First World War had not lived up to their promise, a position he had been repeating since 1919. Baumeister quickly dismisses Hausenstein by referring to newspaper reviews that condemn the book as fogeyish and senile.[24] The quarrel with Sedlmayr is taken, however, more seriously. He rejects Sedlmayr's notion that a vital centre has been lost, not, however, by challenging this transcendent concept, but by substituting his own, perhaps even vaguer concept of *Mitte*, based on a mix of philosophical speculation concerning the identity of subject and object, a sort of oneness with the *Weltstoff* (world-material) that artists can achieve by facing the unknown, abandoning habit and prejudice. This was the idea that he had advanced in his book *Das Unbekannte in der Kunst* written in 1943, and published in 1947.[25] Baumeister's *Mitte*, informed by his reading of Taoist and, significantly, medieval philosophy during the war, suggests a holistic apperception of the world, a timeless solution to the subject-object divide. The concept of *Weltanschauung* that arises from the subject-object divide has led, Baumeister suggests, to despotic views of art and nature: 'This harmless term [*Weltanschauung*] subsequently came to denote narcissism and despotism, as much as it came to stand for Nazism and the wholesale judgements of Spengler, Rosenberg and Sedlmayr'.[26] Sedlmayr's place in this lineage is, for Baumeister, indisputable. His secret longing for the forms of absolute dictatorship in past architecture made him accommodating to the most recent dictatorship. The spiritual belonging that he felt to this 'Goebbels-like perfidy and inflammatory rhetoric' (*Goebbelscher Perfidie und Hetze*) is now appearing again, barely five years after the end of the regime. This reminder of the fate of the prewar avant-garde would have struck his audience as an uncompromising public statement: 'Feeling this oppression, Kirchner shot himself in Switzerland. Unbearable depression led to Schlemmer's death in Baden. Ridiculed by Hitler's youth association, Barlach was attacked by stone-throwers in Güstrow. His home having been repeatedly turned upside down by the Gestapo, Klee died in exile'.[27] Despite these piercing observations, Baumeister withdrew from complete criticism of those implicated with the Nazi regime, stating that a line could be drawn with the past for those who had changed, although in Sedlmayr's case this was not possible. Apart from his involvement with Nazism, Baumeister attacks Sedlmayr for his conservative Catholicism, suggesting that he was attracted only to a type of figurative art, 'more papal than the Pope',[28] but then suggesting, more pertinently, that the Catholic view on modern art was in any case changing. He refers to the lectures given by the Abbé Morel at the Sorbonne in 1949 concerning modern art; to an exhibition of abstract art that the Vatican had overseen in Rome, and to the fact that a Catholic priest had not only opened an exhibition of abstract art in Freiburg, but had also written an approving article in a newspaper. Sedlmayr and Hausenstein had been left behind: 'Their opinions are subjective, and anyway out of date and therefore irrelevant'.[29] As such, Sedlmayr does the Catholic faith a disservice: his theories are more akin to the *Rassentheorie* (racial theories) of Alfred Rosenberg.

The limitations of Baumeister's position are as revealing as the substance of his argument. He does not recognise, for instance, that Sedlmayr may have exaggerated the Catholic sources of his anti-modernism to detract from his implication with Nazism. He also avoids the possibility that Sedlmayr's views could have arisen out of his formative experiences at Vienna University as a student of Alois Riegl and his position within the Vienna School tradition of stylistic cultural history – his pessimism, as one recent commentator has observed, was certainly Viennese, somewhere between the *Radetzky March* and Karl Krauss's *Letzten Tagen der Menschenheit* (The last Days of Mankind, 1919).[30] Others associated with this school are not noted for their enthusiasm for modern art. The tradition of anti-modernism is not just limited to those tainted by extreme political beliefs. Above all, there is no recognition of the possibility that Sedlmayr's views may be more representative of public opinion than Baumeister's own. George Grosz's positive response to Sedlmayr, which resulted in an enthusiastic exchange of letters between the Munich-based art historian and Grosz in New York, is one indication of Sedlmayr's often unexpected contemporary appeal.[31] Despite Baumeister's unique public recognition of Sedlmayr's Nazi sympathies, his own argument is limited and contained; that he himself promotes a concept of *Mitte* based on a transcendent identity of subject and object comes hardly as a breath of fresh air.

To this extent, the affinities between Baumeister and Sedlmayr's position may become more pressing than the differences. What Roland Recht describes as the '*religion du visible*', the idealist belief in the possibilities of intuitive engagement with pure form that links Baumeister with the nineteenth-century art historian Konrad Fiedler, can also describe his affinity with Sedlmayr.[32] As Hans Belting has suggested, the proximity of religious and artistic positions derived from their contribution to the search for a reconstructed self-consciousness.[33] Indeed, the defenders of abstraction believed that this art was the modern alternative to religion. The basis for the defence of abstraction was therefore carried out on religious grounds, the language of the discussion inflected by traditional ideas of belief and redemption, religion forwarded as the *legitimationsbasis* for contemporary art. The favoured notions of modern, abstract art look backwards to the 'transcendentalist claims characteristic of European abstraction in its first phase', rather than pre-empting the 'later structural model of abstraction which comes to dominate American art by the 60s'.[34]

Such 'transcendentalist claims' are strongly evident in the views of other participants. In the course of an open discussion, Gustav Hartlaub observed that in the face of the enormous presence of the Marxist threat, those who can no longer speak of a personal God see in art a successor to religious binding.[35] For Walter Winkler, speaking a short time later, modern art answers to the need of a deepening of inner life, through a concern with the forces of the unconscious, with primal symbols and the irrational, in the face of superficiality and kitsch, the materialism of technology, and the massification of man. Kurt Leonhard contests Sedlmayr's reading of modern art as atheistic by pointing to the fact that most of the founders of modernism used religious ideas as part of their effort to renew artistic form, at least in the shape of metaphysical or mystical thought, giving Kandinsky, Marc, Gleizes and 'even Mondrian' as examples.[36] Hans Hildebrandt quotes Oskar Schlemmer's remark that in the place of the symbols lacking for a public religious culture, private symbols, undoubtedly created by artists, have to operate.[37]

The attempt to counter Sedlmayr's arguments with a positive model of modernism led, as Adorno's contribution towards the end of the discussion made clear, to a failure to move beyond totalising categories. Adorno claims that, instead of rejecting Sedlmayr's argument and countering it with a *kosmischen, harmonischen* art, it should be accepted but subjected to a dialectical reasoning whereby the broken, fractured quality of modernism is seen as a true reflection of 'unreconciled' reality:

> As much as I oppose the cultural conservatism that Sedlmayr articulates, in this place he observes something very correct, something that those pursuing a linear and naive commitment to progress tend to neglect. In dialectical terms I would say that harmony in a modern work of art rests in its uncompromised expression of the irreconcilable, an expression that it refuses to cede, and that it is in this stubbornness, in this 'finding words for that which are ineffable' that lies the only true reconciliation, whereas every attempt to achieve harmony directly in modern art, such as by the appeal to the idea of the cosmic, really only means that we attempt, out of embarrassment with our exposure to the irreconcilable, to establish the type of relation to the past that should in fact be broken with.[38]

The lack of resonance and response to Adorno's words at the time points to a broader inability to think in such critical terms. His contributions were deemed by certain reports to have been completely unfathomable.

The content of the Darmstädter Gespräch and the success of *Verlust der Mitte* demonstrate that the history of modern art was still associated in Germany, both on a scholarly and a popular level, with the continuing legacy of Western Christianity – in particular with the legacy of an ideal Christian society that had existed before the Renaissance and the Reformation, and which after 1945 appeared as an island in the past to which troubled consciences could flee. It also shows what those advocating a reconciliation of religious and modern idiom were up against – what amounted in the case of Sedlmayr to a veritable inquisition of the avant-garde.

The poet Stephen Spender made two visits to occupied Germany in the first months after the war. His task was to gather information about the 'lives and ideas of German intellectuals', and to discover if there was any 'surviving talent' in German literature. In August of 1945, he visited the ruins of Cologne and interviewed the former Mayor, Konrad Adenauer. Considering Adenauer's subsequent role as the first Chancellor of the Federal Republic and spiritual father of West Germany, this was a felicitous encounter. Adenauer explained the tasks facing postwar Germany:

> There are two aspects of reconstruction which we consider of equal importance. One, the material rebuilding of the city. But just as important is the creation of a new spiritual life. You can't have failed to notice that the Nazis have laid German culture just as flat as the ruins of the Rhineland and the Ruhr. Fifteen years of Nazi rule have left Germany a spiritual desert, and perhaps it is more necessary to draw attention to this than to the physical ruins, for the spiritual devastation is not so apparent. There is a hunger and a thirst now for spiritual values in Germany. This is

especially true in Cologne because here, in the past, we have had such a significant spiritual life and activity.[39]

In his diary of the period, Adenaeur notes that the 'hardly bearable' conditions of the first few years after defeat were redeemed by 'a search for strength to come to terms with life, a search that led to religion and art'.[40]

The turn to 'spiritual life' was on one hand a compensation for the moral disaster of Nazism, as well as the dark surrealism of everyday life; and on the other, more prosaically, a Catholic restoration. As a prominent figure in the founding of the CDU, and its subsequent leader, Adenaeur was motivated by the goal of rebuilding the Catholic church to a position of strength that it had not enjoyed in Germany since the historical challenges of Luther in the fifteenth century, as well as those of the liberal/Protestant/Prussian Bismarck, in the *Kulturkampf* of the late nineteenth century. Cologne as *Hauptstadt* (capital) of the Rhineland was an important centre of this effort. Adenauer had been mayor of Cologne for the duration of the Weimar Republic, and was also significant after 1945 in establishing the seat of the Federal Republic in Bonn, on the banks of the Rhine just to the South. What Berlin once was for Bismarck's Prussian-dominated Germany, Cologne and the Rhenish West were intended to be for the western-integrated Catholic restoration.

As part of the gathering assertion of conservative political structures, Adenauer's CDU was quick to shake off the strong element of Christian Socialism that had formed an important part of its beginnings in 1945. In 1964 Walter Dirks, a prominent representative of Socialist Catholicism after 1945, looked back to the widespread excitement at the possibility of Christian renewal and the re-spiritualisation of society: 'Many Catholics dreamt at the time of a Christian society, along the lines of a renewal of a Christian Abendland'.[41] The efforts of those such as Walter Dirks and Eugen Kogon, who founded the newspaper *Frankfurte Hefte* in 1946 as a mouthpiece for a Socialism based on Christian responsibility were, however, soon marginalised and the development of the party, rather than prioritising social needs, led inexorably to the neo-liberal principles of the social market economy.

Such conservatism was further distinguished by an inclusive, composite character. At the time of the founding of the Cologne CDU in 1945, Adenauer recognised that several strong political constituencies – both Catholic and Protestant groups, the remnants of the prewar Centre Party, and liberals – could concorporate to counter Communist and Socialist forces with a Christian, occidental conservatism.[42] The political ideal was one of ecumenicalism, though under a Catholic umbrella. The move to include Protestants in a non-denominational Christian party was aimed at overcoming the political split between the two Christian camps that had marred relations ever since the formation of the predominantly Catholic Centre Party, after the *Kulturkampf*, a split that had weakened centrist, liberal forces in the face of Marxism and nationalism.[43] It also avoided exclusion on the basis of class, aiming to represent all *Volksschichten* (levels of the populace). A Christian basis for a reconstructive party was, for Adenauer, the only way of unifying the German people, resisting the 'form of state and world ideas of the East', and providing the 'conceptual and cultural link, and hence also a link in foreign policy' with the wider western world.[44] Such a western orientation, strongly linked with the spiritual concept of the *Abendland*, which functioned as a quasi-religious binding concept for North-West Europe, led the philosopher Karl Jaspers to christen Adenauer the *Staatsman des Abendlandes*. Noel Annan recalls meeting Adenaeur in December 1945 and hearing him express 'concern that *Westliches Christentum* and *Abendländische Kultur* should be preserved'.[45]

The *Abendland* was the 'Evening Land', the part of the world in which the sun set, by contrast with the *Morgenland* of the East. As a descriptive synonym for 'occident' however, the term came to acquire strong overtones of conservative nostalgia as it figured in the title of Oswald Spengler's enormously influential book *Der Untergang des Abendlandes* (The Decline of the West), published in two parts in 1918 and 1922. Conservative nostalgia continued to underpin the word as it was used in political and cultural contexts after 1945, as did the influence of Spengler: for Willibald Sauerländer, Hans Sedlmayr was 'a second Spengler in neo-Thomist form'.[46] For art historians, the notion of *Abendland* provided a link to an acceptable tradition of pre-modern German art, and to a German Reich – the Holy Roman Empire – unpolluted by modernity. It also looked forward to the scenario of European unification, by creating the possibility of a pan-European common culture. In the journal he founded and edited from 1946–51, *Geistige Welt*, the medievalist art historian Hans Jantzen wrote of the possibilities the tradition of *abendländischer* art presented for surmounting political and linguistic differences.[47] The two central references for this tradition, by which the *abendländische Völke* could find a common cause, were Christianity and Antiquity. Jantzen concised a reactionary idealism that was to find elaboration in numerous exhibitions and publications, all of which drew on a sweeping vision of world culture. As Hans Belting has described, the 'escape into Occidental culture' was based on the idea of a pre-modern, pre-national Latin West that, like the empires of antiquity, had declined in the face of barbarism, but (unlike Imperial Rome) could be politically resurrected.[48] The idealised Latin West was, as Belting puts it, synonymous with Catholic Europe before the Reformation. Thus the Occidental ideal was supposedly antithetical not only to modernism but also to the Protestant Church. Hans Jantzen's own survey of Ottonian art published in 1947, whose photographs of churches taken before the Allied Bombardments appear as melancholy apparitions of buildings that at the time of publication were in ruins, was a part of this postwar tradition of art history that found solace in an undisturbed past.

It would seem, then, that modern art – non-naturalistic, abstract or Surrealist – had no place in the continental region of the *Abendland*. Sedlmayr's anti-modern position, it has been argued, was 'admirably suited to represent the aesthetic of the Adenauer era'. In fact, the reverse was true – it was precisely around the stylistic banner of abstraction that the political restoration in the West coalesced. In the 'Heideggerian' abstraction of those artists associated with Zen 49, led by the patriarch of abstraction, Willi Baumeister, reality was subsumed into free-floating emblems of democratic consciousness. Official sanction of this idiom continued the promotion of abstraction by the Western Allies as part of the re-education programme.

Underlying this liberalising spirit was the broader move after 1945 for reconciliation of Catholicism with the modern world. Baumeister's short description of this reform in the case of the visual arts, mentioned above, can be extended. On an official level, the Catholic Church had not been slow in condemning the apostasies of modernity in the early part of the century. In a definitive encyclical of 1907, Pius X had decried the 'profane novelties' of theological modernism, a position that was developed by his successor, Pius XI, who, on being made Pope in 1922, identified 'a species of moral, legal, and social modernism' that was to be fought against as much as theological modernism.[49] Hans Sedlmayr, howling against the disintegration of the post-Kantian world from his imaginary Gothic cathedral, provided the full elaboration of this position in his *Verlust der Mitte*.

Sedlmayr's views were, however, increasingly marginalised in relation to the general position of the Catholic Church on 'modern' art. This change was largely motivated by the need to regain lost constituents, and counter the mass appeal of Communism. An encyclical promulgated by Pius XII in November 1947, *Mediator Dei*, reversed the Vatican's policy concerning modernism, this time making the connection to the fine arts clearer than in previous statements. 'Recent works of art which lend themselves to the materials of modern composition, should not be universally despised and rejected through prejudice', the letter ran, though it asserted that such art should preserve a balance between 'extreme realism' and 'excessive "symbolism"', a prescient comment in light of the gathering public confrontation of abstraction and realism as political styles.[50]

Although moving beyond the postwar decade, the denouement of these developments in the early 1960s is worth mentioning – if only because it is part of a history of modern art that has not yet been told. The Second Vatican Council, which ran from 1962 to 1965, was unprecedented both in its scale, and in the extent to which it directly addressed the question of the place of the Catholic Church in the modern world. It was also the moment when liturgical adornment achieved an importance it had not known since the Counter Reformation – the Constitution *Sacrosanctum Concilium*, promulgated by Pope Paul VI on 4 December 1963, contained a chapter dealing with 'Sacred Art and Furnishings'. Still, the question of sacred art was dealt with in a highly allusive manner: 'The Church has not adopted any particular style of art as her own; she has admitted styles from every period [...] The art of our own days, coming from every race and region, is also to be given free scope, provided that it adorns the sacred buildings and holy rites with due reverence and honour'. Such openness to contemporary styles was not, however, combined with an overtly democratic attitude: the rights of censorship were retained. 'Bishops should carefully and insistently remove from churches and other holy places the works, produced by some artists, which do not accord with faith, morals and Christian piety, and which offend true religious sense either by depraved forms or by lack of artistic worth, mediocrity or pretense'. In addition, the constitution advocated the founding of 'schools or academies of sacred art [...] so that artists and craftsmen may be trained'.[51] The liberalising spirit of Vatican II was nevertheless shown by the suppression of the *Index librorum prohibitorum*, the list of books proscribed by the Catholic

Church, finally announced in December 1966, though the last condemnation had taken place in 1961, and the last publication of the list of forbidden books had appeared in 1948.[52] During the 1950s the complete works both of Jean-Paul Sartre and André Gide had been declared, *opera omnia*, out of bounds.

If this was a reconciliation of artists with the Church, then it was not without compromise. On 7 May 1964, Pope Paul VI gave an address to a group of Italian artists gathered in the Sistine Chapel, during which he admitted the mutual alienation of Church and artists, trying in the process to balance the blame:

> You have, as artists, somewhat abandoned [our] friendship: you have gone far afield to drink at other fountains, seeking to express other things. You know that we carry a certain unease at heart as we see you intent on artistic expressions which offend us, the guardian of the whole mankind, the guardian of the complete definition of man, of his soundness and stability.

But the Church was also at fault for imposing on artists 'as a first canon' the imperative of 'conventional imitation'.[53] The watershed for Catholic attitudes towards modern religious art came with the opening of the Collezione vaticana d'arte religiosa moderna in 1973.[54]

In the late 1940s, authoritarian Catholicism was increasingly superseded by liberal attitudes geared to retaining popular support in the face of Communism (in France, the larger political presence of Communism resulted in a *rapprochement* policy adopted by the Communists towards the Catholics) and the acceleration of consumer culture in the 1950s.[55] Oskar Kokoschka's (falsely) rumoured visit to Rome in 1949 to portray Pius XII, following his visit to Florence in December of the previous year, when he painted the portrait of the Archbishop of Florence, Cardinal Elia dalla Costa, was symptomatic of a broadening interest in modern art from the Catholic Church, and would have sent a shiver down the spines of conservative Catholics such as Sedlmayr.[56] It was largely due to these reforms that the question of reconciling the Catholic Church with the distinctive forms of twentieth-century art could be raised. Adenauer's search for religion and art implied not only that Catholicism could provide an ethical basis for the art of a new era, but also that Catholicism itself could be, to a certain extent, re-imagined in a new era of international relations. The lacuna between advanced art and general public opinion highlighted by Sedlmayr's text meant, however, that it was down to the concerted efforts of certain individuals to create the frame within which modern religious art could become effective.

In 1947, the Catholic art historian Hugo Schnell (1904–81) founded the journal *Das Münster*, a 'Journal for Christian Art and Art History' (*Zeitschrift für Christliche Kunst und Kunstwissenschaft*). This followed his activities as a publisher before the war; in 1934 he had created a publishing house for the production of small, scholarly guides to the art and architecture of churches in Germany.[57] Both before and

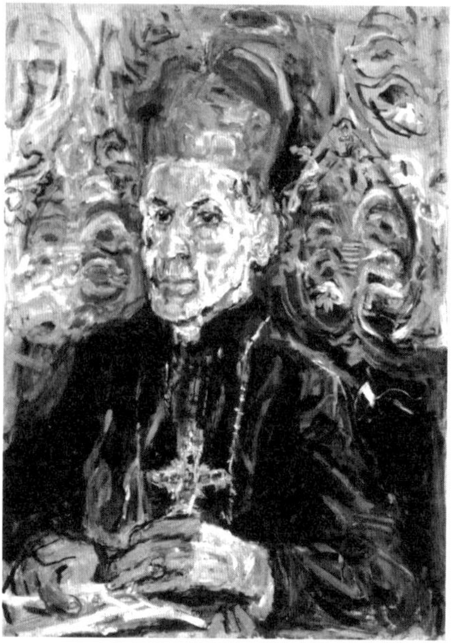

Oskar Kokoschka, *Cardinal Elia dalla Costa*, 1948, oil on canvas, 98.1 × 71.7 cm, The Phillips Collection, Washington, DC

after the war, Schnell was deeply interested in the possibility of a Catholic avant garde, and was keenly aware that a model for such a movement could be found in France. He was an attentive reader of the journal *Cahiers de l'art sacré*, a valuable source of information about developments further west, where a revival of Catholic thought in literature, the *Renouveau catholique*, provided the background for a more general revitalisation of culture from religious premises. A French tradition of modern religious art could be traced back not only to Maurice Denis, who was able in his work both as an artist and a theorist to reconcile Catholic piety and a Symbolist aesthetic, but also to the younger artist Georges Rouault, whose depth of religious intention, as we shall see, was a particularly rich example for the post-1945 generation. This was a continuous tradition that had developed through the agency of major artists. During a lecture given in Munich in 1960, on the centenary of the Verein für Christliche Kunst in München (Association for Christian Art in Munich), Schnell perceived the possibility for such a tradition in Germany, but was aware that it had suffered many frustrations. Franz Marc, for instance, had stood at the beginning of the 'New Era' of modern religious art, but due to his early death had been unable to fulfill his promise.[58]

Schnell was not only active in promoting religious art, but also in documenting modern religious architecture, on which subject he was later to publish a comprehensive book.[59] The exhibitions of religious art and architecture that he organised, in particular *Arte Liturgica in Germania 1945–55* (Liturgical Art of Germania) at the Lateran in Rome during Spring 1956, and *Kirchenbau der Gegenwart in Deutschland* (Contemporary Church Architecture in Germany), held in Munich in 1960, emphasised architecture and conservative decoration at the expense of more avant-garde works in sculpture or painting. The modern religious art movement that had arisen in the 1920s had indeed found its most forward looking expression in church architecture – for Schnell, a successful idiom had been achieved soon after 1918 – 'clear cubic forms, austere in their lines'[60] – a tradition that was successfully rehabilitated after 1945, primarily in the Rhineland.

The architect Dominikus Böhm (1880–1955) was clearly the major source of energy both in creating the movement of 'clear cubic forms', and sustaining it through to the postwar period. Böhm built a number of churches in the early 1920s characterised by a simplicity of form and novel use of materials such as poured concrete. In an extensive programme of church building throughout the following two decades, he incorporated the austere formal impulses of *Sachlichkeit* culture, but also ideas from the Liturgical Movement, a movement designed to reform the Catholic liturgy and make it more accessible to a broad congregation. He was to provide illustrations for Josef van Acken's important 1922 publication *Christozentrische Kirchenkunst. Ein Entwurf zum liturgischen Gesamtkunstwerk* (Christocentric Ecclesiastical Art: Towards a Liturgical Gesamtkunstwerk), which set out these reforms for artists and architects, in particular the requirement that the altar should be

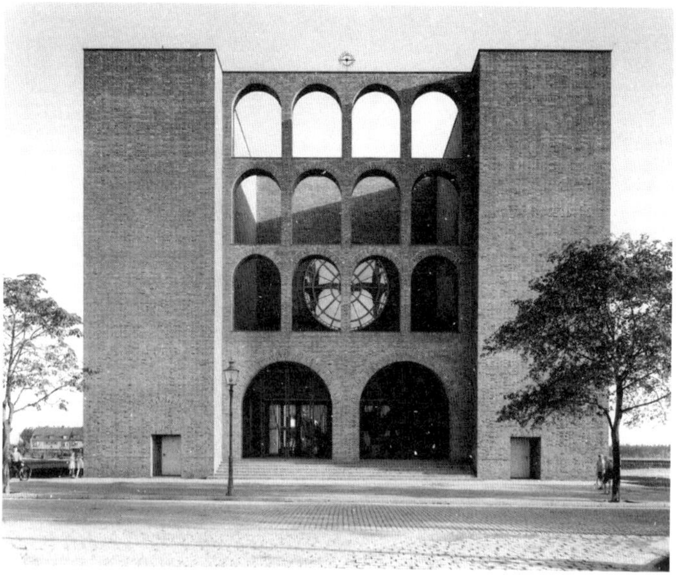

Dominikus Böhm, St. Josef, Hindenburg (now Zabrze, Poland), 1929–31. Photo: Hugo Schmolz

placed in a central position. In 1926, Böhm was called by Konrad Adenauer, at that point, Mayor of Cologne, to be professor of sacred art at the newly-formed Werkschulen in Cologne. With his churches of the early 1930s, in particular St Engelbert's at Köln-Riehl (1930–2), Böhm achieved a new level of international attention, but also found himself at the centre of a debate about the use of such innovatory styles – a use most Catholic authorities clearly abhorred. Although he was strongly criticised by Catholic authorities, his modernising impulses were combined with a historicism that looked back to Romanesque and early Christian sources and therefore made it difficult to condemn his buildings as outright modern. His early membership of the Werkbund was as much an influence as the visits he had made to North Italy just before the First World War. Böhm avoided all debates about modern or traditional styles, the kind of debates that were held in the journal *Die Christliche Kunst*, the organ of the Munich-based Deutsche Gesellschaft für Christliche Kunst (German Society for Christian Art), one of the leading societies for the promotion of religious art in Weimar Germany. Despite this aversion, he was nevertheless lauded after 1945 as a leading modernist, and seen as a precursor for Corbusier's rebuilding of the pilgrimage chapel of Notre-Dame-du-Haut at Ronchamp (1950–54). Böhm's position 'Between God and Cubism' was confirmed in the most important manifestation of modern religious art in Germany just after the War, the exhibition *Christliche Kunst der Gegenwart* (Christian Art of our Times), staged in Cologne in 1948, despite the recent currency reform, as part of celebrations marking the seven hundredth anniversary year of the founding of Cologne Cathedral.

The exhibition had sections devoted to twentieth-century church building, religious art from six European countries, including 275 German and fifty-three English artists, and a central gallery conceived as a memorial to, amongst others, Ernst Barlach, Käthe Kollwitz and Christian Rohlfs. With over 1,000 objects, it was also the largest exhibition to be staged anywhere in Germany during the period 1945–9. The religious purpose of the exhibition was by no means hidden behind the range of modern art on display. Visitors were met at the entrance with an excerpt from Pius XII's 1947 encyclical *Mediator Dei*, expressing the new climate of liberalism in attitudes towards modernism. *Christliche Kunst der Gegenwart* was shown in a changed format the next year in Ravensburg and then in Freiburg.[61]

Hugo Schnell's long report of the 1948 exhibition, published in *Das Münster*, makes clear the documentary intent of the display, and the broad coverage given to works by both religious and non-religious artists.[62] As a gathering together of ranks and a stock-taking of tradition, *Christliche Kunst der Gegenwart* looks forward to the first documenta exhibition, held in Kassel seven years later – though Schnell was critical of the Kassel exhibition for ignoring the broad tradition of Christian iconography in modern art.[63]

Alongside the architecture of both Böhm and Rudolf Schwarz on display in the 1948 exhibition, a tradition of modern Christian iconography was also evident in figurative sculpture. The allusive imagery of works by Kollwitz, who had died in 1945, and Barlach, who had died in 1938, meant that both artists were being claimed for a tradition of Realism in the East (although religious modernism was not absent here, as we shall see), and also in the

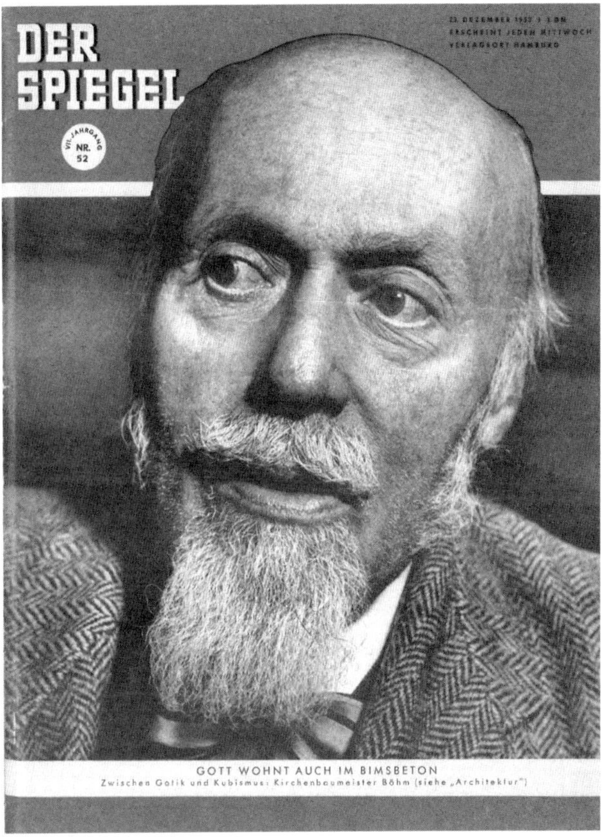

'Gott wohnt auch im Bimsbeton. Zwischen Gott und Kubismus: Kirchenbaumeister Böhm' (God Dwells also in Concrete. Between God and Cubism: Böhm the Church Architect), front cover of *Der Spiegel*, nr. 52, 1953

West as representatives of religious modernism. Much the same can be said for Gerhard Marcks (from 1946 active as a teacher in Hamburg), works by whom were also exhibited in the 1948 exhibition.[64] Marck's five terracotta figures made in 1947 for the Katharinenkirche in Lübeck are typical of his neutral figuration, semi-caricatured and ideologically available. They also represent a direct, unruffled continuation of prewar sculpture, since they complete the commission originally given to Barlach, who was only able to finish three of the eight figures to be displayed on the church's facade. Marcks also added a *Schmerzensmann* (Man of Sorrows) figure in the niche that Barlach had intended to leave empty.[65] Ewald Mataré, by contrast, produced work from a religious position, with explicit Christian iconography and ecclesiastical function. Works by Mataré exhibited in the 1948 exhibition show the type of inoffensive compromise that characterised ecclesiastical commissions at the time, which provoked little disagreement.

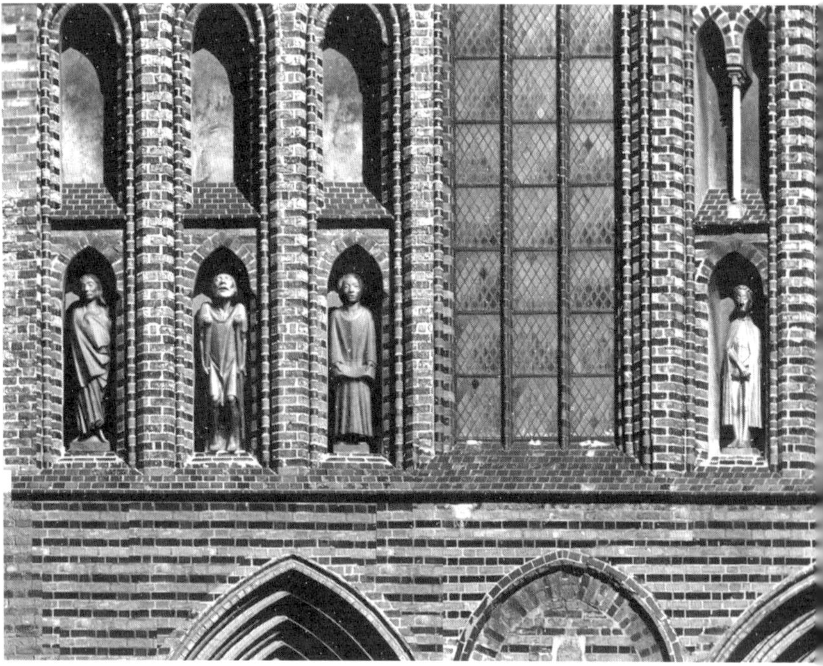

Modern religious painting appeared more problematic in the 1948 exhibition. Like many visitors, Schnell held that one of the central works on display, Emil Nolde's polyptich *Das Leben Christi* (The Life of Christ) was 'questionable'. Schnell was joining a long tradition of resistance to the departure from naturalism evident in Nolde's painting. In 1910, Max Liebermann had demanded the withdrawal of the work from the Berlin Secession exhibition, and two years later, Karl Ernst Osthaus was required to remove the work from the *International Exhibition of Modern Religious Art* in Brussels. It was again criticised as part of the negative reaction that met the

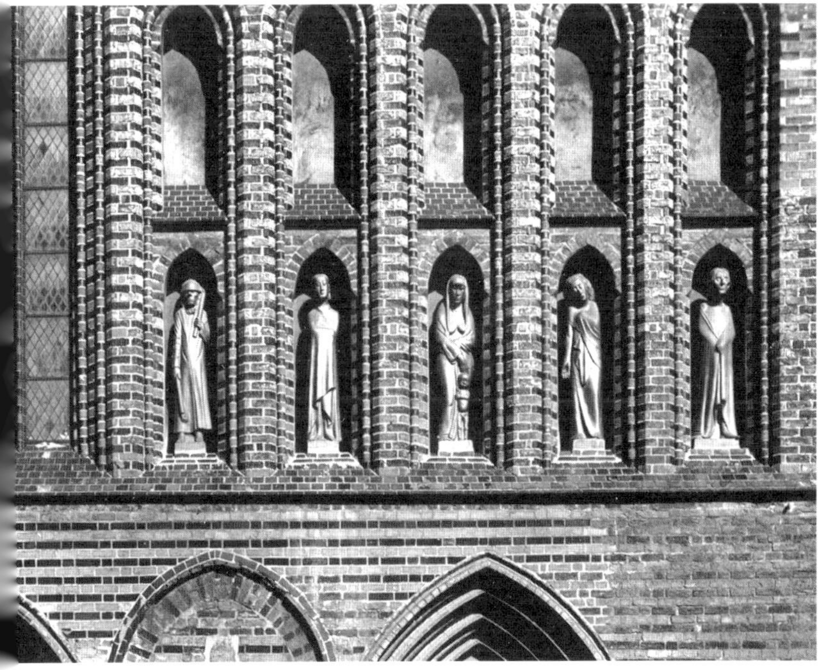

Figures by Ernst Barlach (three on far left; 1930–32) and Gerhard Marcks (1947) on the façade of the Katharinenkirche, Lübeck

exhibition *Religiöse Bilder Emil Noldes*, mounted in the Katharinenkirche in Lübeck by Carl Georg Heise in 1921.[66] The culmination of this discontent was without doubt the inclusion of the work in the 1937 *Entartete Kunst* exhibition. Despite this history, Nolde appears to have been less a test-case for religious painting than Otto Dix, represented in the exhibition by three paintings made after 1945. Although the themes of Dix's paintings belong to Christian iconography, Schnell observes, he retains a 'sociological' engagement with his time. *Hiob* (Job, 1946) represents a beleagured figure lying amongst the ruins, with barely any trace of the biblical Job's continued confidence in God in the face of misfortune.

A liberal definition of sacral art meant that artists such as Dix, who, rather than making cult images, used Christian imagery, could be included. Here was raised the problem of religious effect, and the ineluctable fact that the most powerful works were by artists who did not position themselves as Christian artists. Further, there was a conflict between works being attached to a particular artist's name, and the ecclesiastical demand that they function as impersonal inspirations to religious piety – a conflict between the 'author-function' and the 'devotional-function'. This was further complicated by the association of religious art with traditional, handmade techniques: it would have appeared strange to ask if there could ever be such a thing as religious photography, or a religious film. Indeed, Canon Law at that time forbade the decoration of churches with images reproduced in series.[67] Questions about the artistic status of mechanical reproductions could not be reconciled with questions of religious effect.

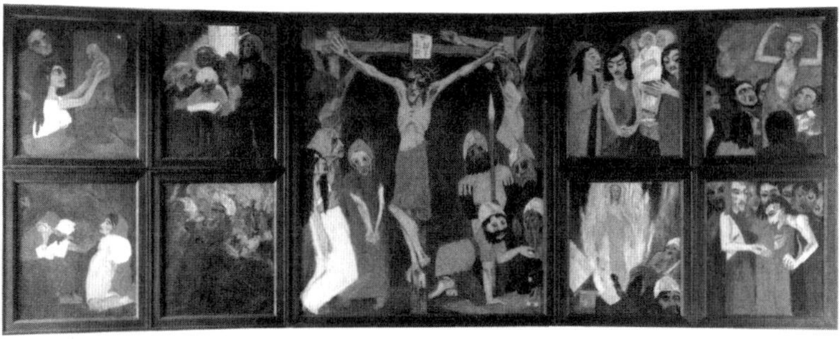

Emil Nolde, *Das Leben Christi*, (The Life of Christ), 1911-12, 9 paintings, oil on canvas, 200 × 535 cm, Nolde-Stiftung, Seebüll

With all these sticking points, it is not surprising that there was resistance to the claims for a modern religious art. For Werner Haftmann, none of the works in the 1948 exhibition could fulfil such a role. Schnell cites Haftmann's cogent summary of this dilemma: 'The cult image, the devotional image – where are they?! It must be said that nowadays it is only possible for artists to produce religious art as church decoration. What is barred to them is the possibility of producing true religious art – with true emotion'.[68]

'True religious art' was in the first place determined, as Haftmann suggests, by whether it was produced with true emotion; a matter then of artistic intention. To be effective as cult or devotional images, however, such art would also have to provoke a specific type of contemplation, not orientated by rational judgement, but as an inspiration to piety. By this argument, both artist and viewer had to submit to a 'religious emotion' that took the place of considered aesthetic reflection. The fault line between requirements for liturgical art and characteristics of the modern movement becomes acute; simply put, the modern work of art had struggled for its independence, and was reluctant to be replaced within an authoritarian schema. Put another way, the fault line between spiritual and critical definitions of art finds two aesthetic ideologies grinding against each other: the demand that the artist function as a sort of secular priest, with the museum as his church, meshes awkwardly with the notion that modern art should constitute a philosophical exercise in individual freedom.

Such problems are the result of the distinctions made between 'sacred' and 'profane' art, and as such exist solely on the level of ideas. Most of the *Kirchliche Kunst* debated and displayed around 1950 was not necessarily destined for liturgical use; the concept was employed more to cover the general utilisation of Christian motifs in modernism, and the notion that there could be some kind of equivalence between the religious and expressive charge of a work of art, both qualities being based on the avant-garde status of the work. As Martin Papenbrock has observed, the Church's use of non-Christian art, often by those who had been branded *entartet*, was a way of securing broad public resonance for exhibitions organised by the Church, and to demonstrate the social and cultural role played by the Church in reconstruction.[69]

Distinctions were nevertheless debated and upheld. Christian art produced outside of formal religious structures was termed by the former *bauhäusler* Lothar Schreyer *Außerkirchliche christliche Kunst* – Christian art made outside the church.[70] This distinction was keenly upheld by those within the Church who felt that simply depicting religious subject matter did not necessarily produce devout art. A short commentary on exhibitions of contemporary Christian art in the journal *Das Münster*, in 1948, pointed to the conflict between 'free' artistic production and the demands and responsibilities of making art for the church.[71] But if those within the Church wanted to reinforce the boundary between sacred and profane, critics from the outside were more interested in eliding the distinctions.

Contributing to the *Kirche und Kunst* debate in 1951, Will Grohmann suggests that it is the Church's responsibility to accept existing traditions of religious painting: neither Nolde nor Beckmann had found their way into the visual liturgy, hanging instead in museums and private collections. For Grohmann, only Barlach managed to make the transition from a secular to a religious setting, for instance with the ceramic figures in the niches of the Lübeck Katharinenkirche. There is a sense of frustration in Grohmann's article that the affinity between modern art and religion, which he describes mostly in terms of the spiritual, transcendent claims of Expressionist painting, had not been formalised by the placing of works of art in churches. Moreover, the type of art that exemplifies this *Einbruch des Ewigen in die Gegenwart* (the appearance in the everyday of eternal values) is now to be found elsewhere – Henry Moore has taken the mantle from Barlach, Rouault is the equivalent of Nolde, and the Swiss Louis Moilliet is the heir of Marc and Klee (Louis Moilliet, 1880–1962, had been a close friend of Klee and Macke, travelling with them to Tunisia in 1914. Moilliet represented continuity as the only survivor of this particular friendship-circle, rather than through his work as an artist. He largely stopped working as an artist around 1936, with the exception of a handful of church commissions for stained glass windows).[72] Grohmann appears to be lamenting the loss of a specifically German combination of formal innovation and spirituality, blaming it on the lack of any organisation dedicated to this essentially romantic tradition.

Such a description appears accurate. In comparison with the Art Sacré movement in France, centred on the journal *Cahiers de l'art sacré* and the project to commission works by modern artists such as Léger, Rouault and Pierre Bonnard for the Eglise Notre-dame-de-toute-grâce at Assy,[73] there was no combined effort to create a movement of Christian modernism in postwar Germany. However, this did not mean that there were fewer artists involved in making religious art. Leopold Zahn makes this point in the issue of *Das Kunstwerk* dedicated to Art Sacré in 1951, in an article framed as a reply to Hans Sedlmayr's identification of modern art with atheism. As evidence for the rapprochement between the Church and artists, he refers to the 1948 Cologne exhibition *Christliche Kunst der Gegenwart*, which he describes as a dress-rehearsal for the exhibition *Esposizione internationale Arte Sacra* in Rome two years later.[74] However, despite a list of German artists working '*ad majorem dei gloriam*', Zahn concludes that there is no single project able to bring these artists together in the same way that the Assy project had done in France. A series of exhibitions in postwar Paris had served to consolidate the Art Sacré movement, including the exhibition organised in 1947 by the Abbé Morel at the Galerie René Drouin, *Pour un Art religieux*; the 1951 retrospective exhibition of *Art Sacré* held at the Musée national d'Art Moderne; and the first and second Salons for *Art Sacré*, held in 1951 and 1952. There were at least as many exhibitions of *Kirchliche Kunst* in Germany during this period. One of the earliest was *Christliche Kunst der Gegenwart*, organised by the Cologne-based Gesellschaft für Christliche Kultur in December 1946.[75] The Munich-based society Deutsche Gesellschaft für Christliche Kunst e.V. instated the exhibition *Zeitgenössische Christliche Kunst* (Contemporary Christian Art) the next year.[76] Although *Das Münster* reviewed six exhibitions of contemporary religious art in 1950, this count decreased dramatically over the following five years, suggesting that this year was the high point for enthusiasm and debate about the possibility of contemporary religious art. Nevertheless, the insistence in Germany on distinguishing between 'authentic' and 'inauthentic' art hampered any attempt to rival the liberal, ecumenical balance that had been delicately struck in France. Rather than create a contemporary ecclesiastical *Gesamtkunstwerk* like Assy, the emphasis in Germany was more on determining which art was acceptable as church art, and trying to establish this, via exhibitions such as the 1948 Cologne *Christliche Kunst der Gegenwart* in an international context.

It was clear that for art to be a source of salvation, it could not remain in the clouds of transcendence or otherwise recall the simple morality of biblical examples. For painting or sculpture to transform the depleted life-world, it had to have some critical impulse, some historical viewpoint. It had also to confront the question of realism, 'visual democracy' and the dangers of kitsch. The struggle against kitsch had in fact motivated much modern religious art in France, against the background of the *Saint-Sulpicien* aesthetic of popular Catholic art; described by William Rubin as the 'special brand' of kitsch 'produced commercially in series' and sold around the church of Saint-Sulpice in Paris.[77] In Germany, *Kirchliche Kunst* also became a key referent in the debate concerning kitsch during the 1940s and 50s. Heinrich Schüling's bibliography of publications on kitsch reveals that interest in the phenomenon reached a high point in the postwar decade.[78] A correlation could certainly be drawn between the number of books published from the late nineteenth century on the subject of religious art and those dealing with kitsch. That the two were concrescent is also not surprising: Richard Egenter's *Kitsch und Christenleben* (Kitsch and Christian Life), first published in 1950, stands out as one of the most sustained attacks on the threat posed by kitsch to Catholicism, and begins by asking the rather pointed question: 'Is Kitsch a Sin?'

The long list of books bibliographed by Schüling attests to a significant ongoing debate about kitsch since the late 1900s. The progressive wish to collide art and life – to ennoble everyday life with the forms of high culture, or to create a meaningful mass culture – stands at the root of this debate. Kitsch was perceived as the antithesis of high culture, and as such required substantial definition as a type of necessary evil. The debate in Germany was certainly part of a broader climate of discriminating the *echt* from the *unecht* (the true from the false). The dangers of *pseudo-kunst* were present for a generation of artists caught on the wave of renewal that culminated in the First World War. More prosaically, as we have seen, artists distinguished between amateur and professional work by the use of quality-control stamps. Identification of quality was once the legislative domain of connoisseurs who would exercise an intuitive apperception of authenticity (Max Friedländer's account of his own experiences as a connoisseur was published in 1929 as *Echt und Unecht: aus den Erfahrungen des Kunstkenners* – True and False: from the Experiences of an Art Connoisseur). The distinction between true and false was drawn differently according to the ends of those involved in making or interpreting art. In the Soviet Zone, as we shall see, kitsch was allied with formalism as the political style of Western Imperialism, although was not subject to any more precise definition. For those artists concerned with a Christian avant garde, the moment of self-definition depended on identifying and reacting to the insidious kitsch that had infiltrated the great European traditions of religious painting.

The stained-glass windows created by Rouault for the famous artists' church at Assy were exhibited in Germany before finally being installed. In the exhibition devoted to contemporary French painting, *Meister Französischer Malerei der Gegenwart*, which opened in Freiburg in 1947, a separate room was reserved for Rouault's windows in order, as the organisers explained, to ensure that the works achieved their proper effect. As one of the leading religious modernists, Rouault's presence in this exhibition along with that of Braque, Chagall, Gris, Léger, Matisse and Picasso would have lent weight to the assertion of a French Catholic avant garde.

Above all it was Rouault who succeeded in forging a modern religious artistic idiom. This impression was confirmed by the tour of his *Miserere* print portfolio through the western zones during 1949–50. The exhibition contained forty-five etchings and aquatints (of a series of fifty-eight), originally commissioned in 1912 by the art dealer Ambroise Vollard for publication in two separate series, *Miserere* and *Guerre*, to be accompanied by texts by the poet André Suarès. The plates arose from drawings made during the First World War that were reworked using a complex and laborious combination of photomechanical and manual procedures. They were eventually cancelled by Vollard after disagreements with Rouault.[79] It was not until 1948, nine years after Vollard's death, that the series was published in Paris by L'Étoile filante, and exhibited at the Galerie des Garets. After this showing, it travelled straight to Germany, stopping at Cologne, Freiburg, Munich (shown by Günther Franke, July–August 1949), Stuttgart, Hamburg, Mannheim, Frankfurt, Ulm, Münster, Kaiserslautern and Karlsruhe, whence it travelled to the Berlin Haus am Waldsee in April/May 1950.[80] The tour was organised by the Direction générale des affaires culturelles, Service des relations artistiques, and was thus part of the cultural propaganda mounted by the French in occupied Germany. The 1949–50 exhibition took place as Rouault's reputation was being firmly established on an international level: following a retrospective at the Museum of Modern Art, New York, in 1945, his work was shown in the French Pavilion at the 1948 Venice Biennale. These came in the wake of a spate of exhibitions in Paris and America around 1940, the year in which Lionello Venturi's monograph on the artist appeared. Despite this enthusiasm, Rouault was still being condemned on an official level by the Catholic Church – in 1950, a print from the *Miserere* series was rejected from the large exhibition of religious art staged in Rome

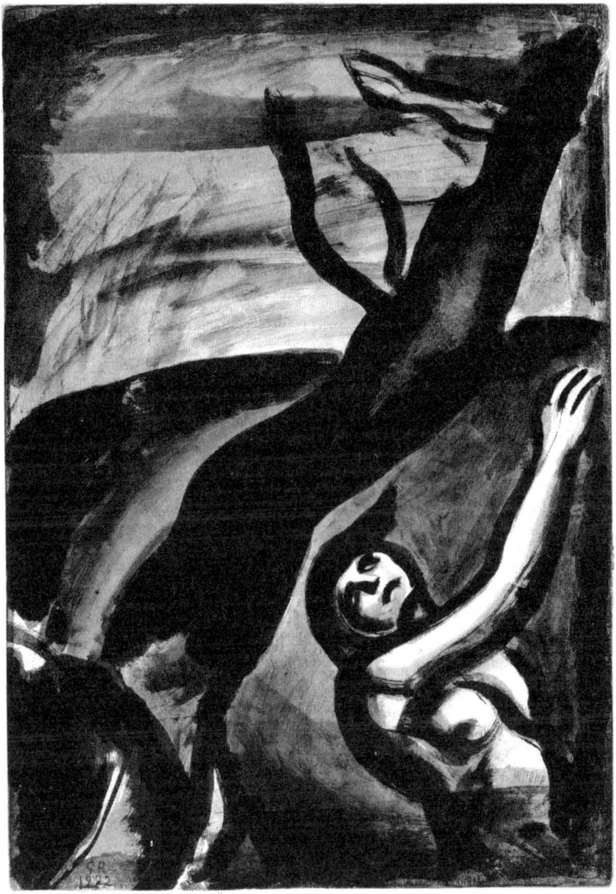

Georges Rouault, *Demain sera beau, disait le naufragé* (Tomorrow will be beautiful, said the shipwrecked man), plate 11 of the print portfolio 'Miserere', 1912–1927, aquatint, roulette, and drypoint over heliogravure, 63.5 × 48.3 cm

that year, and the Vatican was vocal in its condemnation of his work as insufficiently religious in feeling; in 1954 Cardinal Costantini described his work as contributing to the 'anti-catholic offensive'.[81] It was, as William Rubin describes, his tendency to see religious

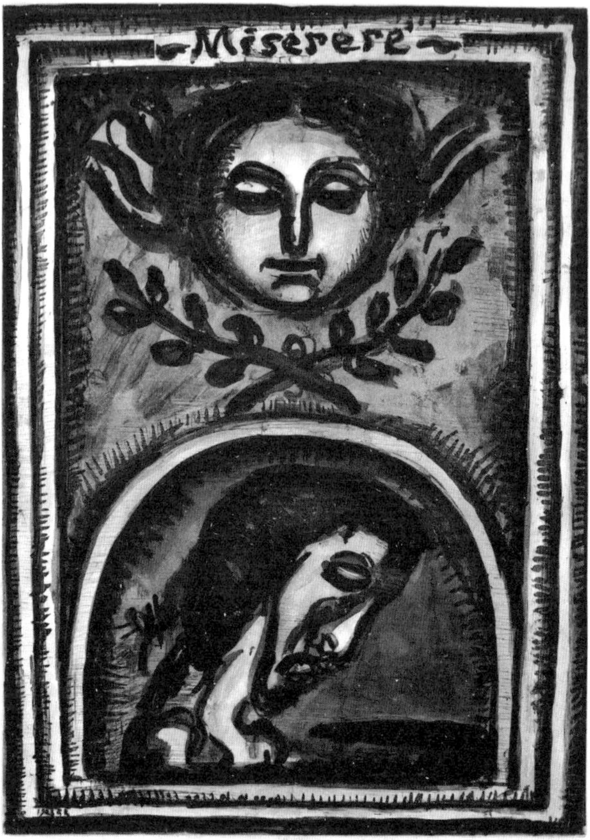

Georges Rouault, *Miserere mei, Deus, secundum magnam misericordiam tuam* (Have mercy upon me, O God, according to thy loving-kindness), frontispiece of the print portfolio 'Miserere', 1912-1927, aquatint, roulette, and drypoint over heliogravure, 63.5 × 48.3 cm

devotion as arising through commitment to and practice of painting that was antithetical to the Church's emphasis on formal religious devotion. Rubin himself agrees with this criticism, describing Rouault's 'oblique' relation to the Church as preventing any possibility of the work having a liturgical function.[82]

The dominant theme of Rouault's portfolio is suffering, expressed not only through traditional religious iconography but also by more allusive themes such as in the print 'Tomorrow will be beautiful, said the shipwrecked man', or the frontispiece to the second part, 'Guerre', captioned by Rouault: 'The very ruins have been destroyed.' That Rouault included sections commenting on contemporary French life may have suggested a comparison with the print portfolio created by Otto Dix in 1924, *Der Krieg*, which offered with a comparable lack of narrative, though with much more descriptive scenery, the effects of war on human life. In his review of the 1948 exhibition Hugo Schnell had praised Dix for his ability to produce works that are acceptable as sacral works but also manage to fulfill the task of Zeit-reportage ('*Zeitaufgeschlossen*'). Much the same could be said of Rouault.

The *Miserere* prints had a remarkably positive reception in Germany. For Werner Haftmann, who, as we have seen, fostered brooding doubts that authentic religious feeling could be distilled in a modern artwork, Rouault represented the forefront of the neo-Catholic movement, the *Renouveau catholique*, that reached from the writers Charles Péguy to Paul Claudel and the thinkers Léon Bloy to Jacques Maritain.[83] Following Bloy (though Bloy says this not of Maritain, as Haftmann suggests, but of Rouault himself), Haftmann describes Rouault as the 'Job on the dung heap of modern civilisation'. Further, though the merciless picture of the world that the artist provides in these prints may have chimed, so wrote Haftmann, with a hardened Protestant viewpoint, Rouault's religious sensibility is somehow deeper than confessional allegiance: 'And yet there is such eagerness, seriousness and severity in these prints, a quality which appears to rest in something other than the mercy and security so characteristic of Catholic man. The secret of the artist's doleful vision can be found in an underlying differentiation of sensation'.[84]

Rouault's success in Germany was noted by a report produced by the French High Commission citing the approval of the Berlin press, both East and West. The *Neue Zeitung* deemed Rouault the only expressive painter in France, who had more affinities with Nolde, Beckmann and Kokoschka than with his compatriots, though he was a product of the radical Catholic milieu of Bloy, Maritain, Suarès and Huysmans. A similar response – Rouault as French Expressionist – had been elicited by the inclusion of his work in the exhibition *Die Meister Französischer Malerei*.[85] The *Telegraf* reported that this 'Celtic Breton', though spiritually affined with the mediaeval cathedral, could nevertheless express the torments of contemporary history.[86] Adolf Weis, writing in the Catholic journal *Hochland*, declared Rouault the leading Christian artist of his time, since he was able to combine authentic religious expression with modern art: 'Indeed, profound freedom allowed religious vision and artistic form to merge in his best works, to such an extent that it was unsure whether a significant Christian was expressing himself as a great artist, or whether the much disputed modern art had here, for once, opened its very core to Christianity'.[87]

Such resonance can be ascribed not only to Rouault's Catholicism, but also to the allegorical nature of the *Miserere* images. Although they had originally been inspired by the First World War, in fact no direct references to war can be found in the fifty-eight images; even the word *Guerre* was suppressed for the 1948 publication and exhibition tour. Here, it appeared, were images that could float above the broken landscape and tortured divisions, images that evoked, in a modern, privatised language, an ancient Catholic unity.

An extraordinarily fragile drawing made in 1951 by a young, unknown artist from the Rhineland may be read as an expression of penitence, or of lamentation; or simply as a comment on the miserable circumstances of postwar life. It appears to have been inspired by the print *Miserere mei, Deus, secundum magnam misericordiam tuam*, from Rouault's *Miserere* portfolio. In the absence of known documentary sources it can only be supposed that the artist, Joseph Beuys, saw the print during its Cologne or Münster showing, or perhaps through a reproduction in circulation. The motif surfaces again in a watercolour of 1956, again showing a depleted head inclined to the right with the inscription '*Miserere*'. Beuys may have been moved, though we do not know, by Rouault's spiritual commitment, and the spiritual authenticity of his print, encrusted with pious labour, intended to inspire devotion by its very physical presence. He may also have been inspired by Rouault's ambiguous relationship with the Roman Catholic Church.

While a student of Ewald Mataré at the Düsseldorf Kunstakademie (1947–51) and for a few years afterwards, Beuys made sculptures and drawings that were strongly shaped by contemporary trends in *Kirchliche Kunst*. In the late 1940s, he assisted Mataré with a number of ecclesiastical sculptural commissions,

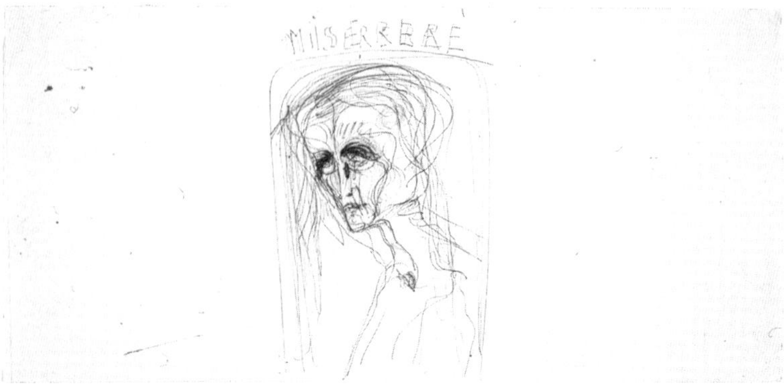

Joseph Beuys, *Miserere*, c.1951, pencil on paper, 23.6 × 50.2 cm, Stiftung Museum Schloss Moyland

including, in 1948, a new set of doors for the south portal of Cologne Cathedral.[88] Mataré, who was strongly associated with religious art, was impressed by the 'rhythmic feeling' of the young artist as he helped him with a number of commissions, and foresaw that he would become a successful sculptor.[89] Although religious imagery, particularly the crucifix, continued to play an important role in his work, that he stopped at the doors of the Cathedral in 1948 is telling. His criticisms of the Church were recorded in an interview that he gave to Rainer Rappman in 1975 – Christianity has developed, he suggests, not within the Church but within the arena of scientific endeavour, and the confessional Church since Luther has been nothing but a hindrance.[90]

Rouault's *Miserere* portfolio raises the question whether religious art should function purely as an aid to devotion, or whether it should also mirror the anguished spiritual status of modern man. Both the anti-establishment character of Rouault's belief in aesthetic experience, and the strength of his individual vision, epitomise the French model that was made available at this time as part of the cultural occupation of Germany. Beuys's engagement, however, echoes the closer connections that had existed between Rouault and Max Beckmann before the Second World War, summarised at the time by Will Grohmann: 'The Catholic Rouault remains at the source of Christianity, the Protestant Beckmann still seeks it'.[91]

The development of religious themes in Beuys's work over the next thirty years occurred as general interest in the possibility of modern religious art dwindled. If anything, Beuys's political stance put him in conflict with the Church: on his dismissal from the Düsseldorf Kunstakademie in 1972, Norbert Kricke, at that time the director, complained that Beuys saw himself as a 'representative of the suffering: he plays the Messiah; he wants to convert us, he wants to let the Academy take over the role of the Church – that is, for me, his *Jesu-Kitsch*'.[92] Certainly his famous action at the 1964 *Fest der neuen Kunst* (Festival of New Art) in Aachen, where, after being struck by a dissatisfied member of the audience, he held aloft a crucifix and saluted the audience, does not dispel this impression. We may take this as proof that the *Nachleben* of religious iconography in twentieth-century art constitutes a type of secular theology: 'a mentality which rejects dogmatic substance and moral rules yet conserves the exterior forms of a rational edifice and retains its instinctive fascination for rites and liturgical figuration'. Yet this would suggest a mere decorative intent, and ignore the religious, expressive effect required of otherwise mute works of art by their creators or interpreters.

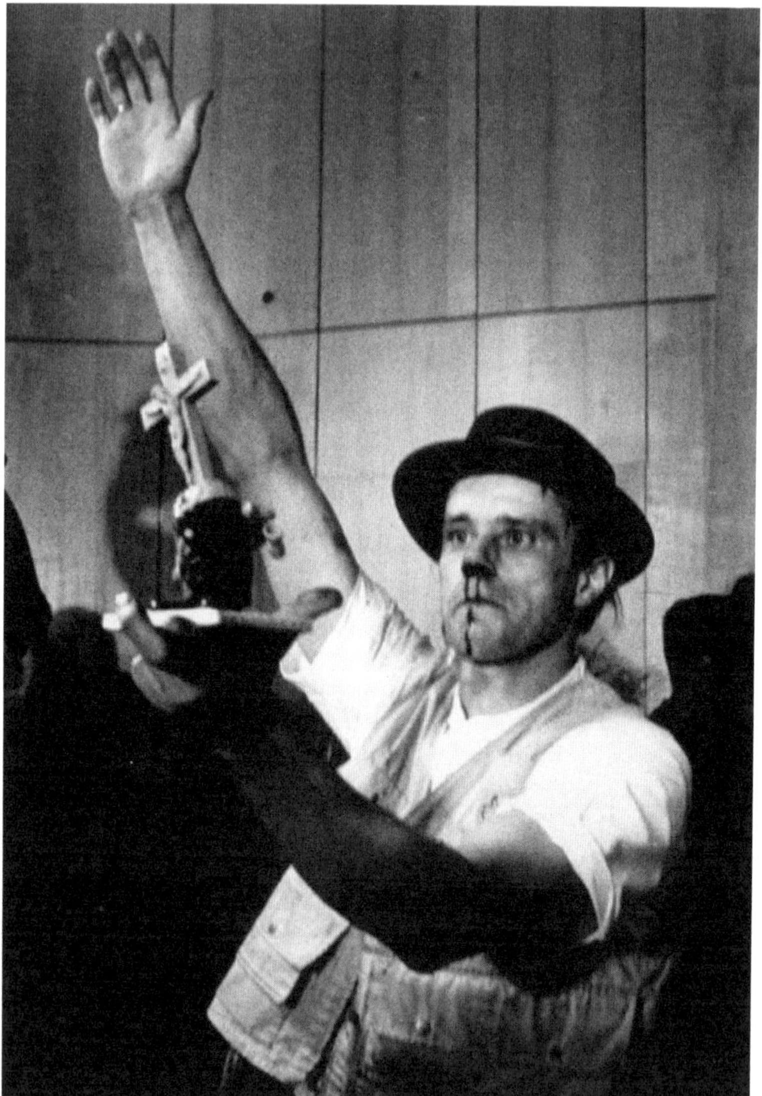

Joseph Beuys during the action *Kukei, akopee-Nein! Braunkreuz, Fettecken, Modellfettecken*, Festival der Neuen Kunst, 20 July 1964, Technische Hochschule, Aachen

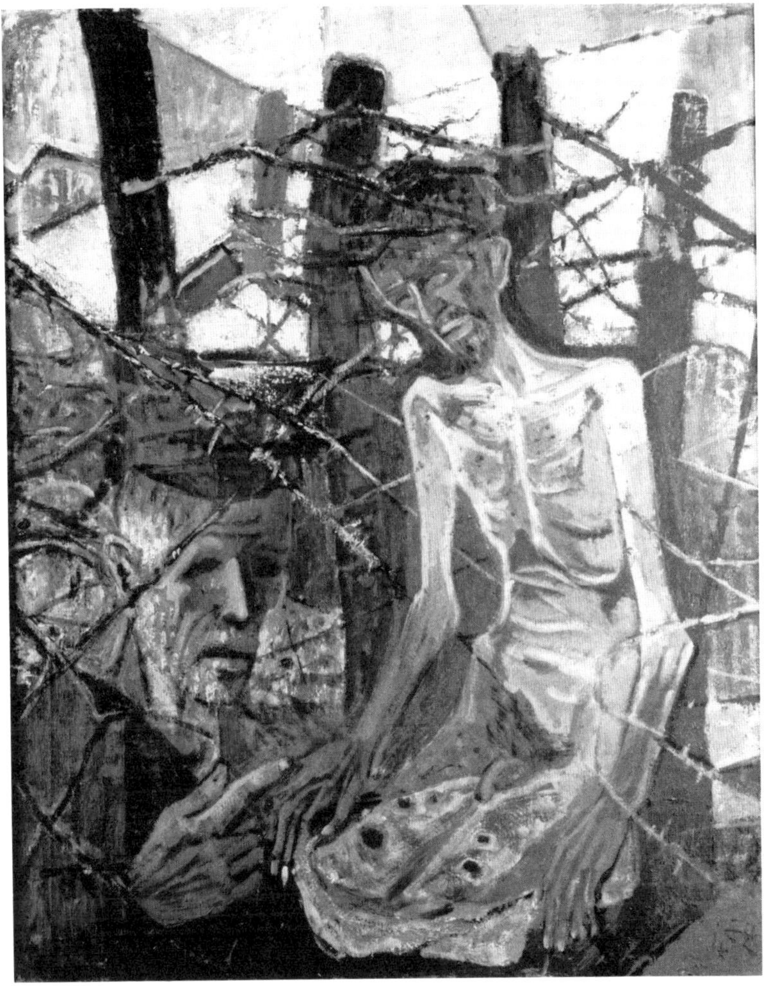

Otto Dix, *Ecce Homo II*, 1948, oil on canvas, 100 × 81 cm, Museum Ludwig, Cologne

Interest in modern religious art was far less in evidence in the Soviet Zone, and had relatively little significance in the cultural life of East Germany. The numinous claims for paintings or sculptures as modern relics with social healing properties were, of course, far from the requirements of Socialist Realism. Paintings with religious themes were still, however, exhibited after 1945, and could be assimilated into the anti-fascist aesthetic, particularly, as Martin Papenbrock has pointed out, those made during the Third Reich, such as the series of paintings of St Christopher made from 1938 to 1944, or the painting depicting the desolation of Flanders from 1936.[93] Otto Dix's *Kreuztragung* (Carrying the Cross), painted in 1946, was one of the three works shown in the *Allgemeine Deutsche Kunstausstellung* of the same year. Perhaps more than any other painting made at this moment, the *Kreuztragung* demonstrates Dix's ability to work between East and West. The faltering Christ is helped by a worker wearing a cap, a figure reminiscent of Dix's proletariate paintings of the 1920s and 30s. Will Grohmann may have been thinking of this painting when he noted, in March 1947: 'There are West Germans and others who are attached to the East and its mentality, its social structure and human qualities, its scarce yet succinct messages, its instinctive and thus immediate position regarding all questions of life. Dix is one of them; his pictures are testimony to this fact.' Grohmann, rector of the Hochschule für Werkkunst and professor of Art History at the Kunsthochschule in Dresden from 1947–9, had invited Dix to become a Professor at the Dresden Academy, an invitation (not taken up) that when made public caused heated exchanges between artists and critics. This debate picked at the potential kitsch-status of works made during and after the war, and the degree to which this affected Dix's role as a model for the younger generation. Hans Eckstein, in February 1947, draws attention to the wartime landscapes and prewar works such as *Nelly mit Spielzeug* (Nelly with Toy), the sickly sweet portrait of Dix's daughter, paintings that were first seen in 1946 at an exhibition held at Tübingen-Reutlinger. He could equally have mentioned any of the numerous religious works that Dix made at this moment, for instance *Auferstehungen Christi II* (Resurrection II). For Eckstein, the recent change in Dix's style and the questions of quality that it raises are no surprise – he claims to have been in full agreement with Carl Einstein in 1931 over Dix's status as a 'Reactionary painter of left-wing motifs'.[94] Dix was subject to many other criticisms at this moment, most of them focusing on the 'emptiness' of his technique, some conceding that his work was at least an accurate reflection of the depleted life-world.[95]

A spirited defence of Dix's work, including his output after 1939, was published by Fritz Löffler in 1949, who discerned a resurfacing of the earlier revolutionary period in Dix's painting around 1914.[96] But the religious themes that now replaced the proletarian imagery of the earlier period could hardly sustain this comparison. In response to the large exhibition of works by Dix held at the Dresdener Staatliche Kunstsammmlungen in 1949, a review in *bildende kunst* described the disappointment of those who had admired Dix's bold social criticism of the 'Dresden years'.[97] The promise of *kulturelle Einheit* (cultural unity) held out by Dix's work, often on the basis of religious subject matter, was largely unrealised.

The paintings submitted by Dix for the *Dritte Deutsche Kunstausstellung* (Third German Art Exhibition) were rejected by members of the jury (although it should be noted that it was the Western jurors who turned Dix down). Although he was to receive many honours, including election to the East Berlin Deutsche Akademie der Künste in 1956, and another large exhibition of his work the next year in East Berlin that contained many postwar paintings,[98] his work ceases to have any relevance to contemporary developments. Dix was strongly against abstraction, as his argument with Grohmann over the latter's support of Kandinsky and Klee demonstrates, but this derived from a diffuse conservatism rather than from Soviet sympathies.[99] His late religious work, despite strong support from Fritz Löffler, seems emblematic of this retreat, and emblematic perhaps of the wider failure to translate traditional religious themes into a modern idiom.

Conservative Catholicism, and modern religious art are linked, but not coterminous. The former opens into the reception and construction of the Middle Ages in twentieth-century thought. This in turn quickly leads attention away from Sedlmayr's censorious views and the history of the Index: as Bruce Holsinger has recently shown, even a theorist as radical as Georges Bataille is grounded in medieval literature, citing, appropriately enough for this context, his essay *Notre-Dame de Rheims*, a 'pious encomium' to the ruins of a cathedral destroyed by German bombs during the First World War.[100]

This reading of medieval sources presents an intriguing challenge and counter to Sedlmayr's anathema. If what contemporary theorists take from Aquinas, Augustine and others is an alternative to the Enlightenment model of progress and rational mastery, modern religious art may also be considered a distinct tradition, establishing a relation to the past not on rational interpretation and technological overcoming, but rather on a liturgical, sacramental basis, more like a musical echo than a measured development. This by no means implies a Gothic revival, but an alternative history of modern art, rooted in French and German traditions, and reaching a crescendo in the decade after 1945.

1 Cf. Lecoq-Ramond, 1995, 62–89.
2 Lankheit, 1959, 43.
3 Cf. Bahr, 1996.
4 Schlemmer, 1958, 148.
5 Cf. Pollack,D., 'Secularisation in Germany after 1945', in: Klessman, 2001, 105–25, here 105.
6 Germanisches Nationalmuseum, 63–87; Ruhrberg, 1986, 138–44.
7 'Die 10 Preisträger des Blevins-Davis Kunst-Wettbewerbes', *Das Kunstwerk*, no. 2, 1950, 62.
8 Grohmann, 1958, 184.
9 Haftmann, W., 'German Abstract Painters', trans. Donald A. McKenzie, *College Art Journal*, vol. 14, no. 4, Summer 1995, 332–9, here 339.
10 Domnick, 1947.
11 Sedlmayr, 1957 (1948).
12 Press and Information Office of the German Federal Government, 336.
13 Nietzsche, F., excerpt from the fragment 'Der Tolle Mensch', *Die fröhliche Wissenschaft*, Leipzig, 1887, 153.
14 Jünger, E., *Das Abenteuerliche Herz*, Hamburg 1938.
15 Kenneth Clark to T.S. Boase, 30 May 1951. TGA 8812.1.2.784.
16 Schwartz, 246.
17 Sedlmayr, 1948, 192.
18 Sedlmayr, 1957 (1948), 172.
19 Sedlmayr, 1961 (1955).
20 Cf. Glaser, 1985, 240.
21 Evers, 14.
22 Ibid., 28.
23 Ibid., 146–55.
24 Ibid., 148.
25 Baumeister, 1947; Hirner; Recht, R., 'Le combat pour l'art de Willi Baumeister', in: Lecoq-Ramond, 1999, 183–203.
26 Evers, 147.
27 Ibid., 149.
28 Ibid., 148.
29 Ibid., 149.

30 Sauerländer, W., 'Von den 'Sonderleistungen Deutscher Kunst' zur 'Ars Sacra'. Kunstgeschichte in Deutschland 1945–50', in: Pehle, 183.
31 Flavell, 264.
32 Recht, R., 'Le combat pour l'art de Willi Baumeister', in: Lecoq-Ramond, 1999, 183–203, here 189.
33 Belting, H., 'Bilderstreit: ein Streit um die Moderne', in: Gohr and Gachnang, 1989, 15–28, here 20.
34 Fer, 9.
35 Evers, 93.
36 Ibid., 111.
37 Ibid., 122.
38 Ibid., 215–6.
39 Spender, 50–1.
40 Adenauer, 1966 (1), 66–7.
41 Dirks, W., 'Das Gesellschaftspolitik Engagement der deutschen Katholiken seit 1945', *Frankfurter Hefte*, no. 11, 1964, 761. Cf. Ruhl.
42 Schwarz; Annan, 1983.
43 Schwarz, 335–6.
44 Letter to Schlarnagh, Mayor of Munich, 21 August 1945, cited in Schwarz, 1995, 339. Cf. also: Adenauer, 1965, 50.
45 Annan, 1983, 12.
46 Sauerländer, W., 'Von den 'Sonderleistungen Deutscher Kunst' zur 'Ars Sacra'. Kunstgeschichte in Deutschland 1945–50', in: Pehle, 182.
47 Jantzen, H., 'Die Einheit Europas in der Geschichte Seiner Kunst', *Geistige Welt*, no. 3, December 1948, 115–7.
48 Belting, 1998.
49 Pope Pius X, 'Pascendi Dominici Gregis', in: Ihm, 71–98, here 71; Pope Pius XI, 'Ubi arcano Die consilio', in: ibid., 225–39, here 237.
50 Pope Pius XII, 'Mediator Dei', in: Ihm, 119–54, here 149.
51 'Of Sacred Arts and Furnishings', Chapter VII of the *Constitution on the Sacred Liturgy*; trans. Fr. Clifford Howell and reprinted in: Rothenstein, 16–20.
52 DeBujunda, 29.
53 'Address of Pope Paul VI to a group of Italian artists, given in the Sistine Chapel, 7 May 1964', in: Rothenstein, 5–10, here 6–7.
54 Fallani.
55 Cf. Coleman, 1993.
56 Anon., 'The Pope in the Expressionist style', *bildende kunst*, no. 5, 1949, 168.
57 Lothar Altmann, 'Schnell, Hugo Karl Maria', *Neuen Deutschen Biographie*, vol. 23 (in preparation).
58 Schnell, 1962, 30.
59 Schnell, 1974 (1973).
60 Ibid., 84.
61 Ibid., 83.
62 Hugo Schnell, 'Christliche Kunst der Gegenwart. Internationale Ausstellung Köln im Domjahr 1948', *Das Münster*, vol. 2, no. 7/8, January/February 1949, 193–218.
63 Schnell, 1962, 104.
64 Rudloff, 1989, 294–305.
65 Rudloff, 1978.
66 Reuther, M., 'Emil Noldes religiöse Bilder. Das Werk und sein geistiger Ort', in: Chiappini, 1994.
67 Rubin, 11.
68 Hugo Schnell, 'Christliche Kunst der Gegenwart. Internationale Ausstellung Köln im Domjahr 1948', *Das Münster*, vol. 2, no. 7/8, January/February 1949, 193–218, 214.
69 Papenbrock, 1996, 20.
70 Schreyer, 1959.
71 Klimoff, E., 'Ein Wort zu Ausstellungen Christlicher Kunst', *Das Münster*, no. 3/4, 1948, 113–4.

72 Grohmann, W., 'Einbruch des Ewigen in die Gegenwart. Kirche und Kunst, Erneuerung und Ewigkeit', *Die Neue Zeitung*, 15 July 1951. Mss copy deposited in FMS.

73 Rubin. Billot, M., 'Le père couturier et l'art sacré', in: Centre Georges Pompidou, 1981, 196–200. Cf. also: Wilson, S., 'Catholics, Communists and Art Sacré', unpublished essay.

74 Zahn, L., 'Kirche und Moderne Kunst', *Das Kunstwerk*, no. 1, 1951, 32–9, here 32. For the Rome exhibition cf. Régamey, R.P., 'Die Moderne Christliche Kunst im Drama Unsere Zeit', *Das Münster*, no. 1/2, Jan/Feb 1951, 49–55.

75 Cf. Braunfels, W., 'Kölner Christliche Kunst der Gegenwart', *Das Münster*, no. 1, July/August 1947, 58.

76 Schnell, H., 'Zeitgenössische Christliche Kunst. Ausstellung der Deutschen Gesellschaft für christliche Kunst e.V. München', *Das Münster*, no. 3/4, September/October 1947, 94–9.

77 Rubin, 10.

78 Schüling.

79 Cf. Schniewind, C.O., 'The Technique of George Rouault's Prints', in: Soby, 29–32.

80 Haus am Waldsee, unpaginated; Blunt, 1963.

81 Rubin, 95.

82 Ibid.

83 Cf. Bahr, 92–125.

84 Haftmann, W., 'Hiob der modernen Zivilisation', *Der Zeit*, 11 August 1949, 4.

85 Gießler, R., 'Kunst des 20. Jahrhunderts. Zur Freiburger Ausstellung Die Meister französischer Malerei', *Badische Zeitung*, 31 October 1947, 7.

86 'Les expositions françaises. Le "Miserere" de Georges Rouault à Berlin', Archives d'occupation française en Allemagne et en Autriche, Colmar, AC 460/7. Copy deposited in HAW.

87 Weis, A., 'Georges Rouault', *Hochland*, 1949/50, 310–12, here 312.

88 Cf. Mataré, entry for 22 July 1948, 153; Cologne, 1987, 153; Trier, E., 'Matarés Neues Domportal', *Das Kunstwerk*, 3/4, 1953, 83.

89 Mataré, entry for 2 December 1948, 376.

90 Harlan, 17.

91 Grohmann, 1930.

92 Translation from Moffit, 14.

93 Papenbrock, 1996, 20.

94 Einstein, 185.

95 Eckstein, H., 'Revolutionär oder Reaktionär? Wiederberufung von Otto Dix an die Dresdener Akademie', *Der Tagesspiegel*, no. 45, 22 February 1947, unpaginated. Variant published as 'Otto Dix – eine bestätigte Enttäuschung', *Süddeutsche Zeitung*, 27 September 1946, 5; 'P.G.', 'Der Maler Otto Dix', *Sächsische Zeitung. Organ der Sozialistischen Einhietspartei Deutschlands. Land Sachsen*, no. 39, 8 March 1947, 2. Cf. Frank, T., 'Otto Dix und die DDR, oder ein deutscher Künstler beharrlich zwischen den Stühlen sitzend', in: Herzogenrath, 295–9.

96 Löffler, F., 'Otto Dix', *Zeitschrift für Kunst*, no. 3, 1949, 173–93.

97 Wiemann, H., 'Die Wandlung des Maler Otto Dix', *bildende kunst*, no. 10, 1949, 342–7.

98 Cf. Pommeranz-Liedtke, 11–16.

99 Gutbrod, 21.

100 Holsinger, 26–56.

Swan Songs

Should you happen at any time [. . .] to feel like derogating from the general to the particular, remember I am here, and on the alert.

Samuel Beckett, *Murphy*, London, 1938, 37

In March 1950, the East German Prime Minister Otto Grotewohl gave an address to the Volkskammer, 'Die deutsche Kultur ist Unteilbar' (German Culture is Indivisible), which reiterated the importance of a unified national culture, and the threat of American *Kosmopolitanismus*. Grotewohl's address was part of an increasing determination on the part of the East German government to bring artists in line, and to alienate those who did not produce art that reflected the collective will to build a Socialist state. Centralisation in the sphere of culture was most clearly expressed by the founding of the Deutsche Akademie der Künste in East Berlin, in March 1950, and in June of that year the founding of the Verband Bildender Künstler Deutschlands (Association of German Artists). This mirrored developments in Moscow, specifically the founding of the Academy of the Arts of the USSR in 1947, and was part of the imposition of the Soviet model in each satellite state: monopolistic artists' unions, centralised control of exhibitions and publicity, state prizes and annual 'national' exhibitions.

German unity, and the threat of America, were also behind the increasingly vehement SED campaign against 'formalism' in the arts, which began with the publication in the *Tägliche Rundschau* of a two-part article by Alexander Dymschitz in November 1948.[1]

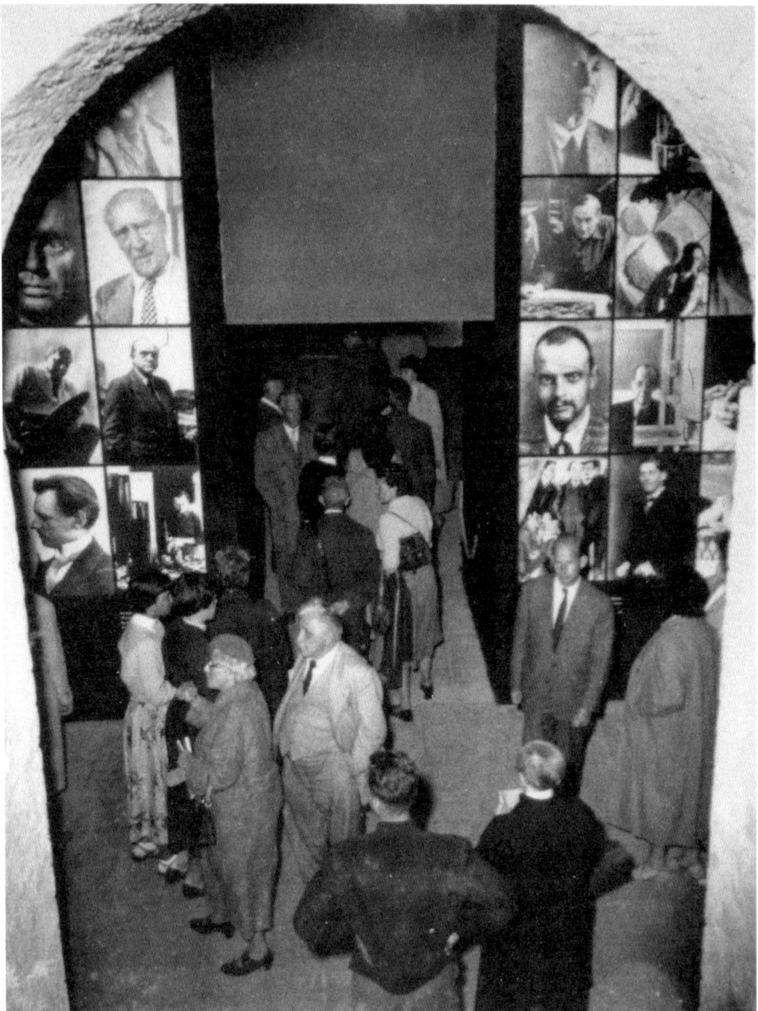

Photograph of visitors to *documenta 1*, Kassel, 1955

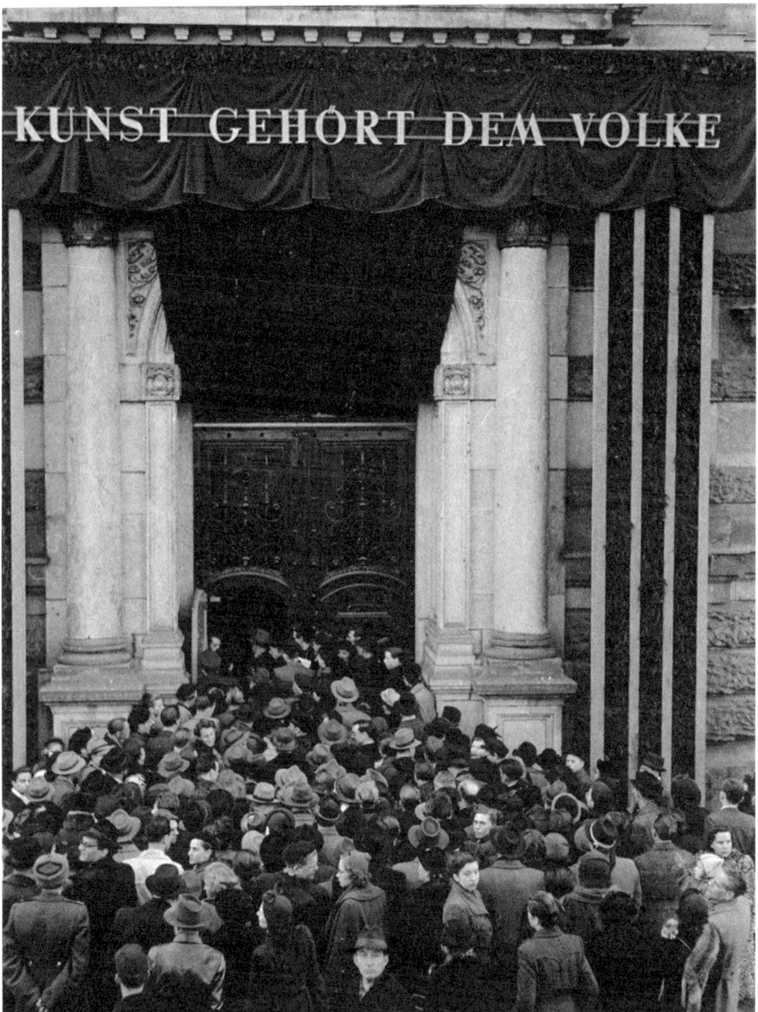

Photograph of visitors to the *Dritte Deutsche Kunstausstellung*, Dresden, Albertinum, 1953. Photo: Erich Höhne/ Erich Pohl

The main tenet of this argument, repeated many times over the coming years, was simple: art that stressed formal concerns of the medium, rather than naturalistic content, was morally reprehensible. The formal revolutions of modern art have destroyed the nature of art, wrote Dymschitz, because art depends on the harmony of form and content. In departing from the tradition of German painting that remained motivated both by progressive social ideals – and here Dymschitz cites Dürer, Grünewald, Bosch and Cranach, as well as Heinrich Zille and Käthe Kollwitz – modern German 'formalists' have become nothing more than the epigones of French modernists, decadent, irrational and pessimistic in their outlook. (That German artists were the artless followers rather than originators of the pathology of modern art was of some significance, as we shall see). As a result of their unhealthily pessimistic outlook, formalists are unable to fulfill the social role ascribed to artists in the wake of war, which is to contribute towards the rebuilding of a democratic society, and so on. 'After a short while', the sculptor Herbert Volwahsen reflected, 'we realised that by it [Socialist Realism] was meant quite simply the naturalistic illustration of party ideology'.[2]

The anti-formalist campaign was launched with renewed vigour after the founding of the East German state by the publication of two articles, N. Orlow's 'Wege und Irrwege der modernen Kunst' (True and False Paths of Modern Art), in the *Tägliche Rundschau*, January 1951, and the next month with W. Girnus's 'Wo Stehen die Feinde der deutschen Kunst?' (Where are the Enemies of German Art?) in *Neues Deutschland*. After its fifth general assembly in March 1951, the first official statement on anti-formalism was issued by the central committee of the SED, *Der Kampf gegen den Formalismus in Kunst und Literatur, für eine fortschrittliche deutsche Kultur* (The Struggle against Formalism in Art and Literature, for a Progressive German Culture),[3] the clearest statement of SED cultural policies in the new climate of confrontation. After recounting the 'cultural successes' of East Germany, notably those writers who had returned from emigration such as Arnold Zweig, Johannes Becher, Bertolt Brecht and Anna Seghers, the bulk of the statement is a condemnation of the 'cultural barbarism' of American Imperialism and the false paths taken by certain East German artists. In comparison to advances in the political and economic spheres, artists are strongly criticised for not coming up to scratch. The root cause of this is the infiltration of 'formalist' tendencies, threats to the 'national character' that lead to cosmopolitanism, rearmament and war:

> Cloaked by such excuses or even misled intentions to develop 'something totally new', the most prominent aspect of formalism rests in the aim to break away from the classical tradition. This leads to the dislocation of national culture, to the destruction of national consciousness and the promotion of cosmopolitanism; in short, it amounts to a direct support of a US-imperialist agenda for war.[4]

A list is provided of those cultural events and works of art that have been infected by this formalism, including Horst Strempel's mural in the Friedrichstraße Station (which had been overpainted by SED officials in February 1951), and work by the painter Max Lingner. Allied with the dangers of formalism, the *pseudo-kunst* of kitsch is also singled out as a method by which the 'Imperialistic culture-destroyers' poison the consciousness of the masses: 'In the interest of an Imperialism directed against humanity and its incendiary politics towards war, both formalism and kitsch serve a specific function'.[5] The true Soviet-German artist must not only be against formalism and kitsch, however, but also against *Proletkult*, the revolutionary proletarian art established in the Soviet Union in 1917, that would 'burn Raphael and trample the flowers of art in the name of our tomorrow'.[6]

To ensure that East German artists appreciated the dangers of an art deficient in naturalistic content, the 1951 SED assembly called for the founding of a central body to deal with all cultural matters. The Staatliche Kommission für Kunstangelegenheiten, 'Stakoku' (State Commission for Artistic Affairs) was established later that year in August, with the official line of promoting an 'All-German progressive culture' based on the classical heritage and humanistic tradition.[7] These ideals found expression not only in the newly reinstated journal *Bildende Kunst*, but also in the *Dritte Deutsche Kunstausstellung* (organised under the auspices of Stakoku and the Verband Bildender Künstler), in which a stringently determined *Staatskunst* took centre stage. Particularly acute was Otto Grotewohl's address for the inauguration of the Stakoku in 1951, 'Die Eroberung der Kultur beginnt' (The Conquest of Culture Begins), which, for its summary of a view of cultural unity, by no means solely a result of Soviet propaganda, is worth citing at some length:

One nation – one culture. The reversal of the forced disintegration of Germany and the maintenance of peace dominate our considerations of the survival of the German nation. The culture of the German people and their artistic expression is central to this struggle. A glance at German history illustrates the extent to which a culture informed by progressive and humanistic traditions has influenced the national consciousness of the German people. Our mother tongue alone prohibits that we speak of an East and a West Germany. We have one language and are one people. Whether it is works by Dürer, Holbein, Altdorfer, Grünewald or Tilman Riemenschneider, or texts by Luther and Thomas Münzer that set us in awe, not to mention the impact of our classical literature, the German people will always perceive a reflection of their character in these achievements. They are neither Bavarians, Thuringians, Saxons nor Rhinelanders, but Germans, and their culture is a German culture. When the first attempts to establish a united nation drowned in blood at the time of the peasant wars in the sixteenth century, it remained culture that kept the ideal of a united nation alive in German minds. In the eyes of the world it is texts by Lessing, Goethe, Schiller and Heine that shape our nation and provide it with a valuable heritage. Long before Bismarck's so-called 'blood and iron politics' effected German unity, German artists, poets, painters

> and musicians had already sketched the German nation. It is this classical heritage and humanistic tradition we mean when we think of developing a progressive German culture in the name of peace and national unity. As in past centuries the role of art has to be to serve the unity of our fatherland and peace. To counter the psychological precursors of an adventurous war driven by US hegemonic-imperialistic interests based on confusion, lies and diversions, we need to mobilise all counter-forces, also in the arts. All our efforts have to be directed against the further expansion of cultural barbarity, gangster- and murder-films relying on unrestrained sensation, mystic revelations, death cults, and all sorts of erotica and perversity. Such anti-culture pollutes minds and souls, our youth in particular, only to blur through the glorification of the adventure of a disgusting and dirty legionary's death on foreign soil the interest of Wall Street dollars.[8]

Importantly, the battle was being waged not against West Germany, but against American Imperialism. For this reason, German unification was still considered feasible: during 1952 the East Germans made a number of overtures towards the Federal Republic, offering to accept their proposal of a pan-German executive, provided certain conditions were met, such as the complete withdrawal of foreign troops, and the recognition of the Oder-Neisse line as the Eastern border of Germany. In addition, political unification should not begin with a free-election (a sure disaster for the Soviets with such an ideologically unprepared electorate), but the formation of an all-German committee.[9]

Unification rhetoric, or *Deutschlandpolitik*, was similarly important for the political constitution of the West, though in a more muted fashion. The *Grundgesetz* (Basic Law), confirmed that the Federal Republic was a temporary substitute for a unified German state. Suspicion of advances from the East was countered by this permanent, if highly legalistic and formalised, commitment to unification. Mirroring Soviet attitudes, it was essential for the Bonn government to maintain that the division of the country had been imposed from the outside, and that the 'spiritual nation' remained as one. Two official reports issued by the Bonn Bundesministerium für gesamtdeutsche Fragen (Bonn Federal Ministry for All-German Affairs), both in 1953, document this in a revealingly partisan spirit. One of the reports, written by the critic Lothar von Balluseck, covered the arts in the Soviet Zone of Occupation (as the West still referred to the DDR, refusing political recognition of the East German state). Balluseck describes the manipulation of East German artists by the Soviet authorities, repressive policies imposed upon artists simply unable to grasp the true nature of the political situation. Members of the Klub der Kulturschaffenden (Club of Creative Culture), for instance, had been asked to sign a protest against the release of certain Nazi officials after the conclusion of the Nuremberg Trials – not, however, as a genuine protest against Nazism but as a gesture calculated to stir up discord with the American authorities.[10] The second anonymous report, *Polit-Kunst*, was a direct reaction to the *Dritte*

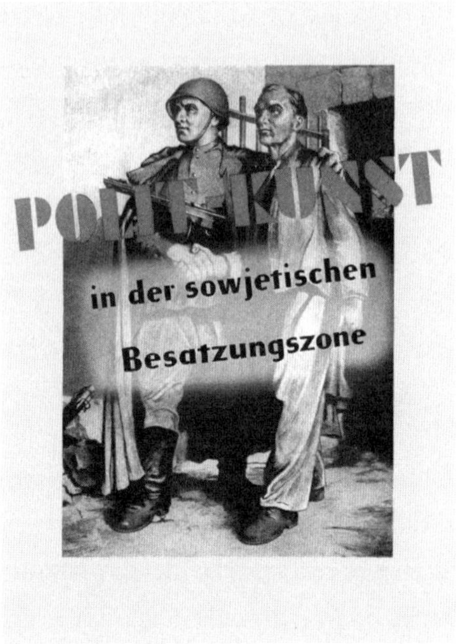

Cover of book *Polit-Kunst in der sowjetischen Besatzungszone* (Political Art in the Soviet Zone of Occupation), Bonn, 1953, with Werner Ruhner, *8. Mai 1945*, c.1953, etching, 96 × 74 cm, location unknown

Deutsche Kunstausstellung, a large exhibition of Socialist painting mounted in Dresden in 1953. This booklet contains a short summary of how the series of 'all-German' exhibitions in Dresden (1946, 1949, 1953) had changed from a relatively pluralistic affair to an illustration of Andrei Zhdanov's crusade against formalism.[11] German artists were not to blame, however, for this state of affairs, the report held – even those who believed in the Stalinist cause were manipulated by their Soviet administrators. Examples of this were the artists who had submitted appropriately Socialist Realist works for the exhibition, such as the sculptor Gustav Seitz (who had travelled through the West gathering support for the exhibition), but who had nevertheless fallen foul of the selection procedure. German artists were at the mercy of culture officers who knew only one thing about art: hard-line Socialist Realism. The report concludes with an extended selection of excerpts from East German newspapers such as *Neues Deutschland* and the *Tägliche Rundschau* that, behind the gushing praise for the achievements of Soviet art (the report suggests), reveal reservations and criticism.

It is clear that animosity and suspicion were not only mutual but based on the same premise. Just as the 'barbarism' of Western artists was a result of American *Kosmopolitanismus*, the predicament of those in the East was explained by Soviet manipulation. In all cases, German artists retain a quality, however hidden, that keeps them German before anything else, capable of creating works of art that had the capacity to 'mirror' the nation.

The 1953 *Dritte Deutsche Kunstausstellung* was intended as a showcase of East German Stalinist Socialist Realism. It did indeed demonstrate the extent of Soviet control of the arts, although, as many of the exhibited works showed, this control was by no means saturated. It left in the end the choice between either sentimental didactic works such as the graphic artist Werner Ruhner's *8 Mai* 1945 (c.1953), or works that betrayed a longing for a different type of art, with roots not in Muscovite *diktats* but a German tradition of realism. This was a tradition derived not only from nineteenth-century painting, but also from a prewar tradition of proletariat imagery, unique to Germany. If the exhibition shows the interaction of Soviet and German ideals of painting, then it also shows the complete failure of the former to take root in East German soil.

This was by no means a result of lack of ideological preparation on the part of the East German authorities. Extensive measures had been taken to prepare artists, and to inculcate Socialist Realist attitudes, following the perceived failure of the first two Dresden exhibitions as manifestations of Socialist art. The 1953 exhibition was to be an exemplary showing of art that accorded to the Leninist-Stalinist idea of using a classical heritage to provide the foundation for the collective project of building a Socialist state, evinced in the works of painters such as Repin.

The publication of Lukács' *Goethe and his Age* in 1947 exemplified the idea of Socialist reconstruction on the basis of a classical German heritage (although Lukács, as an advocate of the critical autonomy of the artist, was certainly not supportive of Stalinism and was in turn rejected by the regime).[12] The 'Goethe-Year' in 1949 was a further vehicle by which, as Stefan Heymann observed, the *klassische nationale Tradition* could be inculcated into the populace. Heymann's criticisms of the 1949 2. *Deutsche Kunstausstellung* were centred on the lack of clarity concerning the constitution of this tradition and its poor reflection in contemporary Socialist art. Does the German national tradition begin and end with the art of the Reformation? Are Dürer, Grünewald, Holbein, Cranach and Riemenschneider the only representatives of the German tradition? Even so, 'the [1949] Dresden exhibition shows with shocking clarity that the spiritual basis of almost all the paintings and sculptures is cosmopolitan, that is to say, with no roots in national feeling'.[13]

Goethe, genius of Weimar classicism, underpinned not only debates about national tradition but also those concerning the imperative of *tipichnost* (the typical), one of the key tenets of Zdhanovian Socialist Realism. Debates about the political importance of the 'typical' were conducted in professional arts publications both before and after the 1949 and 1953 exhibitions. Particularly important in 1949 was Goethe's idea that all organisms arose in relation to a generic type, an '*urbild*'. These ideas were concisely expressed by Walter Benjamin, who cites Goethe's views during his discussion of allegory:

> There is a great difference between a poet's seeking the particular from the general and his seeing the general in the particular. The former gives rise to allegory, where the particular serves only as an instance or example of the general; the latter, however, is the true nature of poetry: the expression of the particular without any thought of, or reference to, the general. Whoever grasps the particular in all its vitality also grasps the general, without being aware of it, or only becoming aware at a later stage.[14]

During preparations for the 1953 Dresden exhibition, these ideas were proclaimed as central to the successful production of Socialist Realist art, particularly that artists should represent the *Neuen*

Menschen (new man) announced by the SED-leader Walter Ulbricht in July 1952: 'Central to artistic activity must be the New Man, the fighter for a unified, democratic Germany, the activist and hero of socialist development'.[15] The concept of the 'typical' that underlay this Socialist *Menschenbild* was spelt out by the Soviet Communist and Politburo member Georgi Malenkow during his address to the Nineteenth Party Congress in Moscow, 1952:

> In creating artistic images, our artists, writers and art workers must always remember that the typical is not only that which is most frequently encountered but that which most fully and pointedly expresses the essence of the given social force. In the Marxist-Leninist understanding, the typical by no means signifies some sort of statistical average. Typicalness corresponds to the essence of the given social-historical phenomenon; it is not merely the most widespread, frequently occurring, and ordinary phenomenon. Conscious hyperbole and accentuation of an image does not exclude typicalness but discloses it more fully and emphasizes it. The typical is the basic sphere of manifestation of the Party approach in realistic art. The problem of typicalness is always a political problem.[16]

Malenkow's address was reported in the *Mitteilungsblatt* (news sheet)of the VBK in April 1953 as part of a criticism of the 'superficial conception of the typical', clearly directed at submissions to the *Dritte Deutsche Kunstausstellung*. German efforts, it was reported, failed to rival Soviet examples, such as the paintings of Boris Ioganson and Aleksandr Gerassimow, since they presented a one-dimensional view of society, avoiding any conflict that would stir up debate.[17] Successful depiction of *Helden*, (heroes) relied on a poetic penetration of appearances and a grasp of essential nature that should not, however, lead to idealising or beautification.

The notion of 'typical' did not thus imply 'collective'. The 1949 Dresden exhibition had been marked by the inclusion of thirteen murals on Socialist themes commissioned from artists' collectives, an important evolution of the attempt at state control. Articles on mural painting – *Wandmalerei* – appeared in Socialist art journals throughout the year, promoting such work as the solution to the dead-end of bourgeois easel painting: 'Representative of a new type of human being dedicated to the human community, we are now witnessing the beginning of a new culture of mural painting', ran a typical announcement.[18] The Mexican muralists, José Clemente Orozco, David Alfaro Siqueiros and Diego Rivera, provided a model, knowledge of whose work was transmitted to the Soviet Zone by those German intellectuals formerly exiled in South America, principally Anna Seghers and Bodo Uhse, as well as the painter Gert Caden (one of the nine artistic directors of the 1949 Dresden exhibition). Anna Seghers compared Horst Strempel's ill-fated mural in the Berlin Friedrichstraße station with Rivera's work.[19] Gert Caden, on his return in March 1948 from Cuba, where he had been active in German exile organisations, reported enthusiastically on the activities of the Mexican 'painter-syndicates'.[20]

The sources for the murals were factories in Saxony, where the artists lived and worked during May and June of 1949, preparing sketches and compositional drawings for approval by the exhibition committee. Unsurprisingly, it was difficult to accord the tenets of Socialist Realism with reality – the Dresden artists Erich Gerlach and Kurt Schütze recorded their dismay at seeing the working conditions of an iron foundry at Freital. Their initial sketches were rejected by the exhibition committee – they were not optimistic enough, and the figures were too schematic. The final, corrected mural, *Berufschulung* (Apprenticeship), strikingly shows the disparity between the ideals of Socialist Realism and the reality of postwar Germany. All but one of the murals were destroyed during the 1950s, after having been rejected for purchase by the SED central committee in Berlin.

The failure in 1949 not only of the *Wandbildaktion* (mural policy) but of all the works on display to fulfil aesthetic requirements was clearly recognised and commented on in a number of articles and speeches. Helmut Holtzhauer, writing the preface for the 1953 Dresden catalogue, made the reasons for the failure clear in 1949: theoretical grounding was too weak, and most of the artists were still under the yoke of formalism. Whereas the emphasis in 1949 was on collective works, leading to what was widely considered to be a failed interpretation of the 'typical', the emphasis in the 1953 exhibition was far more on the 'typical' as depicted, however insufficiently as it transpired, by images of heroic individuals, but also by individual, professional artists.

The works exhibited in the 1949 and 1953 shows were not then simply static expressions of Soviet dogma. There remained

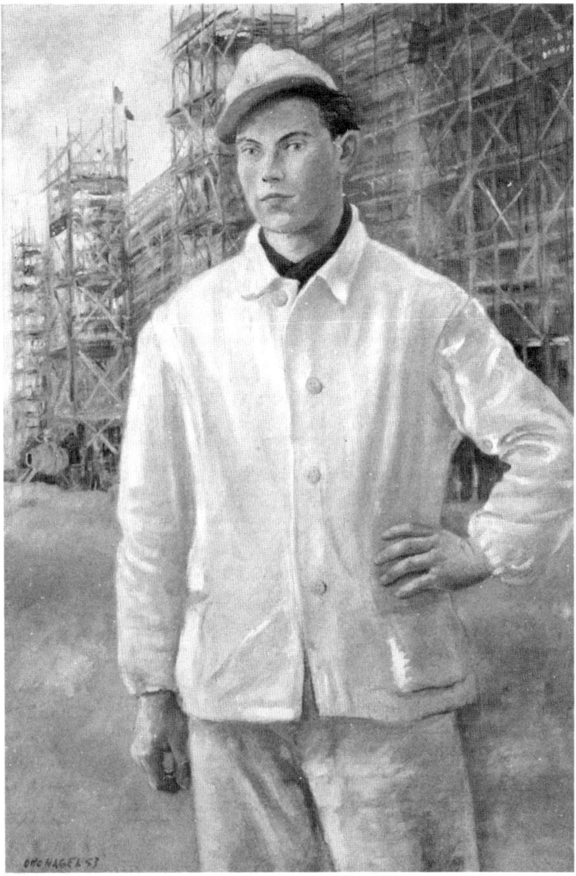

Otto Nagel, *Junger Maurer von der Stalinallee* (Young Bricklayer on the Stalinallee), 1953, oil on canvas, 116 x 79.5 cm, Märkisches Museum, Berlin

a difficult friction between Soviet demands and German traditions. The East German painter Otto Nagel's submission for the 1953 Dresden exhibition, *Junger Maurer von der Stalinallee* (Young Bricklayer on the Stalinallee), indicates the most diplomatic balance that was reached between German traditions of proletariat painting and the demands of Soviet Socialist Realism. The Stalinallee, begun in 1952 as the 'first Socialist street' of the DDR, was intended as a showcase of Soviet architecture and a symbol of national reconstruction. Nagel's image of a young worker standing at ease in front of the scaffolding does not lack undertones of defiance: the Stalinallee was a huge drain on East Germany's resources, and demands for its quicker construction led to the workers' uprising in June 1953, which was put down by Soviet tanks. This occurred just after the Dresden exhibition closed. In comparison to Werner Ruhner's sentimental depiction of a Red Army soldier releasing a German Socialist from Nazi captivity, Nagel's is a more sophisticated image, hovering between an individual portrait and a 'typical' worker. He appears detached and self-contained, more an allegory of youthful vanity than of Ulbricht's *Neuen Mensch*. His idealisation was certain to have been perceived by some as a failure of *tipichnost*, though such views were probably suppressed in light of the painter's high official rank. Nagel was a central figure in the reconstruction milieu, one of the prewar radicals who best adapted to the changed postwar situation. He had been a member of the Arbeitsrat für Kunst after 1918 and was closely associated with Adolf Behne, Käthe Kollwitz and the painter Heinrich Zille. Despite his strong Communist affiliation, he remained in Germany after 1933, continuing his own painting until shortly before the outbreak of war, in the face of persecution that included a short internship in KZ Sachsenhausen. From 1935–41 he ran a private painting school; during this time he also produced his well-known series of *Berliner Bilder*, images of Berlin before the destruction. He held many official positions after 1945, and was co-founder of the Kulturbund zur demokratischen Erneuerung Deutschlands, the Deutsche Akademie der Künste and later president, co-founder and first chairman of the Verband Bildender Künstler.[21] Though his work remained rooted in prewar revolutionary formats, he was a model of success in the postwar Socialist state. His postwar work nevertheless stands as a continuation of the proletariat style of the 1920s, and suggests a form of native resistance to Soviet aesthetic demands. His *Steinträger*, depicting a hodman carrying bricks up a ladder, was made in 1947 to recreate a work destroyed during the war. The latter version recreates the awkward, crude realism of his proletariat paintings of the 1920s and 30s, a quality also evident in other works submitted by the artist for the 1949 exhibition. A pallid jauntiness, deliberate refusal of finish, a rough, almost amateurish caricature, ally these paintings to a prewar tradition associated above all with the work of Otto Dix, rather than with Socialist Realism.

German traditions were evident in other works included in the 1953 exhibition. Carl Lange's *Werkkonzert* (Workers' Concert) and Edmund Götz's, *Im Gaswerk Reick* (In the Reick Gasworks) show the centrality of work to the image of man (*Menschenbild*) according to Soviet/Socialist requirements, but also evoke a type of realism based on atmospheric effects and dramatic illumination, exemplified in paintings by Adolf Menzel, such as *Iron-rolling Mill*, painted during the *Gründerzeit* of the 1870s, a period of industrial expansion aided by war reparations from vanquished France. Herbert Gute, writing in *Der Bildende Künstler*, the organ of the Verband Bildender Künstler, of which he was General Secretary, elucidated the connection between art and work for the benefit of those artists preparing for the 1953 exhibition. Citing Goethe, Engels and Marx, Gute describes the importance of 'critical realism' in the depiction of industrial activities, pointing to Menzel's *Iron-rolling Mill*. Menzel depicts the workers not as *Giganten* (giants) but 'true to reality, in their miserable existence'.[22]

Such references to German traditions make it clear that the 1953 exhibition, contrary perhaps to expectations, was far from being a model of Stalinist propaganda. In the face of Soviet imperatives, and the mutual political non-recognition of eastern and western States, the organisers continued the policy of the previous two exhibitions and attempted to forge links with the West. In fact, 275 works by artists from West Germany were submitted to the jury of Dresden exhibition, 117 of which were accepted. Most of these were innocuous portraits and landscapes that, if not according to the tenets of Socialist Realism, at least did not directly contradict them.

Whereas the first two Dresden exhibitions were held out of necessity in the unassuming Stadthalle, one of the few large buildings that had survived the war intact, the *Dritte Deutsche Kunstausstellung* was staged in the historic Albertinum, extensively damaged by Allied bombing in 1945. Originally the Saxon royal arsenal, the building had been converted in the late nineteenth century to house the Saxon state archive and sculpture collection. The decision to hold the 1953 exhibition in such an important building reflects the prestige attached to the first exhibition of 'true' German art in the newly founded Socialist State.

Two years later, across the still open border, the first documenta exhibition was installed in the still semi-ruined Fridericianum in the town of Kassel, one of the oldest purpose-built public galleries in Europe, which had also been extensively damaged by Allied bombing. In both cases, the buildings were highly symbolic, 'phoenixes rising from the ashes', but also made clear a connection with historic traditions of public exhibition and regional patronage.

The Kassel documenta has received far more attention than the *Dritte Deutsche Kunstausstellung*, and has become part of the 'collective memory' of postwar Germany.[23] Alongside Werner Haftmann's 1954 publication, *Malerei im. 20 Jahrhundert*, the Kassel exhibition anchored the triumph of a type of abstraction or non-narrative painting, rooted in French modernism, and potently symbolised Western economic success: it was a picture of the 'economic miracle' that had settled like snow on the ruins of the previous decade. Yet documenta was also intended as a vehicle by which a link could be re-established between German traditions of modern painting and those from abroad, particularly French. As such, it stands as a loose counterpart to the *Dritte Deutsche Kunstausstellung*. Like the series of exhibitions in Dresden, which continued for another three decades, by its third manifestation in 1964, documenta was integral to the history of the postwar Federal Republic.

The Kassel exhibition was in fact devised in conscious antipathy to East German cultural politics. In a plan for the exhibition, first drafted in late 1954, the instigator of the exhibition Arnold Bode made clear the importance of Kassel as a *Zonengrenzgebiet*, a town on the border with the East that could act as a symbol of western confidence and recovery: 'It would no doubt be an excellent idea to alert the world to the pan-European dimension of art in a location just 30 kilometres away from the Soviet Zone', he wrote.[24] Documenta also reacted against the frequently strained organisation politics of professional associations in Germany, particularly the static authoritarian structures of Soviet cultural organisations, such as the Kulturbund. As such, Bode continued, the neutral location of Kassel was 'neither linked to artists' associations nor political-cultural interests which could in any way be questioned. Kassel does not aim to connect with any traditions that would bring with them the danger of party-political strife'.[25]

Details of the preparation of the exhibition, in particular the naming of the event, are in this respect revealing. Bode had been asked by the organisers of the 1955 *Bundesgartenschau* (Federal Horticultural Show) in Kassel to stage an exhibition of art. As the *Bodeplan* shows, he immediately formed an organising committee, the Abendländische Gesellschaft der Kunst des 20. Jahrhunderts, formally convened on 6 April 1954, with Heinz Lemke as chairman.[26] The founding of an institution as a legally registered bureaucratic structure through which to legitimise the exhibition referred back to prewar traditions, with which Bode had been involved.[27] This committee existed as a means of representing not only the organisers but also politicians and industrialists who were funding the exhibition. Further, Bode saw the necessity of an *Ehrenausschuss*, an honorary committee consisting of political figures who would provide further support. Documenta was in this sense a revival of such traditions of

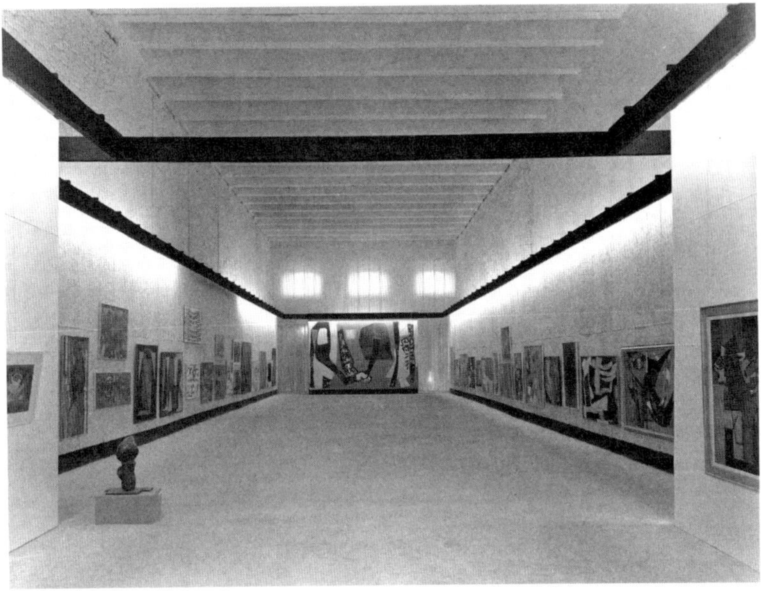

Installation shot of *documenta 1*, Kassel, 1955

sponsorship and legitimation, dependent on a type of public/private milieu that had been absent in the postwar decade since 1945.

The naming both of the society and the exhibition went through a number of changes. In a letter to the *Ministerpräsident* dated 23 April 1954, Bode refers to the exhibition as *Abendländische Kunst des 20. Jh.* Other drafts made during the preparation time suggest *Europäische Kunst des 20. Jahrhunderts* (European Twentieth-century Art), *Kunst Europas seit 1900 – Ausstellung europäische Kunst in Deutschland* (European Art Since 1900 – an Exhibition of European Art in Germany), and *Europa55*.[28] The final choice of 'documenta' suited the impression of political neutrality that Bode sought, a more apt symbol of transnationality than the idea of 'Abendländische', or even 'Europa'. The name 'documenta' also made clear the feeling that an appropriate moment had been reached to take stock of, or document, twentieth-century art, and to present it in terms of a comprehensive overview. Although the concept of abstraction as a 'trans-national' language was central to the thinking behind the exhibition, so too was the intention to create a story of 'modernism continued' after the aberration of Nazism. The entrance to the Fridericianum was surrounded by photographs of the artists whose work was displayed within, creating the impression less of an art exhibition and more of the entrance to a shrine. One contemporary newspaper reported:

> It is touching to observe how entranced visitors are before these photoportraits of mostly ill-fated painters, sculptors and architects. They spend longer in front of them than in front of the actual works themselves; the faces of these artists are so absorbing as they so directly contradict the impression still widely held about the way artists look (criminals, mentally ill etc.). They appear elegant, serious, thoughtful and sensitive types, more like scientists, poets in labcoats with slide-rules.[29]

Nevertheless, the works on display inside reflected not so much a document of twentieth-century art, as a record of the priorities of the postwar decade, fulfilling in particular the task of rehabilitating German artists. Through the entrance hall, a semi-circular apse-like stairwell showed, against the roughly finished white-washed brick work, a series of paintings by Oskar Schlemmer and sculptures by Wilhelm Lehmbruck. Despite the documentary intentions of the exhibition, most of the works on the ground floor were from the early 1950s, and a clear priority was given to German artists. An exception was the large sculpture room, dominated by Henry Moore's *Two Sitting Figures* of 1952–3, displayed in a group with works by other British artists such as Ben Nicholson, Reginald Butler, Kenneth Armitage and Lynn Chadwick. The prestigious placement of these works was at least in part a result of the propaganda exhibitions mounted by the British Council, in particular of works by Moore, during the previous decade. It was only in the rooms devoted to Constructivism, with works by Theo van Doesburg, Max Bill, Josef Albers, Antoine Pevsner and Piet Mondrian, that a significant insight into prewar modernism was given. Upstairs, a large room was devoted to a mini-retrospective of paintings by Max Beckmann made between 1930 and 1945. By contrast, a neighbouring room that contained a largely incoherent sampling of works from artists associated with Expressionism in Dresden and Munich did not provide a significant representation of any one artist, Kirchner and Marc faring particularly badly, and Kandinsky not appearing at all. Four paintings by Wols, curiously faced with a suite of small-format paintings by Raoul Dufy, suggested another reintroduction of a German artist who was, as we have already seen, otherwise unknown in his native land. The heart of the exhibition was undoubtedly the large painting room that dominated the second floor, and which was itself centred around the confrontation of Fritz Winter's monumental *Komposition in Blau und Gelb* (Composition in Blue and Yellow), finished earlier that year, and Picasso's *Girl in front of a Mirror* of 1932. The room was otherwise dominated by examples of postwar abstraction by lesser-known figures such as Guiseppe Capogrossi, Gérard Schneider and Antonio Corpora, although a number of earlier works by Picasso including the 1915 *Harlequin* and four paintings by Matisse, such as *The Red Studio* of 1911, reinforced the primacy given to French painting as representative of prewar modern art. A comparison of Léger and Rouault confirmed this in an adjoining room that also contained a small group of works by Miró, all but one of which were painted after 1947. The most touching and revealing insight into the French section of the exhibition was a small room that contained, preciously displayed on a thin-metal stalk, Henri Rousseau's *Eva* of 1906. The impact of Rousseau on German art – which could have been demonstrated with works by Kandinsky, Marc and Gabriele Münter, works by Beckmann from the 1920s, and further with the Naïve Sachlichkeit of painters such as Wilhelm Schnarrenberger, Georg Scholz, Heinrich Maria Davringhausen, Georg Schrimpf and Carlo Mense – was, however, not to be seen. Other German artists associated with trends of critical realism, such as Otto Dix and Georg Grosz, were also absent. Those German artists who could demonstrate the presence of 'international modern art' in Germany were given a clear preference, as was a type of painting that suggested a development, fired in the 1920s and 30s by French painting, towards an abstract style, taken up after 1945 largely by German artists. In comparison with the pan-German reach of the *Dritte Deutsche Kunstausttellung*, the 1955 Kassel exhibition, like the 1948 *Christliche Kunst der Gegenwart*, did not show any work by East German artists.

The national resonances of the exhibition were by no means underplayed by the organisers, for whom it was the continuation of an interrupted tradition. Bode himself was keen to compare his exhibition to the 1927 *Internationale Ausstellung* in Dresden, which had similarly documented the 'paths and points of achievement to date'.[30] The genealogy had been extended by the time Werner Haftmann came to write his introduction to the exhibition catalogue. Not only the 1927 Dresden exhibition, but also the Cologne *Sonderbund* exhibition of 1912, and Herwarth Walden's *Herbstsalon* in Berlin, 1913, were part of the lineage.

Haftmann's *Malerei im 20. Jahrhundert* itself, the seminal statement of postwar abstraction in the West, and the most immediate textual equivalent for documenta, may be readily placed in a tradition of German art historiography, to which Julius Meier-Graefe's *Entwicklungsgeschichte der modernen Kunst* (The Development of Modern Art, 1904) and Carl Einstein's *Die Kunst des 20. Jahrhunderts* (1926) belong. Meier-Graefe and Einstein were both advocates of French modernism and foils to those, such as Ferdinand Möller, who wished to promote a 'German' avant garde.[31] Haftmann, however, is more on the side of *entente*. Although the historical basis for the spiritually unified postwar 'European whole' he identifies is French modernism, reaching back to Cézanne – an influence confirmed by exhibitions of French art in occupied Germany from 1945 to 1949 – his account is also a sustained plea for the primacy of modern German painting. His 'European whole' is effectively centred around a Franco-German pact, an 'underground connection' that produced a tradition of abstract painting, emblem of the political freedoms evolved in Europe since

1789. Haftmann could not have picked his moment better: the signing, in 1954, of an agreement on cultural co-operation and exchange was part of a 'treaty regime' culminating in the 1964 Elysée Treaty, which established the European architecture for postwar Franco-German co-operation. The ideas behind and content of documenta were in great part cultural recognition of this new parity. The Franco-German focus of documenta can clearly be seen from the nationality of the participants, as listed in the catalogue: fifty-eight Germans and forty-two French far outweighed any other country, although the twenty-eight Italians indicated the importance of Futurism, if as an annex to the story of modernism. (Two Dutch, six Swiss, eight English and three Americans, two of whom, Josef Albers and Kurt Roesch, were German expatriates, complete the count).[32]

The political distinction that Haftmann makes between abstraction and realism is also revealing of this special relationship. In his hands, abstraction became a kind of European folk-art. Though Paris led the way after 1945, achieving a swifter consolidation of artistic groupings, as in the 1947 *Salon des réalités nouvelles*, the younger generation of German artists was soon able to take up the baton of modern art by opting for abstraction. Ludwig Grote's comprehensive exhibitions *Blaue Reiter* and *Maler am Bauhaus* in Munich, Haftmann writes, were the first overviews of German painting after the war that made this continuity possible.[33] Abstract art after 1945 also showed a new understanding of realism: the visible world was represented in the light of science and technology rather than as the result of direct observation. Haftmann cites Klee's idea of 'cool romanticism' approvingly – abstraction providing the cool, techno-sophisticate solution to the old romantic problem of the disparity of subject and object.[34] Contemporary realism, writes Haftmann, is informed by a rational tradition reaching back to Kant and Descartes, rather than by a tradition of non-European Socialist ideas. The various instances of successfully engaged representational painting that were seen favourably at the time, such as work by Renato Guttuso or Diego Rivera, were influenced by a form of European realism distinct from the Soviet Socialist model: 'Their realism has nothing in common with the Soviet realism contrived by the political simplifiers, but it has a great deal in common with the mastery of reality achieved by modern European painters, with what Beckmann called "transcendent realism"'.[35] André Fougeron's Socialist Realism, for example, was derived from Picasso and Matisse rather than a Soviet model.[36] Even so, this acceptable 'transcendent realism', based as it was on a European, modernist foundation of transcendent realism, had little future. For Haftmann, representational art in the postwar era has so far 'failed to produce a new vision of reality'.[37] This is equally the case with 'Existentialist' neo-realist painting, such as the French artists in the group L'homme témoin, Giacometti, and also (in the 1960 translation of Haftmann's book) an English contingent: Graham Sutherland, Francis Bacon, and the 'kitchen-sink' painters of the mid-1950s. Theirs is a realism of *fischkalten Gebilde* (fish-cold images), disassociated by Haftmann from the more positive, totalising model of international abstraction. Objects in the world – kitchen sinks, factories, pot-plants – in themselves appear unable to carry meaning; only the transcendent striving of poetic metaphor is able to reconcile a broken reality with an idea of man and a sense of purpose.

For Kurt Leonhard, *Malerei im 20. Jahrhundert* represented a 'transcendence of human alienation through a holistic experience'.[38] The usefulness of Heidegger's terminology for descriptions and conceptualisations of abstract art is certainly evident in Haftmann's writing. His turn away from *fischkalten Gebilde* mirrors the postwar transition in Heidegger's thought from nihilism to a philosophy of reconciliation. This reconciliation, however, was conceived of by Haftmann as the global dominance of European culture: Europe as the foundation for a world culture that may not itself be called 'European', but is certainly not Soviet or American:

> The European outlook, developed in the last half century and reflected in modern art and architecture, has today been accepted all over the world. In Europe and America, Canada and Brazil, Persia and Japan, it has overwhelmed the bastions of folk culture, many of which have been built up and preserved over thousands of years, and destroyed them at any rate on the surface. A world culture is beginning to be discernible. Today Klee, Kandinsky, Picasso are recognised the world over.[39]

Thus the internationalism of his original argument is really a European Imperialism, defined at heart by a Franco-German axis, spilling over the traditional boundaries. Within the 1955 exhibition, this was most clearly demonstrated by the confrontation of Winter's *Komposition vor Blau und Gelb* and Picasso's *Young Girl in front of a Mirror* of 1932. The inclusion of Wols' 1948 painting *Manhattan*, which must have sat in curious relation to Mondrian's *Broadway Boogie Woogie* of 1942–3, also on display, suggested the simmering of a new type of confrontation. If 'the spittle was replacing the square' and 'Wols was replacing Mondrian',[40] then it was a short-lived victory. Haftmann's 'European outlook' of a new type of technological realism was as ill-fated as the Socialist Realism that had been on display in the *Dritte Deutsche Kunstausstellung* three years earlier. The direction of vision was soon dislocated from this inward-looking 'European' affair, westwards over the Atlantic ocean.

The salvage of national culture after 1945 was a shoring up of national '*mystique*', to re-cite Charles Péguy, that was soon doused and impeded by the developments of '*politique*' around the mid-1950s. These developments put an end to many of the longings of the postwar decade. Attempts to create a national mystique were certainly being overtaken by the time of the 1955 Kassel exhibition. The signing of the Paris treaties in January 1955, by which the Federal Republic from May of that year formally regained sovereignty, led the Soviet Union to announce that it could no longer negotiate for political reunification. Further events made this split apparently irrevocable. The day after the opening of documenta, a summit began in Geneva that for the first time since Potsdam in 1945 brought the 'Allied' leaders and their foreign ministers together. They discussed questions of European security, rearmament and German unification. The failure of these talks led to Kruschev's announcement, on 26 July, of the

Zweistaatentheorie (Two-State Theory), turning away from previous efforts to unify the two halves of Germany. Later that year, the foreign ministry of the Federal Republic announced the Hallstein Doctrine, 'that useless and costly instrument', according to Günther Grass, affirming non-recognition of the East German state and refusal to enter into diplomatic relations with any other state that recognised DDR sovereignty over eastern Germany. This precarious question of recognition led to many difficulties: Finland's special relation with the Soviet Union obliged it to recognise neither German state; the Ceylonese Prime Minister caused consternation by recognising both. When the DDR became a signatory of the nuclear test ban treaty of July 1963, President Kennedy declared paradoxically that it still did not officially exist.[41]

The *Zweistaatentheorie* and Hallstein doctrine confirmed that postwar hopes of reconciliation had come to an end, and a new period of confrontation and separation was beginning, of which the Berlin Wall was to become the painful symbol. This sense of an ending can be read into both the 1953 Dresden and 1955 Kassel exhibitions: both can be read as high-points of certain 'narratives' of style – Stalinist Socialist Realism and Classic (Franco-German) Modernism – which were intended to signal a new beginning. In retrospect, they appear more as strangely harmonised swan songs. Stalin's death four days after the opening of the *Dritte Deutsche Kunstausstellung* looked forward to the (short-lived) 1956 Kruschchevian thaw, and the end of the *zhdanovschina*, the decade after 1946 in which the anti-formalist decrees of Zhdanov dictated the new Socialist art.[42] The strike by construction workers on the Stalinallee, and the subsequent uprising across East Germany on 17 June, signalled the failure of the SED to achieve the goal of imposing political control.

In the West, the dominance of French painting was being superseded by the new American painting. The distinction between the Schools of Paris and New York had become, by 1950, the 'war horse of an entire generation'– not only were American painters defining a national tradition that did not rely on the European model, but that tradition was now (after anti-modern voices in Washington had been dealt with), being exported as 'international art' in the spirit of a universal humanism.[43] Although American painting had been shown in Germany from 1948 (Hilla Rebay's *Gegenstandlose Malerei in Amerika* – Non-objective Painting in America was shown in Karlsruhe during that year), exhibitions such as those staged by French cultural officers had more influence at that moment in defining avant-garde painting. From 1950, the export of American art as dominant model became a reality, and the centrality of Paris as arbiter of taste was incrementally challenged. The first indication of prestige awarded to painters of the New York School by the journal *Das Kunstwerk*, for instance, came in a special issue on Tachism in early 1956. An article on 'Taschists in the USA' located the New York School painters in a broader international field in which Paris was pre-eminent.[44] After the first indications of rain, the storm was inevitable. The exhibition *Amerikanische Malerei. Werden und Gegenwart* (American Painting. Past and Present), which travelled from Berlin to Munich in late 1951, showed a small number of works from the eighteenth and nineteenth centuries, as well as 120 paintings and prints from contemporary artists, including William Baziotes, Jackson Pollock,

Mark Rothko and Mark Tobey. Though the emphasis was not on abstraction, the exhibition asserted a successful and coherent national tradition of American painting.[45] *Hundert Jahre Amerikanische Malerei* 1800–1900 (One Hundred Years of American Painting), which toured Germany throughout 1953, continued this trend. Between 1953 and 1955, a series of exhibitions of American art in Paris marked the end of the Parisian hegemony in the cultural sphere: *Douze peintres et sculpteurs américains*, toured Europe and was shown in Düsseldorf in autumn 1953, *Dessin contemporain aux États-Unis* was shown at the Musée d'Art Moderne in Paris during 1954, and *50 ans d'art aux États-Unis* at the same location during 1955, which travelled to Frankfurt at the end of the year.[46] Daniel-Henry Kahnweiler lamented the decline of the École de Paris: 'True, many a painter has sought refuge in America', he wrote in 1945, 'but so numerous are those who have written to me bewailing their exile (not all of them Frenchmen even) and begging me to hasten their return, that I have not a moment's doubt about the attraction which Paris still holds for them'. But his hopes for Paris were in vain.[47] The colonised, as Serge Guilbaut put it, were becoming the colonisers.[48] By the time of *Moderne Kunst aus USA* (Modern Art from the USA), another MOMA exhibition, which began its European tour in Paris, March 1955, stopping in Frankfurt at the end of that year, it was clear, as Ernst Holzinger stated at the opening, that American art had 'come of age', and was now in a position to influence European trends.[49] The exhibitions *The New American Painting* and a show of drip paintings by Jackson Pollock that toured Europe during 1958–9 were victory laps for art from the New World.[50] The presence of fully developed Abstract

Expressionism at documenta 2 in 1959, with works such as Willem de Kooning's *Suburb in Havana* (1958), sixteen paintings by Jackson Pollock, works by Mark Rothko, Clifford Still, Franz Kline and Barnett Newman, as well as stirrings of post-Abstract Expressionist developments – a 'neo-avant garde' – with three works by Robert Rauschenberg, confirmed to a German audience that the centre of aesthetic gravity had irrevocably shifted from Paris to New York. The challenge of the New York school was by no means the only factor. In 1952, a German critic commented on the central role of the dealer-independent Venice Biennale in providing an alternative to the 'Art-dealer politicking and dictatorship of taste' that characterised the Parisian art scene,[51] and reference must also be made to Peggy Guggenheim's permanent presence in Venice. However, the New York school was incontestably the most important element. With all the moral backing of a recent military victory, and incomparable material resources of a nation undepleted by the war effort, New York had become what Paris had still been for one writer in mid-1945: 'the market place for the human spirit, the central world exchange on civilised values'.[52]

1 Dymschitz, A., 'Über die formalistische Richtung in der deutschen Malerei', *Tägliche Rundschau*, no. 271, 19 November 1948, and no. 275, 24 November 1948.

2 Herbert Vorwahsen, letter to Karin Thomas, 22 February 1983; cited in: Martin-Gropius-Bau, 360.

3 *Einheit*, no. 8/9, 1951. Reprinted in: Schubbe, 178–86.

4 Resolution of the Central Committee of the SED, 'Der Kampf gegen den Formalismus in der Kunst und Literatur für eine fortschrittliche deutsche Kultur', 15–17 March 1951. Reprinted in: Balluseck, 55–67, here 58.

5 Ibid., 61.

6 Cited by Groys, 1992, 39.

7 Grotewohl, O., 'Die Kunst im Kampf für Deutschlands Zukunft', *Neues Deutschland*, no. 203, 2 September 1951; reprinted in: Schubbe, 205–9.

8 Grotewohl, O., 'Die Eroberung der Kultur beginnt', *Der Bildende Künstler*, supplement to issue no. 7, 1951, 3.

9 Cf. Vali, 31–3.

10 Balluseck, 8–9.

11 Bundesministerium für gesamtdeutsche Fragen, 8.

12 Farrely.

13 Heymann, S., 'Kosmopolitismus und Formalismus', *Neues Deutschland*, no. 28, 1 December 1949. Reprinted in: Schubbe, 127–30.

14 Benjamin, 161.

15 Ulbricht, W., 'Kampf um ein realistisches Kunstschaffen', speech to the II Party conference of the SED, 9–12 July 1952, reprinted in: Schubbe, 239–40, here 239.

16 Ebon, 227.

17 Dmitrijewa, N., 'Das Problem des Typischen in der bildenden Kunst', *Der Bildende Künstler*, no. 4, April 1953, 7–12.

18 Lex-Nerlinger, A., 'Das Wandbild als Forderung Unserer Zeit', *bildende kunst*, no. 3, 1949, 92–3, here 93.

19 Seghers, A., 'Diego Rivera', *bildende kunst*, no. 3, 1949, 90–1.

20 Caden, G., 'Zwölf Wandbilder Entstehen', *bildende kunst*, no. 9, 1949, 269–70.

21 Forster, 5–10; Akademie der Künste der DDR, 9–38.

22 Gute, H., 'Kunst und Arbeit, ein Grundproblem der marxistischen Ästhetik', *Der Bildender Künstler*, 1952, no. 1, 10–24, here 19.

23 Schieder, M., 'Die *Documenta* 1 (1955)', in: François, 637–730; Schneckenburger; Wollenhaupt-Schmidt; Kimpel, 1997; Grasskamp, W., 'Die Unbewältigte Moderne: Entartete Kunst und documenta 1. Verfemung und Entschärfung', in: Merkert, 13–24.

24 Arnold Bode *et. al.*, 'Bodeplan', Dokumenta-Archiv, folder 20, d1.

25 Ibid.

26 'Gründungsprotokoll', DA folder 13. d1, 'Abendländische Gesellschaft der Kunst des 20. Jahrhunderts'.

27 Schwarze, D., 'Arnold Bode und der Impuls zur documenta', in: Heinz, 24–29.

28 Dokumenta-Archiv, folder 20, d1.

29 Kiaulehn, W., 'documenta. Fünfzig Jahre moderne Kunst im Spiegel der großen Kasseler Ausstellung', *München Merkur*, 30 June 1955.

30 'Programm-Ankündigung', March 1955, Dokumenta-Archiv, folder 8, d1.

31 Selz, P., 'Painting in the Twentieth Century; The Unknown Shore', *Art Bulletin*, no. 4, December 1963, 389–94, here 390; Hoffmann, E., 'Twentieth Century Painting', *The Burlington Magazine*, no. 686, May 1960, 214–5, here 214.

32 Museum Friedericianum, 26–7.

33 Haftmann, 1954, 436. Cf. chapter four for Grote's exhibitions.

34 Ibid., 439.

35 Ibid., 446 (translation from Haftmann, 1960, 320).

36 Ibid., 445.

37 Ibid., 448 (translation from Haftmann, 1960, 447).

38 Leonhard, K., 'Malerei im 20.Jahrhundert. Zu dem Buch von Werner Haftmann', *Das Kunstwerk*, no. 1, 1955/6, 59–61.

39 Haftmann, 1954, 479 (translation from Haftmann, 1960, 375).

40 Guilbaut, 1990, 51.

41 Cf. Vali, 141–57.

42 Cf. Cullerne-Bown, 165–227; Johnson.

43 Guilbaut, 1985, 176; Saunders, 2000, 253–6.

44 Wankmüller, R., 'Tachisten in USA', *Das Kunstwerk*, no. 5 1955/6; Fischer, K.J., 'Was ist Taschismus?', *Das Kunstwerk* no. 5, 1955/6, 17–21.

45 Ruby, 292–4.

46 Wilson, 387.

47 Kahnweiler, D-H., 'The State of Painting in Paris. 1945 Assessment', *Horizon*, vol. XII, no. 71, November 1945, 333–41, here 338.

48 Guilbaut, 1983, 174.

49 Ruby, 340.
50 Ruby, 372–402.
51 Hodin, J-P., 'Bedeutung der Biennale', *Das Kunstwerk*, no. 5, 1952, 43–4.
52 Spender, 109.

Artists, Art Historians and Critics

Notes are restricted to artists, art historians and critics mentioned in this book, and emphasis is given to their activities in the decade after 1945. In the case of artists, the city or region with which they are most strongly associated is indicated.

Balden, Theo [Koehler, Otto]
(1904–1995) *Berlin*

After training as a technical draughtsman, Koehler studied from 1922–3 at the Bauhaus under László Moholy-Nagy and Oskar Schlemmer. He moved to Berlin and joined the KPD (1928) and ASSO (1929). He was interned by the Gestapo in 1934, and then, after adopting the name Theo Balden in 1935, spent his first years of exile in Prague, where he was co-founder of the Oskar-Kokoschka-Bundes, an anti-fascist artists' collective established in late 1937 to support German émigrés, which also counted the artist Heinz Worner (b. 1910) and John Heartfield (1891–1968) amongst its members. In 1939, with the help of the Artists' Refugee Committee (co-founded by Roland Penrose and Fred Uhlmann), he escaped by plane to London, and became involved with the Free German League of Culture, a prominent refugee organisation, and the Artists' International Association. From June 1940 to January 1941, he was interned as an enemy alien in Canada. He returned to Britain, and lived in Derby, where his work was influenced in particular by Henry Moore. An exhibition of Balden's work toured Derby, Stoke-on-Trent and Nottingham during 1946–7. In January 1947 he returned to Berlin, and shortly after had his first solo exhibition at the Galerie Franz. He was a regular contributor to the satirical journal *Ulenspiegel* from 1948–50, and was involved in East German cultural institutions in the early 1950s, teaching and exhibiting. His work, influenced by western abstraction, was never fully accepted in the East until the mid-1960s, when he gained widespread recognition within the official East German art world.

Baumeister, Willi
(1889–1955) *Stuttgart*

Baumeister was the most prominent modern painter working in an abstract manner during the 1920s and early 1930s who was not formally associated with the Bauhaus. He studied and worked in Stuttgart, then in Frankfurt, where he taught at the Städelsche Kunstschule from 1928. His paintings from this time are often compared with those of Fernand Léger, figurative works based on a classicising, mechanical aesthetic. From around 1930 his paintings became more abstract, coded and concerned with metaphysical or allusive subject matter. Four of his works were included in the 1937 *Entartete Kunst* exhibition, and in 1941 he was banned from exhibiting. With Oskar Schlemmer he worked at Kurt Herbert's paint factory in Wuppertal, enabling him to remain in Germany during the Third Reich. He was appointed professor at the Kunstakademie, Stuttgart, in 1946. His postwar paintings were made as themed groups, an approach reminiscent of Kandinsky. He published a resumé of his ideas about painting in 1947 under the title *Das Unbekannte in der Kunst* (The Unknown in Art), in which he elaborated the idea of a spiritual underpinning for abstract painting.

Behne, Adolph Bruno
(1885–1948)

Behne studied architecture for two years at the Technischen Hochschule Berlin-Charlottenburg, before studying art history at the Friedrich-Wilhelm Universität in 1907, completing a thesis *Inkrustationsstil in der Toskana* (The Incrustation Style of Tuscany), under tuition from Heinrich Wölfflin and the philosopher and social theorist Georg Simmel. He was then active as a freelance writer and editor, contributing to many left-wing journals, notably the organs of the International Socialist movement, *Sozialistische Monatshefte*, and *Die Hilfe*. He also taught at the Hochschule, promoted adult education and was part of the *Volksbildungbewegung* (People's Education Movement), and a lifelong advocate of the reformist principles of the Volkshochschule movement. By 1913, he was a member of the Werkbund. He was also associated with Herwarth Walden and the Sturm circle, publishing his first book *Zur neuen Kunst* (On New Art), a survey of modern art with an emphasis on German Expressionism, with Walden in 1915. In 1919 he was one of the founder members of the Arbeitsrat für Kunst, acting as business manager and contributing to its publications. He visited Russia in 1923, following his activities as founder of the Gesellschaft der Freunde des neuen Russland (Society of Friends of New Russia), and contributions to the journal *Neues Russland*. His most important book, *Der Moderne Zweckbau* (Modern Functional Building), was published in 1925 (though completed two years earlier), and has been compared to Gustav Hartlaub's 1925 *Neue Sachlichkeit* exhibition in establishing a new focus on functionalism and objectivity. Behne was banned from teaching by the Nazis in 1933, due to his position on the executive committee of PEN (Poets, Essayists, Novelists, an international free-speech organisation founded in 1921). During the Third Reich, Behne remained in Berlin, acting as a correspondent for the English magazine *The Studio* (as he had been since 1921) and writing inoffensive articles for non-political journals and similarly neutral books, including the series *Kunst der Gegenwart* (Art of the Present). In 1946, Behne was called by the painter Karl Hofer to teach at the newly instituted Hochschule für bildende Künste in Berlin. Realising that Nazi propaganda had made a profound impact on general opinion, Behne was also extremely active in promoting public consciousness of modern art. He lectured and published a book with the title *Entartete Kunst* (Degenerate Art), an exposé of Nazi propaganda and the Reich's defamation of the modern movement. His concepts of art and art history were given a concise expression in the foreword written for the exhibition catalogue *150 Jahre soziale Strömungen in der bildenden Kunst* (150 Years of Social Currents in the Fine Arts), Berlin 1947, the year before his death.

Breitenbach, Edgar
(1903–1977)

Breitenbach studied art history and German and Scandinavian literature at Munich and Hamburg, the latter under Erwin Panofsky and Fritz Saxl. He completed his dissertation in 1929 under Panofsky. He worked as an assistant in the Warburg Library in Hamburg 1926–7, then studied librarianship in Göttingen and Berlin 1927–9. He worked until 1933 in the Frankfurt Stadtbibliothek, but was dismissed in 1933 by the Nazis on the basis of the 'Gesetzes zur Wiederherstellung des Berufsbeamtentums', the law removing 'non-Aryans' from the civil service. From 1933–7, he lived in Basel and London, emigrating finally to the USA in 1937. In 1943, the same year he took up American citizenship, he worked for the Federal Communications Commission, monitoring German radio broadcasts, and from 1944–5 was Chief of Documentary Operations in the Office of War Information. He returned to Germany with the American Military Government in 1945, based first in Berlin, and from 1946–9 in the Central Art Collection Point in Munich as MFA&A officer, researching the provenance of Nazi loot. He was one of the founders of the Zentralinstituts für Kunstgeschichte. From 1949–53 he worked in the American High Commission in Bad Neuheim and Frankfurt, within the Cultural Relations Division, Section for Fine Arts, Museums, Libraries and Archives, where he played an important part in the reconstruction of German libraries. He returned to Washington in 1956, where until 1973, he was head of the Prints and Photographs division of the Library of Congress in Washington.

Caden, Gert
(1891–1990) *Berlin*

Caden studied in Dresden and Munich and was from 1921 a member of the International Constructivist Group. From Constructivism, he moved to experimentation with photomontage, and also produced set and costume designs for theatres in Berlin. He joined the KPD in 1930, and was involved in anti-fascist activities until his emigration to Paris in 1938. He was interned at Les Milles in the South of France, 1939–40. In 1942 he emigrated to Cuba, via Morocco, and founded the Komitees deutscher Antifaschisten (Committee of German Anti-Fascists), as well as the Freundeskreises Alexander von Humboldt (Society of Friends of Alexander von Humboldt). He was influenced by the work of Diego Rivera and David Alfaro Siqueiros. He returned to Soviet-occupied Germany in 1948, where he became involved with cultural activities in East Germany. He was the artistic director of the 2. *Deutsche Kunstausstellung* in Dresden, 1949.

Cavael, Rolf
(1898–1979) *Munich*

Cavael was a self-taught painter, whose brief association with the Bauhaus in 1930 led to a lasting friendship with Kandinsky. His first exhibition, held in Braunschweig, together with works by Josef Albers, was closed by the Nazis on the opening day. He continued working in retreat in Southern Bavaria after an official ban on painting from the Nazis, and as a result was interned in Dachau for nine months during 1937. Much of his work was seized and destroyed. Cavael remained in South Germany throughout the war. He was interned by the Americans in Munich after 1945 for refusing to take part in denazification. He was a founder member of Zen 49, and participated in all exhibitions mounted by the artists' group.

Claasen, Hermann
(1899–1987) *Cologne*

Claasen worked as a commercial photographer before the war. On the 31 May 1942 his studio and photographic archive was completely destroyed during a bombing raid on Cologne. He continued taking photographs of the attacks on Cologne, despite an official ban on photography. After the war, he was commissioned to document the destruction of the Rhenish towns Düren, Jülich and Hürtgenwald, published in the book *Verbrannte Erde* (Burnt Earth, 1949) and also produced a series on the destruction of Cologne, *Gesang im Feuerofen* (Songs of the Furnace, 1947). Konrad Adenauer was a friend and keen supporter. During the 1950s Claasen exhibited at the *Photokina* exhibitions, and worked both as a portrait and industrial photographer.

Dahmen, Karl Fred
(1917-1981) *Rhineland*

Dahmen studied graphic art in Aachen in the early 1930s, and also worked as a painter. He served in the Wehrmacht from 1939–45, and was active in France, the Balkans and Russia. He had his first solo exhibition in Aachen in 1946. The next year he was able to visit Paris and made contact with artists who influenced the development of abstract painting in his work. His paintings until around 1949 were loosely naturalistic, often depicting townscapes or interiors. After this moment, he painted in an exclusively abstract manner. He exhibited with the junger westen group from 1950, and in 1952 co-founded the Neue Aachener Gruppe with Carl Schneider, Fritz Martin, Franz Josef Herold and Engelbert Mainzer. In 1953, he co-founded the Düsseldorf-based Gruppe 53, with Peter Brüning, Gerhard Hoehme and others.

Dix, Otto
(1891–1969) *Dresden, Hemmenhofen*

Dix's depiction of Dresden burning in the background of his painting *Lot und seine Töchter* (Lot and his Daughters, 1939) was an extraordinary prediction of the disaster to come, comparable to Ludwig Meidner's visions of destruction before the First World War. He was relieved of all honours, teaching posts and permission to exhibition when the Nazis came into power in 1933. He moved away from the city, eventually settling in Hemmenhofen, a small town near Konstanz on the Zeller See, in 1936. His works during the Third Reich employed a highly refined technique, and dwelt on biblical themes and landscapes. His fate as a prisoner of war and the nature of his work after 1945 is described above.

Duda, Fritz
(1904–1991) *Berlin*

Duda studied at the Folkwangschule in Essen from 1922–3, and then in Berlin as a student of Karl Hofer and Paul Plontke. He joined ASSO in 1928 and the KPD in 1929. He was banned from exhibiting in 1936, and from 1939 to 1944 worked as a draughtsman in the office of an architect. During this time, he was also engaged in illegal anti-fascist action. His studio and work were destroyed in a bombing raid in 1944. After the war, he made efforts to re-establish ASSO, but was soon willingly incorporated into the newly devised Socialist art structures of the Soviet Zone and subsequently of East Germany, for instance as a co-founder in 1950 of the Verband Bildender Künstler. He had his first postwar exhibition at the Galerie Franz in Berlin-Wilmersdorf in 1948. Whereas his work of the 1920s and 30s shows the influence of French painting, in particular of Henri Rousseau, after the war he adopted a more illustrative manner that accorded both in style and subject matter to Socialist Realist requirements.

Ende, Edgar
(1901–1965) *Munich*

Ende developed a reputation as a Surrealist painter in Germany during the 1920s and 1930s, making figurative paintings with dream-like imagery, influenced by Giorgio de Chirico and René Magritte, and also by his early interest in the occult and anthroposophy. He served with the German infantry during the war. In April 1944 his studio in Munich, and numerous paintings, drawings and prints, were destroyed by Allied bombs. After 1945 Ende returned to work in Munich, taking up his pictorial concerns from the 1930s in a manner that reflected little on his experiences during the war, or the changed political circumstances. He was involved in cultural reconstruction in Munich, and was a founding member of the Neue Gruppe, which also counted Rudolph Schlichter and Fritz Winter amongst its members. His work was included in many of the survey exhibitions of German art that appeared at this time, including the *Allgemeine Deutsche Kunstausstellung in Dresden*, 1946, and the German contribution to the 1948 Venice Biennale, organised by the Director of the Munich Staatsgemäldesammlung, Eberhard Hanfstaengl. He also took part in the exhibition of surrealist painting, *Vision und Magie* (Vision and Magic), mounted in the Galerie Egon Günther, in Mannheim, 1948. In 1951 he was a founding member of the Internationalen Vereinigung der Surrealisten, a group instigated by the Swiss painter Walter Grab (1927–1989), which included Rudolph Schlichter and the young Arnulf Rainer amongst its members. The group had an exhibition at the Saarland Museum in 1952, *Peinture Surréaliste en Europe – Surrealistische Malerei in Europa* (Surrealist Painting in Europe), and was dissolved soon afterwards.

Evers, Hans Gerhard
(1900–1993)

Evers studied literature at Göttingen University, writing a thesis on Winckelmann and Lessing. His subsequent move to Heidelberg, and contact with the archeologist Ludwig Curtius, the Egyptologist Hermann Ranke and also Friedrich Gundolf, a member of the Stefan-George circle, influenced him to transfer his attentions to art history. He qualified as a lecturer in Munich with his work *Die Breitrichtung der Basilika* in 1932, written under the aegis of Wilhelm Pinder, and became Professor at Munich University in 1942. In 1950 he accepted a teaching position at the Technischen Hochschule in Darmstadt, where he remained until his retirement in 1968. He was one of the motivating figures behind the 1950 Darmstädter Gespräch. His *Rubens* (1942) is written in the form of a historical novel, and gives an account of Rubens as both artist and statesman. In *Vom Historismus zum Funktionalismus* (From Historicism to Functionalism, 1967), he offered a revisionist account of nineteenth-century historicist architecture. His last publication was an attempt to rescue Ludwig II of Bavaria from popular stereotype as a mad king, casting him rather as the last enlightened monarch, who was able to imprint his stylistic vision on his architectural commissions.

Fechter, Paul Otto Heinrich
(1880–1958)

Journalist, theatre and literary critic, historian, novelist, Fechter studied architecture and natural science in Berlin, completing his doctoral thesis, *Die Grundlagen der Realdialektik* (The Foundations of Material Dialetics) in 1906. He began working as a journalist on the *Dresdner Neuesten Nachrichten*, moving to Berlin in 1911 to work on the *Vossischen Zeitung*. From 1918 until 1933 he was a cultural critic for the *Deutschen Allgemeinen Zeitung*. His 1914 *Expressionismus* (Expressionism) was one of the first descriptions of Expressionism as a spiritual artistic movement. He was known primarily as a theatre critic but also wrote extensively on literature, with a distinct preference for German national traditions. After 1945, he published a monograph on Knut Hamsun (1952), and a three-volume survey of European drama, *Das europäische Drama* (1956–8). His novels are now largely forgotten, with the exception of the play *Der Zauberer Gottes*, published in 1940.

Geiger, Rupprecht
(b. 1908) *Munich*

After studying and then working as an architect, Geiger began painting while a soldier on the Eastern Front in Poland and Russia. During 1943 and 1944 he was a war artist in the Ukraine and Greece. He returned from service in 1945 to live in Munich. He began exhibiting representational picassoesque paintings, notably in the exhibition *Extreme Malerei* (Extreme Painting, 1947), and also three surrealistic works on paper in Paris at the *IIIème Salon des Réalités Nouvelles*, summer 1948. During the same year he began making minimal, brightly coloured abstract works, which he developed in one of the most idiosyncratic and forward-looking oeuvres in abstract painting at this time. In July 1949, Geiger was a co-founder of the Gruppe der Gegendstandlosen süddeutsche Künstler (Group of Non-Objective South German Artists), which received significant support from the British diplomat John Anthony Thwaites, then based in Munich, and the American artist Hilla von Rebay, also the founding director of what was to become the Guggenheim Museum in New York. Before its first exhibition in April 1950, the group renamed itself as Zen 49. Geiger was from 1965 to 1976 Professor of painting at the Kunstakademie Düsseldorf.

Gilles, Werner
(1894–1961) *Munich*

After studying at the Weimar Akademie, Gilles enrolled in the Bauhaus, where he studied, from 1919 to 1923 under Lyonel Feininger. He travelled extensively from the early 1920s, and developed a form of lyrical abstraction influenced in part by Matisse. He frequently visited the Italian island of Ischia, where he was inspired by the antique landscape. He remained in Germany throughout most of the war, travelling occasionally, and served for a period in the Wehrmacht. He settled in Munich in the early 1950s.

Götz, Karl-Otto
(b. 1914) *Rhineland*

During the 1930s, Götz studied in Aachen and Dresden. The modern idiom he adopted led to a painting and exhibition ban from 1935 to 1936. He was nevertheless able to continue working in an experimental manner with painting, photography and film during his military service (1936–8). He settled in Dresden in 1940, and served in the Wehrmacht in Norway from 1941 to 1945. After the war, he moved to Königsförde, near Hamelin, in the British Zone, and continued experimenting with abstract painting and photography. He was the only German artist associated with the COBRA group, and was a co-founder of the German Art informel group Quadriga. Under the pseudonym André Tamm, from 1948–53, he edited the journal *Die Metamorphose*, known from its second issue as *META*. This was largely dedicated to the abstract and surrealist tendencies that interested Götz. In his memoirs (*Erinnerungen*, 3 vols., Aachen, 1994), he describes his interest in Surrealism at this time, writing surrealist poetry and translating Maurice Nadeau's *History of Surrealism*. He was also associated with the painter William Gear, then working as a visiting artist in Celle in the British Zone. The fifth issue of *META* was dedicated to English painters and poets, and contained work by Peter Lanyon, Charles Howard, Alan Davie, William Gear and Stephen Gilbert. Götz was one of the most cosmopolitan of artists working in Germany at this time. In 1959 he began teaching at the Kunstakademie Düsseldorf.

Graetz, René
(1908–1974) *Berlin*

Graetz was a self-taught artist who spent the years 1929–38 living in South Africa, where he became engaged to Hester Henrietta Crouse, who was later to marry the English critic William Empson. He went into exile in Zurich, Paris, and finally London in 1939, where he met and in 1944 married the Irish illustrator Elizabeth Shaw. He was interned as an enemy alien and sent to Canada in the latter half of 1939, but like many others, was soon released. He was involved in anti-fascist activities in London and was a member of the Free German League of Culture. His decision to move to Berlin in 1946 with his wife was by no means a return home, and may be taken as some indication of the excitement emanating from the city at this time. His cosmopolitanism sat uneasily with SED cultural politics, although he was awarded several official honours. Among his best-known works are commemorative sculptures at Buchenwald and Sachsenhausen.

Grohmann, Will
(1887–1968)

After a childhood in Dresden, Grohmann studied art history, literature, philosophy and oriental languages in Leipzig and Paris (1908–13). On completion of his dissertation, in 1914, he turned his attention to art criticism. Following the First World War, Grohmann contributed entries to Ulrich Thieme and Felix Becker's *Allgemeines Kunstlexicon* as well as writing articles for the magazine *Cicerone*.

He was a member of the Novembergruppe in 1919, and became strongly involved in the artistic scene of his home town, Dresden. As well as various teaching positions, from 1926–9 he worked as an Assistant at the Staatlichen Gemäldegalerie in Dresden, and also assisted in the organisation of the 1926 *Internationalen Kunstausstellung*. He was dismissed from all his positions by the Nazis in 1933 as a result of his views on modern art, but was able to continue working as an art critic and journalist by joining, in July 1936, the Reichsschriftumskammer. Prior to gaining an official place as a writer in the Third Reich, he had published a book on his friend the dancer Palucca under a Nordic pseudonym, Olaf Rydberg (*Die Tänzerin Palucca*, 1935). During the war, he contributed a significant number of articles to the newspapers *Deutsche Allgemeine Zeitung* and *Das Reich*. He also worked on a finally unpublished book on the art historian Josef Strzygowski, known for his valorisation of 'Nordic', racially determined art. Lacking a visa, he was unable to take up an offer from the School of the Art Institute of Chicago in 1939. After the war, he initially settled in the Soviet Zone, and took a series of positions in the cultural hierarchies of the Dresden Magistrate. It was in this capacity that he organised, in collaboration with Hans Grundig, the *Allgemeine Deutschen Kunstausstellung*, one of the first significant exhibitions in postwar Germany. He was also professor and rector at the Hochschüle für Werkkunst, Dresden (1947–8), but in 1948, as the tensions between East and West were mounting, he moved to West Berlin and became a Professor at the Hochschüle für Bildende Künste (1948–58). The bitter dispute that developed between Karl Hofer and Grohmann was an aspect of the broader debate that confronted representational with abstract art. Although much of the antagonism was motivated by Hofer's own annoyance at what he saw as the sectarian nature of the support for abstract art, the debate demonstrated that it was not just Soviet political imperatives that were behind the anti-abstraction feeling. Just as Hans Sedlmayr had lamented the 'loss of the centre' in an anthropological sense, so Hofer, at the opening of the fourth Künstlerbund exhibition, lamented the vanishing of the *Menschenbild* (human image) in contemporary painting. Grohmann, surrounded by those painters that had left the Künstlerbund in protest at Hofer's polemical stance, kept aloof from direct engagement with Hofer, though was unwavering in his support for artists such as those connected with the Zen 49 group, Willi Baumeister, Rupprecht Geiger, Theodor Werner and Fritz Winter, the avatars of abstraction in postwar Germany. The debate ceased after Hofer's death in 1955. From that year, Grohmann became editor of the journal *Quadrum*. In 1962, at the age of seventy-five, he was made honorary president of the newly founded Association internationale des critiques d'art. After his death six years later, his widow, Annemarie Zilz, whom he had married in 1966, donated his archive and personal library to the Staatsgalerie Stuttgart.

Grote, Ludwig
(1893–1974)

Grote studied art history in Jena (1912), followed by architecture in Braunschweig (1912–19), during which time he was also on military service, for the duration of the First World War. From 1919–22, he studied art history in Munich and Halle under Paul Frankl, completing a dissertation on the Saxon printmaker Georg Lemberger, published in 1924. He went on to work in Dessau as a conservator, and then as director of the Dessau Gemäldegalerie. He was instrumental in inviting the Bauhaus to move to Dessau after the Weimar premises were closed, leading to extensive contact between Grote and Bauhaus members. This contact led in 1933 to his dismissal by the Nazis, and move to Berlin, where he took up private teaching and consultation work. At this time, he was associated with the circle around Carl Georg Heise, Theodor Heuss and Leopold

Reidemeister. During the Second World War he undertook military service on the Eastern Front. From 1945–9 he was active in Munich as an art dealer. In 1949, he organised the important exhibition *Der Blaue Reiter – München und die Kunst des 20. Jahrhunderts.* This was followed by further exhibitions that played an important role in locating postwar opinion about 'degenerate art': *Die Maler am Bauhaus* (1950), *Oskar Kokoschka* (1950) and *Max Beckmann* (1951). As Director of the Germanischen Nationalmuseums in Nuremberg, he was reponsible for further important exhibitions on a variety of subjects, including monographic exhibitions of Ludwig Kirchner, Walter Gropius and Picasso. He published many works on his specialist areas: German art of the Romantic and Modern periods, and Albrecht Dürer.

Grundig, Hans
(1901–1958) *Dresden*

Hans Grundig studied painting in Dresden during the 1920s. His work at this was influenced both by the realism of Otto Dix and by the *art populaire* exemplified by Henri Rousseau. He joined the KPD in 1926. His painting *Reich of a Thousand Years* (1935–8), a triptych depicting a nightmarish scenario of destruction, is a striking portent of the disasters to come, and is perhaps his best work. From 1940–4 he was interned in KZ Sachsenhausen. After 1945 he was strongly involved in cultural reconstruction in Dresden, acting as the rector of the Hochschule für Bildende Künste from 1946–8.

Grundig, Lea [née Langer]
(1906–1977) *Dresden*

Lea Grundig studied in Dresden in the early 1920s, coming under the influence of Otto Dix. She married Hans Grundig in 1928, and became involved in left-wing organisations. In 1939 she fled to Palestine, where she was interned but able to continue working as an artist. She returned to Germany in 1948 and went on producing works with humanitarian themes. She was President of the Verband Bildender Künstler from 1964–70.

Haftmann, Werner
(1912–1999)

Haftmann studied art history, philosophy and archeology in Göttingen and Berlin, 1932–6. In 1935, he began contributing to the journal *Art and Nation*, soon banned by the Nazis. From 1936, he worked in the Art Historical Institute in Florence, and studied the cultural history of the early Italian Renaissance. He served in the German army from 1940 and was interred. From 1950–5, he was a lecturer at the Staatlichen Hochschule für Bildende Kunst in Hamburg. He published a book on Paul Klee in 1950, and the highly important *Malerei im 20. Jahrhunderts* (Painting in the Twentieth Century) in 1954. He was a member of the committee involved in the organisation of the first three Documenta exhibitions. From 1967–74, he served as director of the National Gallery in Berlin.

Hausenstein, Wilhelm
(1882–1957)

After studies in Heidelberg and Munich, Hausenstein became involved in Socialist politics, joining the SPD in 1907, around the same time that he decided to devote himself to freelance writing. He also began attending lectures on the history of art at the university of Munich. He began publishing broadly on art-historical themes, and quickly became a leading critical supporter of Expressionism. In 1912, he was involved in the founding of the Munich new Secession. In the years leading up to the First World War, Hausenstein was a key supporter of Expressionism. In his *Der nackte*

Mensch in der Kunst aller Zeiten und Völker (The Human Body in World Art), of 1913, he prophesised a new era of art based on Socialist ideas of collective endeavour. With the exception of fellow SPD member Adolf Behne, Hausenstein was one of the only critics to promote Expressionism from a left-wing viewpoint. From early 1916 to late 1917, he was stationed in Brussels, where he edited the German-language journal *Der Belfried*. He continued publishing broadly on art after the war, though moved away from his prewar enthusiasm for Expressionism. His increasing antipathy towards the movement could be heard in lectures he gave in Berlin in March 1918, and published later that year, just before the end of the war, as *Über Expressionismus in der Malerei* (On Expressionism in Painting). By the end of 1919, his disillusion was complete, and he could declare Expressionism a manifestation of decadence, and a causal factor in the doomed war effort. One of the key reasons for this shift was the extreme popularity and vulgarisation of Expressionism by 1918. Although he continued to write about art, his views were predicated on a notion of dissolution and decline. He took refuge in the art of the past, as well as publishing travel books. Both he and his wife Margot converted to Catholicism in 1940. In 1934 he became literary editor for the *Frankfurter Zeitung*, remaining so for most of the Third Reich, until he was dismissed shortly before the liberal and independent newspaper was finally closed down by the Nazis in 1943. In an open letter to Thomas Mann, published in the *Süddeutsche Zeitung* in December 1945, Hausenstein refuted Mann's claim that all literature published in Germany during the Third Reich was worthless, citing many examples, including art-historical literature. He continued his art and literary criticism after the war, writing in particular on nineteenth-century French poetry, as well as publishing an autobiographical novel, *Lux Perpetua*, in 1947. His criticisms of modern art as socially dysfunctional and symptomatic of decline are comparable, at this moment, to those of Hans Sedlmayr. His 1949 *Was bedeutet die moderne Kunst?* (What is Modern Art?), which rehearsed his anti-modernist stance, was criticised by Willi Baumeister in the 1950 Darmstädter Gespräch, in the same breath as Sedlmayr's 1948 *Verlust der Mitte*. Involvement with Franco-German relations at this moment led to his appointment in 1950 as General Consul in Paris, and then in 1953 as German Ambassador to France, a post he held until 1955. An account of his experiences in Paris was published posthumously as *Pariser Erinnerungen. Aus fünf Jahren diplomatischen Dienstes 1950–1955* (Paris Memoirs: Five Years of Diplomatic Service, 1950–1955, 1961). Hausenstein died in Munich in 1957.

Heckel, Erich
(1883–1970) *Berlin, Hemmenhofen*

In the wake of persecution, Heckel left Berlin, spending periods of time in Carinthia, Austria. In 1944, his studio and many works were destroyed in the Allied bombardment. He moved to Hemmenhofen on the Swiss border, near where Otto Dix was living, and stayed there in retirement, apart from a period teaching at the Kunstakademie in Karlsruhe (1949–55).

Heldt, Werner
(1904–1954) *Berlin*

Heldt served in anti-aircraft units during the war, and was interned by the British in 1945. He lived in the Soviet Zone of Berlin from 1946–9, and was strongly associated with the Galerie Gerd Rosen, where he had a solo exhibition in March 1946. Around this time, he began the series of paintings and drawings for which he is best known, entitled 'Berlin am Meer' (Berlin at Sea), showing melancholy scenes of Berlin after an imaginary deluge. These works show above all the strong influence of Ferdinand Léger, but carry none of the French artist's optimism. He moved to West Berlin in 1950.

Höch, Hannah
(1889–1978) *Berlin*

Höch remained in Germany throughout the war, living in Heiligensee in the North of Berlin. Her most notable contributions to postwar reconstruction were her membership of the Fantasten group and her participation in its sole exhibition at the Galerie Gerd Rosen, Berlin, as well as the exhibition that she organised on the theme of Dada and photomontage for the same gallery in late 1946, the sole attempt to revalorise the Dada movement in Germany in the early years after the war.

Hofer, Karl
(1878–1955) *Berlin*

Hofer was a central figure in postwar cultural life, having been appointed director of the newly opened Kunsthochschule of Berlin-Charlottenburg as early as June 1945 by the Soviet authorities. On 3 July of that year, he was made a vice-president of the Kulturbund zur demokratischen Erneuerung Deutschlands. In April 1947, he founded the magazine *bildende kunst* with Oskar Nerlinger, in which one of the first public statements of the realism/abstraction debate appeared. Hofer stood as the first president of the re-instated Künstlerbund 1950, with Karl Schmidt-Rottluff and Karl Hartung as vice-presidents. The purpose of the society, originally formed in 1902 and banned by the Nazis in 1936, is stated in the catalogue of the first exhibition, held at the Hochschule für Bildende Künste, Berlin, in 1951: to represent and promote German artists at home and abroad. Despite his official success, Hofer was nevertheless disillusioned with the reception of his work, and was involved in a public dispute with Will Grohmann and other supporters of abstraction, who disagreed with his support of a realistic painting style. The debate was unresolved at the time of his death. His painting developed an uneasy form of simplified, symbolic realism.

Kesting, Edmund
(1892–1970) *Dresden, Berlin*

Kesting's series of manipulated photographs of Dresden in the wake of the Allied bombardment, entitled *Dresdner Totentanz* (Dresden Dance of Death), are amongst the most memorable responses to the Allied bombing of his native town. He was closely involved in postwar cultural reconstruction, was a founder member of the group Der Ruf, and organised its first exhibition in November 1945. He was a member of the jury for the *Allgemeine Deutsche Kunstausstellung*, held in Dresden the next year. He taught photography at Dresden and then in East Berlin, where in 1953 he was dismissed without notice as a result of the 'formal' tendencies of his work. His work often betrays the influence of Klee. From 1955 to 1960 he taught photography in Potsdam.

Kubicěk, Juro
(1906–1970) *Berlin*

Kubicěk was a self-taught painter, active in Berlin before the war. He served in the propaganda section of the Wehrmacht and took part in the Russian Campaign. He was once again active as an artist in Berlin after 1945, and had his first solo exhibition in the Galerie Franz in 1947. As the first artist in an exchange programme established by the US State Department, he worked at the University of Louisville, Kentucky from December 1947 to July 1949. On his return, he worked in the Amerika-Haus on Nollendorfplatz in Berlin.

Löffler, Fritz
(1899–1988)

Löffler's intimate connection with his native Dresden defined much of his writing as an art historian and critic. After diverse studies, and a dissertation on the poet Eduard von Keserling, he obtained a position at the Staatlichen

Gemäldegalerie in Dresden. Dismissed from this post in 1937 for promoting left-wing art, he was not to regain employment at the Dresden Gallery until 1948 – only to be dismissed two years later by the East German government for 'reactionary' tendencies. From 1951 until his retirement in 1968, he worked at the Institut für Denkmalpflege (Institute for the Care of Monuments). During this time, he published many accounts of Dresden architecture, and was actively involved in the restoration of the Baroque city. He wrote the first catalogue raisonnée for the paintings of Otto Dix in 1981. Löffler's friendship with Dix dated from the 1920s and 30s, when he was a member of the Hirsch circle around Fritz Beinert, son of the collector Ida Beinert. Löffler organised the first exhibition of Dix's works in Dresden in 1933.

Mammen, Jeanne
(1890–1976) *Berlin*

Educated in Paris, Mammen worked as an artist in Berlin, gradually acquiring a reputation for her socially engaged realism, which has been compared to that of Dix and Grosz. Her success at this time was confirmed by a solo exhibition at the Galerie Fritz Gurlitt in 1930. She survived the Third Reich in Berlin by working in advertising and also as an itinerant bookseller. She continued making work after the war, and was associated with the circle of artists around the Galerie Gerd Rosen in Berlin, having an exhibition there in 1947. She also participated in the exhibition *Zone 5* at the Galerie Franz in late 1948, and the next year in the 'existential cabaret' founded in Berlin as *Die Badewanne*.

Marcks, Gerhard
(1889–1981) *Rhineland*

Marcks led the pottery workshop at the Bauhaus from 1920 to 1925, and then taught in Halle. During the war, which he spent in Germany, many of his works were destroyed in air raids. After the war, he taught in Hamburg, before settling in Cologne in 1950. He created a number of memorials for soldiers and civilians killed during the war, and completed Ernst Barlach's frieze for the facade of the Katherinenkirche in Lübeck.

Martin, Kurt
(1899 –1975)

Martin studied philosophy and art history in Freiburg after the First World War, with, amongst others, Martin Heidegger, Edmund Husserl and Hans Jantzen. Under Heinrich Wölfflin, he wrote a doctoral thesis on fourteenth-century stone sculpture from Nuremberg, and then worked at the Mannheim Kunsthalle under Gustav Hartlaub. During the Second World War, Martin was in charge of museums and the protection of monuments in the Upper Rhien region. After 1945, he assisted the Allies with the restitution of works, particularly those that had been seized from the Karlsruhe Kunsthalle, of which he was appointed director. He was involved in exhibitions in collaboration with the Allies, including an exhibition of German art that toured the USA in 1948. From 1956–7, he was director of the Academy of Fine Arts in Karlsruhe, from where he moved to become Director of the Munich Gemäldesammlungen, a post he held until 1964.

Mataré, Ewald
(1887–1965) *Rhineland*

Mataré was Professor of sculpture at the Kunst-akademie Düsseldorf for a very brief period before being dismissed by the Nazis in 1933. He took up a post at the same institution after 1945, and continued his work as a sculptor, producing many public commissions, particularly for churches. Alongside his involvement with the postwar Kirchliche Kunst movement, he is noted for the influence he had on his pupil, Joseph Beuys.

Nagel, Otto
(1894–1967) *Berlin*

Nagel's activities as a painter in Berlin during the 1920s and 1930s were strongly influenced by his commitment to Communism. He was associated with other artists living in Berlin who were engaged with proletarian themes, notably Heinrich Zille and Käthe Kollwitz. In 1925, he became secretary of the Internationale Arbeiterhilfe (an International Communist affiliate, established in Berlin by Willi Münzenberg in 1921, which produced and distributed propaganda films and provided social security for workers), and was strongly involved in cultural exchanges with Russia. In 1933, he was banned by the Nazis from painting in his studio, and took instead to working outside, creating a series of works that are important documents of Berlin before the Allied bombardment. In 1937 he spent a short time in the Sachsenhausen concentration camp. After 1945, he was a key figure in the Socialist cultural reconstruction, and was involved with many of the key institutions. Despite these official engagements, his work remained rooted in the outmoded proletarian style of the 1920s, a style in conflict with the more classical demands of Socialist Realism.

Nay, Ernst Wilhelm
(1902–1968) *Rhineland*

A successful painter in a semi-abstract style before the war, Nay later served in the German infantry in France, and was subsequently interned by the Americans. After his release in 1945, he lived in Hofheim, near Frankfurt, moving to Cologne in 1951. The paintings he produced during the war, and in the first years after 1945, introduced expressive, figurative elements into an oeuvre that had hitherto been dominated by a calm, largely decorative abstract manner. These postwar works are often referred to as the 'Hekaten-Bilder' (Hecate Paintings), a name derived from two works made during 1945 and 1946, *Tochter der Hekate I* and *Tochter der Hekate II* (Hecate's Daughter I and II), showing Nay's interest at this time in themes of classical mythology. His paintings were exhibited in 1946 by Günther Franke in Munich and Gerd Rosen in Berlin, and thereafter in numerous exhibitions throughout the western zones. Around 1947–9 his work developed in tandem with contemporary trends, once again employing decorative abstract motifs, for instance with the series of paintings 'Fugalen Bilder' (Fugal Paintings).

Pechstein, Max
(1881–1955) *Berlin*

Pechstein spent much of the war in retreat in Leba, a small town in Middle Pomerania on the Baltic coast. He returned with his wife to Berlin in September 1945, to find his house and studio destroyed. He nevertheless remained in Berlin, taking up a teaching post at the Hochschule für bildende Künste, and writing his memoirs, published after his death in 1960.

Querner, Curt
(1904–1976) *Dresden*

From 1926–30, Querner studied at the Dresden Kunstakademie under Otto Dix, amongst others. Although he joined ASSO and the KPD in 1930, he retained a distance from overtly political painting. From 1940, he served in the Wehrmacht and was in interned until 1947 in various French prisoner-of-war camps, returning to his native Börnchen near Dresden in 1947. In his postwar work, he developed his interest in the Saxon landscape, and also in portraiture, including a number of self-portraits. His realist style was indebted to the Neue Sachlichkeit trends of the 1920s.

Radziwill, Franz
(1895–1983) *Dangast*

After studying architecture and undertaking a period of military service during the First World War, Radzwill turned to painting, and in 1923 settled in the small town of Dangast on the North Sea Coast near Wilhelmshaven. His work was influenced by the Neue Sachlichkeit movement, in particular Dix, with whom he worked in Dresden for a short time in the late 1920s. Radziwill joined the Nazi Party in 1933, and was appointed to a Professorship at the Düsseldorf Kunstakademie. He was dismissed from his teaching post in 1935, and from the Nazi Party in 1938, his works having been declared degenerate. He continued painting after the war, producing surrealist-influenced works that dwelt on the destruction of war, often showing aircraft, a motif recurrent in his work. His paintings are particularly memorable for their vivid colouration.

Rave, Paul Ortwin
(1893 –1962)

After studies in Bonn, in 1922 Rave was called by Ludwig Justi to the Berlin National Gallery. He was to make his name in connection with both the museum and the city. When Justi was dismissed by the Nazis in 1933, Rave carried on working under the new director, Eberhard Hanfstaengl, who in turn was dismissed in 1937. Rave took over the directorship, and in 1949 published an invaluable account of the fate of museums during the Third Reich, *Kunstdiktatur im Dritten Reich* (The Arts under the Third Reich). Rave gave up his position in 1950, after the division in 1948 of the National Gallery into eastern and western parts. From 1954 until 1961, he was the director of the Kunstbibliothek in West Berlin.

Reidemeister, Leopold
(1900–1987)

On his return from war service in 1918, Reidemeister studied architecture at the Technischen Hochschule in Braunschweig, moving after one year to the University of Berlin. To fund his studies, Reidemeister worked as an assistant in the Galerie Van Diemen, where he came into contact with many young artists. From 1924, he worked in the East Asian department of the National Gallery, soon becoming head curator. He studied Chinese and travelled to the Far East. His researches into Asian art culminated in 1929 in a large exhibition on Chinese Art that contained many valuable loans from around the world. In 1945, Reidemeister became director of the Wallraf-Richartz Museum in Cologne, at that moment in ruins, with the task of reconstructing the museum and collection. When it was reopened, Reidemeister moved back to Berlin, where he was, from 1957–65, the general director of the Staatlichen Museens and then, following Paul Ortwin Rave, director of the National Gallery in the West. His acquisitions for the National Gallery, reflecting his own taste for classic modernism, compensated for many of the losses due to the Nazi campaign of confiscation.

Roh, Franz
(1890 – 1965)

Roh studied philosophy, literature, history and art history in Leipzig, Berlin, Basel and Munich, completing his dissertation, *Holländische Malerei des 17. Jahrhunderts* (Dutch Painting of the Seventeenth Century) under Heinrich Wölfflin in Munich. He subsequently worked as a freelance critic and writer, beginning also to practise as an artist, producing photo-collages influenced by Max Ernst. He published two important books in the 1920s, *Nach-Expressionismus, Magischer Realismus. Probleme der neuesten europäisches*

Malerei (After Expressionism, Magic Realism: Problems of New European Painting, 1925) and *Foto-auge – 76 fotos der zeit zusammengestellt von franz roh und jan tschichold* (Foto-auge – 76 images of the time assembled by Franz Roh and Jan Tschichold, Stuttgart 1929). He spent the war in 'inner emigration', working on a book that was published in 1948 as *Das Verkannte Künstler – Geschichte und Theorie des kulturellen Mißverstehen* (The Unrecognised Artist – History and Theory of Cultural Misunderstanding). In the same year, he began teaching art history at the University of Munich, a position he held until his death. In 1951, he became the first president of the German branch of the International Association of Art Critics. His book, *Der Streit um die moderne Kunst* (The Controversy Over Modern Art), published in 1962, reviewed many of the debates concerning the public acceptance of modern art, focusing particularly on adversaries of the modern movement, such as Hans Sedlmayr, with whom he clashed at the 1950 Darmstädter Gespräch.

Rudolph, Wilhelm
(1889–1982) *Dresden*

Rudolph moved from his native Chemnitz to study in Dresden in 1908. He remained in the city, and was closely associated with the local art scene. He is remembered chiefly for the series of 150 drawings of Dresden that he began just after the bombardments of February 1945, which destroyed his studio, and finished in early 1946. These drawings depict in detail the destruction of the city, and constitute one of the few artistic documents that show the effects of Allied bombardment. Although he was awarded many honours for his subsequent work as a painter and printmaker in East Germany, he was never again to repeat the achievement of the series 'Das Zerstörtes Dresden' (Dresden in Ruins).

Sedlmayr, Hans
(1896 –1984)

After service with the Austrian army in the Near East during the First World War, Sedlmayr studied architecture at the Technische Hochschule, Vienna, and then art history at Vienna university under Max Dvořák and his successor Julius von Schlosser, completing his dissertation on the architect Fischer von Erlach. He published one of his most important essays in 1931, 'Zu einer strengen Kunstwissenschaft' (Towards A Rigorous Study of Art), which outlined the approach that he and his colleague Otto Pächt had been developing, an analysis of the structural properties of works of art. This approach was strongly influenced by the work of Alois Riegl, and his notion of *Kunstwollen*, as well as by Gestalt psychology, in particular the work of Max Wertheimer. Sedlmayr edited a collected volume of Riegl's essays in 1929. Three years later, he joined the Austrian Nazi party. In 1933, with his study *Die 'macchia' Breugels*, he received his habilitation from the Vienna Technische Hochschule. In 1934 he moved again to the university to become Schlosser's assistant. He followed Schlosser in the chair of art history 1936–45. The exact extent of Sedlmayr's involvement with the Austrian Nazi party during the Third Reich remains a grey area. He published his best-known work, a vehement critique of modern art, *Verlust der Mitte* (The Loss of the Centre), in 1948. His last position was at the University of Munich, where he taught from 1951. Working within a Viennese tradition of stylistic analyis established by Alois Riegl, Sedlmayr, along with his colleague Otto Pächt, established at the beginning of the 1930s a 'second' Vienna School, in which many of the structural aspects of Riegl's thought were developed. The notion that an age expressed itself synthetically through a style, giving artistically formed objects the quality of historical documents, can be read both in *Verlust der Mitte*, and his work on Gothic architecture, in which he ascribed the architectural choices made by Gothic cathedral builders to their desire to create a version of heavenly Jerusalem on earth.

Schlichter, Rudolf
(1890–1955) *Munich*

Schlichter was associated with the Dada group and the Novembergruppe after 1918, and was in 1924 a co-founder of the Rotte Gruppe, a communist artistic grouping. In 1927, he converted to Catholicism. Although a member of the Reichskammer der Bildende Künste, he was banned from exhibiting his works as a result of the 1937 painting *Blinde Macht* (Blind Power). He spent the war in Munich. His postwar paintings reflect on the ruins of Germany. In 1949 he published *Das Abenteuer der Kunst* (The Adventure of Art).

Schmidt-Rottluff, Karl
(1884–1976) *Berlin*

After the destruction of his studio and work in Autumn 1943 by Allied bombs, Schmidt-Rottluff went to live in his parent's house in Rottluff, where he remained until 1946. He resided initially in Chemnitz after the war, where he was made President of the local branch of the Kulturbund, then, on being offered a teaching post at the Hochschule für Bildende Künste by Karl Hofer, he moved to Berlin at the end of 1946. He continued teaching until 1954.

Schultze, Bernard
(1915–2005) *Rhineland*

Schultze studied painting in Berlin and Düsseldorf. He served in the German army in Russia and Africa. All his early works were lost when his Berlin studio was destroyed by a bomb in 1945. He moved to Frankfurt in 1947, and from 1951 began making frequent trips to Paris, where he encountered the work of Wols and Jean-Paul Riopelle, both of whom had a strong influence on his painting. With Karl-Otto Götz, Otto Greis and Heinz Kreutz, he exhibited 'Neo-Expressionist' work at the Galerie Klaus Franck in Frankfurt in 1952, on which basis the artists' group Quadriga was founded. He was a leading representative of German Art informel.

Schumacher, Emil
(1912–1999) *Rhineland*

Schumacher studied graphic design in Dortmund from 1932–5. His first exhibition as a painter in Witten in 1934 was shut down by the Nazis. He worked as a technical draughtsman during the war in Hagen, but after 1945, became active once again as a painter, and was a founder member of the group junger westen. He worked in a figurative manner, painting a variety of domestic subjects with varying degrees of naturalism, until the early 1950s, when his work became abstract. He travelled to Paris in 1951 and met Pierre Soulages. His work was included in the exhibitions *Deutsche Kunst nach 1945* (German Art After 1945), Stedelijk Museum, Amsterdam (1954) and *Peintres et sculpteurs non-figuratifs en Allemagne d'aujourd'hui* (Non-figurative Painters and Sculptors in Germany Today), Cercle Volney, Paris (1955). He was strongly influenced by Wols in the second part of the 1950s.

Sitte, Willi
(b.1921) *Halle*

In his autobiography, *Willi Sitte. Farben und Folgen* (Willi Sitte: Colours and Consequences), published in 2003, Sitte describes his experiences as a German soldier involved in the first Russian winter campaign in 1941, and then in Italy, where he came into contact with anti-fascists. After 1945, he lived and worked for a short while in Milan, where he had his first exhibition. On returning to his home town of Kratzau, in Czechoslovakia, at the end of 1946, he joined the Komitee deutscher Antifaschisten. He soon moved to Halle, where he joined the SED and was involved in the Socialist cultural life of the newly formed East German State. In 1948, Sitte joined the Halle-based, Socialist artists' group Die Fähre, and in 1951 began teaching at the Institut für künstlerische Werkgestaltung at Halle-Burg Giebichenstein. He was strongly involved in SED cultural politics, painted murals, and made works that despite their Socialist Realist content showed the strong influence of Picasso and French modern painting in general.

Simson, Otto Georg von
(1912–1993)

Simson studied with Wilhelm Pinder in Munich, completing a dissertation on Baroque art, published as *Zur Geneaologie der weltlichen Apotheose im Barock, besonders der Medicigalerie des Peter Paul Rubens* in 1936. He emigrated to America on the outbreak of war, teaching for a short time in New York, then, from 1945–57, as a Professor of Art History at the University of Chicago. Two major publications produced in exile were *Sacred Fortress. Byzantine Art and Statecraft in Ravenna* (1948) and *The Gothic Cathedral* (1956), the latter placing him in dialogue with publications on Gothic architecture by Hans Sedlmayr and Erwin Panofsky. Simson returned to Germany in 1957, taking up a position first in Frankfurt, and then in the Freien Universität in Berlin, where he worked from 1964–79. In his 1986 *Der Blick nach Innen*, Simson dwelt on the concept of *innerlichkeit*, as manifest in the work of four German painters, Caspar David Friedrich, Carl Spitzweg, Wilhelm Leibl and Ludwig Richter. The posthumous *Peter Paul Rubens (1577 – 1640) Humanist, Painter, Diplomat* (1996) brought together Simson's work on the artist with whom he had been preoccupied for much of his career.

Sintenis, Renée
(1888–1965) *Berlin*

Sintenis studied at the Kunstgewerbeschule (School of Applied Arts) in Berlin, 1908–12, and soon afterwards acquired a reputation for small figurative sculptures, in particular of animals. She joined the Prussian Academy in 1931 but was ejected in 1934 due to the Jewish origins of her grandparents. She nevertheless continued living and working in Berlin, and in 1947 began a teaching job at the Hochschüle der Künste.

Steinert, Otto
(1915–1978) *Saarbrücken, Essen*

After studying and practising medicine, Steiner set up a photography studio in Saarbrücken in South-West Germany in 1947, at that time under French administration. He co-founded the fotoform group the next year, and was a leading figure in the Subjektive Fotografie movement.

Strempel, Horst
(1904–1975) *Berlin*

Strempel studied in Breslau under Oskar Moll and Otto Müller, then in Berlin under Karl Hofer. He became involved in revolutionary politics and joined the KPD. He emigrated to Paris in 1933, where he met Max Ernst and Frans Masereel. After 1939, he spent time in various prison camps in the South of France, and then in 1941 he was interned by the Gestapo in Berlin. He then served with the Wehrmacht and was interned by the British in 1944. From 1945–7 he lived and worked in Berlin, contributing drawings to the magazine *Ulenspiegel*. During this time he painted *Nacht über Deutschland* (Night Over Germany, 1945–6), a grim image of prisoners and ordinary people during war time that carried a clear anti-fascist message. Despite his left-wing allegiance, the semi-abstract nature of his work caused disfavour with the SED. His mural at the Berlin Friedrichstraße station was painted over, and in 1953 he moved to West Berlin, where he remained.

Thiemann, Hans
(1910–1977) *Berlin*

The earliest notable works by Thiemann are the 1929 series of parodies of work by famous German artists such as Schwitters, Grosz, Klee and Schlemmer, done so well as to have been considered forgeries. Thiemann then studied at the Dessau Bauhaus, the Kunsthochschule in Dresden, and again at the Bauhaus in Berlin. He remained in Berlin throughout the war, exempt from military duty due to bad health. He achieved widespread success after 1945 with his paintings, illustrations and set designs. He was associated with the Galerie Gerd Rosen, where his works were frequently to be seen, particularly in the *Fantasten-Ausstellung* (Fantasten Exhibition) of February 1946. In 1949, Thiemann was one of the founding members of the Berliner Neuen Gruppe, a Berlin-based exhibition society.

Trökes, Heinz
(1913–97) *Berlin*

Trökes' first solo exhibition, at the Galerie Nierendorf in Berlin in 1938, was shut down by the Nazis. He remained in Germany during the war, as a *Flaksoldat* in Berlin. In 1945, he was co-founder of the Galerie Gerd Rosen in Berlin, where he worked for a short while. His paintings were strongly influenced by prewar Surrealism, above all by Max Ernst, and he published a number of articles explaining and defending modern art. His paintings became more explicitly abstract around 1950, reflecting the ascendance first of a geometric abstraction, in the manner of Willi Baumeister, and later of a less decorous approach influenced by contemporary trends of informel painting.

Uhlmann, Hans
(1900–1975) *Berlin*

Uhlmann began working as sculptor in 1925, and had his first exhibition at the Galerie Gurlitt in Berlin in 1930. His work was strongly influenced by Constructivism. After arrest for distributing anti-fascist leaflets, he was interned for eighteen months. He remained in Germany throughout the war, developing designs for technical instruments. After 1945, he was strongly involved in cultural reconstruction in Berlin, at first working as head of the Fine Arts Department of the Peoples' Education department of Steglitz. He was closely involved with the Galerie Gerd Rosen from 1946, and had a solo exhibition of sculptures and drawings there in 1947. Although according with the general trend towards a less rigorous abstraction in the late 1940s, his work nevertheless remained true to his original Constructivist ambitions. He began teaching at the Hochschule der Künste in Berlin in 1950.

Winter, Fritz
(1905–1976) *Munich*

Winter studied at the Bauhaus under Schlemmer, Kandinsky and Klee. Between 1929 and 1931 he frequently visited Ludwig Kirchner in Davos. He served in the Wehrmacht and was interned by the Russians as a prisoner-of-war from 1945 to 1949. His well-known series of abstract paintings referring to terrestrial forces, *Triebkräfte der Erde*, were begun while serving at the Front in 1944. These works, amongst the most important produced by a German artist at this moment, have been considered as a link between the work of Franz Marc and Paul Klee earlier in the century, and the work of Joseph Beuys after 1945. In 1949, Winter was a co-founder of the Munich-based group later known as Zen 49, a focus for interest in prewar traditions emanating from the Blaue Reiter and the Bauhaus.

Sources Consulted

Archives

British Council Archives, London [BC]
Dokumenta Archiv, Kassel [DA]
Ferdinand-Möller-Stiftung Archiv [FMSA]
Haus am Waldsee Archiv, Berlin [HAWA]
Kunstakademie Düsseldorf Archiv
Public Record Offices, London [PRO]
Stiftung Archiv der Akademie der Künste, Berlin
Washington National Archives II, Maryland [NA]

Unpublished sources (excluding theses)and articles are cited in the footnotes. Exhibition catalogues, when not obviously authored, are indexed under exhibition venue. Official publications are listed under location and institution. The date of first publication is indicated in brackets when a later edition is cited.

Journals

Die Aussprache. Mitteilungsblatt für die Mitgleider und Freunde des Kulturbundes zur Demokratischen Erneuerung Deutschlands
bildende kunst (1947–9)
Bildende Kunst (1953–90)
Der Bildende Künstler. Mitteilungsblatt für Mitgleider des Verbandes Bildender Künstler
Das Blatt des Verbandes Bildender Küstler Deutschlands
Kulturaufbau. Aussprache und Mitteilungsblatt für Freunde und Mitgleider des Kulturbundes zur Demokratischen Erneuerung Deutschlands e.V.
Kulturaufbau. Monatszeitschrift für Kunst, Literature, Wissenschaft, Kulturpolitik und Unterhaltung
Das Kunstwerk
Mitteilunsblatt des Kulturbundes zur Demokratisches Erneuerung Deutschlands Landesverband Nordrhein-Westfalen e.V.
Der Monat. Eine internationale Zeitschrift für Politik und geistiges Leben
Das Münster
Zeitschrift für Christliche Kunst und Kunstwissenschaft
Zeitschrift für die Kunst. Vierteljahreshefte für künstlerische Gestaltung, Malerei, Graphik, Plastik, Architektur, Kunsthandwerk

Books and Catalogues

Adenauer, K., *Erinnerungen*, vol. 1 1945–53; vol. 2 1953–55, Stuttgart, 1965, 1966.
Adenauer, K., *Memoirs 1945–53*, trans. Beate Ruhm von Oppen, London, 1966 (1).
Adorno, T., *The Jargon of Authenticity*, trans. K. Tarnowski and F. Will, Evanston, 1973 (1964).
Akademie der Künste der DDR, Berlin, *Otto Nagel 1894–1967. Gemälde, Pastelle, Zeichnungen*, exh. cat., 1984.
Albertinum, Dresden, *Dritte Deutscher Kunstausstellung*, exh. cat., 1953.
Amerika-Haus Gallery, Munich, *Amerikanische Malerei. Werden und Gegenwart*, exh. cat., 1951.
Améry, J., *Preface to the Future: Culture in a Consumer Society*, trans. Palmer Hilty, London, 1964 (1961).
Annan, N., *How Dr. Adenauer Rose Resilient from the Ruins of Germany*, London, 1983.
Annan, N., *Changing Enemies. The defeat and regeneration of Germany*, London, 1995.
Arp, H., and El Lissitzky, *Die Kunstismen/Les ismes de l'art/The isms of art*, Zurich, Munich and Leipzig, 1925.
Bahr, C., *Religiöse Malerei im 20. Jahrhundert am Beispiel der religiösen Bildauffassung im gemalten Werk von Georges Rouault (1871–1958)*, Stuttgart, 1996.
Baker, K.L., Russel J. Dalton and Kai Hildebrandt, *Germany Transformed. Political Culture and the New Politics*, Cambridge and London, 1981.

Balluseck, L.v., *Zur Lage der Bildende kunst in der Sowjetischen Besatzungszone*, Bonner Berichte aus Mittel- und Ostdeutschland, Bundesministerium für gesamtdeutsche Fragen, Bonn, 1953.

Bance, A. (ed.), *The Cultural Legacy of the British Occupation in Germany*, Stuttgart, 1997.

Bark, D.L. and Gress, D.R., *A History of West Germany*, vol. 1; *From Shadow to Substance 1945–63*, Oxford, 1989.

Barron, S. (ed.), *Entartete Kunst. Das Schicksal der Avantgarde im Nazi-Deutschland*, Munich, 1992.

Baumeister, W., *Das Unbekannte in der Kunst*, Cologne, 1947.

Behne, A., *1. Kunstausstellung der Kammer der Kunstschaffenden*, exh. cat., Kammer der Kunstschaffenden, Berlin, July/August 1945.

Behne, A., *Entartete Kunst*, Berlin, 1947.

Belting, H., *The Germans and their Art: a troublesome relationship*, trans. Scott Kleager, New Haven, 1998.

Benjamin, W., *Ursprung des deutschen Trauerspiels*, Frankfurt, 1963; English trans. John Osborne, *The Origin of German Tragic Drama*, London, 1977.

Benn, G., *Primal Vision. Selected Writings of Gottfried Benn*, London, 1976 (1960).

Berlin, Sowjetische Militär-Administration in Deutschland, *Befehle des Obersten Chefs der Sowjetischen Militärverwaltung in Deutschland. Sammelheft 1. 1945*, 1946.

Betthausen, P., et. al., *Metzler Kunsthistoriker Lexicon. Zweihunder Porträts deutschsprachiger Autoren aus vier Jahrhunderten*, Stuttgart and Weimar, 1999.

Billeter, F., *Max Beckmann und Günther Franke*, Bayerische Staatsgemäldesammlungen, Hefte des Max Beckmann Archivs 4, Munich, 2000.

Birke, A.M., Hans Booms and Otto Merker, *Akten der britischen Militärregierung in Deutschland Sachinventar 1945–1955 / Control Commission for Germany British Element Inventory 1945–1955*, vols 1–6, Munich, New Providence, London, Paris, 1993.

Blume, E., and Roland März, *Kunst in der DDR. Eine Retrospective der Nationalgalerie*, exh. cat., Nationalgalerie, Berlin, 2003.

Blunt, A., *Georges Rouault. Miserere*, Boston, 1963.

Böll, H., *Missing Persons and other Essays*, trans. Leila Vennewitz, London, 1977.

Bourke-White, M., *"Dear fatherland, rest quietly" A report on the collapse of Hitler's 'Thousand years'*, New York, 1946.

Bourke-White, M., *Deutschland, April 1945*, Munich, 1979.

Brady, J.S., Beverly Crawford and Sarah Elise Williarty (eds), *The Postwar Transformation of Germany*, Michigan, 1999.

Brenner, H., *Die Kunstpolitik der Nationalsozialismus*, Reinbeck, 1963.

Breton, A., *Peinture Surréaliste en Europe/ Suurealistische Malerei in Europa*, exh.cat., Saarbrücken, Saarland Museum,1952.

Brion, M., et. al., *Art since 1945*, London, 1958.

British Council, *Ausstellung über Graphische Kunst von zeitgenössischen Britischen Künstlern*, exh. cat., touring exhibition (Hamburg, Hanover, Berlin, Kiel), 1948.

Brubaker, R., *Citizenship and Nationhood in France and Germany*, Cambridge MA, 1992.

Buchanan, T. and Conway, M., *Political Catholicism in Europe 1918–1965*, Oxford 1996.

Bundesministerium für gesamtdeutsche Fragen, Bonn, *Polit-Kunst in der Sowjetischen Besatzungszone: 'III Deutsche Kunstaustellung 1953' Dresden*, 1953.

Bundesminister für Vertriebene, Flüchtlinge und Kriegsgeschädigte, Bonn, *Dokumente deutscher Kriegsschäden. Evakuierte, Kriegssachgeschädigte, Währungsgeschädigte. Die geschichtliche und rechtliche Entwicklung*, vol. 1, 1958.

Buruma, I., *The Wages of Guilt*, London, 1994.

Bushart, M., *Die Geist der Gotik und die expressionistische Kunst*, Munich, 1990.

Bushart, M. (ed.), *Adolf Behne. Essays zu seiner Kunst- und Architektur-Kritik*, Berlin, 2000.

Caspers, E., Wolfgang Henze and Hans-Jürgen Lwowski (eds.), *Nolde, Schmidt-Rottluff und ihre Freunde: die Sammlung Martha und Paul Rauert, Hamburg 1905–1958*, exh. cat., Ernst-Barlach Haus, Hamburg, 1999.

Cassou, J., *Moderne Französische Malerei. Vom Impressionismus bis zur Gegenwart*, exh. cat., Kurhaus, Baden-Baden, September, 1946.

Central Art Collecting Point, Munich, *Zen 49*, exh. cat., 1950.

Centre Georges Pompidou, Paris, *Paris-Paris 1937–1957*, exh. cat., 1981.

Chiappini, R. (ed.), *Emil Nolde*, exh. cat., Lugano, Museo d'Arte Moderna, Lugano, 1994.

Claasen, H., *Gesang im Feuerofen. Köln – übereste einer alten Stadt*, Cologne 1947; revised edition: Claasen, H., *Gesang im Feuerofen. Köln, Überreste einer alten deutschen Stadt*, Josef Rick (ed. and preface), Düsseldorf, 1979.

Clare, G., *Before the Wall. Berlin Days 1946–1948*, New York, 1989.

Coleman, J., *Beyond Catholicism: Pierro Manzoni and the Society of the Miracle 1958–63*, unpublished MA thesis, Courtauld Institute, London, 1993.

Cullerne-Bown, M., *Art under Stalin*, Oxford, 1991.

Damus, M., *Kunst in der BRD 1945–1990. Funktionen der Kunst in einer demokratisch verfasten Gesellschaft*, Hamburg, 1995.

de Beauvoir, S., *La force des choses*, Paris 1963; English trans R. Howard, *Forces of Circumstance*, London, 1965.

de la Motte, M. (ed.), *Dokumente zum deutschen Informel*, Bonn, 1976.

DeBujunda, J. M., *Index Librorum Prohibitorum 1600–1966*, Geneva and Sherbrook, 2002

Demisch, F., *Franz Marc – der Maler eines Neubeginns*, Hannover, 1948.

Derenthal, L., *Bilder der Trümmer- und Aufbaujahre. Fotografie im sich teilenden Deutschland*, Marburg, 1999.

Deres, T., and Martin Rüther, *Fotografieren verboten! Heimliche Aufnahmen von der Zerstörung Kölns*, Cologne, 1995.

Deutsche Akademie der Künste, Berlin, *Patriotische Kunst aus der Zeit der Volkserhebung 1813*, exh. cat., 1953.

Diefendorf, J.M., *In the Wake of War: The Reconstruction of German Cities after World War II*, New York and Oxford, 1993.

Dilly, H., *Deutsche Kunsthistoriker 1933–1945*, Munich and Berlin, 1988.

Dilly, H., *Altmeister moderner Kunstgeschichte*, Berlin, 1990.

Domnick, O., *Die Schöpferischen Kräfte in der Abstrakten Malerei – Ein Zyklus*, Bergen, 1947.

Domnick, O. and Greta Domnick, *Die Sammlung Domnick. Ihre Entstehung, ihre Aufgabe, ihre Zukunft, eine Dokumentation*, Stuttgart, 1982.

Durth, W. and Gutschow, N., *Architektur und Städtebau der Fünfziger Jahre, Schriftenreihe des Deutschen Nationalkomitees für Denkmalschutz*, vol. 33., Bonn, 1988.

Durth, W. and Gutschow, N., *Träume in Trümmern: Planungen zum Wiederaufbau zerstörter Städte im Westdeutschlands, 1940–1950*, 2 vols, Brunswick, 1988 (1).

Easton, L. M., *The Red Count. The Life and Times of Harry Kessler*, Berkeley, 2002.

Ebon, M., *Malenkow, Stalin's successor*, New York, Toronto and London, 1953.

Egenter, R., *Kitsch und Christenleben*, Ettal 1950; English trans. Edward Quinn, *The Desecration of Christ*, London, 1967.

Einstein, C., *Die Kunst des 20.Jahrhunderts*, Propyläen-Kunstgeschichte, vol. xvi, Berlin, 1931.

Evers, H.G. (ed.), *Das Menschenbild unserer Zeit. Das Darmstädter Gespräch*, Darmstadt, 1951.

Fallani, G., V. Mariani and G. Mascherpa, *Collezione vaticana d'arte religiosa moderna*, Milan, 1974.

Farrely, D.J., *Goethe in East Germany, 1949–1989. Toward a History of Goethe Reception in the GDR*, Columbia, 1998.

Fechter, P., *Der Expressionismus*, Munich, 1914.

Feist, G., and Eckhart Gillen, *Kunstkombinat DDR. Daten und Zitate zur Kunst und Kunstpolitik der DDR 1945–1990*, Berlin, 1990.

Feist, G. et. al., *Kunstdokumentation SBZ/DDR 1945–1990. Aufsätze, Berichte, Materialien*, Cologne, 1996.

Fer, B., *On abstract art*, New Haven and London, 1997.

Flavell, M. K., *George Grosz. A Biography*, New Haven and London, 1988.

Forster, R., Anna Scheer and Jens Thiel, *Otto Nagel (1894–1967) Bibliographie*, Berlin, 2000.

François, E. and Hagen Schulze, *Deutsche Erinnerungsorte*, vol. 2, Munich, 2001.

Frankfurter Kunstverein, Frankfurt, *Zwischen Krieg und Frieden. Gegenständliche und realistische Tendenzen in der Kunst nach 45*, exh. cat., 1980.

Friedrich, G., *Der Kulturbund zur Demokratischen Erneuerung Deutschlands. Geschichte und Funcktion*, Cologne, 1952.

Friedrichsbau, Freibourg, *Die Meister französischer Malerei der Gegenwart*, exh. cat., 1947.

Fuchs, P., *Josef Haubrich. Sammler und Stifter moderne Kunst*, Cologne, 1979.

Fulbrook, M., *The Two Germanies 1945–90*, London, 2000.

Fulbrook, M., *History of Germany 1918–2000. The Divided Nation*, Oxford, 2002.

Gallwitz, K. (ed.), *Max Beckmann Briefe*, vol. 1, 1899–1925, Munich and Zurich 1993.

Gee, M., Tim Kirk and Jill Steward (eds), *The City in Central Europe. Culture and Society from 1800 to the Present*, Cambridge, 1999

Geiss, I., *The Question of German Unification 1806–1996*, London, 1997.

Germanisches Nationalmuseum, Nuremberg, Archiv für Bildende Kunst am Germanischen Nationalmuseum, *Georg Meistermann, Werke und Dokumente*, exh. cat., 1981.

Gillen, E., and Diether Schmidt (eds), *Zone 5. Kunst in der Viersektorenstadt 1945–51*, exh. cat., Berlinische Galerie, Berlin, 1989

Gillen, E., and Haarman, R. (eds), *Kunst in der DDR*, Cologne, 1990.

Gillen, E. (ed.), *German Art from Beckmann to Richter. Image of a Divided Country*, Berlin, 1998, published to accompany the exhibition *Deutschlandbilder. Kunst aus einem geteilten Land*, Martin-Gropius-Bau, Berlin, 1998.

Glaser, H., *Kulturgeschichte der Bundesrepublik Deutschland*, vol. 1, *Zwischen Kapitulation und Währungsreform 1945–48*, Munich and Vienna, 1985; vol. 2, *Zwischen Grundgesetz und Großer Koalition 1949–1967*, Munich and Vienna, 1986.

Glaser, H., Lutz von Pudendorf and Michael Schöneich (eds), *So Viel Anfang war nie. Deutsche Städte 1945–1949*, Stuttgart, 1989.

Glaser, H., *Deutsche Kultur 1945–2000*, Munich and Vienna, 1997.

Gloszer, L., *Westkunst. Zeitgenössische Kunst seit 1939*, exh. cat., Messehalle, Cologne, 1981.

Gohr, S. and Gachnang, J., *Bilderstreit. Widerspruch, Einheit und Fragment in der Kunst seit 1960*, exh. cat., Museums Ludwig, Rheinhallen der Kölner Messe, Cologne, 1989.

Golan, R., *Modernity and Nostalgia. Art and Politics in France between the Wars*, New Haven and London, 1996.

Gollancz, V., *Germany Revisited*, London, 1947.

Gollancz, V., *In Darkest Germany*, London, 1947 (1).

Grass, G., *Two States – One Nation?*, trans. Krishna Winston and A.S. Wensinger, London, 1990.

Grasskamp, W., *Die unästhetische Demokratie. Kunst in der Marktgesellschaft*, Munich, 1992.

Grayling, A.C., *Among the Dead Cities. Was the Allied Bombing of Civilians in WWII a Necessity or a Crime?*, London, 2006.

Greene, H.C., *The Third Floor Front. A View of Broadcasting in the Sixties*, London, 1969.

Grigson, G., *Moderne Englische Zeichnungen und Aquarelle*, exh. cat., British Council touring exhibition (Stuttgart, Wiesbaden, Munich) 1950–1.

Grigson, G., *Henry Moore. Zeichnungen und Kleine Plastik*, exh. cat., Haus am Waldsee, Berlin, 1951.
Grisebach, L., and Annette Meyer zu Eissen, *Ernst Ludwig Kirchner 1880–1938*, exh. cat., Nationalgalerie, East Berlin, 1979–80.
Grohmann, W., *Georges Rouault, Munich Exhibition 1930*, exh. cat., Munich, 1930.
Grohmann, W., *Art Since 1945*, London, 1958.
Grohmann, W., *The Art of Henry Moore*, trans. M. Bullock, London, 1960.
Grosser, J.F.G. (ed.), *Die große Kontroverse*, Hamburg, 1963.
Grote, L., *Der Blaue Reiter*, exh. cat., Haus der Kunst, Munich, 1949.
Groys, B., *Gesamtkunstwerk Stalin. The Total Art of Stalinism*, Princeton, 1992.
Grundig, H., *Künstlerbriefe aus den Jahren 1926 bis 1957*, Rudolstadt 1966.
Guggenheim Museum, New York, *Max Beckmann in Exile*, exh. cat., 1996.
Guilbaut, S., *How New York Stole the Idea of Modern Art. Abstract Expressionism, Freedom, and the Cold War*, London and Chicago, 1985 (1983).
Guilbaut, S. (ed.), *Reconstructing Modernism. Art in New York, Paris and Montreal 1945–64*, Cambridge MA and London, 1990.
Gutbrod, K. (ed.), *Lieber freund. Künstler schreiben an Will Grohmann*, Cologne, 1968.
Haftmann, W., *Plastik im Freien. Ausstellung anläßlich der Internationalen Gartenbau-Ausstellung auf dem Alstervorland am Harvestehuder Weg vom 30. April bis zum 31.Oktober 1953*, exh. cat., Alstervorland am Harvestehuder Weg, Hamburg, 1953.
Haftmann, W., *Malerei im 20. Jahrhundert*, Munich, 1954 (2nd edition, 1957; 4th edition, 1965).
Haftmann, W., *Painting in the Twentieth Century*, vols 1 & 2, trans. Ralph Mannheim, London, 1960.
Halbrehder, C., *Die Malerei der Allgemeinen Deutschen Kunstausstellung / Kunstausstellung der DDR I-VIII*, Europäische Hochschulschriften, Frankfurt, 1995.
Harlan, V., Rappman, R. and Schatta, P., *Soziale Plastik – Materialen zu Joseph Beuys*, Achberg, 1976.
Haus am Waldsee, Berlin, *Georges Rouault. Miserere*, exh. cat., 1950.
Hausenstein, W., *Was bedeutet die moderne Kunst? Ein Wort des Besinnung*, Munich, 1949.
Hearnden, A. (ed.), *The British in Germany. Educational Reconstruction after 1945*, London, 1978.
Heibel, Y., *Reconstructing the Subject. Modernist Painting in Western Germany, 1945–50*, New Jersey, 1995.
Heidegger, M., *Vorträge und Aufsätze*, Pfullingen, 1954.
Heidegger, M., *The Question Concerning Technology and other Essays*, trans. William Lovitt, New York, Hagerstown, San Francisco, London, 1977.
Heidegger, M., *Basic Writings from Being and Time (1927) to The Task of Thinking (1964)*, London and Henley, 1978 (1977).
Heidegger, M., *Holzwege*, Frankfurt, 1950. trans. Julian Young and Kenneth Haynes, *Off the Beaten Track*, Cambridge, 2002.
Heinz, M., *Arnold Bode 1900–77 Leben und Werk*, Kassel, 2000.
Heinzelmann, M. and Krempel, U., *Emil Nolde und die Sammlung Sprengel 1937–1956. Geschichte einer Freundschaft*, exh. cat., Sprengel Museum, Hannover, 1999.
Held, J., *Kunst und Kunstpolitik in Deutschland 1945–49. Kulturaufbau in Deutschland nach dem 2. Weltkrieg*, Berlin, 1981.
Hentzen, A., *Henry Moore/Englische Farblithographien*, exh. cat., Kestner-Gesellschaft E.V., Hannover, 1953.
Hermand, J., *Kultur im Wiederaufbau. Die Bundesrepublik Deutschland 1945–65*, Munich, 1986.

Hermand, J., *Avantgarde und Regression. 200 Jahre deutsche Kunst*, Leipzig, 1995.

Herzogenrath, W., and Johann-Karl Schmidt, *Dix*, exh. cat., Galerie der Stadt Stuttgart, 1991.

Hiepe, R., *Gewissen und Gestaltung. Deutsche Kunst im Widerstand*, Frankfurt, 1960.

Hinkel, H. (ed.), *Handbuch der Reichskulturkammer*, Berlin, 1937.

Hochschule für Bildende Künste, Berlin, *Deutscher Künstlerbund 1950. Erste Ausstellung Berlin 1951*, exh. cat., 1951.

Hofer, K., *Erinnerungen eines malers*, Berlin, 1953.

Holsinger, B., *The Premodern Condition. Medievalism and the Making of Theory*, Chicago and London, 2005.

Holz, K., *Modern German Art for Thirties Paris, Prague, and London*, Ann Arbor, 2004.

Honnef, K. and Hans M. Schmidt (eds), *Aus den Trümmern. Kunst und Kultur im Rheinland und in Westfalen 1945–52: Neubeginn und Kontinuität*, exh. cat., Rheinisches Landesmuseum, Bonn, Kunstmuseum Düsseldorf and Museum Bochum, Cologne, 1985.

Honnef, K., and Ursula Breymayer (eds), *Ende und Anfang. Photographen in Deutschland um 1945*, exh. cat., Deutschen Historischen Museum, Berlin, 1995.

Honnef, K., Rolf Sachsse and Karin Thomas (eds), *German Photography 1870–1970. Power of a Medium*, Cologne, 1997.

Hornstein, S. and Florence Jacobowitz (eds), *Image and Remembrance: representation and the Holocaust*, Indiana, 2003.

Ihm, C. C., *The Papal Encyclicals 1903–1939*, Raleigh, 1981.

Isaacs, J., *Turner Watercolours*, exh. cat., British Council touring exhibition 1949–51 (Düsseldorf, Wiesbaden, Mannheim, Munich, Nuremberg), London, 1949.

Jameson, F. (ed.), *Aesthetics and Politics. Ernst Bloch, Georg Lukacs, Bertolt Brecht, Walter Benjamin, Theodor Adorno*, London and New York, 1998 (1977).

Jaques, R., *Expressionismus in Malerei und Plastik*, exh. cat., Kaiser Wilhelm-Museum, Krefeld, 1946.

Jaspers, K., *Die Schuldfrage*, Heidelberg, 1946, trans. E.B. Ashton, *The Question of German Guilt*, New York, 1947.

Jaspers, K., *Tragedy is not Enough*, trans. Harald A.T. Reiche, Harry T. Moore and Karl W. Deutsch, London, 1953.

Jay, M., *Permanent Exiles. Essays on the Intellectual Migration from Germany to America*, New York, 1986.

Joachimedes, C., Norman Rosenthal and Wieland Schmied, *German Art in the 20th Century: Painting and Sculpture 1905–85*, exh. cat., Royal Academy, London, 1985.

Johnson, P., *Kruschev and the Arts. The Politics of Soviet Culture 1962–64*, Cambridge, Mass., 1965.

Judt, Tony, *Postwar. A History of Europe since 1945*, London, 2005.

Junge Kunst, Hamburg, *An Exhibition of Recent Paintings by Major W. Gear, Royal Signals, Monuments, Fine Arts and Archives Control Commission for Germany*, exh. cat., 1947.

Junge, H. (ed.), *Avantgarde und Publikum. Zur Rezeption avantgardischer Kunst in Deutschland 1905–1933*, Cologne, Weimar, Vienna, 1992.

Kaiser, P., and Karl-Siegbert Rehberg, *Enge und Vielfalt – Auftragskunst und Kunstförderung in der DDR*, Dresden, 1999.

Karl & Faber, Munich, *William Gear. Arbeiten aus dem Atelier des Künstlers 1946–1986*, exh. cat., 1988.

Kästner, E., *Der Tägliche Kram. Chanson und Prosa 1945–1948*, Zurich, 1949.

Kimpel, H., and Karin Stengel, *documenta 1955. Erste Internationale Kunstausstellung – eine fotografische Rekonstruktion*, Bremen, 1995.

Kimpel, H., *documenta. Mythos und Wirklichkeit*, Cologne, 1997.

Klemperer, V., *LTI. Notizbuch eines Philologen*, Berlin, 1947, trans. Martin Brady, *The Language of the Third Reich. LTI – Lingua Tertii Imperii, A Philologist's Notebook*, London and New Jersey, 2000.

Klemperer, V., *The Lesser Evil. The Diaries of Victor Klemperer 1945–59*, trans. Martin Chalmers, London, 2003.

Klessman, C., Misselwitz, H. and Wichert, G. (eds), *Deutsche Vergangenheit – eine gemeinsame Herausforderung*, Berlin, 1999.

Klessman, C., *The Divided Past. Rewriting Post-War German History*, Oxford and New York, 2001.

Kluge, A., *Neue Geschichten: Hefte 1–18. 'Unheimlichkeit der Zeit'*, Frankfurt, 1977.

Kober, K.M., *Die Kunst der frühen Jahre 1945–1949*, Leipzig, 1989.

Koebner, T., Wulf Köpke und Joachim Radkau (eds.), *Exilforschung, Ein Internationales Jahrbuch. Vol.2., Erinnerungen ans Exil — kritische Lektüre der Autobiographien nach 1933 und andere Themen*, Munich, 1984.

Koenig, T., *Otto Steinerts Konzept Subjektive Fotografie (1951–1958)*, Munich, 1988.

Koops, T. and Vogt, M. (eds), *Das Rheinland in zwei Nachkriegszeiten: 1919–30 und 1945–9*, Koblenz, 1995.

Kracauer, S., *The Mass Ornament. Weimar Essays*, trans. Thomas Y. Levin, Cambridge MA and London, 1995.

Kracauer, S., *Theory of Film. The Redemption of Physical Reality*, Princeton, 1997 (1960).

Krause, M., *Galerie Gerd Rosen. Die Avantgarde in Berlin 1945–50*, Berlin, 1995.

Kuhirt, U. (ed.), *Kunst der DDR. 1945–1959*, Leipzig, 1982.

Kunsthalle, Hamburg, *Deutscher Künstlerbund 1950. Dritte Ausstellung Hamburg 1953*, exh. cat., 1953.

Kunsthaus, Zurich, *Kunst in Deutschland 1930–1949*, exh. cat., 1949.

Lambourne, N., *War Damage in Western Europe. The Destruction of Historic Monuments During the Second World War*, Edinburgh, 2001.

Landesmuseum, Mainz, *Abstrakte Maler der inneren Emigration*, exh. cat., 1985.

Lankheit, K., *Franz Marc*, Berlin, 1950.

Lankheit, K., *Das Triptychon als Pathosformel*, Heidelberg, 1959

Lauren, P. G., *Diplomats and Bureaucrats. The First Institutional Responses to Twentieth-Century Diplomacy in France and Germany*, Stanford, 1976.

Lauterbach, I., (ed.), *Bürokratie und Kult. Das Parteizentrum der NSDAP am Königplatz in München, Geschichte und Rezeption*, Munich and Berlin, 1995.

Lecoq-Ramond, S. (ed.), *Regards contemporains sur Grünewald*, Colmar, 1995.

Lecoq-Ramond, S. (ed.), *Willi Baumeister et la France*, exh. cat., Musée d'Unterlinden, Colmar and Musée d'Art moderne Saint-Étienne, Paris, 1999.

Lee, M. and Ruth Emily McMurry, *The Cultural Approach. Another Way in International Relations*, North Carolina, 1947.

Lewy, G., *The Catholic Church and Nazi Germany*, New York, 1965.

Löffler, F., *Otto Dix 1891–1969. Oeuvre der Gemälde*, Recklinghausen, 1981.

Lord Methuen, *Normandy Diary*, London, 1952.

Loth, W., *The Division of the World 1941–1955*, London, 1988.

Lüdecke, H., *Otto Dix. Der Krieg*, Berlin, 1963.

Maier, C.S., *The Unmasterable Past. History, Holocaust and German National Identity*, Cambridge and London, 1997.

Mann, T., *Doktor Faustus. Das Leben des deutschen Tonsetzers Adrian Leverkühn, erzählt von einem Freunde*, Berlin, 1947; English trans H.T. Lowe-Porter, *Doctor Faustus. The Life of the German Composer Adrian Leverkühn as told by a Friend*, London, 1949.

Marc, F., *Briefe aus dem Feld*, Berlin, 1940.

Martin-Gropius-Bau, Berlin, *Stationen der Moderne*, exh. cat., 1988.

Mataré, E., *Tagebücher 1915 bis 1965*, Cologne, 1997.

Mathieu, G., *Au-dela du Tachisme*, Paris, 1963.

McEwen, J., *William Gear*, London, 2003.

Merkert, J., et. al., *Museum der Gegenwart – Kunst in öffentlichen Sammlungen bis 1937*, exh. cat., Kunstsammlung Nordrhein-Westfalen, Düsseldorf, 1987.

Merrit, A.J. and Merrit, R.L., *Public opinion in occupied Germany: the OMGUS Surveys, 1945–49*, Chicago, 1970.
Messegelände, Cologne, Messe- und Ausstellungs-G.m.b.H. (ed.), *Photo-Kino Ausstellung*, exh. cat., 1950.
Messegelände, Cologne, Messe- und Ausstellungs-G.m.b.H. (ed.), *photokina 1960. Bilder und Texte*, exh. cat., 1960.
Meyer-Ellinger, H., *'Privatbesitz Hofheim'. Sammlung Hanna Bekker vom Rath. Künstler der Brücke, des Blauen Reiters und des Bauhauses. Urspring und Entwicklung*, exh. cat., Jahrhunderthalle, Hoechst, 1984.
Miesel, V.H. (ed.), *Voices of German Expressionism*, London, 1970.
Moffit, J.F., *Occultism in Avant-Garde Art: The Case of Joseph Beuys*, Ann Arbor and London, 1988.
Möller, F., *Die Alten Meister der Modernen Kunst in Deutschland II 'Brücke' 'Blauer Reiter' 'Bauhaus' u.a.*, exh. cat., Galerie Ferdinand Möller, Cologne, 1952.
Morris, L., and Robert Radford, *The Story of the Artists International Association 1933–1953*, exh. cat., Museum of Modern Art, Oxford, 1983.
Müller, H., *10 Wandbilder Entstehen*, Dresden, 1949.
Mumford, L., *Art and Technics*, London, 1952.
Murken, A. H., *Edgar Ende. Sein Leben und sein Werk (1901–1965). Seine kunsthistorische Stellung in der Malerei des 20. Jahrhunderts*, Herzogenrath, 2001.
Musée d'Art Moderne, Saint-Etienne, *L'Art en Europe 1945–53, les années décisives*, exh. cat., 1987.
Museum Fridericianum, Kassel, *documenta. kunst des XX Jahrhunderts internationale ausstellung im museum fridericianum in kassel*, exh. cat., 1955.
Nationalgalerie, East Berlin, *1945–1985. Kunst in der Bundesrepublik Deutschland*, exh. cat., 1985.
Neunzig, A. (ed.), *Hans Werner Richter und die Gruppe 47*, Munich, 1979.
Nicholas, L.H., *The Rape of Europa. The Fate of Europe's Treasures in the Third Reich and the Second World War*, London, 1994.
Niederhofer, U., *Die Auseinandersetzung mit dem Expressionismus in der Bildende Kunst im Wandel der politischen Realität der SBZ und der DDR 1945–89*, Europäische Hochschulschriften, Frankfurt, 1996.
O'Brian, J. (ed.), *Clement Greenberg. The Collected Essays and Criticism*, vol. 4, Chicago and London, 1993.
Offenburg, Dokumente-Verlag, *Revue mensuelle des questions allemandes. German Contemporary Art*, 1952.
Palmier, Jean-Michel, *Weimar in Exile*, trans. David Fernbach, London, 2006.
Papenbrock, M., *'Entartete Kunst,' Exilkunst, Widerstandskunst in westdeutschen Ausstellungen nach 1945: eine kommentierte Bibliographie*, Weimar, 1996.
Papenbrock, M., and Saure, G. (eds), *Kunst des frühen 20. Jahrhunderts in deutschen Ausstellungen. Teil 1. Ausstellungen deutscher Gegenwartskunst in der NS-Zeit: eine kommentierte Bibliographie; Teil 2: Antifaschistische Künstler/innen in Ausstellungen der SBZ und der DDR: eine kommentierte Bibliographie*, Weimar, 2000.
Pechstein, M., *Erinnerungen*, Wiesbaden, 1960.
Pehle, W.H., and P. Sillem, *Wissenschaft im geteilten Deutschland. Restauration oder Neubeginn nach 1945?*, Frankfurt, 1992.
Peter, R., *Dresden – Eine Kamera Klagt An*, Dresden, 1949.
Piel, F., *Hans Sedlmayr: 1896–1984. Verzeichnis seiner Schriften*, Munich, 1996.
Pike, D., *The Politics of Culture in Soviet-Occupied Germany 1945–49*, Stanford, 1992.
Poetter, J. (ed.), *Villa Stuck. Franz von Stuck 1863–1928*, exh. cat., Villa Stuck, Munich, 1984.
Poetter, J. (ed.), *Zen 49: Die ersten zehn Jahre – Orientierung*, exh. cat., Staatliche Kunsthalle, Baden-Baden, 1986.
Pommeranz-Liedtke, G., *Otto Dix. Gemälde und Graphik von 1912–1957*, exh. cat., Deutsche Akademie der Künste, Berlin, 1957.

Press and Information Office of the German Federal Government, Bonn, *Germany Reports*, 1953.

Rave, P.O., *Kunstdiktatur im Dritten Reich*, Hamburg, 1949.

Read, H., *Zeitgenössische Britische Malerei*, exh. cat., British Council touring exhibition (Düsseldorf, Hamburg), London, 1948.

Read, H., *Concise History of Modern Painting* (revised and enlarged edition), London, 1968 (1959).

Reidemeister, L., *Sammlung Haubrich*, exh. cat., Alten Universität, Cologne, 1946.

Reidemeister, L., *Vierundzwanzig Deutsche Zeichnungen des XX. Jahrhunderts aus der Sammlung Haubrich-Köln*, exh. cat., Alten Universität, Cologne, 1946 (1).

Reidemeister, L., *Neuerwerbungen des Wallraf-Richartz-Museums Köln für die Sammlung Haubrich*, exh. cat., Walraf-Richartz-Museums, Cologne, 1948.

Rogoff, I. (ed.), *The Divided Heritage. Themes and Problems in German Modernism*, Cambridge, 1991.

Roh, F., *Kommentare zur Kunst*, Rundfunk-Kritiken, Munich, 1948.

Roh, F., *'Entartete Kunst'. Kunstbarbarei im Dritten Reich*, Hannover, 1962.

Romanus, P., *Im Kampf um die moderne Kunst. Das Schicksal einer Sammlung in der 1. Hälfte des 20. Jahrhunderts*, exh. cat., Staatliche Galerie Moritzburg, Halle, 1985.

Roters, E., *Galerie Ferdinand Möller, Breslau, Berlin, Köln, 1917–56*, Berlin, 1984.

Rothenstein, J., *The Church and Art. Pope Paul's Talk to Artists*, London, 1964.

Rubin, W., *Modern Sacred Art and the Church of Assy*, New York and London, 1961.

Ruby, S., *'Have we an American Art?' Präsentation und Rezeption amerikanischer Malerei im Westdeutschland und Westeuropa der Nachkriegszeit*, Weimar, 1999.

Rudloff, M., *Ernst Barlach, Gerhard Marcks. Der Lübecker Figurenfries*, Bremen, 1978

Rudloff, M. (ed.), *Gerhard Marcks 1889–1981 Retrospektive*, exh. cat., Josef-Haubrich Kunsthalle, Cologne; Nationalgalerie, Berlin; Gerhard Marcks-Haus, Bremen, 1989.

Rudolph, W., *Das Zerstörte Dresden*, Leipzig, 1988.

Ruhl, K-J. (ed.), *"Mein Gott, was soll aus Deutschland werden?" Die Adenauer-Ära 1949–63*, Munich, 1985.

Ruhrberg, K., *Georg Meistermann, Die Kirchenfenster*, Freiburg, Basel, Vienna, 1986.

Ruhrberg, K. and Schäfke, W., *Georg Meistermann. Monographie und Werkverzeichnis*, Cologne, 1991.

Rumpf, H., *Das War der Bombenkrieg. Deutsche Städte im Feuersturm. Ein Dokumentarbericht*, Oldenburg and Hamburg, 1961; English trans Edward Fitzgerald, *The Bombing of Germany*, London, 1963.

Saunders, F.S., *Who Paid the Piper? The CIA and the Cultural Cold War*, London 1999; American edition: *The Cultural Cold War. The CIA and the World of Arts and Letters*, New York, 2000.

Schaezler-Palais, Augsburg, *Malerei der Gegenwart III. Extreme Malerei*, exh. cat., 1947.

Schelsky, H., *Die skeptische Generation: Eine Soziologie der deutschen Jugend*, Düsseldorf, 1957.

Scheurer, H.J. and Jan Thorn-Prikker (eds.), *Nichts erinnert mehr an Frieden: Bilder einen zerstörten Stadt / Hermann Claasen*, Cologne, 1985.

Schieder, M., *Expansion/Integration. Die Kunstausstellungen der französischen Besatzung im Nachkriegsdeutschland*, Berlin and Munich, 2003.

Schieder, M., *Im Blick des Anderen. Die Deutsche-Französischen Kunstbeziehung 1945–1959*, Berlin, 2005.

Schivelbusch, W., *In a Cold Crater. Cultural and Intellectual life in Berlin, 1945–48*, trans. Kelly Barry, Berkeley, Los Angeles and London, 1998.
Schlemmer, O., *Briefe und Tagebücher*, ed. Tut Schlemmer, Munich, 1958.
Schmidt, W., *Ausgebürgert. Künstler aus der DDR und aus dem Sowjetischen Sektor Berlins 1949–1989*, exh. cat., Staatliche Kunstsammlungen, Dresden, 1990.
Schmitt, C., *Politische Theologie: Vier Kapitel zur Lehre von der Souveränität*, Berlin, 1922.
Schmitt, C., *Ex Captivitate Salus: Erfahrungen der Zeit 1945/47*, Cologne, 1950.
Schmitt, C., *Hamlet oder Hekuba. Der Einbruch der Zeit in das Spiel*, Stuttgart, 1985 (1956).
Schmitt, C., *Der Begriff des Politischen*, Munich, 1932; English, trans. George Schwab, *The Concept of the Political*, New Jersey, 1976.
Schmitt, H-J., ed., *Die Expressionismusdebatte. Materialien zu einer marxistischen Realismuskonzeption*, Frankfurt, 1973.
Schneckenburger, M., *Documenta – Idee und Institution: Tendenzen Konzepte Materialen*, Munich, 1983.
Schnell, H., *Zur Situation der Christliche Kunst*, Munich, 1962.
Schnell, H., *Der Kirchenbau im. 20 Jahrhundert in Deutschland*, Munich and Zurich, 1973; English trans. P.J. Dine, *Twentieth Century Church Architecture in Germany*, Munich, 1974.
Schreyer, L., *Christliche Kunst des XX. Jahrhunderts in der Katholischen und Protestantischen Welt*, Hamburg, 1959.
Schubbe, E. (ed.), *Dokumente zur Kunst-, Literatur- und Kulturpolitik der SED, 1946–1970*, Stuttgart, 1972.
Schüling, H., *Zur Geschichte der ästhetischen Wertung: Bibliographie der Abhandlung über den Kitsch*, Giessen, 1971.
Schulmeister, K.H., *Auf dem Wege zu einer neuen Kultur. Der Kulturbund in den Jahren 1945–49*, Berlin, 1977.
Schulz, B., *Grauzonen Farbwelt. Kunst und Zeitbilder 1945–1955*, exh. cat., Neuen Gesellschaft für Bildende Kunst, Berlin, 1983.
Schwartz, F.J., *Blind Spots. Critical Theory and the History of art in Twentieth-Century Germany*, New Haven and London, 2005.
Schwarz. H-P., *Konrad Adenauer. A German Politician and Statesman in a Period of War, Revolution and Reconstruction, Vol. 1: From the German Empire to the Federal Republic 1876–1952*, trans. L. Willmot, Providence and Oxford, 1995.
Sebald, W.G., *Luftkrieg und Literatur*, Munich, 1999; English trans. Anthea Bell, *On the Natural History of Destruction*, London, 2003.
Sedlmayr, H., *Verlust der Mitte*, Berlin, 1948; English, trans. Brian Battershaw, *Art in Crisis*, London, 1957.
Sedlmayr, H., *Die Revolution der modernen Kunst*, Hamburg, 1961 (1955).
Soby, J.T., *Georges Rouault. Paintings and Prints*, exh. cat., Museum of Modern Art, New York, 1945.
Spender, S., *European Witness*, London, 1946.
Spies, W., *Max Ernst. Life and Work – an autobiographical Collage*, London, 2006.
Staatenhaus, Messegelände, Cologne, *Deutscher Künstlerbund 1950. Zweite Ausstellung: Deutsche Malerei und Plastik der Gegenwart*, exh. cat., 1952.
Staatliche Kunsthalle, Berlin, *30 Jahre BBK*, exh. cat., 1980.
Stadthalle Nordplatz, Dresden, *Erste Allgemeine Deutsche Kunstaustellung*, exh. cat, 1946.
Stadthalle Nordplatz, Dresden, *150 Jahre Soziale Strömungen in der bildenden Kunst*, exh. cat., 1948.
Stadthalle Nordplatz, Dresden, *2. Deutsche Kunstausstellung*, exh. cat., 1949.
Stallabrass, J., *Henry Moore. Mutter und Kind/Mother and Child*, exh. cat., Cologne, Unna, Norden, Ratzeburg and Huddersfield, 1992.
Taylor, B., *Art for the Nation. Exhibitions and the London Public 1747–2001*, Manchester, 1999.

Taylor, P. M., *The Projection of Britain. British overseas publicity and propaganda 1919–1939*, Cambridge, 1981.
Theunissen, G.H., *Berlin im Bilde Seines Wesens. Zu den Zeichnungen Werner Heldts. Ein Versuch zur phänomenologischen Methode der Kunst*, Berlin, 1948.
Thomas, Karin, *Zweimal deutsche Kunst nach 1945*, Cologne, 1985.
Thomas, Karin, *Kunst in Deutschland seit 1945*, Cologne, 2002.
Thorn-Prikker, J., *Hermann Claasen: Das Ende. Kriegszerstörung im Rheinland*, exh. cat., Rheinischen Landesmuseum, Bonn, 1983.
Turner, I.D. (ed.), *Reconstruction in Post-War Germany. British Occupation Policy and the Western Zones, 1945–55*, Oxford, New York and Munich, 1989.
Turner, J. (ed.), *The Dictionary of Art*, 36 vols, London, 1996.
Uhlmann, H., *Nach 12 Jahren*, exh. cat., Kamillenstrasse 4, Berlin, 1945.
Vali, F.A., *The Quest for a United Germany*, Baltimore, 1967.
van Laak, D., *Gespräche in der Sicherheit des Schweigens: Carl Schmitt in der politischen Geistesgeschichte der frühen Bundesrepublik*, Berlin, 1993.
Vellinghausen, A.S. and A. Schröder, *deutsche kunst nach baumeister. junger westen*, Recklinghausen, 1958.
Voigt, W. and I Flagge (eds), *Dominikus Böhm 1880–1955*, Tübingen and Berlin, 2005
Volkmann, B. (ed.), *Zwischen Widerstand und Anpassung: Kunst in Deutschland 1933–1945*, exh. cat., Akademie der Künste, Berlin, 1978.
von Simson, O., *The Gothic Cathedral. The Origins of Gothic Architecture and the Medieval Concept of Order*, London, 1956.
Wendland, U., *Biographisches Handbuch deutschsprachiger Kunsthistoriker im Exil*, 2 vols, Munich, 1999.
Werner, W., *Reichskulturkammer und ihre Einzelkammer*, Findbücher zu Beständen des Bundesarchivs, vol. 31, Koblenz, 1987.
Weyrauch, W. (ed.), *Tausend Gramm, Sammlung neuer deutscher Geschichten*, Hamburg and Stuttgart, 1949.
Widmer, U., *1945 oder die 'Neue Sprache'. Studien zur Prosa der 'Jungen Generation'*, Düsseldorf, 1966.
Wilhelmi, C., *Künstlergruppen in Deutschland, Österreich und der Schweiz seit 1900. Ein Handbuch*, Stuttgart, 1996.
Willman, H., *Zwei Jahre Kulturbund*, Berlin, 1947.
Wilson, S., *Art and the Politics of the Left in France c. 1935–1955*, PhD thesis, Courtauld Institute of Art, London, 1992.
Wofsy, A., *George Rouault. The Graphic Work*, London, 1976.
Wollenhaupt-Schmidt, U., *documenta 1955. Eine Ausstellung im Spannungsfeld der Auseinandersetzungen um die Kunst der Avantgarde 1945–1960*, Frankfurt, 1994.
Wood, C. (ed.), *The Vienna School Reader. Politics and Art Historical Method in the 1930s*, New York, 2000.
Worringer, W., *Form in Gothic*, intro. Herbert Read, London, 1927.
Züchner, E., *Kunst ist ein Spiel, das Ernst macht. Eberhard Roters Briefe und Texte 1949–1994*, Berlin, 1999.

Copyright Notices / Photo Acknowledgmets

The publishers would like to thank the following for permission to reproduce photographs:

Werner Heldt, (1904–1954), *Berliner Häuser, im Vordergrund Masken*. Berlinische Galerie, Landesmuseum für Moderne Kunst, Fotografie und Architektur, © DACS 2007, page 14.

Jeanne Mammen, (1890–1976), *Die Tür zum nichts*. Berlinische Galerie, Landesmuseum für Moderne Kunst, Fotografie und Architektur, © DACS 2007, page 15.

Hermann Claasen, (1899–1989), *Fronleichnams-prozession*, 1946, (in two parts) [D 6639, Nr. 424] Photo: Estate Hermann Claasen, Rheinisches LandesMuseum Bonn, pages 16/17.

Theo Balden, (1904–1995), *Landschaft*, chalk on paper. Academy of Arts, Berlin, Fine Arts Collection, © DACS 2007, page 21.

bpk /Kunstbibliothek – Staatliche Museen zu Berlin, page 37.

Heinz Trokes, (1913–1997), *Mit der offenen Tür*. Berlinische Galerie, Landesmuseum für Moderne Kunst, Fotografie und Architektur, © DACS 2007, page 38.

Juro Kubicěk, (1906–1970), *Berlin*, 1946. Berlinische Galerie, Landesmuseum für Moderne Kunst, Fotografie und Architektur, page 42.

Berlinische Galerie, Landesmuseum für Moderne Kunst, Fotografie und Architektur, page 43.

Franz Radziwill, (1895 –1983), *Der Riß im Hof*, 1945. Städtische Galerie Wolfsburg, © DACS 2007, page 45 top.

Werner Heldt, (1904–1954), *Gewitternachmittag an der Spree*, 1951, Öltempera, Akademie der Künste, Berlin, Kunstsammlung, © DACS 2007, page 45 bottom.

Wilhelm Rudolf, (1889–1982), *Figuren vom Mozartbrunnen an der Bürgerwiese*. © Kupferstich-Kabinett, Staatliche Kunstsammlungen Dresden, page 50 top.

Wilhelm Rudolf, (1889–1982), *Prager Straße*. © Kupferstich-Kabinett, Staatliche Kunstsammlungen Dresden, page 50 bottom.

Otto Dix, (1891–1969), *Pragerstrasse*, 1920 (oil on canvas), Staatsgalerie, Stuttgart, Germany/ Peter Willi/The Bridgeman Art Library, © DACS 2007, page 51.

Hermann Claasen, (1899–1989), *Christus König vor der Kirche St. Maria in der Kupfergasse*. [D 6630] Photo: Estate Hermann Claasen, Rheinisches LandesMuseum, page 57.

Hermann Claasen, (1899 –1989), *Blick vom Wallraf-Richartz-Museum auf die Straße An der Rechtsschule*. [D 6624] Photo: Estate Hermann Claasen, Rheinisches LandesMuseum Bonn, page 58,

Hermann Claasen, (1899 –1989), *Vor dem Dom Hotel Monopol*. [D 6624, Nr. 70] Photo: Estate Hermann Claasen, Rheinisches LandesMuseum Bonn, page 59,

Hermann Claasen, (1899 –1989), *Elendskirche* [D 6654, Nr. 478] Photo: Estate Hermann Claasen, Rheinisches LandesMuseum Bonn, page 60.

August Sander, Collage for New Year's greeting, 1948–1949. © Die Photographische Sammlung/SK Stiftung Kultur - August Sander Archiv, Cologne/VG Bild-Kunst, Bonn and DACS, London 2007, page 63.

Reproduced from the Collections of the Library of Congress. Copyright © 1951, by Margaret Bourke-White, copyright renewed 1979, by the Estate; photographs used by permission of the author's agent, Barry N. Malzberg, pages 67, 68, 69.

Werner Gilles,(1894–1961), *Nach der Bombennacht*, 1950, bez. u.r. Gilles, Öl / Leinwand, 67 x 95 cm, Inv. Nr.1704 – Kunstmuseum, Mülheim an der Ruhr in der Alten Post, page 78.

Andrea della Robia, *Portrait of a Youth* c. 1470. bpk / Skulpturensammlung und Museum für Byzantinische Kunst, SMB / Christa Begall, page 79.

bpk / Staatsbibliothek zu Berlin, page 92.

Georges Rouault, (1871–1958), *Homo homini lupus (L'homme est un loup pour l'homme)* Titre attribué: *Le pendu* – 1944–1948. Musée national d'Art moderne – Centre Georges Pompidou, Paris. © Photo CNAC/MNAM Dist. RMN /© ADAGP, Paris and DACS, London 2007, page 111.

British Council, page 115.

Willi Sitte, (1921–), *Raub der Sabinerinnen*. bpk / Nationalgalerie, Staatliche Museen zu Berlin. Photo: Jörg P. Anders, © DACS 2007, page 128.

Theo Balden, (1904–1995), *Lesender*, 1948. Academy of Arts, Berlin, Fine Arts Collection, © DACS 2007, page 131.

The image on page 133 has been reproduced by permission of the Henry Moore Foundation.

bpk / Zeitungsabteilung, Staatsbibliothek zu Berlin – Preußischer Kulturbesitz, page 147.

Fritz Duda, (1904–1991), *Ruhendes Paar*, bpk / Nationalgalerie, Staatliche Museen zu Berlin, © Friedrich Bronsart, Weiden, page 153.

Rudolf Schlichter (1890–1955), *Lebendiges Sprengt Totes*. © Viola Roehr v. Alvensleben, Munich, page 154.

Willi Baumeister (1889–1955), *Bild mit farbigen Zonen*. SLUB Dresden / Deutsche Fotothek, © DACS 2007, page 155 top.

Curt Querner (1904–1976), *Märzbild* 1933. Oil on canvas, 134 × 146 cm. Stiftung Moritzburg, Kunstmuseum des Landes Sachsen-Anhalt. Photograph: Klaus E. Göltz, Halle(Saale). © DACS 2007, page 155 bottom.

Otto Dix, (1891–1969), *Dr Josef Haubrich*, 1951. Rheinisches Bildarchiv, © DACS 2007, page 191.

Fritz Winter, (1905–1976), *Komposition III*, 1950. Märkisches Museum Witten, © Fritz-Winter-Haus, Ahlen, page 213.

Ernst Wilhelm Nay (1902–1968), *Gespräch*, 1946. Westfälisches Landesmuseum für Kunst und Kulturgeschichte, Münster / Rudolf Wakonigg, © Elisabeth Nay-Scheibler, Cologne, page 221.

Bernhard Heiliger, *Martin Heidegger*, 1964. photo by: Mathias Michaelis / DLA-Marbach. © Bernhard-Heiliger-Stiftung, Berlin, page 223.

Otto Dix, (1891–1969), *Madonna mit Stacheldracht* (Madonna with barbed wire), © DACS 2007, page 240.

Max Beckmann, (1884–1950): *The Descent from the Cross*. 1917. New York, Museum of Modern Art (MoMA). Oil on canvas, 59 × 50" (151,2 × 128,9cm). Curt Valentin Bequest. 328.1955. © 2006. Digital image, The Museum of Modern Art, New York / Scala, Florence. © DACS 2007, page 242.

Max Beckmann, (1884–1950), *Deposition*, 1946. Pfalzgalerie Kaiserslautern. Photo © Gunther Balzer. © DACS 2007, page 243.

Georg Meistermann, (1911–1990), *Der Neue Adam*. Germanisches Nationalmuseum, Nürnberg. © DACS 2007, page 246.

Karl Schleswig, (1898–1955), *Das Gleichnis von den Blinden*, 1947. Galerie Remmert und Barth, Dusseldorf/Germany, page 248.

Oskar Kokoschka, *Cardinal dalla Costa*, 1948 – Acquired 1949. The Phillips Collection, Washington, DC, page 268.

Fotowerkstätte Hugo Schmölz, (1879 –1938), © Archiv Wim Cox, Köln, page 270.

Der Spiegel, nr 52, 1953. bpk / Zeitungsabteilung, Staatsbibliothek zu Berlin – Preußischer Kulturbesitz, page 273.

Terracotta figures, *Katharinenkirche*, Lübeck. Photograph: Gerhard-Marcks-Stiftung, Bremen, pages 274/275.

Emil Nolde, (1867–1956), *Das Leben Christi* (The Life of Christ), 1911/12, 9 paintings/oil on canvas, © Nolde Stiftung Seebüll, Wvz Uban 421–423 and 477–482, page 277.

Georges Rouault. *Tomorrow will be beautiful, said the shipwrecked man*, 1948. Aquatint, roulette, and drypoint over heliogravure. Collection of Robert and Sandra Bowden (Photo: Gina Fuentes Walker). Courtesy of Museum of Biblical Art, New York. © ADAGP, Paris and DACS, London 2007, page 285.

Georges Rouault. *Have mercy upon me, O God, according to thy loving-kindness*, 1948. Aquatint, roulette, and drypoint over heliogravure. Collection of Robert and Sandra Bowden (Photo: Gina Fuentes Walker).

Courtesy of Museum of Biblical Art, New York. © ADAGP, Paris and DACS, London 2007, page 286.

Joseph Beuys, (1921–1986), *Miserere*, ca.1951. © Stiftung Museum Schloss Moyland; Maurice Dorren. © DACS 2007, page 290.

Joseph Beuys, (1921–1986), (Aktion „Kukei, akopee-Nein!, Braunkreuz, Fettecken, Modellfettecken"), Festival der neuen Kunst, Technische Hochschule Aachen, 20.7.1964 (aus der Serie Happenings, 1964–1965), Silbergelatineabzug © VG-Bild Kunst, Bonn 2004 © Heinrich Riebesehl Archiv Heinrich Riebesehl / Dauerleihgabe des Landes Niedersachsen im Sprengel Museum Hannover, page 292.

Otto Dix (1891–1969), *Ecce Homo II*, 1948. Rheinisches Bildarchiv, © DACS 2007, page 293.

© by documenta Archiv-photographer: Günther Becker, page 304.

SLUB Dresden / Deutsche Fotothek / Höhne – Pohl, page 305.

University of Wisconsin Digital Collections. http://uwdc.library.wisc.edu, page 312.

Otto Nagel, (1894–1967), *Junger Maurer von der Stalinallee*. Stiftung Stadtmuseum Berlin, © Sybille Schallenberg-Nagel (Daughter of Otto Nagel), page 319.

© by documenta Archiv-photographer: Günther Becker, page 325.

Every effort has been made to contact the holders of copyright material, but if any have been inadvertently overlooked the publishers will be pleased to make the necessary arrangements at the first opportunity.

Index